Women
Political Leaders
in Africa

Women
Political Leaders
in Africa

Rosemarie Skaine

McFarland & Company, Inc., Publishers
Jefferson, North Carolina, and London

Library of Congress Cataloguing-in-Publication Data

Skaine, Rosemarie.
Women political leaders in Africa / Rosemarie Skaine.
p.   cm.
Includes bibliographical references and index.

ISBN-13: 978-0-7864-3299-8
softcover : 50# alkaline paper ∞

1. Women in politics — Africa.   2. Women politicians — Africa.   I. Title.
HQ1236.5.A35S53 2008   960.09'9 — dc22   2007039866

British Library cataloguing data are available

Cover photograph: Nigeria's Finance Minister Ngozi N. Okonjo-Iweala,
chairman of the Development Committee of the World Bank and
International Monetary Fund (left) at a 2004 press conference,
with World Bank President James Wolfensohn (center) and
IMF Deputy Managing Director Agustín Carstens
(AP Photo/J. Scott Applewhite)

Manufactured in the United States of America

*McFarland & Company, Inc., Publishers
Box 611, Jefferson, North Carolina 28640
www.mcfarlandpub.com*

To Esther Kawira, M.D., FAAFP,
Medical Director of SHED Foundation,
Shirati, Tanzania

Acknowledgments

I am grateful to L. Muthoni Wanyeki, the executive director of FEMNET (the African Women's Development and Communication Network) in Nairobi, Kenya. Her guidance and information were pivotal to the proper development of this book. FEMNET members Wa Christine Butegwa, programme officer in communications, and Rose Akinyi provided critical initial assistance. I appreciate Edna Adan Ismail, the former minister for women and family issues in Somaliland, who provided valuable information about women leaders in Somaliland.

Friends and colleagues shared their special talents. Professor Jerry Domatob gave inspiration and encouragement; Esther Kawira, M.D., FAAFP, Medical Director of Shirati Health, Education, and Development Foundation (SHED), Shirati, Tanzania, offered sound advice; Christopher M. Schulte, instructor of art education, University of Northern Iowa, Cedar Falls, Iowa, drew maps; and Robert Kramer, professor emeritus and founder of the Center for Social and Behavioral Research, University of Northern Iowa, Cedar Falls, advanced the book through his expertise in technology.

For his tireless assistance with editing and proofreading this, my tenth book, I thank and hold dear James C. Skaine, professor emeritus in communication studies at the University of Northern Iowa.

For assistance in acquiring their photographs, I am grateful to: the Honorable Fatoumata Jahumpa-Ceesay, the Speaker of the Gambian National Assembly, and Ambassador Dodou Bammy Jagne and Tijan Masanneh-Ceesay, the people's servant, at the Embassy of The Gambia in the United States; the Honorable Maria do Carmo Trovoada Silveira, former prime minister of São Tomé and Príncipe, and Domingos Ferreira, minister counsellor, Permanent Mission of São Tomé and Príncipe to the United Nations; and the Honorable Dr. Farkhonda Hassim, member of parliament and secretary-general of the National Council for Women, Egypt, Azza Mahfouz, press and information counselor for the Embassy of Egypt, Washington, D.C., Dr. Amina Abdel Aziz, National Women's Council, Cairo, the Egyptian Consulate, Chicago, and Edward W. Lempinen, senior writer, American Association for the Advancement of Science, Office of Public Programs.

For help, I thank Kalifa Gadiaga, information specialist at the United States Embassy in Bamako, Mali; the Embassy of Rwanda, Washington, D.C.; Patricia Adams, USAID/LPA/ SCP, the photo librarian at the United Nations; and Jorge A. Jaramillo and Kimberly D. Waldman, Associated Press.

I value the guidance and research resources given by Faiza Jama Mohamed, Africa Regional Director, Equality Now — SOAWR Secretariat; Margot Gould, programme officer for Africa and Middle East, and Rita Taphorn, programme officer for political parties and women in politics, International Institute for Democracy and Electoral Assistance (IDEA), Stockholm,

Sweden; Litha Musyimi-Ogana, Advisor, gender, parliamentary affairs and civil society organizations, NEPAD Secretariat, South Africa; Julie Ballington, programme officer, Programme for Partnership between Men and Women, Inter-Parliamentary Union (IPU), Geneva, Switzerland; Tacko Ndiaye, economic affairs officer, United Nations Economic Commission for Africa, Addis Ababa, Ethiopia; Martin K.I. Christensen, chief editor/redaktør, www.guide2 womenleaders.com; and Atar Markman, Distribution Africa Section, Strategic Communications Division, Department of Public Information, United Nations, New York.

Richard L. Kuehner and Nancy L. Craft Kuehner and William V. Kuehner and Carolyn E. Guenther Kuehner provide ongoing support of my work.

I am forever grateful to Cass Paley, my friend of yesteryear, who came and gave without taking.

Table of Contents

Acknowledgments vii

Preface 1

PART I. WOMEN AND GOVERNANCE IN AFRICA

Chapter 1. African Women Leaders: Historical Roles and Present-Day Status 5

Chapter 2. Women of Africa in New or Changing Roles 13

Chapter 3. Leadership and Globalism 27

Chapter 4. Profiles of African Women Leaders 33

PART II. PROGRESS OF AFRICAN WOMEN BY COUNTRY

Introduction 61

NORTH AFRICA

People's Democratic Republic of Algeria	65	Kingdom of Morocco	71
Arab Republic of Egypt	67	Republic of the Sudan	72
Great Socialist People's Libyan Arab Jamahiriyah	68	Tunisian Republic	73
		Western Sahara	75
Islamic Republic of Mauritania	69		

CENTRAL AFRICA

Republic of Cameroon	77	Equatorial Guinea	82
Central African Republic	78	Gabonese Republic	83
Republic of Chad	79	Democratic Republic of São Tomé	
Republic of the Congo	80	and Príncipe	84

EAST AFRICA

Republic of Burundi	87	Republic of Madagascar	97
Union of the Comoros	89	Republic of Rwanda	98
Democratic Republic of the Congo	89	Republic of Seychelles	100
Republic of Djibouti	91	Somalia	101
State of Eritrea	93	Republic of Somaliland	102
Federal Democratic Republic of Ethiopia	94	United Republic of Tanzania	105
		Republic of Uganda	107
Republic of Kenya	96		

WEST AFRICA

Republic of Benin   109   Republic of Liberia   120
Burkina Faso   110   Republic of Mali   122
Republic of Cape Verde   111   Republic of Niger   123
Republic of Côte d'Ivoire   113   Federal Republic of Nigeria   125
Republic of The Gambia   114   Republic of Senegal   127
Republic of Ghana   116   Republic of Sierra Leone   128
Republic of Guinea   117   Togolese Republic   129
Republic of Guinea-Bissau   119

SOUTHERN AFRICA

Republic of Angola   132   Republic of Namibia   141
Republic of Botswana   133   Republic of South Africa   143
Kingdom of Lesotho   135   Kingdom of Swaziland   145
Republic of Malawi   137   Republic of Zambia   146
Republic of Mauritius   139   Republic of Zimbabwe   148
Republic of Mozambique   140

Conclusion: Leadership, Power and Decision Making   153

Appendix: Women in Parliaments   157

Abbreviations and Glossary   163

Chapter Notes   165

Bibliography   187

Index   201

Preface

The women of Liberia and the women of Africa ... must ... succeed and we will.[1]
— Ellen Johnson-Sirleaf to supporters before her
inauguration as president of Liberia.

All across Africa, women are being trained to take leadership positions with positive results. Countries are evaluating progress and bringing about change, some more rapidly than others. These are exciting times in Africa.

The goal of a study by *Women's eNews*, and one of my goals, is to deliver the underreported story of committed leadership of women leaders in Africa. As *Women's eNews* explains, "Almost without exception, the U.S.-based media covers Africa only during a crisis of genocidal ethnic conflicts, famine, [or] AIDS. Thus, many would argue, those of us in the U.S., Western Europe, and even Africans who rely on international media for information about their continent could easily come to the conclusion that the entire continent is beyond hope and that assistance is ineffective."[2]

Uncovering the story is framed in a sociocultural theoretical context. Sociocultural change in Africa requires social reconstruction of gender roles and will ultimately have to build upon cultural reconstruction. Sociocultural reconstruction is taking place because the people have power to chart their own course and "rid themselves of ... negative cultural traits ... and go to work replacing them creatively with positive alternatives."[3]

The Beijing Platform for Action in 1995 outlined 13 strategic objectives and actions. My focus is one target: women in power and decision making. Some consideration is given to a second target: the institutional mechanism for the advancement of women.[4] When examining the countries' reports, I focus on parity issues that produce elected or appointed women in public office. A tendency in the reporting of progress is to synthesize country reports. Part of the reasoning for synthesizing may be to view Africa as a whole. I have chosen to examine individual reports for each country[5] and have uncovered a mosaic of progress for women as leaders.

African women in elected or appointed positions on the national level is my primary focus. According to Femmes Africa Solidarité, "no gains are made without struggle. We are standing today on the shoulders of many of our sisters who sacrificed so much in the past."[6] The organization believes that we owe these sisters a huge debt and we owe them our continuance of that struggle. Such leaders include Aline Sitoe Diatta of Senegal. Diatta was a Diola woman considered by many the only female who stood against the French colonialist push into Casamance (the southern province of Senegal).[7] Another leader, Lina Magaia of Mozambique, led women in the struggle for peace. Femmes Africa Solidarité reminds us that a leader also can be a woman in a market selling food to pay for her daughter's education. Because the highest positions remain the greatest challenge, I have sought to explore why.

1

PART I

WOMEN AND GOVERNANCE IN AFRICA

1. African Women Leaders: Historical Roles and Present-Day Status

If you want to be a leader, you have to be clear what you want and what you stand for. You must stand for principle. Principle will never let you down.... You have to be able to choose what are the principles worth dying for.... And you have to add on a little sacrifice. Leadership needs a lot of sacrifice — personal and public sacrifice.
— Gertrude Ibengwe Mongella, President, Pan African
Parliament at its first Session, March 2004[1]

In almost all nations, women have made progress as leaders of governments. In Africa, women have not yet reached the highest levels of decision-making in the same proportion as they have in parliaments elsewhere. Africa's strong legacy of women rulers, however, is a positive backdrop for their current successes.

Women's Worldwide Progress as Leaders of Government

In January 2006, women were the leaders of the government in 10 countries: Bangladesh, Finland, Germany, Ireland, Latvia, Liberia, Mozambique, New Zealand, the Philippines and São Tomé and Príncipe. In March 2006, Chile's newly elected president assumed her position, bringing the total number of women leaders of 11.[2] In 1999, Sweden became the first country to have more female ministers than male, 11 women and 9 men.[3] Only Monaco and Saudi Arabia have never had a female member of government, even in a sub-ministerial position.[4] One-third of women who came to power were in "legacy positions" or were chosen on the basis of family name.[5]

After World War I, a few women became members of governments. Nina Bang, Danish Minister of Education from 1924 to 1926, became the world's first female to be a full cabinet minister.[6] Progress was slow until the end of the 20th century when female ministers became more common.[7] In 1960, Sirimavo Bandaranaike of Sri Lanka became the first woman elected prime minister.[8] In 1974, Isabel Perón of Argentina became the first woman president.[9] In 1985, the number of women presidents was six; in 1993, 15; and in 2006, 11.[10]

In September 2006, the United Nations General Assembly chose its first Muslim woman president, Haya Rashed Al Khalifa of Bahrain[11] and the United Nations Secretary General, Ban Ki-moon, appointed Tanzanian Foreign Minister Asha-Rose Mtengeti-Migiro as his Deputy Secretary General.[12]

Women are beginning to assume high leadership positions in their own right, in part because we are seeing more women in parliaments.[13] Yet the Inter-Parliamentary Union (IPU) reports that, in the highest positions in the state, including executive positions and presiding officers of parliament, women "have not reached the highest levels of decision-making in the same proportions as in parliaments."[14] Globally, the number of heads of state and government has decreased from 12 in 1995 to eight in 2005. The number of women presiding officers decreased from 10.0 percent in 1995 to 8.0 in 2005 but increased in 2006 to 27, or 14.4 percent of 187 parliaments. Countries with presiding officers are: Albania, Antigua and Barbados (both houses), Austria, the Bahamas, Belgium, Belize, Burundi, Colombia, Dominica, Estonia, Georgia, Greece, Grenada, Hungary, Iceland, Jamaica, Japan, Latvia, Lesotho, Netherlands, New Zealand, Saint Kitts and Nevis, South Africa, Trinidad and Tobago, Uruguay and Zimbabwe.[15]

African Women's Progress as Leaders of Government

In Africa, women leaders have a strong legacy. This tradition includes women pharaohs in ancient Egypt, such as Hatshepsut; ruling queens and queen mothers throughout Africa today, like Nzingha of Angola and Yaa Asantewa of Ghana; and the women leaders in the modern liberation movements, like Winnie Mandela and Elizabeth Sibeko in South Africa.[16]

Egyptian queens are believed to have governed from around 3000 B.C.[17] In 51 B.C., Ptolemy Auletes died and left his kingdom in his will to his eighteen year old daughter, Cleopatra, and her younger brother Ptolemy XIII, who was twelve.[18] Cleopatra became the ruler.

In the last one thousand years, Africa has had numerous female leaders from the legendary queens of Ethiopia to the president of Liberia, elected in 2005. African women have held the offices of Empress, Queen, Queen Mother, Queen Sister, Paramount Chieftainess, Chiefess, Sultan, Prime Minister and President.[19]

FEMALE HEADS OF STATE IN AFRICA

African women are part of the global progress of women leaders today. One woman serves as an elected head of state and queens govern other countries. Female prime ministers are serving.

Elected Women Presidents In 2006, Liberia became the first African country to have an elected female head of state, Ellen Johnson-Sirleaf.[20]

Queens Recently Lesotho and Swaziland have been governed by queens. Lesotho's Queen "MaMohato Tabitha" Masentle Lerotholi ruled from June to November 1970 and January to February 1996.[21] "MaMohato Tabitha" Masentle Lerotholi in Lesotho[22] becomes the Regent in the absence of the King.[23] The Queen Mother of Lesotho served an additional brief period from November 6, 1990, to November 12, 1990. It was the second of three times she has served as a Regent when the office of King was vacant. She appears to have been the first woman to head an African independent state in recent times.[24]

Swaziland has had two queens: Dzeliwe Shongwe from 1982 to 1983, and Ntombi Thwala from 1983 to 1986.[25] King Mswati has ruled since 1986 and, by tradition, the king reigns along with his mother, referred to as the Indlovukaz (the Great She-Elephant). The King is the administrative head of state and his mother is the spiritual and national head of state. The

Presidential candidate Ellen Johnson-Sirleaf from the Unity Party waves at her supporters during a rally in Monrovia, Liberia, on Thursday, October 6, 2005. Twenty-two candidates were running for president, including African soccer legend George Weah and former rebel leader Sekou Conneh, whose deadly mid–2003 siege of Monrovia helped drive warlord-turned-president Charles Taylor into exile (AP/Wide World Photos/Schalk van Zuydam).

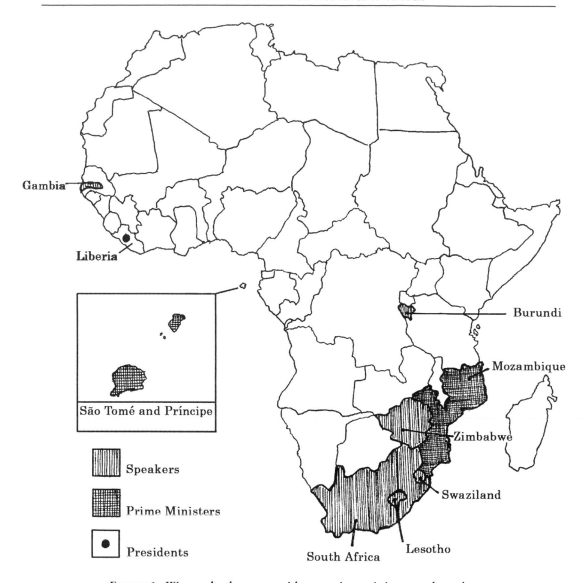

FIGURE 1. Women leaders as presidents, prime ministers and speakers.

Indlovukaz is considered a joint head of state as well as the Queen Mother. As the monarch, the king appoints the prime minister, the head of government.[26]

Dzeliwe Shongwe, the senior wife of King Sobhuza II, was also co–Chairperson of the Libandla, the Swazi National Council. Ntombi Thwala, one of the youngest wives of King Sobhuza II and mother of the future king, was a regent queen. As Queen Mother, she was the Deputy Head of State and co–Chairperson of the Libandla, the Swazi National Council, together with the king.[27]

There is some doubt who may be in the office of Queen in Angola's monarchy. Some claim the Queen Regent (the Ntolia aNtino ne Kongo) is still in office. Others report that the Queen ruled only from 1962 to 1975. She succeeded her husband, King Dom Antonio III. In 1962, her son Dom Pedro VIII Mansala was king during September and October, but after that period, she retook power.[28]

Prime Ministers As of February 2006, two female prime ministers served in Africa: Maria do Carmo Trovoada Silveira of São Tomé and Príncipe and Luisa Diogo of Mozambique.[29] Mozambique's prime minister was one of eight out of 191 sovereign states in January 2005. In March 2006, the country was one of eleven along with São Tomé and Príncipe.[30] Silveira's party was defeated in April 2006.[31]

Examples of past prime ministers include Elisabeth Domitien, Central African Empire (1975–1976), Agathe Uwilingiyimana, Rwanda (1993), Madior Boye, Senegal (2001–2002), Maria das Neves, São Tomé and Príncipe (2002–2004).[32]

Deputy and Acting Heads and Vice Presidents Women sometimes hold office as deputy head of state. Benin has not had a recent woman head of state, but from 1998 to 2002, Ouinsou née Denis was Deputy Head of State and President of the Cour Constitutionelle Conceptia.[33] Women also serve as acting heads of state and vice presidents. As one of seven acting heads in the world, Carman Periera of Guinea-Bissau served from May 14–16, 1984.[34] Aisatou N'Jie Saidy, Vice President of The Gambia since 1997, is one of five in the world.[35]

Women Cabinet Members One importance of cabinet positions is that they often lead to higher positions of leadership. (See country reports for examples of numbers of women in cabinet positions.)

PRESIDENTS OF PARLIAMENT OR PARLIAMENTARY BODIES

Before 1945, Austria was the only country to have elected a woman to the presidency of one of its chambers. From 1945 to 1997, 42 of the 186 states with a legislative institution have selected a woman to preside over Parliament or a house of Parliament; this has occurred 78 times. Those countries include 18 in Europe, 19 in the Americas, three in Africa, one in Asia and one in the Pacific. As of February 2007, 35 women preside over one of the houses of the 189 existing Parliaments, 73 of which are bicameral. Women hold 13.4 percent of the total number of 262 posts of presiding officers of Parliament or of one of its houses. Of these posts African countries include: Burundi (Inama Nshingmateka); The Gambia (National Assembly); Lesotho (National Assembly); South Africa (National Assembly); Swaziland (Senate); and Zimbabwe (Senate).[36]

For the first time in Africa's parliamentary history, nine women became presiding officer of Parliament or of one of its houses in the following countries: São Tomé and Príncipe, 1980; South Africa, 1994; Ethiopia, 1995; Lesotho, 2000; Liberia, 2003; Burundi, 2005; Zimbabwe, 2005; The Gambia, 2006; and Swaziland, 2006. Between Austria in 1927 and the United States in 2007, a total of sixty-six countries in the world had a woman become presiding officer of Parliament or of one of its houses.[37]

Significant numbers of women have also been elected to their respective parliaments. South Africa and Mozambique began the upswing with elections in 1994 that produced 25 percent women elected to parliament, and in 2004 the percentage of women elected to national legislatures increased to more than 32 percent. In 2005, Seychelles, Namibia and Uganda had at least 24 percent of the seats in the lower or single houses of parliament held by women.[38] Gretchen Bauer and Hannah E. Britton write, "This is a noteworthy development in a world in which regional averages for women's representation in parliaments range from six percent in the Arab states to only 18 percent in the Americas (approaching 40 percent only in the ...

West Africa

(1) Guinea, 19.3%
(2) Senegal, 19.2%
(3) Cape Verde, 15.3%
(4) Sierra Leone, 14.5%
(5) Guinea-Bissau, 14.0%
(6) Liberia, 12.5%
(7) Niger, 12.4%

(8) Burkina Faso, 11.7%
(9) Ghana, 10.9%
(10) Mali, 10.2%
(11) Gambia, 9.4%
(12) Togo, 8.6%
(13) Côte d' Ivoire, 8.5%
(14) Benin, 7.2%
(15) Nigeria, 6.1%

North Africa

(16) Tunisia, 22.8%
(17) Mauritania, 17.9%
(18) Sudan, 17.8%
(19) Morocco, 10.8%
(20) Libyan Arab Jamahiriy, 7.7%
(21) Algeria, 6.2%
(22) Egypt, 2.0%
(23) Western Sahara, 0.0%

East Africa

(35) Rwanda, 48.8%
(36) Burundi, 30.5%
(37) Tanzania, 30.4%
(38) Uganda, 29.8%
(39) Seychelles, 29.4%
(40) Eritrea, 22.0%
(41) Ethiopia, 21.9%
(42) Djibouti, 10.8%
(43) Dem. Rep. Congo, 8.4%
(44) Somalia, 7.8%
(45) Kenya, 7.3%
(46) Madagascar, 6.9%
(47) Comoros, 3.0%

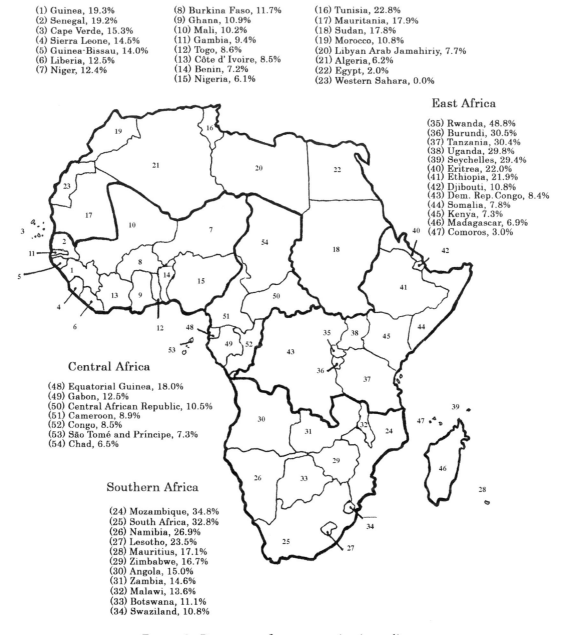

Central Africa

(48) Equatorial Guinea, 18.0%
(49) Gabon, 12.5%
(50) Central African Republic, 10.5%
(51) Cameroon, 8.9%
(52) Congo, 8.5%
(53) São Tomé and Príncipe, 7.3%
(54) Chad, 6.5%

Southern Africa

(24) Mozambique, 34.8%
(25) South Africa, 32.8%
(26) Namibia, 26.9%
(27) Lesotho, 23.5%
(28) Mauritius, 17.1%
(29) Zimbabwe, 16.7%
(30) Angola, 15.0%
(31) Zambia, 14.6%
(32) Malawi, 13.6%
(33) Botswana, 11.1%
(34) Swaziland, 10.8%

FIGURE 2. Percentage of women serving in parliament.

Nordic states)."[39] Figure 2 denotes the percentages of women in the parliaments of African countries as of February 2007. The countries are grouped according to the classification of the United Nations Economic Commission for Africa (ECA).[40]

The IPU has developed a World Classification of women in parliaments. (See Appendix.) Bauer and Britton point out the particular significance of Rwanda's percentage of women. In October 2003, ten years after genocide had taken the lives of almost one million people, Rwanda elected 39 women to its 80-member Chamber of Deputies. In one night, Rwanda surpassed Sweden as the country with the highest percentage of women in its national legislature. The increase of Scandinavian and European countries was slow and steady, ranging from 35 to 45 percent female in early 2000. By contrast, in just one election, Rwanda's percentage of women jumped to 48.8 percent.[41]

In the last ten years, several African countries have moved from the bottom to the top of the list of countries in women's representation in national legislatures.[42] Gender balance moved more towards equality with the inauguration in 2006 of Ellen Johnson-Sirleaf as president of Liberia and more women being elected in countries such as Kenya, Somalia, Zimbabwe, Lesotho, Swaziland, Rwanda, Zambia and South Africa.[43]

WOMEN VICE PRESIDENTIAL CANDIDATES FROM 2000

Women in many countries in Africa have been denied the opportunity to seek higher office, such as president and vice president. The situation is changing. In 2006, Ellen Johnson-Sirleaf became President of Liberia. Since 2000, an increasing number of women have been candidates for vice president. Some examples are, in 2005, six women who unsuccessfully aspired for the office. From Liberia, two women sought office: Amelia Ward and Parleh D. Harris, a civil servant in the Gender Affairs Ministry, and a former senatorial candidate. Four women sought election in Tanzania: Rukia Omar Kiota, vice chairperson of the Labour Party; Naila Majid Jidawi; Anna Valerian Komu, the Chadema Party; and Naila Jidawi, who in 2000 was barred from running for president of Zanzibar.[44]

In 2003, four women from Nigeria contended for vice president: Hajiya Asmau, Hajia Maira Baturiya Habib, Asmau Aliyu Mohammed, and Maimunatu Lata Tombai.[45] Sierra Leone had two women compete in 2002: Deborah Salaam, running mate of Zainab Hawa Bangura, and Satta Kumba Amara.[46]

WOMEN AMBASSADORS AND REPRESENTATIVES TO THE UNITED NATIONS

The offices held by women as representatives and ambassadors are too numerous to list. I have selected a few to demonstrate the breadth of their leadership. In many cases, women who served as permanent representatives and ambassadors to the United Nations came to their current office with broad experience. Before her 2004 position, María de Fátima Lima Veiga from Cape Verde was Ambassador to Cuba from 1999 to 2001; Secretary of State of Foreign Affairs, 2001 to 2002; and Minister of Foreign Affairs, 2002 to 2004.[47]

In 2003, Judith Mbula Bahemuka from Kenya was chairperson of the Social and Human Sciences National Committee at the United Nations Educational, Scientific and Cultural Organization (UNESCO) National Commission. Serving from 2001 to 2003, Luzéria Dos Santos Jaló, Guinea Bissau, held offices in her country's Ministry of Finance from 1986 to 1995, and from 1999 to 2000 she was the president of the Institute of Women and Children.[48]

Neh Rita Sangai Dukuly-Tolbert of Liberia served from 1999 to 2001. Dukuly-Tolbert held ambassadorships to France, UNESCO, Switzerland, Luxembourg and Spain. Her term as ambassador to China began in 2004.[49]

Mahawa Bangoura Camara from Guinea served from 1999 to 2000 and subsequently was the ambassador to the United States and Foreign Minister, 2000–02.[50]

Three women served in the 1980s: Biyémi Kekeh, Togo, from 1982 to 1983; Simone Mairie, Cameroon, from 1982 to 1985; and Hanna Abedou Bowen Jones, Liberia, from 1981 to 1985. She had served as Liberia's Minister of Post, 1975–78; Minister of Communication,

1977–78; and Minister of Health and Social Security, 1978–81; and she was Vice-President of the General Assembly of the United Nations, 1983–84.[51]

During the 1970s three women served. Gwendoline C. Konie from Zambia served from 1977 to 1979. Previously she was ambassador to Denmark, Sweden, Norway, Finland and Iceland. After her service, she was ambassador to Belgium, the European Union and Germany from 1992 to 1999 and in 2000. In 2000, she established the Social Democratic Party, and in 2001, she announced her candidacy for the presidency. She did not win.[52]

From 1975 to 1977, Angie Brook-Randolph from Liberia served as Ambassador to the U.N. Some of her previously held offices include: Assistant Secretary of State of Liberia, delegate to the U.N., and Vice President. She became President of the United Nations General Assembly, and has served as a judge in the Supreme Court from 1977.[53]

Jeanne Martin-Cisse from Guinea served from 1972 to 1976. For one month in 1972 she was President of the Security Council. Previously she also held the offices of deputy president of Assemblée Nationale and Minister of Social Affairs in Guinea.[54]

Conclusions

Merely counting the number of women in politics does not measure the difference they make.[55] "Numbers matter simply in terms of women's right to participate in decision-making. But that numbers are not sufficient to ensure women's human rights are taken on board in terms of decision-making," is the philosophy of L. Muthoni Wanyeki, the Executive Director for the African Women's Development and Communication Network (FEMNET) located in Nairobi, Kenya.[56] Wanyeki also believes: "That many women 'leaders' exist outside of the political domain, particularly among female activists. That female artists, particularly singers and writers, probably do more to shape the consciousness of African women (and men) than female politicians."[57]

Ellen Johnson-Sirleaf, President, Republic of Liberia, would agree that numbers alone are insufficient. She writes that it is critical "to target all stages of women's political participation, from the moment they decide they want to run for public office, through each step till they reach that designated office, and thereafter to ensure that as members of parliaments, they have the means and needed resources to impact positively and constructively on the advancement of their nation."[58]

Yet, the evidence the International Institute for Democracy and Electoral Assistance (IDEA) has collected "suggests that increasing numerical representation is an important first step towards facilitating real change in power relations throughout the world."[59]

Statistics help represent the exciting activity taking place all over the world. The special concentration on Africa shows that women are making stronger inroads into decision-making positions. Numbers do not tell the entire story of the difference women are making, but it is one way to focus on the change taking place. The incidence picture presented is limited in that it addresses primarily women leaders in some national and international government positions. Many more women serve in other national and international positions and on the local level. Still more women serve in leadership positions in the private sector, such as law enforcement, religious offices, and business.

2. Women of Africa in New or Changing Roles

Women's presence in parliaments around the world is a reality that is impacting on the social, political and economic fabric of nations and of the world. Yet, their access to these important legislative structures, learning how to work within them, and the extent to which they impact on and through them, remain serious challenges.
— *Ellen Johnson-Sirleaf, President, Republic of Liberia*[1]

Insights into questions of leadership are revealed through examinations of formation of women-headed households, the rhetoric that strong women use, and the expansively professed view of African women versus what actually is the case. In spite of progress, the leadership challenges coexist with post colonial cultural tradition. Yet, Africa now has a higher percentage of women in government than developed nations. Africa's rising female leaders and reasons for the breakthrough are interesting because the breakthrough is not without opposition and limitations.

Leadership Challenges

At the beginning of the 21st century women throughout the world have partly succeeded in combating discrimination based on gender, writes Nadezhda Shvedova. Legal and political context barriers also remain. Gender challenges that persist are:

• balancing work and family obligations;
• segregation into lower-paid jobs;
• inequality of pay between men and women;
• the feminization of poverty;
• increases in violence against women; and
• exclusion from post-conflict peace negotiations and rehabilitation and reconstruction efforts.[2]

Heading Shvedova's list of legal barriers is the fact that the governments of many countries remain male-dominated. Other legal obstacles include: lack of party support, the type of electoral system, the type of quota provisions and the degree to which they are enforced, the many institutions that reflect male standards and political attitudes, lack of coordination with and support from women's organizations and other NGOs, women's culturally enforced low self-esteem and self-confidence, and lack of proper media attention to women's contributions and potential.[3]

Shvedova writes, "in all countries women need to be able to compete on a level playing field with men." Indicators of success of women's participation in politics include: political, institutional and financial guarantees so that female nominees in electoral campaigns have equal participation; formulating legislative regulations for implementing effective quota mechanisms; creating educational programs and centers to prepare women for political careers; and developing and supporting schools for these centers.[4]

"The increase in women's participation on the African continent in the past few years has been greater than that experienced at any other time in the past four decades, rising tenfold to over 14 percent in 2003,"[5] writes Karen Fogg, Secretary-General of the International Institute for Democracy and Electoral Assistance (IDEA). Gender quotas are seen as important for increasing women's access to decision-making bodies throughout the world. Fogg reports that observations of Africa are very encouraging. More than 20 countries either have legislated quotas or political parties that have voluntarily adopted them. These measures have contributed directly to the increased number of women who have accessed the legislature. The average representation of women in sub–Saharan Africa in 1995 was 9.8 percent; it had increased to 15.1 percent by 2004.[6]

The African Landscape: Generations of Activism

Africa's long legacy of female leaders that began in antiquity is well established. From the mid 1980s and after the early 1990s, women's organizations and other groups have increased throughout Africa. In these associations women can state such concerns by taking claims to land, inheritance and associational autonomy to court; challenging laws and constitutions that do not uphold gender equality; and moving into political openings previously limited to men.[7]

The shift in women's independence movements in the late 1990s is due to a variety of reasons including the rise of multi-partyism and demise of military rule; the growing influence of the international women's movement; shifting donor strategies; the expansion of the use of the cell phone and of the Internet along with increased secondary and university educated women.[8]

Women's collective action often represented the largest organized group within society. All women and all issues pertaining to women were included. Aili Mari Tripp writes that these groups drew upon "women's identification with motherhood and the private sphere to make claims on participation in the public sphere. But it also worked the other way around as women saw that participation in the public sphere gave them entitlements to make claims for greater decision making within the home."[9]

As a consequence, Tripp believes the most important change occurred in the late 1980s and 1990s. These organizations began to challenge "the stranglehold clientelism and state patronage had on women's mobilization in the post independence period."[10] And even though the cultural and political changes are far from over and associational autonomy is under threat, Tripp believes women "have set in motion important and unprecedented societal transformation."[11]

Tripp's analysis provides understanding in addressing some of the African women who are now serving in high positions. (See also Chapter 4.)

African Women Leaders

The 2006 election of Ellen Johnson-Sirleaf, a Liberian woman, as president marked a first for Africa. Slvia Tamale writes that to meet the need for more women in the highest offices of their countries, some African women are giving "men a run for their money."[12] In addition to Johnson-Sirleaf, Tamale includes women such as: Specioza Wandira-Kazibwe from Uganda, as the first woman to ascend to the second highest political position in her country; Rose Rugendo as Foreign Affairs Minister of Tanzania; Charity Ngilu, Minister of Health for Kenya; Inonge Mbikusita-Lewanika, 2001 and 2002 Ambassador of the Republic of Zambia to the United States of America; and Margaret Dongo, who is a parliamentarian and ex-freedom fighter for Zimbabwe.[13]

This list of notable women expands greatly when we examine the international non-governmental organization, Femmes Africa Solidarité's work in progress, *African Women Pioneers*. This praiseworthy work lists six presidents and vice presidents, three presidential candidates, and 13 ministers, as well as the numerous women who serve in African mechanisms such as commissioners, directors and leaders of organizations, governmental and non-governmental. Six international representatives are featured as well as 40 women active in international organizations and civil society.[14]

L. Muthoni Wanyeki, who is the Executive Director of the African Women's Development and Communication Network (FEMNET), maintains it is next to impossible to specify who are the most successful women in the government and politics in Africa. She says, "There are 53 countries in Africa, each with women who've made a difference to other women in one way or another. And 'success' might not be defined in those terms in any case."[15]

Challenges for Parliamentarians

Holding office presents challenges. Former ambassador from Mexico to the United Nations, Rosario Green, believes that women are sometimes subjected to more scrutiny at work than are men. This close inspection slows down women's advancement. To advance to positions of authority, women sometimes have to be overqualified to get noticed. And sometimes, after an appointment, a woman is said to be just like a man.[16]

Inonge Mbikusita-Lewanika, ambassador to the United States for Zambia, believes that multiple roles make getting into and staying in positions of power difficult. If the husband of a female parliamentarian doesn't support her, her life becomes hard. Mbikusita-Lewanika told *Africa Renewal*, "When you have young children, you have to rush home while your male counterparts carry on with discussions in the bars or in the chambers."[17]

THE PATH TO ELECTED OFFICE

Just as holding office presents challenges, the path to that office is often not easy. Gender quotas can help assure women will hold office. Gumisai Mutume writes that in Washington, D.C., Mbikusita-Lewanika is one of 16 female ambassadors to the United States. Out of the eight that are African, seven are from Southern Africa. These results are no coincidence, because of the Southern African Development Community (SADC) declaration on gender and development that required each country to reach at least 30 percent female representation in decision making by 2005, writes Mutume.[18]

"In no country do women have political status, access or influence equal to men's,"[19] nor is enfranchisement of women universal. Miki Caul Kittilson would agree that women must play an active role in creating opportunity. But since political parties are the gatekeepers to elected offices, they can facilitate or impede women's participation in parliament. Thus, women's efforts are most effective when they recognize favorable conditions within the party and party system and where they devise strategies to be included. Once in a top-level party position, women can encourage parties to adopt measures to increase the proportion of women in their delegations to parliament.[20]

Positive attitudes of women political elites are essential to getting more women into powerful positions. Kittilson concludes: "Those groundbreaking women must be willing to 'let the ladder down,' and recent surveys point towards a growing recognition of the effectiveness of quota policies."[21]

In Africa, "for many women the path to power has been difficult and even onerous,"[22] writes Alida Brill. Women have the dual responsibilities of the domestic and public spheres. The public woman is the most critical to alleviating gender stereotype and bias necessary to challenge assumptions about gender organization and sex-role assignment.

Even when women are politically active, the road is fraught with difficulty. South African Thenjiwe Mtintso describes and outlines problems faced in her early days of parliament.

In 1994, Mtintso was elected to serve as a member in South Africa's first democratic Parliament, was a member of the select committee for Defense, the study group for the Reconstruction and Development Program and the Rules Committee, and was appointed as chairperson of the Commission on Gender Equality.[23]

Mtintso writes that a significant number of women entered Parliament in 1994, 106 out of 400, but in the cabinet, the idea of proportional representation disappeared. Sixteen out of 90 senators were women, but out of 27 ministers, only two were women, the minister of health, Dr. Nkosazana Zuma-Dlamini, and the minister of public enterprise, Ms. Stella Sigcau. Of 11 deputy ministers, two were women, and of 25 chairpersons of standing committees, six were women. The speaker of the house, Dr. Frene Ginwala, was female. All women were from the ANC.[24]

In this initial period, female parliamentarians experienced three major strains: "gender-role conflict at home; a women-unfriendly Parliament and gender constraints; [and] parliamentary procedures as well as structural and political factors."[25]

Mainly, gender-role conflict arose at home because of society's artificial divide between the personal and the political. Women have always been assigned more work. Women are caregivers to all in the family, responsible for a working and loving home. Men are the head of the family, responsible for financial security and decision-making. A big hurdle for some husbands to accept was that parliamentarians performed their functions in Cape Town. Thus, some families viewed women parliamentarians as not fulfilling their role of caring and responsibility. So women were faced with moving and leaving their children with an unwilling partner, forfeiting personal fulfillment, or taking the children with them and facing the challenge of inadequate child care. The societal definition of division of labor makes it easier for men to move and either take or leave the family. An even bigger hurdle was the reversal of roles when a woman became a parliamentarian; Mtintso found it was stressful for both husband and wife.[26]

Secondly, Parliament is women-unfriendly and imposes gender constraints, writes Mtintso. Women with children were without organized child care, making evening parliamentary responsibilities difficult. Government-organized child care met with resistance when it was first addressed in the parliament.[27]

Lastly, parliamentary procedures as well as structural and political factors constrain women. Mtintso points out that procedures of addressing parliament are easier for the intellectual woman than the majority with less education. A need exists to consider the needs of women from the varied backgrounds and set up different support structures. Structurally, there was no women's ministry, thus, no select committee on gender. Women in other positions must pursue gender issues. This limitation translates into no link with the women on the outside of Parliament. And even though the constitution specifies equality, neither the Cabinet nor the Parliament has addressed the issue of pervasive patriarchy. Coupled with these difficulties, Mtintso believes women parliamentarians had "insufficient preparation about how Parliament operates and what to expect."[28] Along with lack of training, some men perceive their power threatened by women and some women accept male orientation and "play the game according to the rules dictated by male domination instead of trying to change the whole game and its rules."[29] Mtintso believes these behaviors do not help to restructure society and power relations.

Developing Leadership

LEADERSHIP AND WOMEN-HEADED HOUSEHOLDS: BOTSWANA CASE STUDY

We can learn about the development of leadership from different explanations for the formation of women-headed households. Through case studies that included Central America and Botswana, Kavita Datta and Cathy McIlwaine provide insights into questions of leadership.

Women-headed households form for different reasons. Women no longer form households because of male abandonment, but may choose to do so to take control of their lives and the lives of their children. Women taking control because they are poor is not always the case. Social and economic marginalization depends upon the idealization of marriage and motherhood by the community, the church and the state. When it comes to the resulting style of female leadership, the transition from oppressive to empowering forms of leadership may not be natural or immediate when males are replaced by women. Likewise, Datta and McIlwaine maintain, organizations led by women sometimes adopt structures with hierarchies based on age, class, and education as well as gender.[30]

The case study of Botswana in 1995 found that women as household heads do not always adopt egalitarian and enabling patterns of decision making.[31] Permanent female heads of households realize there are benefits that were denied in marriage or cohabitation.[32] Allocation of tasks and resources are two of the central issues in household leadership. Task allocation was decided through use of gender hierarchies in both male and female-headed households. Male-heads assigned tasks, and usually to females. If there were no women, young men did household duties. Female-heads tried to have more egalitarian arrangements, but like male-heads, younger females did most of the work. In some cases, female-heads adopted domineering leadership styles. Requirements made by female-heads on younger relatives frequently produced conflict. Most elderly males were not asked to do domestic work.[33]

Allocation of resources, particularly money and food, has received more attention than sharing space, write Datta and McIlwaine. Gender and age hierarchies were the deciding factors. Male-heads retained their private space. Women heads reinforced this social norm of "male privilege" and favored men's need for space.[34]

Positive images of women's style of leadership have filtered to the grassroots, raising the question whether male and female leadership styles differ, challenging existing gender ideologies that underscore that men are better heads than women.[35] And yet, their study concluded that in spite of encouraging breakthroughs, "gender ideologies — which prescribe that men are 'better' leaders of household than women — are firmly entrenched."[36]

LEADERSHIP AND RHETORIC:
CASE STUDY IN GITHUMU, KENYA

We can learn about the development of leadership from the rhetoric that strong women use through an examination of women's inheritance and rhetoric used in the new era of organizational authority. A case study in Githumu, Kenya, provides additional insight.

Strong women have traditionally learned to use language to influence and persuade, as well as to listen and understand, critical to understanding leadership. Women have had the ability to influence people with their language using whatever available means of persuasion in any given situation. Women had the ability to influence those around them by discovering what the available means of persuasion were.[37] According to Jane Thompson Stephens, one of the ways was "through the art of persuading the persuaders."[38] Women have had to value their influence through indirect means, for example, through a husband or son.

Since women were positioned at the threshold of power, they used the power of language in less open and formal situations such as through songs, stories, letters, conversations and at slumber parties or club meetings. Thompson Stephens concludes, "the leadership of women has been diminished, not only by their lack of access to direct and legitimate authority, but by their lack of connection to a tradition of powerful female voices with direct influence."[39]

Thompson Stephens focuses on a new era of direct access to organizational authority, examining rhetoric women have developed apart from authoritarian infrastructures of male-led institutions. Her interviews revealed strong women leaders who were also tender and lacked a self-protectiveness.[40] She asks what qualities of women's voices we want to bring to leadership as we "reshuffle the deck of power and privilege," and how will leadership affect the quality of women's voices.[41]

Thompson Stephens found women reluctant to tell the truth because they themselves will not allow it. I found a degree of this reluctance when I interviewed Masai women in Tanzania on the subject of female circumcision. I would receive traditional answers such as "we like it" and "it is tradition."[42] Expert African interviewees told me that unless I was accompanied by a female interpreter, the Masai women would be reluctant to talk openly. My interpreter was male.

Esther Njathi worked with *Maendeleo Ya Wana Wake*, a national women's health collective. Her mother was one of the organization's first leaders. When Thompson Stephens asked Esther to tell her about her mother, Esther triumphantly replied, "You know she was not circumcised."[43] Esther's grandmother made a radical choice and had not allowed her daughters to be circumcised. Consequently, Esther's confidence was "the product of a risky investment that her grandmother made in her mother's future."[44]

Women in Kenya and Tanzania were bound to silence by all important relationships. They are free to talk only when they become old women. The voices of these free women are unsettling to the tribal males. One result at the time of Thompson Stephens' writing, prior to 2000, was a rise in witch burning of older women.[45]

The result of such intimidation "is a language which always renders a dichotomy, a 'split world,' in which one side is affirmed while the other is negated," writes Thompson Stephens.[46]

She explains that the father tongue language holds women in place. At times the mother tongue can tumble the house of cards created by patriarchy with a statement, for example, "You broke my heart." The father tongue protects itself with its rule of no talking back. But the women leaders that Thompson Stephens interviewed displayed a lack of self-protectiveness. They were strong, but open, thus engaging in rule changing.[47]

ROLES AND CHANGE IN LEADERSHIP: REALITY VERSUS RUMOR IN NIGERIA

There is a wide discrepancy between what is expansively professed about African women and what actually is the case, writes Nkiru Nzegwu. Because women are not adequately represented in history, "one would think that women did not participate in governance, existed only in shadowy spheres, and meekly accepted whatever their male lords and masters directed."[48] Women's powerlessness is not from culture, but from the male privileged policies and programs since colonization.

Nonetheless, that women are rarely included in historical narratives allows scholars "a stereotypical picture of passive ineffectual women."[49] This position makes it difficult to understand from where women derived the power to act. Scholars "resolve this theoretical dilemma by questioning the authenticity of the powers and challenging the legitimacy of women's actions."[50]

Nkiru Nzegwu maintains that having more honesty in men's roles does African women a service. Equally valuable would be to include the history of women's resistance to male reconstructions of traditional levels of government. In accounting for women's loss of ground in politics and the political arena, one important reason is economic, the lack of equal opportunities with men to accumulate wealth and increase their net worth potential. In addition, campaign costs are formidable. Family responsibilities, disproportionately assigned to women, leave men free to pursue their goals. The result is that women are left out of the competition.[51]

In addition to funds, Nzegwu writes that for male and female politicians, a "godfather" is needed. But for women, the role of the godfather or male politician is potentially of a sexist nature, for they hold the belief that women should defer to men, and if women do not, they are perceived as a threat and things are made difficult for them. In the Nigerian process, this situation occurs because of the prevalence of men at the executive decision-making level of the party. Sexism forces women to rely on their own funds, husbands, significant others, family and godfathers. Nzegwu writes that these barriers prevent a significant number of women from political activity because of the personal compromises that they do not wish to make.[52]

The role of violence and brutalization pervades politics in Africa. Strategies designed to intimidate are used to derail women with political aspirations; for example: "Bands of thugs are freely used to beat up opponents, invade polling centers, and abscond with election result sheets in a process in which women become easy targets. When these tactics fail, there is little hesitation about using state apparatus punitively."[53]

In addition to the economic factor, family responsibility, violence and sexism, Nzegwu believes that the military is a "rarely mentioned institution that has played a formidable role in stymieing women's political advancement."[54] In west Africa, the concern should not be only for Sierra Leone and Liberia, but also for fairly stable governments where military leaders become civilian officials, such as Ghana, Nigeria, Togo and Benin. These leaders bring with them their devaluing attitudes towards women. In these cultures, women rise to and fall from political stature only as wives when they become First Ladies.

In 1994, Advocate Bience Gawanas from the Office of the Ombudsman of Namibia reported that many women participated in the political campaign of 1986 that led to independence. Yet, although law promoted equality, parties did not place women on their lists or elect them into influential positions until subsequent elections.[55]

War is a common occurrence in Africa, writes Madonna Owusuah Larbi. The wars differ in intensity, from simmering in the Western Sahara to severe in Sierra Leone. Either way, when peace is being negotiated, the perspectives of women are not represented in adequate numbers. Often women become the victims in war by rape or violence and death. As African women struggle in society for equal opportunity and social justice, they also provide recruits for armies, through their partners, children and sometimes themselves.[56]

The Challenges Leadership Presents

Opinions differ as to whether gender issues present challenges to leadership. Nzegwu basically believes that leadership problems are due to male role dominance. Agozino holds that we should conclude that leadership problems are not primarily sexually or gender based. Men and women fought against imperialism alongside one another, but men became more powerful and sometimes oppressive following the emancipation.[57]

Leadership challenges the coexistence with postcolonial cultural tradition. Considering that the status of women in Africa is so low, the 2006 election of Ellen Johnson-Sirleaf as Liberian president is an example of progressive change.[58] Jane Thompson Stephens believed that first-generation women leaders in special areas, through the complex and sometimes unconscious work they do, negotiate room for their own voice and style in traditional male-driven fields, such as church, business and higher education. She believes that it is important to "unpack the rhetorical repertoire that women leaders have developed apart from the authoritarian infrastructures of male-led institutions."[59] Thus, it is likely that Johnson-Sirleaf did not lose the memory, language, and images that she inherited from women leaders in her past.

THE CONTINENTAL INITIATIVE

In Accra, Ghana, in December 1995,[60] 23 women from different activist organizations formed the Continental Initiative. The countries represented included Burkina Faso, Cameroon, Ghana, Malawi, Mali, Nigeria, Sierra Leone, Tanzania, Zambia, Zimbabwe, Swaziland and Somalia. The organizations reaffirmed that the "African Renaissance" in the making, is not built on war. Good governance is not built on military regimes.[61]

Progressive women were hopeful, and according to Larbi, "Unlike the era of the leaders of the independence movement, where the handful of men leaders had women fawning over them, the leaders of the African women's movement have to contend with many more politically aware supporters, who are able to question and who will not be blinded by promises that cannot be supported."[62]

TOWARDS WOMEN AND GOVERNANCE

Identification of Potential Leaders Governments in the tropical areas have known the importance of women's formal participation in government. By the mid 1970s, they had concentrated on unifying and consolidating under government women's groups along with other organizations. In addition, some key military regimes, including Nigeria, Upper Volta (renamed Burkina Faso in 1984),[63] Ghana, Mali and Senegal, intended to return their countries to civilian rule.[64] Many reasons were given for the change, but whatever approach governments took, all had in common a knowledge that they could not remain in power unless they addressed the issue of popular participation in the political system.[65]

In 1994, Amina Mama, the chairperson of gender studies at the African Gender Institute at the University of Cape Town, told the African Women and Governance Seminar and Training Workshop in Entebbe, Uganda, that donors to Africa have not addressed the development needs of women. By doing so, they have overlooked an important resource, "women who are in a position to make a difference or women who could get into such positions relatively easy."[66] The seminar and workshops worked to gain African women's participation in development and decision making at various levels.

In addition, an examination of middle-class women reveals that the women who move into top posts are a small minority of the class's elite. Ordinary middle-class women haven't "pulled ahead of the pack and are in competition with a very large pool of men."[67]

Packaging and Winning the Women's Vote Female candidates walk a fine line, write Akwe Amosu and Ofeibea Quist-Arcton. Johnson-Sirleaf made much of her attributes as a homemaker and conciliator, but did not present herself as a feminist. Although her plan of attack appeared to be an effort not to alienate male voters, portraying herself as a feminist may have affected female voters in the same way. A woman candidate's best approach is most likely to argue that she has the best skills for the position rather than emphasizing her gender.[68]

An emerging pattern is that several leading female politicians have backgrounds in finance and economics. Managing government with these theories makes knowledge and intellectual capacity matter. Amosu and Quist-Arcton suggest, "Smart women may have less trouble climbing the ladder in these sectors than in others where gender, political alliances, ethnic and other affiliations matter more."[69] Since Africa suffers a shortage of top-level people, gender is not as significant as it might be in lower-level positions. High-level people like Johnson-Sirleaf and Okonjo-Iweala, Minister of Finance in Nigeria, come to their positions as very accomplished individuals. They are more competent than most men. Amosu and Quist-Arcton conclude that gender is not as important "as an ability to think strategically and a track record of attracting and managing resources."[70]

Reasons Women Are Gaining in Elected Offices in Some Areas and Not in Others L. Muthoni Wanyeki believes Rwanda, South Africa and Uganda represent countries where the progress of women in assuming political and governmental positions has been increasing rapidly. She explains the factors that have contributed to or caused the rapid progress:

> Contributing factors: women's involvement in conflict resolution and transitional justice processes (including constitutional settlements entrenching women's equality); women's advocacy for constitutional and legal provisions around affirmative action; women's advocacy around women's experiences of the electoral/political process; all of the above pre-supposing the mobilization of women around the issues.[71]

Conflict does not automatically change the balance of political and social power, but it can provide opportunities for women, who outnumber the men, writes Gumisai Mutume. In the extreme case of the post–1994 genocide in Rwanda, for every four men, there were six women. In other conflicts such as the war for Eritrean independence from Ethiopia and the wars of liberation of South Africa and Zimbabwe, women gained some equality by fighting alongside men. Although Zimbabwe's gain did not hold, women renewed their efforts through the Beijing conference.[72]

QUOTAS FOR WOMEN BY PERCENTAGE IN PARLIAMENT

Country and Election System	Quota Type(s)	Results last election	% of women in parliament
Rwanda List PR	Constitutional Quota for National Parliaments; Election Law Quota Regulation, National Parliament; Constitutional or Legislative Quota, Sub-National Level	39 of 80	48.8
Mozambique List PR	Political Party Quota for Electoral Candidates	87 of 250	34.8
South Africa List PR	Constitutional or Legislative Quota, Sub-National Level; Political Party Quota for Electoral Candidates	131 of 400	32.8
Burundi List PR	Constitutional Quota for National Parliaments; Election Law Quota Regulation, National Parliament	36 of 118	30.5
United Republic of Tanzania FPTP	Constitutional Quota for National Parliaments; Election Law Quota Regulation, National Parliament; Constitutional or Legislative Quota, Sub-National Level	97 of 319	30.4
Namibia List PR	Constitutional or Legislative Quota, Sub-National Level; Political Party Quota for Electoral Candidates	21 of 78	26.9
Uganda FPTP	Constitutional Quota for National Parliaments; Election Law Quota Regulation, National Parliament; Constitutional or Legislative Quota, Sub-National Level	73 of 305	23.9
Tunisia Parallel	Political Party Quota for Electoral Candidates	43 of 189	22.8
Eritrea N	Election Law Quota Regulation, National Parliament	33 of 150	22.0
Ethiopia FPTP	Political Party Quota for Electoral Candidates	116 of 546	21.2
Senegal Parallel	Political Party Quota for Electoral Candidates	23 of 120	19.2
Equatorial Guinea List PR	Political Party Quota for Electoral Candidates	18 of 100	18.0
Sudan FPTP	Election Law Quota Regulation, National Parliament	66 of 450	14.7
Sierra Leone List PR	Political Party Quota for Electoral Candidates	18 of 124	14.5
Malawi FPTP	Political Party Quota for Electoral Candidates	27 of 188	14.4
Liberia N	Election Law Quota Regulation, National Parliament	8 of 64	12.5
Niger List PR	Election Law Quota Regulation, National Parliament; Political Party Quota for Electoral Candidates	14 of 113	12.4

Country and Election System	Quota Type(s)	Results last election	% of women in parliament
Lesotho MMP	Constitutional or Legislative Quota, Sub-National Level	14 of 120	11.7
Burkina Faso List PR	Political Party Quota for Electoral Candidates	13 of 111	11.7
Botswana FPTP	Political Party Quota for Electoral Candidates	7 of 63	11.1
Ghana FPTP	Quotas existed previously or quota legislation has been proposed	25 of 230	10.9
Morocco List PR	Political Party Quota for Electoral Candidates	35 of 325	10.8
Djibouti PBV	Election Law Quota Regulation, National Parliament	7 of 65	10.8
Zimbabwe FPTP	Political Party Quota for Electoral Candidates	16 of 150	10.7
Mali TRS	Political Party Quota for Electoral Candidates	15 of 147	10.2
Cameroon PBV	Political Party Quota for Electoral Candidates	16 of 180	8.9
Côte d'Ivoire FPTP	Political Party Quota for Electoral Candidates	19 of 223	8.5
Somalia N	Constitutional Quota for National Parliaments	21 of 269	7.8
Kenya FPTP	Constitutional Quota for National Parliaments; Political Party Quota for Electoral Candidates	16 of 224	7.1
Algeria List PR	Political Party Quota for Electoral Candidates	24 of 389	6.2
Egypt TRS	Quotas existed previously or quota legislation has been proposed	9 of 454	2.0

Legend: FPTP   First Past the Post, a plurality/majority election system
List PR   List Proportional Representation, a proportional representation election system
MMP   Mixed Member Proportional, a mixed systems election system
N   No provisions for direct elections
Parallel   Parallel Systems, a mixed election system
PBV   Party Block Vote, a plurality/majority election system
TRS   The Two-Round System, a plurality/majority election system
See abbreviations and glossary for full definition of above systems.

Table Source: International IDEA and Stockholm University, "Country Overview," *Quota Database: Global Database of Quotas for Women*, 2006. Sept. 24, 2006, http://www.quotaproject.org/country.cfm?SortOrder=LastLowerPercentage%20DESC.

Legend Source: International IDEA and Stockholm University, *Electoral System Design: the New IDEA Handbook*, 2005–2006, ix, 173. Sept. 25, 2006, http://www.idea.int/publications/esd/index.cfm.

In countries where the progress of women has been slow or nonexistent, the lack of progress can be attributed to several factors. Wanyeki elaborates,

general lack of respect for democratic principles and human rights, making women's mobilization around the issues difficult; intransigence by political parties on the issues; manipulation of the electorate on the basis of false interpretations of customary/religious law re: women's public roles.[73]

Some reasons for Rwandan women's breakthrough to holding office include quota systems mandated by law and limitations of the opposition. Types of quota systems in Africa include constitutional, election law and political party quotas. Burkina Faso and Uganda are examples of countries that have constitutional provisions reserving seats in the national parliament for women. Election law quotas are provisions written into national legislation, as in Sudan. Political party quotas are internal rules that are adopted to include a certain percentage of women as candidates for office, as is the case in South Africa and Mozambique.[74]

"Gender quotas are now increasingly viewed as an important policy measure for boosting women's access to decision-making bodies throughout the world,"[75] writes Karen Fogg, Secretary-General of International Institute for Democracy and Electoral Assistance (IDEA). One especially relevant conclusion, reached by Professor Drude Dahlerup at Stockholm University, is "that in almost all political systems, no matter what electoral regime, it is the political parties, not the voters, that constitute the real gatekeepers into elected offices. Consequently, the party nomination practices should be kept in focus."[76]

Africa stands out from other parts of the world because it has two particular types of quotas, reserved seats and voluntary party quotas, writes Julie Ballington. Africa's quota systems are in contrast to Latin America with its many legislated political party quotas. She concludes that electoral systems matter because reserved seats exist under First Past the Post (FPTP) systems, whereas Proportional Representation (PR) systems are more suitable for the adoption of voluntary party quotas. Also important are women's mobilization at all levels of government and windows of opportunity for legislative reform.[77]

Julie Ballington gives six results of the quota implementation in Africa: First, women's political representation has increased steadily over the past two decades with Rwanda as the world leader in women's parliamentary representation. Mozambique and South Africa ranked among the top 15 nations. Second, electoral system type has a strong correlation with women's political representation: countries with PR systems have twice the number of women in parliament than those with majority systems. Third, African countries utilized gender quotas either by reserved seats or appointments, and voluntary party quotas. Fourth, regional and international organizations mobilizing and recommending women are critical to promote quotas. Fifth, party leaders' political will is central to the successful implementation of quotas. Finally, more research is needed to determine the political effect of quotas and whether they lead to any real empowerment of women.[78]

In Uganda, the effects of women's participation are mixed. Loyalty to the ruling party prevents women parliamentarians from supporting legislation favored by women's movements. Gumisai Mutume reports that Mozambique and South Africa have similar concerns, but that women, like men, are elected to represent the party, not necessarily to represent the interests of women. The challenge is whether and how to articulate gender issues distinct from party interests and identities. In Zimbabwe, the women's lobby viewed the appointment of the first woman deputy president, Joyce Mujuru, as a politically correct move by an intolerant government.[79]

Opposition often comes from societies with strong patriarchal traditions or where important political participants do not support quotas, as in Zambia. The limitations include the view that quotas are a transitory solution not a cure, and that women are disadvantaged by lack of financial resources.[80]

The success of women in politics and government has had little effect on of the balance of power within the family, says Wanyeki. She says: "Reproductive and community labour in the private realm continues to rest in the hands of women and remain unquantified and un(der)valued in the public realm. Women's success in the public realm has also, in some instances, led to a backlash in the private realm."[81]

Gumisai Mutume writes, "Despite the challenges, a growing proportion of women are breaking through the glass ceiling."[82] Women leaders attribute their success to education and work opportunities, good mentoring by men and women, support from family, employers, supervisors, teachers and colleagues and successful lobbying by gender activists.

Successful Reconstruction of a War-Torn Country: Rwanda Reconstruction in war-torn countries dictates that women fill many positions formerly held by men. For example, Rwanda heads the world rankings of women in national parliaments (189 countries), with 48.8 percent of representation in the lower house to the world average of 17.2 percent, and 34.6 percent in the upper house to the world average of 16 percent.[83] (See Appendix 1.)

Violent conflicts can offer a new way to articulate debate about gender politics while also offering women a chance to live in a different way. This is all the more true when the liberation movement is part of the conflict as in Uganda. Women access a political space of power not previously open. Gretchen Bauer and Hannah E. Britton found their case studies confirmed "a connection between postconflict states and improvements in women's political representation."[84]

The Absence of Women in Senior Positions Despite the advances towards equality, Caroline Sweetman writes that "women are largely absent from senior positions in the national and international institutions that govern our life."[85] This absence marginalizes women from real power. Women must gain civil and political rights and institutional power in order to become leaders. Real change for women necessitates engagement with mainstream institutions.[86]

Organizations and International Conferences Through her study of Senegalese organizations, Amy S. Patterson challenges existing assumptions that organizations and civil society teach democratic values; for example, the idea that civil society organizations promote democratic values so that members can then challenge repressive state actions and promote democratic development. She argues that "groups in civil society rarely teach their members democratic values because most associations do not practice legitimate, inclusive and accountable decision making.... Social hierarchies and power relations that define how people of different genders and classes are to interact in the public realm limit democracy."[87] The result is that groups are not as effective as they might be and often are disorganized, and thus cannot achieve their goals. The groups are affected by the larger civil society's inefficiency and undemocratic systems. This nature of the larger society affects democratic transitions.

Abantu for Development and the many non-governmental organizations (NGOs) like it believe and teach that women's political participation from the grassroots up empowers women.[88] Non-governmental organizations play a vital role as they work to train women for leadership. One of the important functions of organizations is developing leadership skills.[89]

FEMNET, African Women's Development and Communication Network, coordinates African regional participation of NGOs. Its vision is to promote "African women's collective leadership for equality, peace and sustainable development"[90] through networking of African organizations. L. Muthoni Wanyeki explains FEMNET's purpose: "FEMNET works towards African women's development, equality and other human rights through advocacy at the regional and international levels, training on gender analysis and mainstreaming and communications."[91] When asked what are some of its major successes, Wanyeki replied:

> Maintaining a network of African women's organizations to enable the sharing of experiences and coordinated action at the regional and international levels. Providing a platform for engagement

with the United Nations, primarily through the Commission on the Status of Women but also through other relevant policy negotiation processes. Pioneering work by the African women's movement with the African Union, which contributed to the elaboration of the Protocol to the African Charter on Human and Peoples' Rights on the Rights of Women in Africa. Pioneering work on gender analysis and mainstreaming in Africa includes outcomes such as the development of frameworks and tools for the same in both English and French, and sector-specific frameworks and tools. It provides multiple communication channels, in both English and French, for the African women's movement.[92]

Wanyeki believes that the organization might be doing additional activities such as "building stronger national focal points and working more consistently on organizational development and sustainability, and organizational governance issues."[93]

A few other pan–African women's organizations and/or networks work to help women run for office and/or assist them once they are in office, but they tend to focus on specific sectoral work, according to Wanyeki. Examples are the Association of African Women for Research and Development (AAWORD) which focuses on research; Forum for African Women Educationalists (FAWE) concentrates on education; the Federation of African Women's Peace Networks (FERFAP), on peace; Society for Women Against AIDS in Africa (SWAA) on HIV/AIDS; and Women in Law and Development in Africa (WiLDAF) on law. Wanyeki states, "There are none that focus specifically on women's political participation (with the exception of networks of female parliamentarians that exist under, for example, the Commonwealth and the IPU)."[94]

Conclusion

Reaching a position of leadership poses many challenges, but it is also made possible through many avenues, for example, the practice women get through their living experience and the assistance of quota systems and organizations.

The international conferences of the 1980s and early 1990s set the stage for women to enter positions of leadership. Globally, their role was critical, as is discussed in Chapter 3. The international conventions and the world conferences on women of the 1980s and the early 1990s offered goals for the rights of women.

3. Leadership and Globalism

Achieving the goal of equal participation of women and men in decision-making will pro-
vide a balance that more accurately reflects the composition of society and is needed in order
to strengthen democracy and promote its proper functioning.
                        — Fourth World Conference on Women, Beijing, Platform
                        for Action, Women in Power and Decision Making[1]

International Discourses

International law serves as a basis for the concept of equal rights and the inherent human rights of women and men. Regional and local laws seek to model their practices on the international discourses. Those discourses include: the 1995 Beijing Declaration, the Global Platform for Action, the Charter of the United Nations, the Universal Declaration of Human Rights, the Convention on the Elimination of All Forms of Discrimination Against Women, the Convention on the Rights of the Child, the Declaration on the Elimination of Violence Against Women and the Declaration on the Right to Development.[2]

THE 1995 BEIJING DECLARATION

The year 2005 marked the ten-year anniversary of the Fourth World Conference of Women in Beijing. Member states of the United Nations were asked to submit an assessment of their progress and challenges on implementation at the national level and the outcomes of the twenty-third special session of the General Assembly, held in 2000. The Secretary-General's report was presented to the 49th session of the Commission on the Status of Women.

The report identified areas in which progress was lacking. These areas included: high rates of violence against women in all parts of the world, including zones of armed conflict; increasing incidence of HIV/AIDS among women; gender inequality in employment; lack of sexual and reproductive health rights and a lack of equal access under the law to land and property. The Commission's final declaration emphasized that "the full and effective implementation of the Beijing Declaration and Platform for Action was essential to achieving the internationally agreed development goals, including those contained in the Millennium Declaration."[3]

PROTOCOL ON THE RIGHTS OF WOMEN IN AFRICA

The Protocol on the Rights of Women in Africa was adopted at the African Union summit held in Maputo, Mozambique, in July 2003. In 2004, 29 of the African Union's 53 member states had signed the protocol and only one country, the Comoros, had ratified it. African groups launched a petition to African leaders in a continent-wide campaign to mobilize support for the Protocol.[4] Over 200 organizations petitioned the governments of Africa in 2004 to ratify the Protocol. Among them were African Women's Development and Communication Network (FEMNET), Credo for Freedom of Expression and Associated Rights, Equality Now–African Region, Fahamu Networks for Social Justice, and Oxfam GB–Pan African Policy.[5]

Ratification by fifteen countries was necessary for the Protocol to become law in Africa. In 2005, sixteen countries ratified the Protocol. The next step is the implementation of these rights at the national level.[6] The 20 countries that have signed and ratified the protocol as of August 21, 2006, are: Benin, Burkina Faso, Cape Verde, the Comoros, Djibouti, The Gambia, Lesotho, Libya, Malawi, Mali, Mauritania, Mozambique, Namibia, Nigeria, Rwanda, Senegal, Seychelles, South Africa, Togo and Zambia.[7] Eight countries have not signed the protocol and 25 have signed, but have not yet ratified it.

PROTOCOL ON THE RIGHTS OF WOMEN IN AFRICA:
STATUS OF SIGNATORIES AND RATIFICATIONS AS OF AUGUST 21, 2005

Countries		
Signed, ratified (20)	**Signed, not ratified (25)**	**Not signed (8)**
Benin	Algeria	Angola
Burkina Faso	Burundi	Botswana
Cape Verde	Cameroon	Central Africa Republic
Comoros	Chad	Egypt
Djibouti	Côte d'Ivoire	Eritrea
The Gambia	Congo	São Tomé and Príncipe
Lesotho	Democratic Republic of Congo	Sudan
Libya	Equatorial Guinea	Tunisia
Malawi	Ethiopia	
Mali	Gabon	
Mauritania	Ghana	
Mozambique	Guinea-Bissau	
Namibia	Guinea	
Nigeria	Kenya	
Rwanda	Liberia	
Senegal	Madagascar	
Seychelles	Mauritius	
South Africa	Niger	
Togo	Sahrawi Arab Democratic Republic	
Zambia	Sierra Leone	
	Somalia	
	Swaziland	
	Tanzania	
	Uganda	
	Zimbabwe	

Source: Equality Now — SOAWR Secretariat, email from Faiza Jama Mohamed, Africa Regional Director, Aug. 21, 2006.

International discourses are instrumental in bringing about equality. The Inter-Parliamentary Union (IPU) states, "The equal participation of women and men in public life is one of the cornerstones of the 1979 United Nations Convention on the Elimination of All Forms of Discrimination against Women (CEDAW)."[8] The Fourth World Conference on Women in 1995 brought forth a revitalized pressure for carrying out CEDAW provisions. The Conference identified "inequality between men and women in the sharing of power and decision-making at all levels" and "insufficient mechanisms at all levels to promote the advancement of women" as critical concerns where action was vital for the advancement of women.[9]

Intense international lobbying took place after 1995, with other instruments, such as the United Nations Security Council resolution 1325 on Women, Peace and Security, and the Millennium Development Goals (MDGs) making an impact. The IPU states, "The MDGs recognize the fundamental role of women in development, with the proportion of seats held by women in national parliaments being a key indicator in measuring progress on women's empowerment."[10]

The IPU concludes that the provisions of international instruments that relate "to the use of special measures, have proved pivotal for women's movements worldwide."[11]

International Regional Organizational Efforts

International and regional organizations have also contributed to equality. Through the grassroots they have provided information and tools for reform. They accomplish this dissemination "by working directly with political parties, by providing training to women candidates seeking election or those already in parliament, and through technical assistance projects. Promoting women's participation within international organizations is also important."[12]

The Inter-Parliamentary Union (IPU) is the only international organization adopting measures and mechanisms to promote gender equality within the organization. As of 2005, 32 percent of the participants were women, surpassing the 30 percent target set by the United Nations. But IPU states that "underpinning all such efforts, however, is the need for political will, both within and outside parliaments and at the international, regional and local levels."[13]

IPU believes that the incremental change in the past decades is not so much because women claim space, but the result of electoral quotas, political party commitment and will, and "sustained mobilization and emphasis placed on achieving gender equality by the international community."[14] One scholar contends that construction of effective leadership must occur across national boundaries and is thus crucial to the facilitation of leadership globally.[15]

Post 1995 Beijing World Conference

VOCABULARY OF INTERNATIONAL DEVELOPMENT AGENCIES

Language is a critical component of effective leadership skills, but "in the vocabulary of international development agencies 'women's empowerment' is an ill defined concept."[16] Sara Hlupekile Longwe writes that insisting that women are empowered by access to education or by increased access to credit or land is inadequate because power is about increased control over resources. At the national level, this means women control resources through a presence in government, and thus have power to allocate those resources equally.[17] Further, she states, "It is the nature of empowerment that it cannot be given. It has to be taken."[18] Thus, patriarchal claims that women lack education, confidence or leadership qualities should be ignored.

RECOGNIZING DIFFERENT LEADERSHIP STRATEGIES

Transformational leadership and transformation of institutions go hand in hand. And transforming media coverage is an important and necessary supplement.

Transforming Leadership and Individuals Peggy Antrobus suggests that a political view on social change would begin by acknowledging gender imbalances of power and recognize the need to address these disproportions if change is to be equitable. Also acknowledged is the validity of feminist politics to the process of social change.[19]

Women within the structures of government and international agencies must assume some responsibility for social change, according to Antrobus. They must recognize the inherent contradictions in international programs. These programs propose to advance gender equity, lessen poverty, and end violence, "while governments continue to pursue policies and programmes that take them further from those goals."[20] She suggests: "Building bridges is necessary, between women bureaucrats and those women working beyond the structures of government and international agencies, who are therefore better placed to challenge these institutions and to hold governments accountable."[21] A need exists not only to distinguish between different strategies but also "between those women who are most likely to lead us on a transformational path, and those who prefer to remain within the status quo," Antrobus concludes.[22]

Perhaps one of the ways to the path of transformational leadership is through understanding the relationship between spirituality and charisma. Julia Preece explores this relationship in the southern African context of Botswana. She contends that transformative education aids transformative leadership and that the two need to consider the African contexts. One difference between transformative learning and transformative leadership is that leadership focuses on charismatic qualities that inspire motivation to change, but that "a defining conceptual thread of spirituality runs through the transformative learning and leadership literature that resonates with southern African core value systems. It is this thread that provides the overall conceptual link between different strands of thought."[23]

Transforming Leadership and Institutions The challenge of social change is in "changing the rules of the game, not playing by them."[24] Aruna Rao and David Kelleher write that current institutions see power as a commodity that the few used to control the many. Organizations are irrational biased reflections of the larger society. Social change within may be limited because organizations are controlled in part by informal norms which are difficult to break. Often they are hidden. These norms act as unrecognized constraints and can be stronger than formal policies. Leaders who seek to make transformational change will have to provide vision to challenge institutional norms, formal and informal. In part, leaders must challenge hierarchical power.[25]

Examining power at all levels is important. Mid and lower-level women leaders also face challenges. The struggle of professional competence as a basis for authority produces ambiguity when authority no longer resides solely in the office, but rather in qualifications. Thus, someone on a lower official level having more expertise may be difficult to take.[26]

Attention is needed on the form of women's democratic inclusion. Shireen Hassim argues, "how women are included can have effects on how they aggregate as a political power bloc, and on the kinds of political and policy outcomes that are possible through increased representation.... [Q]uota mechanisms can result in demands for representation being disembedded from the processes of constituency formation."[27] Transformative agendas may not be met if quotas are unlinked from the collective mobilization on one hand and intensive debate over meanings of equality and the desirable outcomes of policy on the other.

Therefore, Hassim takes as a starting point "the evidence that there is not an automatic relationship between women's increased political representation and the erosion of gender equalities."[28] The relationship is much more complex. The strategies of participation, representation and gender equality outcome aim to shift debate from quotas to more challenging issues of accountability and equality outcomes.[29]

Transforming Media Coverage Section J of the Beijing Platform for Action emphasized concerns of media content and representation of women. Representation of African women remained a concern ten years after the world conference. L. Muthoni Wanyeki, Executive Director, African Women's Development and Communications Network (FEMNET), provides two reasons for the concern. Although some movement away from traditional reporting is occurring, coverage of the concerns of African women is one of marginalization. Secondly, the media have not deconstructed the notion of the "general" public. Events affect Africa's many publics, for example, young and old, male and female, and rural and urban, differently. Wanyeki explains media policy and skills make certain "women's voices, interpretations and solutions are mainstreamed, are covered as part and parcel of the daily news, economic analyses, political analyses have yet to be evolved. Women are still covered as passive, rather than as active."[30]

Less obvious and more difficult to address is the gendered nature of the realization of the fundamental rights of freedom of expression and information recognized by international law and regional African law. Wanyeki writes that patriarchal law, practice, and conflict constrain most African women's exercise of these fundamental rights.[31]

Neither the international nor regional level recognize the right to communicate. Wanyeki says this issue has been discussed since the 1960s and strategies have given rise to the African rural press and national broadcasters. However, African women have not been featured in these plans.[32]

Africa's Role in International Leadership

In 2003, United Nations Secretary-General Kofi Annan said, "Respect for the rule of law, at home and at the global level, will continue to be a key barometer of Africa's progress."[33] Africa had accepted the importance of international law at the time of independence, and has continued to make the contribution to its codification and progressive development. At the same time, Kofi Annan said that it wasn't enough just to make laws, but African states must also

> respect and implement the obligations embodied in treaties, norms and laws. Indeed, some of the key challenges at the heart of development — including the demands of democratization, governance and accountability; the elimination of discrimination against women and enhancing their role in male-dominated societies; combating corruption, terrorism and other forms of criminality; enhancing judicial reforms — require not only leadership and resources, but a legal response.[34]

The post–1995 Beijing World Conference era and the recognition of different leadership strategies attest to progress but also reveal areas for improvement. In 1998, *African Recovery* reported that many countries had ratified U.N. agreements such as the Convention for the Elimination of Discrimination Against Women, but had not informed policy-making or translated into better living and working conditions for women. This affects half the population. They write, "Without meaningful commitment in the form of policy changes and the provision of resources to deal with the root causes of women's conditions, Africa cannot hope to see a breakthrough in its development and renewal."[35]

Severe economic constraints and poverty prevent many of the United Nations programs from being as successful as they might otherwise be. And perhaps very critical is that governments' macroeconomic policies, such as found in the World Bank and the International Monetary Fund (IMF), fail "to incorporate gender perspectives in their design and ignore the structure of households in Africa and the social relations that influence women's roles in production."[36]

Many governments have ratified conventions and international legal instruments on women's rights. Policy makers in Africa must work with development agencies and women to enact international law into national law that will remove the social, economic and legal constraints on women. In this way, African women can meaningfully participate in the political process and in governance.[37]

Conclusions

International law is a basis to equal rights and the inherent human rights of women and men. International instruments are modeled on international discourses. Construction of effective leadership must cross national boundaries. Regional efforts are important. The vocabulary of international development agencies is influential in giving women power; for example, "women's empowerment" as an ill-defined concept has been questioned. Africa's role in international leadership, in the post–1995 Beijing World Conference era, is critical as each country ratifies international instruments and models its laws accordingly.

4. Profiles of African Women Leaders

I live in a world where the battle for freedom of information and expression is still being fought. The politicians still decide what is good and safe for us [women] to read ... what we need is correct information so that we can make the right decisions and take appropriate actions.
—Wangari Maathai, Kenya, Deputy Minister of Environment and Nobel Laureate[1]

The women of Africa live in a world where the battle for freedom of information and expression is still being fought. The battle began years ago and women all across Africa joined the struggle. Many personally prevailed and hold high office. Of those who rose to high office, I have chosen to profile some who have achieved the highest offices in their countries.

Her Excellency Madam Ellen Johnson-Sirleaf

PRESIDENT OF THE REPUBLIC OF LIBERIA

I hope young girls will now see me as a role model that will inspire them. I certainly hope more and more of them will be better off, women in Liberia, women in Africa, I hope even women in the world.
— President Ellen Johnson-Sirleaf[2]

The election of Ellen Johnson-Sirleaf as the 23rd President[3] of Liberia "is truly a celebration, of which all women of the world and in particular Africa are proud of."[4] She was inaugurated as president on January 16, 2006. The Femmes Africa Solidarité (FAS), an organization that supported Liberian women, regards Johnson-Sirleaf as a sister, mother and friend. Her unifying spirit will help the cause of dignity and respect to women and girls throughout the world and thus bring new strength and stability. Her victory was not a surprise to FAS. After 14 years of civil war, Liberia needs the experience and commitment Johnson-Sirleaf brings.[5] She won the November 2005 elections with 59.4 percent of the vote, compared to George Weah's 40.6 percent.[6]

Of 22 presidential contesters, Johnson-Sirleaf of the Unity Party was the only female.[7] She holds the distinction of being Africa's first elected female leader.[8] In her inaugural address, she commended women, "I want to here and now, gratefully acknowledge the powerful voice of women of all walks of life."[9]

First Lady Laura Bush praised Johnson-Sirleaf as "a magnificent leader and an amazing woman" and said that her "courage and commitment to her country are an inspiration to me and women around the world."[10] That Johnson-Sirleaf is called an amazing woman is not surprising. In 1980, she escaped death when a firing squad killed thirteen Liberian cabinet ministers. In 1985, she served a prison term because she fought for a peaceful Liberia, and a few months later she was put in jail again. In December 2005, the Agenda Africa KCA Think Tank Newsletter named her person of the month "for riding through the macho image of Liberia's politics to become Africa's first woman elected Head of State."[11]

Johnson-Sirleaf comes to her position from a humble background. She was born in Monrovia, the capital of Liberia, on October 29, 1938.[12] She was born among the original colonists of Liberia who were ex–African slaves from America. When the ex-slaves, known in Liberia as Americo-Liberians, arrived, they "set about enslaving the indigenous people using the social system of their old American masters as a basis for their new society."[13] Struggle between indigenous Liberians and the Americo-Liberians has led to much of the political and social strife in Liberia, writes Alistair Boddy-Evans.

Liberia's President Ellen Johnson Sirleaf waves to the crowd as she stands in front of the president's chair during her inauguration at the Capitol Building in Monrovia, Liberia, Monday, January 16, 2006. In a ceremony attended by U.S. First Lady Laura Bush and other dignitaries, Johnson-Sirleaf became Africa's first elected female head of state (AP/Wide World Photos/Charles Dharapak).

She has no American lineage. Three of her grandparents were indigenous Liberians and the fourth was a German who married a rural market woman. Both grandmothers were farmers and village traders who could not read or write any language. Johnson-Sirleaf says that her inspiration is based in her grandmothers' love of country and family and belief in education. She said: "They inspired me then, and their memory motivates me now to serve my people, to sacrifice for the world and honestly serve humanity. I could not, I will not — I cannot — betray their trust."[14]

At the age of 17, Johnson-Sirleaf married James Sirleaf, but later divorced.[15] She is the mother of four sons and grandmother to six children.[16]

She came to the presidency with outstanding accomplishments that began early in her life. From 1948 to 1955,[17] she was educated at the College of West Africa, in Monrovia. In 1961 she came to the United States[18] and earned a B.A. in accounting at Madison Business College in Madison, Wisconsin. She later received a diploma at the Economics Institute at the University of Colorado and in 1971 she earned a master's degree in public administration from Harvard University.[19]

First Lady Laura Bush referred to President Johnson-Sirleaf as "a terrific example of the power of education, and an indication of why it's important to educate women and girls.... Women around the world are proud of Mrs. Sirleaf and ... they are watching her as a role model."[20] On September 21, 2006, Bush and Johnson-Sirleaf were presented the International Republican Institute's 2006 Freedom Award which recognizes their work in encouraging women to participate in democratic process.

The Liberian Embassy in Washington, D.C., describes Her Excellency Johnson-Sirleaf as having "led a distinguished career spanning nearly four decades in local and international public life."[21]

Johnson-Sirleaf's regal, quiet, but commanding presence belies the struggle dotted within many accomplishments, a struggle that no doubt contributed to the special strength she brings to the presidency.

After Sergeant Samuel Doe staged a military coup in 1980, Johnson-Sirleaf left Liberia for several years. During this time she was a loan officer for the World Bank and a director for Citibank in Nairobi. In 1985, she returned to Liberia and President Doe "placed her under house arrest for her criticisms of his repressive rule,"[22] according to *Africa Renewal*. David Harris writes that when Johnson-Sirleaf announced her intention to run as a senatorial candidate in the 1985 elections, she did so "in opposition to the military rule of Samuel Doe. For a brave speech heavily critical of Doe, she was sentenced to ten years imprisonment, of which she served two short periods of detention, one before and one after the 1985 election, before fleeing the country."[23]

Johnson-Sirleaf describes her persecution to the U.S. Congress, before she found refuge in the United States:

> In 1985, after challenging the military regime's failure to register my political party, I was put in jail with several university students who also challenged the military rule. This House came to our rescue with a resolution threatening to cut off aid to the country unless all political prisoners were released. Months later, I was put in jail again, this time in a cell with 15 men. All of them were executed a few hours later. Only the intervention of a single soldier spared me from rape.[24]

During Johnson-Sirleaf's exile, she held high-level positions in banking and investment institutions until 1992 when she was appointed Director of the Regional Bureau of Africa for the United Nations Development Program (UNDP). She also served as Senior Loans Officer at the World Bank.

ACCOMPLISHMENTS
HER EXCELLENCY MADAM ELLEN JOHNSON-SIRLEAF,
PRESIDENT OF THE REPUBLIC OF LIBERIA

Positions	Date
President	Jan. 16, 2006
Standard Bearer and presidential candidate, Unity Party	2005
Chair, Commission on Good Governance, Liberia	2004–2005
Co-chair, dialogue among political currents in the Democratic Republic of the Congo	2002
Appointee to investigate Rwanda genocide by Organization of African Unity	1999
Standard Bearer and presidential candidate, Unity Party, first postwar elections	1997
Assistant Administrator and Director, Regional Bureau of Africa for the UN Development Program (UNDP) with rank of Assistant Secretary General of the United Nations	1992–1997
Leading member of exile government of Amos Sawyer in U.S.	1990–1994
Vice President and member of the Executive Board, Equator Bank, Washington	1986–1992
(House arrest, in prison, then in exile)	1985–1997
Vice President Africa Regional Office, Citibank, Nairobi	1982–1985
World Bank (also an initial member of World Bank Council of African Advisors)	1980–1985
Leading member of the opposition	1980–1985
President, Liberian Bank for Development and Investment	1980
Minister of Finance	1979–1980
Secretary of State of Finance, Government of Liberia	1972–1973 and 1977–1979

Other Positions and Accomplishments

Founder, Measuagon, a community development NGO, Liberia

Founding member, International Institute for Women in Political Leadership

Member of the Advisory Board, Modern Africa Growth and Investment Company, the Hong Kong Bank Group

Member of the Finance Committee, Modern Africa Fund Managers

Founder and President, Kormah Development and Investment Corporation, a financial management advisory consultancy firm

Publications

Assisted in authoring a report by the United National Development Fund for Women on peace building	2002
The Outlook for Commercial Bank Lending to Sub-Saharan Africa	1992
From Disaster to Development	1991

Sources: Agenda for Africa, "Person of the Month — Dec 2005A." Oct. 1, 2006, http://www.agendaafrica.com/site/en/newsletters/potm/dec2005.html; Embassy of Liberia, Washington D.C., "Profile of Her Excellency Ellen Johnson-Sirleaf President of the Republic of Liberia," 2004. Oct. 5, 2006, http://www.embassyofliberia.org/biography.htm; "Ellen Johnson-Sirleaf: Positions; Selected Works," Africa Centre, London: *Contemporary Africa Database*: People: Positions; Selected Works, Sept. 26, 2006. Oct. 11, 2006, http://people.africadatabase.org/en/person/2655.html; Ernest Harsch, "Liberian Woman Breaks the 'Glass Ceiling': Ambitious Agenda for President Ellen Johnson-Sirleaf," *Africa Renewal* 19, no. 4 (Jan. 2005):4. Oct. 8, 2006, http://www.un.org/ecosocdev/geninfo/afrec/vol19no4/194sirleaf.htm; Worldwide Guide to Women in Leadership, "Women Leaders in Africa," May 8, 2006. July 20, 2006, http://www.guide2womenleaders.com/womeninpower/Africa.htm.

President Samuel Doe was killed in Charles Taylor's 1989 invasion to throw out Doe. A tentative peace accord called for elections and Johnson-Sirleaf returned to Liberia after the seven-year civil war to campaign for the presidency as a challenger to Charles Taylor, the strongest warlord. President Taylor was elected.[25] According to David Harris, at first, Johnson-Sirleaf supported Taylor's 1989 invasion to rid the country of Doe; however, since then, she has been his unrelenting opponent. Although she based her campaign on her noninvolvement in the war, because of her financial expertise and her untainted maternity, she was viewed as a former minister in a government with a questionable record and a member of the old urban elite.[26]

Taylor had a sizeable electoral machine and the electorate believed that Taylor kept Liberia out of another war. He won with 75 percent of the vote. Johnson-Sirleaf came in second to Taylor. The Taylor government charged her with treason and she went into exile a second time.[27] Peace did not prevail; civil war again broke out under his dictatorial rule.[28] Taylor went into exile in Nigeria in August 2003. In November 2005, Liberia continued to search for peace, and they elected Johnson-Sirleaf, standard bearer for the Unity Party, after a disputed runoff with football player George Weah. Ellen Johnson-Sirleaf became the first woman to win an African presidential election.[29]

Her commitment to women and gender equality is the theme through her presentations. In September of 2006, when congratulating newly elected President H.E. Sheikha Haya Rashed Al Khalifa of the sixty-first session of the General Assembly, she reiterated her dedication to the United Nations General Assembly: "It is my hope that the establishment of a new, independent UN fund or program for the empowerment of women and gender equality will be fully supported by member states, and that such fund will have sufficient resources to support targeted programmes for women empowerment desperately needed at the national level."[30]

A competent female leader, President Johnson-Sirleaf has made a strong beginning. During her first few weeks in office she suppressed corruption and increased government revenue by 21 percent while, at the same time, the Reconciliation Commission investigated the abuses of war. Included is a resolve to see that justice is done with Charles Taylor in accordance with the requirements of the United Nations and the broad international community while at the same time seeking national unity and reconciliation.[31]

These strong beginnings are no easy feat. Challenges remain in her six-year term. Post-war and post-misrule reconstruction is necessary. No national telephone network, no national electricity grid and no piped water are but a few areas of need.

Reintegrating into civilian life the 100,000 ex-combatants, including many former child soldiers, is another challenge.[32]

In a tribute to President Ellen Johnson-Sirleaf, Mojúbàolú Olúfúnké Okome, summarizes the climate of Liberia met by the skill of its new leader:

> In spite of the plentiful landmines, numerous rivers to cross and mountains to climb, Ellen [Johnson-Sirleaf], here's hoping you can respond to the needs of poor, marginalized, embattled and excluded Liberians. Liberian women and [the] majority of the Liberian people have expressed confidence in you. May you rise to the challenge of leadership and make us proud! The glory, I hope, is in the future. My hope is that Liberia's best is yet to come, and that Ms. [Johnson-Sirleaf] would lay the groundwork upon which future generations of Liberia can build.[33]

Gertrude Ibengwe Mongella

UNITED REPUBLIC OF TANZANIA,
PRESIDENT OF PARLIAMENT OF THE AFRICAN UNION

Gertrude Ibengwe Mongella of Tanzania is a world figure.[34] The Pan African Parliament elected Mongella as president at its Inaugural Session in March 2004, for a term of five years. By virtue of this election, President Mongella is the head of state and chief of government of the African Union. The African Union consists of all 53 African states; 21 percent of the Parliament's 265 legislators are women.[35]

United Nations Secretary General Boutros Boutros Ghali invited Mongella to chair the Fourth United Nations World Conference on Women in Beijing in September 1995. She became known as "Mama Beijing."[36] As of 2006, she holds the positions of Special Advisor to the United Nations Economic Commission for Africa (ECA), Executive Secretary as well as to the UNESCO Director General, and is a member of the African Women Committee on Peace and Development (AWCPD).[37]

In each of these areas, she is strongly committed to women. She is the founder and the 1996 president of an NGO called Advocacy for Women in Africa (AWA).[38] In November 1996, she chaired the Women's Leadership Forum on Peace in Johannesburg. This meeting led to the drafting of the terms of reference of the proposed African Women's Committee for Peace and Development. As part of the African women's peace mission to Burundi, Mongella

Gertrude Ibengwe Mongella from the United Republic of Tanzania is the President of Parliament of the African Union. Shown here at the Commission on the Status of Women: International Women's Day Observance. A Commemoration of Thirty Years of United Nations' Efforts to Promote Gender Equality. In 1975, Gertrude Mongella was the Secretary-General, United Nations Fourth World Conference on Women (UN/DPI Photo/Mark Garten).

visited the Bubanza displaced persons' camps to encourage the women of Burundi. In March 1997, she participated in the Pan-African Conference on Peace, Gender and Development in Kigali to support Rwandan women. Her travel schedule is demanding, but she replies, "I cannot say no to the women when they need me. I meet illiterate women from rural areas who are committed to improving the lives of women. If these women can be so committed to bringing about change, then why not me?"[39]

Other positions Mongella held in support of women include the Tanzania Association of Women Leaders in Agriculture and Environment (TAWLAE) and the Society for Women and AIDS in Africa Tanzania Branch (SWAAT). In 1997, Mongella was the senior advisor to the executive secretary of the Economic Commission for Africa on Gender issues; in 1998 a member of the Organization of African Unity (OAU), Women Committee for Peace and Development in Addis Ababa; and a member of the regional reproduction health task force for WHO Africa Region in 2002.[40]

Other recent memberships held include: Council of the Future, UNESCO, in Paris, France, in 1999; Parliament, Ukerewe Constituency of Tanzania in 2000; high-level advisory panel of Eminent Persons, OAU, in 2002; leader of the OAU election observer team to the Zimbabwe presidential election in 2002; Goodwill Ambassador, WHO Africa Region, in 2003; and a member Pan African Parliament in 2004.[41]

Mongella was born in 1945 on the island of Ukerewe in Lake Victoria in Tanganyika; the island is now part of Tanzania. At age 12, she left home to attend a school operated by Maryknoll nuns. In 1970, she graduated as a teacher from the East Africa University College in Dar es Salaam. From 1970 to 1974, Mongella was a tutor at the Dar es Salaam Teachers' Training College and from 1974 to 1978, she held the position of curriculum developer at the Institute of Education in Dar es Salaam. She is married and the mother of four children.[42]

The number of positions Mongella has held is daunting, and her early life was no different. Formerly, she held membership on the East African Legislative Assembly from 1975 to 1977; Board of Directors of Tanzania Rural Development Bank from 1975 to 1980; Council at the University of Dar es Salaam from 1975 to 1982; Central Committee and National Executive Committee of Chama Cha Mapinduzi (CCM) party from 1977 to 1992; and Parliament of Tanzania from 1980 to 1993.[43]

Mongella held three ministries: Minister of State in the Prime Minister's Office from 1982 to 1988; the Minister of Lands in the Office of Tourism and Natural Resources from 1985 to 1987; and the Minister without Portfolio in the president's office from 1987 to 1990.[44]

Other positions include: vice chairperson of the World Conference to Review and Appraise the Achievements of the U.N. Decade for Women in 1985; Tanzania representative on the Commission on the Status of Women in 1989; member of the Trustee, United Nations International Research and Training Institute for the Advancement of Women (INSTRAW) in Santo Domingo from 1990 to 1993; Tanzania High Commissioner to India from 1991 to 1992; U.N. assistant secretary general and secretary general for the 4th World Conference on Women in Beijing, China, in 1995; U.N. undersecretary and special envoy to the secretary general of the United Nations on women's issues and development from 1996 to 1997; member of the advisory group to the director general of UNESCO for the follow-up of the Beijing Conference in Africa, South of the Sahara; member of the board, Agency for Co-Operation and Research in Development (ACORD) in London in 1996; member of the board, the Hunger Project in New York, United States, in 1996; and member of the board, U.N. University in Tokyo, Japan, in 1996.[45]

In Mongella's address at the Inaugural Session of the Pan African Parliament, she addressed her sisters in Africa:

> [T]he struggle we have started for many years — abolishing slavery on this continent along with men, abolition of colonialism, dismantling of apartheid, we are now in a Union where we can see the practical implementation of gender equality. And this has come together because we have worked together. If you count the men in this gathering they are more than the women ... the partnership between men and women, the struggle for peace on the African continent, will still remain the guiding principles in my heart as I execute my duties as the president of the Pan African Parliament.[46]

Mongella's life of service reflects her vision of leadership shared at the first African Women's Forum in January 1997: "If you want to be a leader, you have to be clear what you want and what you stand for. You must stand for principle. Principle will never let you down.... You have to be able to choose what are the principles worth dying for.... And you have to add on a little sacrifice. Leadership needs a lot of sacrifice — personal and public sacrifice."[47]

Luisa Diogo

PRIME MINISTER, REPUBLIC OF MOZAMBIQUE

Luisa Diogo from Mozambique became prime minister at the age of 47 in February 2004. She is the head of the FRELIMO party (the Frente de Libertação de Moçambique or Liberation Front of Mozambique), which has governed the country since its independence in 1975.[48] In October 2006, Diogo was ranked 96 on the Forbes list of the 100 Most Powerful Women. Forbes states that Diogo "has become increasingly vocal in taking rich nations to task for not following up on aid, trade and debt relief promises to Africa. 'It is no country's destiny to be poor,' she has said."[49]

Mozambique, with its problems of poverty, disasters (drought, floods, and rising HIV/AIDS infection rates) and recovering from approximately 17 years of civil war (1975 to 1992), is fortunate to have a visionary leader. Mozambique experienced slow but steady recovery when Diogo served as minister of finance in the five years (1999 to 2004) prior to her appointment as prime minister.[50] But her history in

Mozambique's Prime Minister Luisa Dias Diogo joins heads of state from over 40 Asian and African countries in a reenactment of a historic walk from 1955, along Asia Africa Street, Sunday, April 24, 2005, in Bandung, Indonesia. Gathering at the birthplace of the Non-Aligned Movement, representatives of African and Asian nations closed out their summit with promises to boost economic and political relations and counter the threat of globalization (AP/Wide World Photos/Suzanne Plunkett).

helping the country began even earlier when, in 1980, she joined the Ministry of Planning and Finance while still in college. In 2004, *Time 100* described Diogo as leading a state with "a government that was once written off as a failed state but that now posts economic-growth rates of an Asian tiger. Income per head in Mozambique has doubled over the past decade."[51]

Diogo was born April 11, 1958, in the Tete Province in western Mozambique. She attended Dona Maria Primary School in Tete City until age twelve and the Tete Commercial School until she was fourteen. She was educated at the Maputo Commercial Institute before receiving a B.A. in economics at Eduardo Mondlane University in 1983 and an M.A. in financial economics at the University of London in 1992. She married an attorney, Albano Silva. She has three children.[52]

In 1986, at the age of 28, Diogo became a department head, and four years later, 1989, she served as national budget director. After she earned her M.A. degree, she served as program officer in the World Bank in Mozambique. In 1994, at 36 years old, Diogo joined the FRELIMO government as deputy finance minister. An able negotiator, she obtained several grants. In 2004 alone, Diogo was able to secure $790 million in aid from the World Bank. In January 2004, *The Banker* named Diogo Finance Minister of the Year.[53]

After the 2004 elections, President Chissano was replaced by FRELIMO candidate Armando Guebuza. Diogo remained prime minister but with newly defined duties. She no longer had finance duties, but she assumed a more extensive leadership role. She had attracted global attention. In October 2004, the general directors of the United Nations chose her, the only prime minister, to represent all of the world's developing countries.[54] Making Mozambique and all developing countries self-sufficient is one of Diogo's major goals. She has established a "poverty observatory," a forum of citizens and media who from time to time evaluate government strategies.[55]

In 2004, it was said, "Perhaps Diogo's greatest success was in debt relief— Mozambique was the third country (after Uganda and Bolivia) to qualify for relief under the World Bank's HIPC (Heavily Indebted Poor Countries) initiative."[56] In 2006, perhaps Forbes is correct in speculating, "Diogo may be positioning herself for a run for her country's presidency in 2009."[57]

Maria do Carmo Trovoada Silveira

PRIME MINISTER, DEMOCRATIC REPUBLIC OF SÃO TOMÉ AND PRÍNCIPE

Maria do Carmo Trovoada Silveira simultaneously served as Prime Minister and Finance Minister of São Tomé and Príncipe from June 7, 2005, to April 21, 2006.[58] In 2005, Silveira was one of two African female prime ministers, the other minister being Luisa Diogo of Mozambique. Silveira was one of five female prime ministers in the world: Helen Clark of New Zealand, Begum Khaleda Zia of Bangladesh and Angela Merkel of Germany were the others. Silveira was the youngest of these women[59]; she was born in 1960.[60] She became the second woman to hold the position in São Tomé and Príncipe.[61] Maria das Neves de Sousa, who was Prime Minister of São Tomé and Príncipe from October 2002 to September 2004, was the first woman to be prime minister.[62]

Silveira was a member of the Movement for the Liberation of São Tomé and Príncipe

Social Democratic Party (MLSTP-PSD). Her term as Prime Minister ended when the opposition defeated the MLSTP-PSD in the 2006 parliamentary elections.[63]

Before she became Prime Minister, Maria do Carmo Trovoada Silveira was the governor of the small West African country's Central Bank from March 1999 to June 2005.[64] She earned a degree in economic sciences at the University of Donetsk in the Ukraine, with the support of the International Monetary Fund. She specialized in macroeconomic policy.

Maria do Carmo Trovoada Silveira simultaneously served as Prime Minister and Finance Minister of São Tomé and Príncipe from June 7, 2005, to April 21, 2006 (reprinted with permission from Maria do Carmo Trovoada Silveira).

Baleka Mbete

SPEAKER OF THE NATIONAL ASSEMBLY, REPUBLIC OF SOUTH AFRICA

Speaker Baleka Mbete has a long career serving as an activist and politician. Since South Africa's first democratic elections in 1994, she has been a member of its parliament. In April 2004, she was elected as speaker of the National Assembly following an eight-year term as deputy speaker (May 1996 to April 2004). She has been a member of the African National Congress's (ANC) National Executive Committee since 1997[65] and Chairperson of ANC Parliamentary caucus since 1995.[66]

Mbete was born on Sept. 24, 1949. She grew up in Durban with four sisters and three brothers. She was enrolled in a seminary in Durban in 1968. She earned a teacher's certificate at Lovedale Teachers' College in 1973. Mbete taught at Isibonelo High School at KwaMashu, Durban, in 1975. While in exile, she taught at Matter Dolorosa High School at Mbabane, Swaziland, from 1976 to 1977.[67] In 1978, while both were exiled in Tanzania, Mbete married poet Keorapetse Kgositsile, an ANC member. The couple are no longer married.[68]

Mbete's political involvement resulted in 15 years of exile, forcing her to live in Zimbabwe, Botswana, Tanzania and Zambia.[69] While in exile, Mbete served the ANC in many different functions, including: the Department of Information and Publicity (Radio Freedom) from 1977 to 1981; the Women's section in Dar es Salaam, Tanzania, from April 1978 to October 1981; the underground political structures in Gabarone, Botswana, from 1983 to 1986; the Regional Women's Committee and Regional Political Committee in Harare, Zimbabwe, from 1986 to 1987; the Executive Committee in the capacity of administrative secretary in Lusaka, Zambia, from 1987 to 1990; the Interim Leadership Core and the Task Force of the ANC Women's League in South Africa, from 1990 to 1991; and as Secretary General of the ANC Women's League, from 1991 to 1993.[70]

Chinese Premier Wen Jiabao, right, shakes hands with South African National Assembly speaker Baleka Mbete during their meeting in Beijing, Wednesday, September 27, 2006 (AP/Wide World Photos/Xinhua, Li Xueren).

As a member of the Panel of Chairpersons of Multi-Party Negotiating Process from 1991 to 1994, and as a member of the Constitutional Committee of the Constitutional Assembly since 1994, Mbete was deeply involved in the drafting of South Africa's interim and final constitutions. In 1995, she became a member of the Presidential Panel on Truth and Reconciliation Commission.[71]

Mbete has continued her work in the ANC and has been a member of its National Executive Committee since 1994.[72] She was a member of UNESCO's International Advisory Panel in 1998 and served on UNIFEM's panel of experts to assist in engendering the Burundi Peace Process for June and July in 2000.[73]

Mbete has a positive flair about her. The European Union Parliamentary Support Programme described Mbete as "a music lover, a poet, a former exile, a mother."[74] Her day as deputy speaker of the national assembly begins at 6:30 A.M. and ends at 7 P.M. on most weekdays. The European Union evoked a strong, positive response when a reader said, "Seeing Ms. Baleka Mbete in her beautiful outfit and reading about her demanding duties as Deputy Speaker of the National Assembly helps break the notion that beautiful women cannot be strong leaders. — Comrade (Mpumalanga)."[75]

In 2005, at the opening of parliament, Mbete walked with style through the crowd with President Thabo Mbeki and his wife Zanele. Mbete was described as looking "gorgeous in a traditionally inspired embroidered burnt-orange gown topped off with a swirling yellow head-piece and looped earrings."[76]

In 2000, as a deputy speaker, Mbete worked for a presence of women in government. She said, "We haven't done too badly, although we need to look at staff and women being at top management level."[77] She also hoped that more women would win in upcoming elections because: "That's when women can be more effective in trying to build a non-sexist society, which we have to strive for."[78]

Of women in parliament, Mbete said that in addition to allocating resources and having policy and law be gender sensitive, the institution needs reforming so that it becomes a place "that makes women feel they want to come here.... Parliament can be very intimidating and we need it to be a place that attracts women and is supportive to women. For instance, recently we made a ruling that no sittings will take place beyond 6 P.M., so that family and children won't be neglected."[79]

In 2004, Mbete presided over the launch of "the people's assembly" as an extension of the belief in a people's parliament. Challenged, parliament was to become relevant to the poor and marginalized — for example, women — and give them a voice in parliamentary committees.[80] In 2006, Mbete shared further her like philosophy on the role of parliament with the National Assembly of Parliament of the Republic of the Côte d'Ivoire. She said, in part: "I cannot overemphasize the importance of the role of Parliament in times like these, in seeking answers to teething problems of nation building and reconciliation. Parliament is a place for civil and meaningful engagement. It is an alternative to solving our problems through violence."[81]

Further, Speaker Mbete presented President Thabo Mbeki the memorandum of recommendations from the Progressive Women's Movement. She further emphasized the need for more work to be done for women's rights. She said, "We recognized the advances that our democracy has registered for women in particular. We appreciate what our government is doing but we believe that there is a lot more still to be done."[82]

Described in *Essence* as one of the "formidable warriors" and "movement women," Mbete and the others "fought the long, hard fight for freedom and lived to now help run the country. As recently as five years ago, their very presence in government was unthinkable."[83]

Fatoumata Jahumpa-Ceesay

SPEAKER OF THE NATIONAL ASSEMBLY, REPUBLIC OF THE GAMBIA

The Honorable Fatoumata Jahumpa-Ceesay became Speaker of the Gambian National Assembly on February 2, 2006. She brings to the office family status and a vast experience of political successes. The Speaker is the daughter of the late Alhagi Ibrahima Muhammadu Garba, a renowned Pan Africanist and Gambian political luminary. She is the second woman to hold the position of speaker and follows Belinda Bidwell, who served in 2006.[84]

Jahumpa-Ceesay is described as "a delight to behold. Everything around her radiates brilliance and love, understanding and peace. No wonder she has become one of few women in the continent whose contributions extend beyond her contributions [of] her immediate environment."[85]

The Gambia News Site is also laudatory of her: "Her quiet, pleasing personality became

The Honorable Fatoumata Jahumpa-Ceesay became Speaker of the Gambian National Assembly on February 2, 2006 (photograph reprinted with permission from Fatoumata Jahumpa-Ceesay).

her strategic weapon in the Honourable House as she engaged her colleagues in the debates of the Assembly, proving her mettle and holding her own against a male-dominated club. Her personality and eloquent contributions soon became a hallmark and unique branding image of popular appeal to all and sundry. She not only became a voice for women's affairs, she was a voice for the voiceless and displayed an admirable sense of political correctness."[86]

Committed to women and youth development, Jahumpa-Ceesay was appointed a Lady Councilor to Banjul City Council in 1985 and became the first woman Deputy Mayor of Banjul in 1989. She served as Director of Public Relations at the Office of the President from 1997 until her nomination by the president to the National Assembly in 2002.[87]

In February of 2002, she was nominated to the West African Community Parliament (ECOWAS). Jahumpa-Ceesay is the coordinator of the Economic Community Female Parliamentarians Association and the first woman to be appointed deputy speaker in the ECOWAS parliament.[88]

Jahumpa-Ceesay's organizational service is extensive. Most notable is that she founded her own NGO for children and women's rights, the Family Rights Advancement and Protection. She is its executive chairperson. Her service in other organizations includes being a former board member of the West African Networking for Peace Gambia Charter, African Parliamentary Union, International Parliamentary Union, Better Life for the African Rural Woman, Voice of Women in Africa, and chairperson for the Women-Children Commission of the NGO Coalition on NEPAD (New Partnership for Africa's Development).[89]

Awards include both local and international honors. In 2000, for her impressive career path, President Jammeh awarded her the Insignia of Medal of the National Order of the Republic of the Gambia. She also received the Paul Harris Fellowship Award sponsored by the President; Child Friendly Award by the Observer Youth Column; Better Life Programme for African Rural Woman Award 2005; and the African Women Leaders Diamond Award 2005.[90]

Jahumpa-Ceesay is a trained broadcaster and print journalist. She began her career as an announcer at Radio Gambia. Later she joined the Gambia Airways Limited. She worked for the *Daily Observer*, *Point*, and *Family Focus* newspapers.[91]

Jahumpa-Ceesay was born October 25, 1957. She completed her secondary education in 1977 at Armitage High School and Gambia High School. In 1995, she received a higher diploma certificate in print journalism at the Centre for Foreign Journalists in Reaton, Virginia. She also has certificates in broadcasting journalism, human rights and public relations.[92]

Jahumpa-Ceesay is married to Mr. Sulayman Masanneh Ceesay, a former Secretary of State for the Interior. As of 2007, her son is studying in the United States.[93]

Wangari Maathai

Deputy Minister of Environment and Member of Parliament, Tetu Constituency, Republic of Kenya, and Nobel Peace Laureate

Biologist Wangari Muta Maathai's accomplishments are exceptional. She was the first woman from East Africa to earn a doctorate, to become a professor and chair of a department — all at the University of Nairobi.[94] At 65, Maathai ranks 69 on the Forbes list of the

Wangari Maathai, 2004 Nobel Peace Prize laureate from Kenya, speaks during the Nobel Peace Prize Forum, Friday, March 10, 2006, at Luther College in Decorah, Iowa. The purpose of the forum was to recognize Norway's international peace efforts and to offer opportunities for Nobel Peace Prize laureates, diplomats, scholars, and the general public to share in dialogue on the dynamics of peacemaking and the underlying causes of conflict and war (AP/Wide World Photos/ Charlie Neibergall).

100 Most Powerful Women.[95] She is the first woman from Africa to receive the Nobel Peace Prize for starting her Green Belt Movement to reforest Africa.[96] This movement began in 1976, with her activism in the National Council of Women of Kenya. Through the Council, she established a tree-planting project, "Save the Land Harambee."[97] According to the Forbes profile, the Green Belt Movement has assisted women in planting over 30 million trees across Africa.

Maathai was born in Nyeri, Kenya, April 1, 1940. She has three children, Waweru, Wanjira and Muta.[98] Her parents were farmers in the highlands of Mount Kenya. Her degrees are in biological sciences from Mount St. Scholastica College in Atchison, Kansas, in 1964, and a master of science degree from the University of Pittsburgh in 1966. She earned a Ph.D. in anatomy from the University of Nairobi in 1971. Also at the university, she taught veterinary anatomy and became chair of the Department of Veterinary Anatomy in 1976 and an associate professor in 1977. She was the first woman in the region to attain these positions.[99]

Introducing her tree-planting concept in 1976 to the National Council of Women of Kenya, she then served on the council from 1976 to 1987, chairing it from 1981 to 1987. From this organization she formed the Green Belt Movement, "a broad-based, grassroots organization whose main focus is helping women's groups plant trees to conserve the environment and improve quality of life."[100] The BBC reports, "Maathai rose to prominence fighting for those most easily marginalized in Africa — poor women."[101]

Maathai is not only a noted environmentalist but also a pro-democracy activist. But her fame has come with opposition. She has been arrested several times for campaigning against deforestation in Africa. The BBC reported, "[Maathai] once was beaten unconscious by heavy-handed police. On another occasion, she led a demonstration of naked women."[102] Unafraid, she questioned male-made decisions. In 1989, she worked to preserve Uhuru Park because it "was the only place in Nairobi where people could spend time with their families outdoors."[103] The city wanted to destroy the park and build a multi-storied complex.

Maathai wrote about her work in the Green Belt Movement. She took her instruction from the Bible, "one publication that has successfully evaded and, indeed, impressed the censors hands down."[104] From it she learned the importance of acquiring and using knowledge for the common good. Maathai has a good sense of humor and encourages women to seek knowledge and information from the tree of life in the center of their garden: their intellect, heritage, libraries, laboratories and Mother Nature —"For that is exactly what Eve did: She took action to seek knowledge, never mind what man had to say about that!"[105]

But even with this sound philosophy, Maathai was on a rigorous journey. Unsure of when she began confronting injustices, she saw nothing wrong in her approach, but some people did. She had asserted her right to be herself, finding nothing wrong with being a woman, a graduate, and a professional claiming rights to have an opinion on all manner of issues, but became labeled an activist, a radical and a rebel. Few men and women in Kenya shared her view that "it was o.k. for women to pioneer on the basis of the information at their disposal."[106] The only way Maathai says she was able to understand the reaction of men and women was by concluding, "Many men wanted to see such women publicly humiliated to teach all women a lesson. In addition, women who were not sympathetic were comforted to know that they were not alone under the stifling oppression of men."[107]

In 1992, the two-party system became legal in Kenya and Maathai tried to unite the opposition party. When her efforts were not successful, she ran for president. Unfortunately, she lost, learning it was difficult to get elected without funds.[108]

In December 2002, Maathai was elected to parliament in Kenya's first democratic elections. After her election, the president appointed her as deputy minister for environment, natural resources and wildlife.[109]

In 2004, the Norwegian Nobel Committee awarded the Nobel Peace Prize to Maathai "for her contribution to sustainable development, democracy and peace."[110] The Committee praised her for her holistic approach and her ability to think globally and act locally. Maathai was the first woman from Africa to be honored with the Nobel Peace Prize and the first African from the sizable area between South Africa and Egypt to be awarded the prize.

In addition to her membership in the Parliament and being the assistant minister for environment, Maathai holds other prestigious positions, including Goodwill Ambassador for the Congo Basin Forest Initiative from 2005 to the present and presiding officer for the Economic Social and Cultural Council of the African Union from 2005 to 2007. She is a member of the United Nations Secretary-General's Advisory Board on Disarmament Matters in the United States and the U.N. Commission on Global Governance, U.S.[111]

Maathai's awards include *Time* magazine's one of the 100 most influential people in the world in 2005 and the New York Women's Foundation, New York Women's Century Award. In 2006, she was awarded the University of Pennsylvania's Medal for Distinguished Achievement; the American Biographical Institute Inc. 2006 Woman of Achievement Award; the Government of France's Legion d'Honneur; International Association for Impact Assessment, Norway Global Environment Award; and the Disney Wildlife Conservation Fund Award.[112]

Times changed and many women found Maathai's leadership in asserting her rights an inspiration to follow. Now Maathai is part of a multitude.[113] She is a leader.

Dr. Farkhonda Hassan

PARLIAMENT AND SECRETARY-GENERAL OF THE NATIONAL COUNCIL FOR WOMEN, ARAB REPUBLIC OF EGYPT

Dr. Farkhonda Hassan is serving her third legislative session of Egypt's Parliament. She was selected to serve in 1979.[114] She first served in the Public National Assembly until 1984 when she became a member of the Shoura Council (Second House of Parliament), serving until 1989. Since 1992, she has served as Shoura's chair of the Human Resources and Development committee and of the Parliamentary Commission on Human Development and Local Administration.[115] In 1980 she became a Holder of the Order of Merit of Arts and Sciences, "First Class."[116] She the first woman from the Third World to be an honorary life member of the International Parliamentary Union.[117]

She is a member of the General Secretarial of the Political Office of the National Democratic Party. President Hosni Mubarak appointed her the Head of the Women's Sector of the Party in 1995.[118] In 2001, she left that post when she became the Secretary-General of the National Council for Women that is led by Mrs. Suzanne Mubarak.[119]

Hassan's international activities are as numerous as her professional, political and social activities. After being a member since 1995, Dr. Hassan became the co-chair of the Gender Advisory Board of the United Nations Commission on Science and Technology for Development in 1998.[120] Some of her other activities include active participation for gender, science, environment and technology in Canada, Italy, the Mediterranean, the United States and the United Nations.[121]

Hassan earned the following degrees: a B.Sc. in chemistry and geology in 1952 at Cairo University, after which she earned a diploma in psychology and education at Ein Shams University; an M.Sc. in solid state science in 1966 at the American University in Cairo; and a Ph.D. in geology in 1970 at the University of Pittsburgh.[122]

Hassan, also a professor of Geology at the American University in Cairo, retired in 2003,[123] after serving at the university since 1964.[124] The department described her: "As a scientist, politician and development specialist, Hassan has dedicated her multi-faceted career to serve women's cause in politics, public services, sciences, and information and technology."[125]

In 1983, Egypt adopted its first conservation legislation. Hassan was widely recognized as the law's prime mover. She said of the law, "Environmental awareness is a form of development."[126] In addition, she gave insight on her successful early efforts to get legislators to discuss what's happening to the environment in parliament:

> When I came to the People's Assembly in 1979 and began preaching ecology to other legislators they smiled and were very polite.... They were also completely unimpressed.... But each time an economic problem was discussed in Parliament, I related it to the environment. If banana crops were down, I talked about soil pollution. If asthma and lung ailments increased, I asked them what else they could expect with the air we breathe in Cairo.[127]

Unswerving, Hassan's recent service reflects innovative leadership abilities. Through the National Council for Women in 2001, Hassan continued to work for women's rights, including political participation and parliamentary representation. The Council favored a return of the system whereby people voted for a party list rather than an individual. Hassan favored a return to this system because she believed it beneficial to women. Women candidates as part of a list would not be considered the risk that they were when they ran as individuals. Respective parties would name more women on the list.[128]

In 2004, in her opening remarks at the African pre-ministerial meeting of experts assessing Africa's implementation of the Beijing Platform for Action, she said that women and girls were still marginalized in education, employment, trade, industry and decision making. She said: "The objective now is not to renegotiate our dreams but to emphasize the accountability of all actors through detailed discussions of goals, achievements and failures within a consolidated African perspective.... We are no longer seeking promises but are demanding action."[129]

In 2005, Hassan continued as a voice for women's representation in government when President Hosni Mubarak, as he had in the past, used a constitutional clause to increase the parliamentary representation of women and minorities. The clause specifies that 444 seats of the 454-member People's Assembly are elected. The remaining 10 seats are to be appointed by the executive.[130]

President Mubarak's appointment of five women and five Coptic Christians to parliament did not fully satisfy many. But the lack of female representation in government runs deeper. Hassan said the National Women's Council was "extremely unhappy with this result. The parties didn't nominate enough women. The people didn't vote for women."[131] She added that the ruling National Democratic Party (NDP) was considering a quota system that would reserve a percentage of each party's seats to women and minorities.

In 1994, the *London Independent* described Hassan, when she defended the Koran and women's rights, as being in "fine form." She said:

> Yes, women in the Middle East lack basic rights, although they are improving in Egypt. But it's the social attitudes of men that are at fault, not the Koran. Before the Koran was written, women were treated like animals, they were bought and sold and kidnapped. And all those rights for

Dr. Farkhonda Hassan is serving her third legislative session of Egypt's Parliament and is the Secretary-General of the National Council for Women, Arab Republic of Egypt (reprinted with permission from Dr. Farkhonda Hassan and the National Council for Women, Egypt).

women that were woven into the Koran were a real support for women at the time. Remember that all those years ago in what is now Saudi Arabia, the Prophet Mohammed wanted women to vote for him. Yes, there are some points in the Koran that some women do not like—but compared to the zero rights they had before the Prophet, the Koran was really something.[132]

The National Council for Women has best summed up Hassan's life of commitment to the advancement of women at the national and international levels in these ways:

As scientist, politician and development specialist, she has dedicated her multi-faceted career to serve women's cause in policies, public services, sciences, information and technology, social work at grass roots level, education and culture, and other disciplines. Her affiliations with national and international organizations, non-governmental organizations, research and knowledge institutions have been directed towards women's empowerment.[133]

Ngozi Okonjo-Iweala

FINANCE MINISTER AND MINISTER OF FOREIGN AFFAIRS, FEDERAL REPUBLIC OF NIGERIA

On June 21, 2006, Ngozi Okonjo-Iweala moved from her post as finance minister that she had held since July 16, 2003. She assumed the position of foreign affairs minister until she resigned amid controversy on August 3, 2006.[134] As foreign affairs minister, Okonjo-Iweala oversaw "the withdrawal of Nigerian troops from the southeastern Bakassi Peninsula and the transfer of the disputed territory to Cameroon."[135] Prior to these governmental positions, she was a corporate secretary and vice president of the World Bank.[136] She joined the World Bank in 1982 through the prestigious Young Professionals Program. Her career there lasted nearly 20 years until, in 2000, she took a leave of absence to serve as an economic adviser to President Olusegun Obasanjo.[137]

In 2003, Okonjo-Iweala co-authored, with Tijan Sallah, a biography, *Chinua Achebe: Teacher of Light* for Africa World Press. Also that year she co-edited with Charles C. Soludo and Mansur Muhtar an academic work, *The Debt Trap in Nigeria: Towards a Sustainable Debt Strategy* for Africa World Press.[138]

Okonjo-Iweala has won many awards across the world, including the Economic Development Award from Vital Voices in 2006[139]; Global Finance Minister of the Year 2005; Hero of the Year by *Euromoney* magazine and *Time* magazine in 2004; the Euromarket Forum Award for Vision and Courage in 2003.[140]

In 2006, Okonjo-Iweala's rank of 62 on the Forbes 100 Most Powerful Women list credits her for "prudent debt management and calls for fiscal discipline."[141] Okonjo-Iweala led the negotiations that resulted in cancellation of nearly two-thirds, $18 billion, of Nigeria's $30 billion Paris Club debt. This debt cancellation was the second largest in the Paris Club of international creditors' 30-year history and Africa's biggest debt write-off.[142]

Okonjo-Iweala gave the government a "transparency" policy. This policy regularly published details of government revenue and financial allocations made to all administration levels. Although she introduced a bill to restrict public expenditures to measurable indices, parliament has not passed the bill.[143]

As finance minister, Okonjo-Iweala led a team of economists and prosecutors on a difficult path which she describes as follows: "We started to publish figures in a bulletin inserted in newspapers, such as the revenue from oil, how much went to local government for what, and people began to ask questions: Why is there no chalk, why are there potholes in our roads? ... It unleashed a whole conversation on how much resources states and local government were allocated and how they used them."[144]

She acknowledged, "But perhaps the simplest and most powerful thing we have done is to publish this.... Every month the federal government pays out money to state governments as their share of Nigeria's oil revenues. But no-one knew what they got and everyone blamed the federal government for everything."[145] The *Washington Post* reports that during this time Okonjo-Iweala's husband received calls warning that her life was in danger, and her character was maligned in some press outlets.

Weeks after her successful negotiation of the cancellation of Nigeria's debt, her government, headed by President Olusegun Obasanjo, moved her to the Foreign Ministry. Soon Okonjo-Iweala disclosed corruption as a major problem in the Foreign Ministry.[146]

Early in life, while Okonjo-Iweala's parents studied at European universities, she lived with her grandmother Dora, a "loving disciplinarian." During the week, she attended a rural school behind the house and on weekdays and on weekends wandered the fields. She also helped weed her grandmother's farm, collected firewood and mushrooms, and brought water from a stream.

In 1963, her parents placed her in a staff school at a university where they taught in western Nigeria. She then attended a select high school that ranked third in the country. She took ballet and piano lessons. In 1967 the Biafran war broke out, and the family fell upon hard times.[147]

Nigeria's Finance Minister Ngozi N. Okonjo-Iweala, chairman of the Development Committee of the World Bank and International Monetary Fund, left, takes a reporter's question, joined by World Bank President James Wolfensohn, center, and IMF Deputy Managing Director Agustín Carstens, at IMF Headquarters in Washington, Sunday, April 25, 2004. World finance ministers promised to do more with relieving the heavy burden of global poverty and debt relief for impoverished nations (AP/Wide World Photos/J. Scott Applewhite).

Although Okonjo-Iweala describes her childhood as "magical and happy,"[148] she is no stranger to hardship. Okonjo-Iweala was born on June 13, 1954. Her father, Professor Okonjo, was a renowned economist at the University of Ibadan and her mother a professor of sociology and economics.[149] She was 14 when the Biafran war began. Her father, who was a brigadier in the Biafran army, chose to keep her in Nigeria. Her family lost everything and experienced significant hardship and had little to eat much of the time.[150]

For three miles to the doctor's, Okonjo-Iweala carried on her back her three-year-old sister who was sick with malaria. Her father was away at war and her mother was ill. Six hundred other people were waiting to see the doctor. Okonjo-Iweala forced her way through the crowd and climbed through a window to see the doctor.[151]

Okonjo-Iweala received her bachelor's degree in economics magna cum laude at Harvard in 1981 and later a Ph.D. in regional economics and development from M.I.T.[152] She is married to her childhood sweetheart, who is a Washington, D.C.-based surgeon.[153] She describes her husband as uncomplaining, a most amazing person, a true partner who is kind and loving. She is the mother of four children whom she considers to be her inspiration. "There's so much love and energy from them, they make it possible for me."[154]

Edna Adan Ismail

MINISTER OF FOREIGN AFFAIRS, REPUBLIC OF SOMALILAND

Edna Adan Ismail served as Minister of Foreign Affairs in Somaliland from June 2003 to August 2006 and Minister of Family Welfare and Social Development from August 2002 to June 2003. She is also the president of two national organizations, the Victims of Torture in Somaliland and the Somali Studies International Association.[155]

In an interview with Ismail, she said that she became involved in politics for two reasons:

> I had been an activist for Human Rights, for the Rights of Women, and for the recognition of Somaliland during all of my adult life. I had also just completed the construction of the first Charity Hospital which I had built with the proceeds from my pension from the U.N. and my own personal funds. The hospital was opened in March 2002 and I was quite reluctant to join politics. I was convinced to accept the nomination of Minister of Family Welfare and Social Development as it would "open the door" to other women to join the government.[156]

And open the doors for women was exactly what Ismail did when she created the position of Director General upon her appointment in 2002. As of 2007, there is only one woman Director General in all of Somaliland, according to Ismail. She explains: "Recently, some women have become involved in politics through political parties because of the female votes that they bring. Their positions are usually subordinate to men and women do not have their rightful access to decision making."[157]

President Dahir Rayale Kahin nominated Ismail to become a minister in August 2002. She was not a member of Parliament, nor belonged to any political party. She shares her insights into her government positions:

> When appointed in August 2002, I became the first and only woman Cabinet Minister. Men jokingly referred to me as "the only terrorist in the cabinet, or Somaliland's Iron Lady" because I spoke my mind and lived by the principles that had served me well throughout my life. In May 2003, I was made Foreign Minister for Somaliland and a second woman Minister was appointed to my old ministry. Until I left politics in August 2006, we were two women in the cabinet, and now there is only one in a cabinet of over 40 men consisting of Ministers, Vice-Ministers, and Ministers of State.[158]

In 2007, Ismail became the recipient of the Medical Mission Hall of Fame Award in association with the Medical College of Ohio for her exceptional, exemplary, and significant contributions to medical mission activities throughout the world.[159] In 2002, she was the recipient of the Amanitare Award (named for a ruling queen of ancient Nubia)[160] for Africa and was also nominated Somalilander of the Year by the Somaliland Forum. She was decorated by the government of the Republic of Djibouti in October 1997, in recognition of the services rendered to the health services of Djibouti while she served as the WHO representative. She was awarded the decoration and title of "Commandeur de l'Ordre National du 27 Juin." Also, in October of 1997 she was a recipient of the United Nations Development Program (UNDP) Manager of the Year Award.[161]

Edna Adan Ismail served as Somaliland's Minister of Foreign Affairs from June 2003 to August 2006 and Minister of Family Welfare and Social Development from August 2002 to June 2003 (reprinted with permission from Edna Adan Ismail).

During the time that Ismail's husband served as Prime Minister of Somalia from August 1967 to October 1969, she undertook numerous state, social and charitable responsibilities both in the country and abroad as the First Lady. Following the Marxist coup of October 1969, she was a political prisoner placed under house arrest for six months. She was frequently detained for a few days at a time as a political activist. Later, from April 1977 to November 1978, Ismail became the first female promoted to the position of Director in Somalia and became Director of the Department of Human Resources Development, Ministry of Health and Labour in Somalia.[162]

Ismail was born on September 8, 1937, in Hargeisa, British Somaliland Protectorate, and holds a dual nationality in Djibouti and Somaliland. Thus, her international career is based in part on her Djibouti nationality status. From March 1991 to October 1997, she served as the WHO Representative for the Republic of Djibouti and from January 1996 to October 1997, she was the president of United Nations AIDS program and "Doyenne" (female senior member) of the U.N. Staff in Djibouti.[163]

Ismail became the founding member and vice president of the Inter-African Committee for Traditional Practices Affecting the Health of Women and Children from 1983 to 1986. She then held several positions with the World Health Organization's Regional Office for the Eastern Mediterranean (WHO/EMRO). From January 1987 to March 1991 she was the Regional Technical Officer for Maternal/Child Health and Family Planning, during which time she was also the focal point for Traditional Practices Affecting the Health of Women and Children (FGM), for safe motherhood initiatives, and for training of midwives and traditional birth attendants (TBAs).[164]

Other WHO/EMRO positions Ismail held include: Regional Nursing Adviser from May 1986 to December 1986; short-term consultant, Human Resources Development, Republic of Djibouti, from February 1982 to September 1982; temporary adviser, Nigeria, in November 1980 and in Sudan in February 1979; and for UNICEF in Zambia in December 1979.[165]

She was a WHO/EMRO member of panel of experts on human resources development for health from 1977 to 1986 and a WHO staff member, nurse/midwife educator in Tripoli, Libya, from October 1965 to December 1967.[166]

Ismail's career is not limited to political activism. She holds the following credentials in health care in the United States: certificate in health care in developing countries from Boston University; BSc. in nursing services management at Clayton University, Atlanta, Georgia; and a certificate as a family planning practitioner at the Margaret Sanger Center in New York City. From the United Kingdom, Ismail is a state certified midwife (SCM); has a Central Midwives Board certificate (CMB); and is a state registered nurse (SRN). In August 1961, following completion of her studies in the U.K., she returned to Somalia as the first qualified Somali nurse midwife and became the first female to become appointed to a senior post in the Civil Service of Somalia.[167]

These qualifications enabled her to construct the Edna Adan Maternity Hospital in Hargeisa, Somaliland. The facility is a non-profit charity and a nurse/midwifery teaching hospital. The first group of 30 registered nurses graduated in 2003. The first group of 27 midwives graduated in 2004. Fifteen assistant laboratory technicians graduated in 2002. A second group of 30 student nurses were in training as of August 2006.[168]

Ismail's medical service is extensive. From February 1984 to May 1988, she also supervised the project and construction of the first privately owned hospital in Mogadishu, Somalia, the Edna Maternity Hospital. Unfortunately, says Ismail, "After my family fled Somalia because of the civil war there, all my property in Mogadishu has been forcibly occupied by warlords."[169]

Earlier, her medical service in Mogadishu included the position of midwife superintendent at Medina Hospital from January 1972 to January 1977; owner and operator of a private pharmacy from July 1970 to January 1972; secretary general and founding member of the Somali Red Crescent Society from 1963 to 1965; and senior national nurse/midwife educator at the Health Personnel Training School from August 1963 to October 1965.[170]

Edna Adan Ismail is an accomplished person whose medical abilities and work in human rights put her in a strong position for a government assignment. When I asked her what the roadblocks are for women in government, she replied, "Roadblocks are there from the start. It's up to you to push them aside and stake your claim and your authority. A woman does not get called to cabinet meetings unless she gets to know about them; or special sessions are held informally over Qat [leaves and twigs of the *Catha edulis* tree[171]] chewing which women do not attend."[172]

Ismail has words of vision for other women based on her role and experience in government and politics:

> Any woman who is working in a male-dominated environment has to concentrate on what needs to be done, how she can do it, and not waste energy on obstructions. Stand by your principles, do not get disheartened, and love your country and people because whatever you are doing, you are doing it for them. Also, know that you are a role model and that other women (both young and old) are watching you and learning from you. Be encouraging, show confidence and determination.[173]

Odette Nyiramirimo[174]

SENATOR, REPUBLIC OF RWANDA

Dr. Odette Nyiramirimo is an influential senator and the president of the Committee on Social Affairs and Human Rights in the Republic of Rwanda. She has been the Secretary General of the Liberal Party or PL (Party Liberal) since 2001. From 2000 to 2003 she was the State Secretary in Social Affairs.[175]

In 1973, Nyiramirimo attended a teachers' college in Cyangugu, but along with other girls, she was expelled because she was a Tutsi student.[176] Later when she sought readmission in Cyangugu, the director would not readmit her. When she enrolled in another school that specialized in the sciences to prepare her for her career in medicine, unlike what happened at Cyangugu, the headmistress kept Nyiramirimo's name out of the enrollment books and hid her when inspectors came looking for Tutsis.[177] Nyiramirimo became a physician and earned a Ph.D. in human medicine. From 1982 to 1999, she was a practical doctor and teacher in nursing and an assistant in the Medicor School in Butare.[178]

Nyiramirimo's life story is profiled in Philip Gourevitch's book, *We Wish to Inform You That Tomorrow We Will Be Killed with Our Families*. Nyiramirimo, an ethnic Tutsi, was born in 1956 in Rwanda in Kinunu, Gisenyi prefecture. She was the seventeenth of her father's eighteen children and was born to his second wife. When she was three years old, many members of her family were killed in the power struggles after independence.[179] In Gourevitch's book, she explains what she saw at an early age,

> I was three when this history of the genocide began. I can't remember it exactly, but I did see a group of men on the facing hill descending with machetes, and I can still see houses burning. We ran into the bush with our cows and stayed there for two months. So there was milk, but nothing else. Our house was burned to nothing.[180]

Nyiramirimo's family lived in poverty and fear, but her father protected them for a while when he took an identity card as a Hutu.[181]

After she became a physician, she married Jean-Baptiste Gasasira, who was also a physician. They had three children. Together, they founded a private maternity and pediatric practice in Kigali called Le Bon Samaritain (The Good Samaritan).[182] She and her husband adopted ten children and treated children survivors of the genocide for free.[183]

By the mid 1980s, the couple had well-paid positions at the Central Hospital of Kigali. In 1991, Nyiramirimo began her service as a physician in the United States Peace Corps mission in Kigali. In 1993 she served in a number of Peace Corps postings in Gabon, Kenya and Burundi. Later that year, due to political unrest in Burundi, she took a position with the Peace Corps in Kigali, Rwanda.[184]

Rwanda was one of the world's poorest and most densely populated countries. In April 1994, when Rwandan President Juvénal Habyarimana's plane was shot down, it marked the beginning of the Rwandan genocide.[185] The United Nations High Commissioner for Refugees (UNHCR) describes the horrifying events of that year:

> [O]ut of a population of some 6.5 million, nearly one half were either murdered or fled the country. Of those who stayed, three-quarters were forced from their homes. Most of the country's basic infrastructure was destroyed. With the possible exception of Somalia, no state was nearer to total meltdown.[186]

Nyiramirimo and her family escaped from Kigali that night in April 1994, but not without a great deal of travail: paying protection money sometimes not honored, signing over their jeep and other belongings in exchange for escort protection, the loss of family, and the capture of her children, her husband and herself.[187] Gourevitch describes this time: "Meanwhile, all across Rwanda: murder, murder, murder, murder, murder, murder, murder, murder, murder...."[188]

In 2001, Nyiramirimo as Minister of Social Affairs presented a report to establish the exact number of genocide victims. From October 1, 1991 to December 31, 1994, 1,074,017 people were killed in massacres and genocide. The report established the names of 951,018 victims. Men represented 66 percent of the victims. The most affected age group for both genders was between one and 21. Of those killed, 97.3 percent were Tutsi.[189]

Philip Gourevitch believes the distinguishing mark of the Rwandan events was the "programmatic effort to eliminate everybody in the Tutsi minority group because they were Tutsis."[190] Gourevitch described the speed of this effort as very rapid. Eight hundred thousand people were murdered in 100 days or 8,000 murders a day or five murders a minute. The murders were committed with extreme brutality. Machetes mostly were used to batter, hack or stab on a one-on-one basis. Gourevitch explains that without much help from the world, the Rwandans, the rebel Rwandese Patriotic Front, ended the genocide and took power. In the most rapid mass exoduses in modern history, Tutsis fled into Tanzania and the Congo.[191]

UNHCR reports that ten years later, although massive problems remain, Rwanda's "efforts to overcome the most dreadful type of violence perpetrated against a perceived enemy, that of genocide, have been admirable."[192]

U.N. Secretary-General Kofi Annan launched an action plan to prevent future genocides and said, "We must never forget our collective failure to protect at least 800,000 defenseless men, women and children who perished in Rwanda."[193]

In 2006, Nyiramirimo added, "Forgiveness is very difficult. The problem is not yet solved. In my deep consciousness, I feel it will not happen again across the breadth of the country. But there are incidents. People are still being killed."[194]

As for the effectiveness of parliament, Nyiramirimo and other women in politics acknowledge that parliament does not play an overly confrontational role with the executive branch because of the divisive politics of the country's past. As a result, only a few pieces of legislation have originated in parliament in recent years. Loyalty to President Paul Kagame, a Tutsi and former rebel leader of the Rwandan Patriotic Front whose forces suppressed the mass killing of Tutsi and moderate Hutu in 1994, is critical for political survival regardless of one's gender.[195]

As of February 2007, the Rwandan Parliament leads the world in percentage of women parliamentarians, with 48.8 percent representation in the lower house and 34.6 percent in the senate.[196] Even so, the efforts of female legislators to have equality in political debates has taken time. Nyiramirimo said in 2006, "Men are watching us.... They wonder if we'll rise up to a higher level. We're learning fast, because we have to. We say to each other that we can't be as good as the men — we have to be better."[197]

Nyiramirimo believes the true test of women's success is how much change occurs in the lives of rural women. She says, "I grew up in a rural area, and every morning before school I had to get up early and fetch water at the river.... It was so painful to balance it on your head. Every time I go to my village I see girls and women still doing it."[198] Nyiramirimo planned an initiative to import and breed donkeys to carry the women's loads.

Women are making progress in passing legislation. In 1999, before the current number of women gained office, but with substantial input from women, Rwanda liberalized the rules restricting inheritance for women. The rules were a major force in keeping women poor. Penalties have been increased for those who rape children, as a result of the brutal genocide of 1994.[199]

Nyiramirimo, as a survivor of genocide at the Hotel des Mille Collines, is featured in the movie *Hotel Rwanda* by the manager of the Hotel des Mille Collines, Paul Rusesabagina, and in Rusesabagina's book, *An Ordinary Man*. The movie and the book are controversial.[200]

Rwanda participated in the International Conference on Population Development (ICPD) in November 2006, in Bangkok, Thailand. Members of Parliament from all over the world attended. Senator Odette Nyiramirimo represented Rwanda.[201]

It is fitting that this highly accomplished woman, Odette Nyiramirimo, is a part of a parliament that is the world's leader in the number of female legislators. She describes the Rwanda Parliament as "renowned for its achievements, including the representation of women."[202]

PART II

PROGRESS OF AFRICAN WOMEN BY COUNTRY

Introduction

We all agree that the advancement of women is essential for true democracy, balanced decision-making and effective management of social and economic resources.
— Suzanne Mubarak, head of Egypt's delegation to the 23rd United Nations General Assembly special session on women.[1]

After the First World Conference on Women was held in 1975 in Mexico, regional commissions of the United Nations evaluated and made recommendations on the international platforms for action on the advancement of women. Since that first conference, the United Nations Economic Commission for Africa (ECA) has organized a review every five years for the African region.[2] The Dakar Platform for Action, known as the African Platform for Action, was adopted by African women and their respective governments, according to Josephine Ouedraogo, Director of the ECA's African Center for Gender and Development (ACGD). The ECA organized the African regional conference to prepare Africa's participation in the Beijing conference.[3]

In 1998, the Economic Commission for Africa issued a separate report on post-conflict countries and gender. Its findings included considerable gains during the evolving process of democratization, especially the inclusion of constitutional equal rights, growth of women's movements and affirmative action plans. A major constraint for female candidates has been lack of information. In addition, women are not sensitized to the ways they can influence government and they usually lack independent resources, making costs of campaigning prohibitive. Third, women councilors are not knowledgeable enough about gender issues or sensitive to the needs of women, especially the need to challenge some traditional values that undermine the status and rights of women.[4]

In 2005, the United Nations Economic and Social Commission for Western Asia (ESCWA) issued a report, *Women in Decision-Making in the Arab Region*. This report included all Arab countries of the world. The ESCWA found that constitutional rights do not necessarily lead to representation. Men control the political, social, economic and legal realms of life through informal and personalized networks. The ESCWA stated, "Women in the Arab world have been largely marginalized from the formal political arena."[5]

Some of the earliest Arab countries in Africa to provide women their political rights were the Comoros, Djibouti, Egypt, and Tunisia. Djibouti became the first to guarantee women's suffrage in 1946. Most Arab countries had upheld such rights by the 1960s and early seventies.[6]

Out of 16 Arab countries (including some countries outside of Africa) that have functioning parliaments and have given women the right to vote and to run for public office, women's share of parliamentary seats does not exceed 4.1 percent on average. Djibouti and Libya have no women at all in their parliaments. Out of the 13 Arab countries in the world that have women in their parliaments, seven have a female representation below the regional average, recording roughly 2 percent women representation in parliament. In Africa, Sudan and Tunisia show the best records of female representation in parliament, listing 9.7 percent and 11.5 percent.[7]

Arab women's representation in ministerial and executive positions is equally low. In 1990, six African Arab countries had women ministers, Algeria, the Comoros, Egypt, Mauritania, Sudan, and Tunisia, ranging between one and two women ministers in each respective cabinet.[8]

The Economic Commission for Africa has issued two major reports on the progress of African women since the Beijing Declaration and Platform for Action adopted by the Fourth World Conference on Women: Action for Equality, Development and Peace in Beijing on September 15, 1995.[9] In 2001, the ECA issued the first report that assessed the progress of women five years after the Beijing conference. This report is often called *Beijing+5*.[10] The second report, issued in 2005, evaluated the achievements of women ten years after Beijing, and is often called *Beijing+10*.[11]

The *Beijing+5* report reviews progress in Africa in the area of women in politics and decision-making since the adoption of the Dakar and Beijing declarations. Progress has been slow in that in 1999, only 11 percent of the members of legislative bodies were women, up from ten percent in 1995, but far short of the 30 percent target.[12] Cultural and traditional barriers are the leading reasons given for the lack of success, along with "the persistent unequal division of labor and responsibilities within households; civil wars and strife; women's inadequate education and training; lack of enforcement of quotas and affirmative action; inadequate generation, dissemination and use of gender research and disaggregated data; the HIV/AIDS epidemic; the serious economic problems facing African economies; lack of political will."[13]

The 2001 report recognized that creating a conducive environment for women to achieve must be accompanied by the philosophy that women should empower themselves to be empowered. Thus, it stresses the importance of judging the non-quantifiable aspects such as increased ability to enter political leadership, as well as the number of women in positions of power and decision-making. In this framework, the report concluded that most African countries demonstrated a national commitment to raising the status of women and increasing their presence in power and decision-making.[14]

The second Beijing report (*Beijing+10*), issued in 2005, evaluates the achievements of women ten years after the Beijing Conference. This report views gender equality in governance as a human rights issue and a democratic imperative. It states, "There is no democracy without gender equality."[15] In general, there is a growing list of countries where peaceful elections took place; for example, in South Africa after apartheid ended. Mechanisms for accountability were created, such as the African Peer Review Mechanism within the New Partnership for Africa's Development (NEPAD).

In 2005, three African countries, out of 14 countries worldwide, reached or exceeded 30 percent of women in parliament: Rwanda, South Africa and Mozambique. All of these countries had a proportional representation election system or a mix of systems that included some proportional representation. Eight African countries had quotas for women candidates. In some countries of Africa, the proportion of women in parliaments increased dramatically. Rwanda headed the countries on the list with an almost 49 percent increase and even the lowest country on the list, Uganda, had an almost 25 percent increase. These increments equaled or surpassed the objectives specified in the Beijing Platform for Action.[16]

COUNTRIES WITH HIGHEST POSITIVE TRENDS IN
TEN YEARS AFTER BEIJING PLATFORM FOR ACTION (BPFA)

Country	Percentage
Rwanda	48.8
South Africa	32.8
Mozambique	30
Seychelles	29.4
Namibia	26.4
Uganda	24.7

Source: United Nations Economic Commission for Africa (ECA), *Promoting Gender Equality and Women's Empowerment in Africa: Questioning the Achievements and Confronting the Challenges Ten Years After Beijing*, Addis Ababa, Ethiopia, Feb. 2005, 19. Dec. 10, 2006, www.uneca.org/acgd/Publications/Gender_Equality.pdf.

The 2005 report found women elected and appointed into powerful decision-making positions. Specifically, the Gambia and Zimbabwe appointed female vice presidents and Mozambique, a prime minister. Governments also appointed women as ministers, ambassadors, speakers and deputy speakers of parliaments and national directors of public prosecution. In South Africa, 42.9 percent of its ministers are women.[17]

The *Beijing+10* evaluation reported that, although there have been increases in numbers of women, women are still underrepresented in all structures of decision-making power in two specific areas. First, policies may be in place, but implementation falls behind. Women who are appointed are often appointed to traditionally female ministries such as health, education, social services, and gender. Second, it raised the question whether the increase in the number of women led to more gender-sensitive development and programs.[18]

The *Beijing+10* report concluded that many African governments have acted on their promises that implement the Beijing Platform for Action, but that there are many unresolved issues: "The empowerment of women and gender equality, commitment to democracy and the right to development continue to be considered as optional and not obligatory," and, "If Africa does not prioritize the promotion of gender equality and continues with 'business as usual,' the continent will continue to struggle with the scourges of poverty, hunger and disease for a long time to come."[19]

In addition to the two Beijing reports and its post-conflict report, the ECA's *African Governance Report* in 2005 concludes that women, especially in the agricultural sector and the informal economy, are marginalized in the political process even though they had active roles in the struggle for decolonization.[20] The overriding reason for women's lack of participation in the political process is the patriarchal nature of African societies. The ECA categorizes African countries into three groups in terms of their efforts to empower women. The "high flyers" are South Africa and Uganda. Countries that have taken moderate steps include Botswana, Burkina Faso, Gabon, Lesotho, Malawi, Mali, Namibia, Senegal, Tanzania, Zambia and Zimbabwe. The third group comprises countries that have taken no or inadequate steps: Benin, Egypt, Ethiopia, the Gambia, Ghana, Kenya, Mauritius, Nigeria and Swaziland. The women in the "high flyers" countries hold more than 25 percent of the seats in their parliaments. In the second group, women hold 10 to 25 percent and in the third group less than ten percent.[21]

The ECA concludes that the level of women's participation in politics is generally low in spite of a "high flyer" group. Encouraging is that African countries are setting minimum standards for themselves. For example, the Southern African Development Community set a target of 30 percent for women's representation in parliament and other state organizations in these countries by the end of 2005.[22]

According to Josephine Ouedraogo in 2004, "no study has been undertaken on the impact of government policies on the advancement of women at the continental level, which would at the same time enable an assessment of the relevance and effectiveness of government strategies and those of other agencies."[23] The ECA has devised a tool to measure disparities between men and women in all priority areas. The index is a series of indicators on the basis of which disparities, in terms of capacities, opportunities and the power to bring about change, can be measured. The new index correlates, for example, the measuring of gender inequalities as well as governmental efforts for the advancement of women. Ouedraogo concludes, "The objective of the African Gender and Development Index is not to classify countries, but rather to provide a common platform for gauging actual progress on the ground, taking into account the social, economic, political and historical context in each country."[24]

Tacko Ndiaye, an ECA officer, explains: "The African Gender and Development Index"[25] was launched and

> has also been piloted in 12 African countries: Benin, Burkina Faso, Cameroon, Ethiopia, Egypt, Ghana, Madagascar, Mozambique, South Africa, Tanzania, Tunisia and Uganda. The national reports will be launched in early 2007. The 12 reports are also synthesized in a publication called the *African Women's Report* to be launched at the same time as the national reports.[26]

Evaluating the progress of women in Africa in positions of leadership is a work in progress. Until this index is fully evaluated and the progress of countries is itemized, the progress of women's participation in decision-making at the office-holding level will not be fully known. Numbers alone at this level do not totally represent women's participation in decision-making. Women participate in many ways, such as political parties, lobbying, and private sector activities. Countries excel in ways not examined here. No systematic way is in place to determine gender progress and governmental efforts at present.

NORTH AFRICA

Algeria, Egypt, Libya, Mauritania,
Morocco, Sudan, Tunisia, Western Sahara

People's Democratic Republic of Algeria

BACKGROUND[1]

Location: Northern Africa, bordering the Mediterranean Sea, between Morocco and Tunisia
Population: 32,930,091 (July 2006 est.)
Per Capita Income: $7,700 (2006 est.)

Government type: republic.

Independence: July 5, 1962 (from France). After more than a century of rule by France, Algerians fought through much of the 1950s to achieve independence in 1962. Algeria's primary political party, the National Liberation Front (FLN), has dominated ever since the country gained independence. Those citizens dissatisfied with the FLN, the Islamic Salvation Front (FIS), were first successful in the December 1991 balloting. The army began a crackdown on the FIS that spurred FIS supporters to attack government targets. The government later allowed elections, but did not appease the activists, who extended their attacks. The fighting escalated into an insurgency between 1992 and 1998 which resulted in over 100,000 deaths. By the late 1990s, the government gained control and in January 2000, FIS's armed wing, the Islamic Salvation Army, disbanded. However, small numbers of armed militants persist in confronting government forces and conducting ambushes and some attacks on villages. The army placed Abdelaziz Bouteflika in the presidency in 1999 in a fraudulent election but claimed neutrality in his 2004 landslide reelection. Longstanding problems continue to face Bouteflika, including the ethnic minority Berbers' ongoing autonomy campaign, unemployment, housing shortage, unreliable electrical and water supplies, government inefficiencies and corruption, and the extremist militants. Algeria needs to diversify its petroleum-based economy, which has yielded a large cash reserve but has not been used to correct Algeria's many social and infrastructure problems.

Constitution: September 8, 1963; revised 1976, 1988, 1989, and November 1996.

Legislature: bicameral Parliament consisting of the National People's Assembly or Al-Majlis Ech-Chaabi Al-Watani (389 seats, formerly 380 seats; members elected by popular vote to serve five-year terms) and the Council of Nations (Senate) (144 seats; one-third of the members appointed by the president, two-thirds elected by indirect vote; members serve six-year terms; the constitution requires half the council to be renewed every three years).

Elections: National People's Assembly — last held 17 May 2007 (next to be held in 2012); Council of Nation (Senate) — last held December 28, 2006 (next to be held in 2009).

Election results: National People's Assembly — percent of vote by party, N/A; seats by party — FLN 199, RND 47, Islah 43, MSP 38, PT 21, FNA 8, EnNahda 1, PRA 1, MEN 1, independents 30; Council of Nation — percent of vote by party, N/A; seats by party — FLN 29, RND 12, MSP 3, RCD 1, independents 3, presidential appointees (unknown affiliation) 24.

Political parties: Ahd 54; Algerian National Front or FNA; National Democratic Rally or RND; Islamic Salvation Front or FIS (outlawed April 1992); National Entente Movement or MEN; National Liberation Front or FLN; National Reform Movement or Islah (formerly MRN); National Renewal Party or PRA; Rally for Culture and Democracy or RCD; Renaissance Movement or EnNahda Movement; Socialist Forces Front or FFS; Social Liberal Party or PSL; Society of Peace Movement or MSP; Workers Party or PT. A law banning political parties based on religion was enacted in March 1997.

STATUS AND PROGRESS OF WOMEN

Algeria nominated the first woman to parliament in September 1962 and elected the first woman in September 1964.[2] The Inter-Parliamentary Union (IPU) lists Algeria as having a setback with the number of women in parliament. In 1995, 12 women served out of 178 seats (6.74 percent) and in 2006, 24 out of 389 (6.17 percent). The difference was -0.57 percent.[3]

Although the participation of women in decision making is guaranteed by the constitution and the law, Algeria's *National Report on the Solemn Declaration on Equality of Men and Women* notes that their participation compared to men remains modest. A little over 46 percent of women voted in the 2002 local elections.[4]

In the higher levels of government in 2004, women held such positions as: three in the government; four ambassadresses, including two in service abroad; one first-time named governor in 1999 followed by two other governors, one of whom was a deputy governor; one secretary-general of a ministry; three secretaries-general of governors' offices, and three general inspectors of governors' offices.[5]

Algeria's *Beijing+10* report indicated women were making a substantial political contribution, an important gain in democratic openness and multiple parties. In legislative elections, women's changing situation is shown in the table below.

ALGERIA'S LEGISLATIVE ELECTIONS AND
WOMEN'S PARTICIPATION, 1997 AND 2002[6]

	1997		2002	
	Candidates	Elected	Candidates	Elected
Communal People's Assemblies	1,281	75	3,679	147
Wilaya People's Assemblies	905	62	2,684	113
National People's Assembly	322	11	694	27
Council of the Nations	—	—	—	3

In 2006, the official government information shows three women held positions of minister: Mme. Khalida Toumi, Minister of Culture; Mme. Nouara Saâdia Djaffar, Minister for Health, the Population and the Hospital Reform, Responsible for the Family and the Female Condition; and Mme. Souad Bendjaballah, Minister for Higher Education and Scientific Research.[7]

Algeria stated its main challenges are that cultural stereotypes and restrictions still prevail and women are reluctant to participate in political life and appear to find their traditional roles satisfactory.[8]

Arab Republic of Egypt

BACKGROUND[9]

Location: Northern Africa, bordering the Mediterranean Sea and the Red Sea, between Libya and the Gaza Strip, north of Sudan, and includes the Asian Sinai Peninsula
Population: 78,887,007 (July 2006 est.)
Per Capita Income: $4,200 (2006 est.)
   Government type: republic.
   Independence: February 28, 1922 (from U.K.). The regularity and richness of the annual Nile River flood, coupled with semi-isolation provided by deserts to the east and west, allowed for the development of one of the world's great civilizations. A unified kingdom arose circa 3200 B.C., and a series of dynasties ruled in Egypt for the next three millennia. The last native dynasty fell to the Persians in 341 B.C., who in turn were replaced by the Greeks, Romans, and Byzantines. It was the Arabs who introduced Islam and the Arabic language in the 7th century and who ruled for the next six centuries. A local military caste, the Mamluks, took control about 1250 and continued to govern after the conquest of Egypt by the Ottoman Turks in 1517. Following the completion of the Suez Canal in 1869, Egypt became an important world transportation hub, but also fell heavily into debt. Ostensibly to protect its investments, Britain seized control of Egypt's government in 1882, but nominal allegiance to the Ottoman Empire continued until 1914. Partially independent from the U.K. in 1922, Egypt acquired full sovereignty following World War II. The completion of the Aswan High Dam in 1971 and the resultant Lake Nasser have altered the time-honored place of the Nile River in the agriculture and ecology of Egypt. A rapidly growing population (the largest in the Arab world), limited arable land, and dependence on the Nile all continue to overtax resources and stress society. The government has struggled to ready the economy for the new millennium through economic reform and massive investment in communications and physical infrastructure.[10]
   Constitution: September 11, 1971; amended May 1980 and May 2005.
   Legislature: bicameral system consists of the People's Assembly or Majlis al-Sha'b (454 seats; 444 elected by popular vote, 10 appointed by the president; members serve five-year terms) and the Advisory Council or Majlis al-Shura, which functions only in a consultative role (264 seats; 176 elected by popular vote, 88 appointed by the president; members serve six-year terms; mid-term elections for half of the elected members).
   Political parties: National Democratic Party or NDP (Mohammed Hosni Mubarak [governing party]); National Progressive Unionist Grouping or Tagammu; New Wafd Party or NWP; Tomorrow Party. Formation of political parties must be approved by the government.

STATUS AND PROGRESS OF WOMEN

In July 1957, Egypt elected the first woman to parliament.[11] The United Nations Commission for Africa's (ECA) *Beijing+5* report found Egypt's parliament to have nine women out of 454 seats (2.2 percent); two women out of 23 cabinet members (8 percent); 22 women out of 360 local authorities (6.1 percent); and women representing 5.7 percent of senate members. The report stated, "Major obstacles faced are difficulties in implementing legislation that challenges religious forces and the effects of economic liberalization/structural adjustment policies and programs. NGOs also claimed that they were not consulted in the formulation of policies on women."[12] The Inter-Parliamentary Union lists Egypt as having a setback with the number of women in parliament. In 1995, ten women served out of 454 seats (2.20 percent) and in 2006, nine out of 442 (2.04 percent). The difference was -0.16 percent.[13]

By presidential decree, the National Council for Women was formed in 2000 as the governmental institution responsible for the advancement of women. The council's president is Egypt's First Lady, H.E. Mrs. Suzanne Mubarak. The council developed the fifth national plan and established a standing mechanism to ensure gender mainstreaming in the National Plan (2002–2007). It has also developed gender-sensitive indicators to monitor the benefits to women. The Council established a Centre for the Political Empowerment of Women, as a pilot initiative.[14]

Although a woman was elected as deputy speaker of the First House of the Parliament, the number of female parliamentarians was very low, 2.2 percent in the First House and 5.7 percent in the Second House.[15] The low numbers reveal "that there are constraints, many of which are hard to overcome."[16]

Improvement was noted in the appointment of more women in higher decision-making positions, reaching 34.6 percent in 2002, compared to only 15.3 percent in 1996. Efforts were being made to build a group of politically and technically qualified women with knowledge and experiences to be able to run for the parliamentarian elections in 2005. The representation of women in the political spheres is still lagging behind in spite of the marked increase in the rate of females appointed to higher decision-making positions. These appointments nearly doubled from 15 percent in 1996 to 34 percent in 2002.[17]

The report listed challenges to women's political participation: societal perceptions regarding the traditional division of labor, where women are seen as bound to certain functions only; the famous "glass ceiling"; and the high cost of running campaigns.[18] Some of Egypt's proposed methods of improvement include: political parties' support of the campaigns for women candidates and revision of party law to obligate parties to set a specific percentage for women and youth on their electoral lists; the continuation of awareness campaigns and activities of pressure groups and non-governmental organizations; working towards implementation of Article 4 of the CEDAW, in connection with the possibility to resort to temporary measures, pending that Egyptian women acquire their right to a fair representation in the legislative councils; revisiting the current election system to increase the chances for women and youth to win seats in elected councils; and supporting the Programme for the Political Empowerment and other existing avenues.[19]

Great Socialist People's Libyan Arab Jamahiriya

BACKGROUND[20]

Location: Northern Africa, bordering the Mediterranean Sea, between Egypt and Tunisia
Population: 5,900,754 (note: includes 166,510 non-nationals; July 2006 est.)
Per Capita Income: $12,700 (2006 est.)

Government type: Jamahiriya (a state of the masses) — in theory, governed by the populace through local councils, in practice an authoritarian state.

Independence: December 24, 1951 (from U.N. trusteeship). The Italians supplanted the Ottoman Turks from the area around Tripoli in 1911 and did not relinquish their hold until 1943 when defeated in World War II. Libya then passed to U.N. administration and achieved independence in 1951.

Constitution: none; note: following the September 1969 military overthrow of the Libyan government, the Revolutionary Command Council replaced the existing constitution with the Constitutional Proclamation in December 1969; in March 1977, Libya adopted the Declaration of the Establishment of the People's Authority.

Legislature: unicameral General People's Congress (N/A seats; members elected indirectly through a hierarchy of people's committees).

Political parties: none.

STATUS AND PROGRESS OF WOMEN

In 1996, women accounted for 4.5 percent of Libya's ministerial positions.[21] The *Contemporary African Database* lists ten women who serve or who have served as political figures or government officials, primarily as ministers.[22] In February 2001, out of 20 countries, Libya had a woman ambassador to the United Nations in Geneva.[23] Although Libya replied to the questionnaire on the implementation of the Beijing Platform for Action five years after the conference, the country report for the ten-year review is not available.[24] However, in 2005, the United Nations Economic and Social Commission for Western Asia (ESCWA) reported that although women gained suffrage in 1964, Libya has no women at all in its parliament, but had one woman minister. In 1989, Libya became a signatory to the Convention on the Elimination of all Forms of Discrimination Against Women (CEDAW).[25]

Islamic Republic of Mauritania

BACKGROUND[26]

Location: Northern Africa, bordering the North Atlantic Ocean, between Senegal and Western Sahara

Population: 3,177,388 (July 2006 est.)

Per Capita Income: $2,600 (2006 est.)

Government type: republic.

Independence: November 28, 1960 (from France). In 1976, Mauritania annexed the southern third of what is now the Western Sahara. The Polisario guerrilla front sought independence for the territory and Mauritania relinquished it after three years of raids. In 1984 Maaouya Ould Sid Ahmed Taya successfully staged a coup and took power in 1985. Opposition parties were legalized and a new constitution approved in 1991. The two multiparty presidential elections since then were defective, but the October 2001 legislative and municipal elections were free and open. A bloodless coup in August 2005 deposed Taya, and a military council headed by Colonel Ely Ould Mohamed Vall took over. The council said he would remain for up to two years while the government created conditions for democratic institutions and organized elections. Successful parliamentary elections were held in December 2006 and senatorial and presidential elections were held in January and March 2007. Until the new government takes power, Mauritania remains an autocratic state, and the country experiences ethnic tensions among its black population and different Moor (Arab-Berber) communities.

Constitution: July 12, 1991.

Legislature: bicameral legislature consists of the Senate or Majlis al-Shuyukh (56 seats; a portion of seats up for election every two years; members elected by municipal leaders to serve six-year terms) and the National Assembly or Majlis al-Watani (95 seats; members elected by popular vote to serve five-year terms).

Elections: Senate — last held January 21 and February 4, 2007 (next to be held 2009); National Assembly — last held November 19 and December 3, 2006 (next to be held 2011).

Political parties: Alternative or Al-Badil; Coalition for Forces for Democratic Change or CFCD (coalition of political parties including RFD, United Forces of Progress or UDP, APP, Islamists, HATEM-PMUC, RD, UDC); Democratic Renewal or RD; Islamists (Centrist Reformists); Mauritanian Party for Unity and Change or HATEM-PMUC; National Rally for Freedom, Democracy and Equality or RNDLE; Popular Front or FP; Popular Progressive Alliance or APP; Rally of Democratic Forces or RFD; Rally for Democracy and Unity or RDU; Republican Party for Democracy and Renewal or PRDR (formerly ruling Democratic and Social Republican Party or PRDS); Union for Democracy and Progress or UDP; Union of Democratic Centre or UCD.

STATUS AND PROGRESS OF WOMEN

Women received the right to vote and to stand for election in 1961.[27] In 1965, five years after Mauritania became a sovereign state, it had its first legislature, and ten years later, in 1975, it elected the first woman to parliament.[28] The constitution of July 20, 1991, guarantees women rights and liberties on the same level as men. In addition, Mauritania has adhered to a number of international and regional legal texts which protect the fundamental rights of women.[29]

In February 2007, 26 women held seats in parliament, nine of which were newly elected. Prior to the 2005 coup, the government included only ten women. Colonel Ely Ould Mohamed Vall's transitional government established a 20 percent quota of women at the parliamentary and municipal levels. Parity for men and women must be achieved on candidate lists where two seats are at stake. Where three or more seats are at stake and voting is proportional, candidates must alternate between male and female on the list.[30]

Mauritania's *Beijing+10* report stated "socio-political participation remains limited, despite certain advances."[31] In 2004, four women were at the highest level of ministerial departments or the equivalent; women were 3.7 percent of deputies in government; women were five percent of senators in government; one political party was led by a woman. For the first time in Mauritania, a woman candidate ran for office in the presidential elections in November 2003.

Mauritania's strategies for improvement include: "the creation of a gender approach to reduce the gap between the sexes with regard to access to education, legal and judiciary services and economic and financial resources; strengthen the participation of women in decision making at all levels; strengthen the participation of women in decision making through their presence in key sectors, such as diplomatic corps or even in the military or paramilitary sectors; [and the] development of a program to advocate in favor of the reinforcement of the participation of women in decision making."[32]

Kingdom of Morocco

BACKGROUND[33]

Location: Northern Africa, bordering the North Atlantic Ocean and the Mediterranean Sea, between Algeria and Western Sahara

Population: 33,241,259 (July 2006 est.)

Per Capita Income: $4,400 (2006 est.)

Government type: constitutional monarchy.

Independence: March 2, 1956 (from France since 1912). The internationalized city of Tangier and most Spanish possessions were turned over. Morocco annexed Western Sahara during the late 1970s, but final status of the territory remains unresolved.

Constitution: March 10, 1972; revised September 1992, amended (to create bicameral legislature) September 1996.

Legislature: bicameral Parliament consists of an upper house or Chamber of Counselors (270 seats; members elected indirectly by local councils, professional organizations, and labor syndicates for nine-year terms; one-third of the members are renewed every three years) and a lower house or Chamber of Representatives (325 seats; 295 by multi-seat constituencies and 30 from national lists of women; members elected by popular vote for five-year terms).

Political parties: Action Party or PA; Alliance of Liberties or ADL; Annahj Addimocrati or Annahj; Avant Garde Social Democratic Party or PADS; Citizen Forces or FC; Citizen's Initiatives for Development; Constitutional Union or UC; Democratic and Independence Party or PDI; Democratic and Social Movement or MDS; Democratic Forces Front or FFD; Democratic Socialist Party or PSD; Democratic Union or UD; Environment and Development Party or PED; Front of Democratic Forces or FFD; Istiqlal Party (Independence Party) or PI; Justice and Development Party or PJD; Moroccan Liberal Party or PML; National Democratic Party or PND; National Ittihadi Congress Party or CNI; National Popular Movement or MNP; National Rally of Independents or RNI; National Union of Popular Forces or UNFP; Parti Al Ahd or Al Ahd; Party of Progress and Socialism or PPS; Party of Renewal and Equity or PRE; Party of the Unified Socialist Left or GSU; Popular Movement Union or UMP; Reform and Development Party or PRD; Social Center Party or PSC; Socialist Union of Popular Forces or USFP.

STATUS AND PROGRESS OF WOMEN

The Inter-Parliamentary Union (IPU) reports that Morocco elected the first woman to parliament in June 1993.[34] The IPU lists Morocco as making progress with the number of women in parliament. In 1995, two women served out of 333 seats (0.60 percent) and in 2006, 35 out of 325 (10.77 percent). The improvement was 10.17 percent.[35] Improvement in representation of women in the Arab states was due to quotas adopted in some states, including Morocco.[36] The country's *Beijing+10* review reported that in February 2002, the government adopted a national list of 30 seats reserved for women for the legislative elections in September 2002. This policy increased the number of female deputies from 0.5 percent to 10.8 percent.[37]

The report states, "For the first time in the history of Morocco, there is political mobilization around women's issues."[38] Laws reflecting international law are in place and now the
need is to gradually integrate the gender dimension in the elaboration of the country's socio-
economic development programs. A cabinet ministry created in part for the status of women
strengthens the mechanisms of support for the advancement of women.

Women have been "long almost absent from the political arena and the decision-making sphere,"[39] but are now organizing and advocating for improved legal status. Their objective is to remove the major contradiction between the constitution that grants women the
same rights as men, and the old Personal Status Code which ranks them with minors. In 1993,
the Code was revised, changing an "untouchable" area: the appointment of women to higher
decision-making positions.

The Declaration of the Government in November 2002 and the speech by the King in
October 2003 clearly expressed the political will for the advancement of women. Results
included legislative reform and the creation of institutions and gender focal points in several
departments. Advances were significant: women began to appear at the highest level of the
hierarchy as counselors to the King (one in 2000), secretary of state (two in 1998), minister
(one in 2000), ambassadors (two in 2000), as well as deputies and counselors in the two
chambers (37 in 2002); in September 2002, the new Electoral Code facilitated the access of
35 women to Parliament, 30 of which were by quota and five from local lists. This figure is
almost 10 percent of the members of the Chamber of Deputies. Also for the first time, Morocco
witnessed the election of a woman president of a parliament group, and a vice president of
the house of representatives; and the Moroccan Center of Information, Documentation and
Studies on Women was created.[40] The government realizes the need to strengthen existing
institutional structures, strengthen and enforce legislation, and to support women in their
efforts.[41]

Republic of the Sudan

BACKGROUND[42]

Location: Northern Africa, bordering the Red Sea, between Egypt and Eritrea
Population: 41,236,378 (July 2006 est.)
Per Capita Income: $2,300 (2006 est.)

Government type: Government of National Unity (GNU); the National Congress Party
(NCP) and Sudan People's Liberation Movement (SPLM) formed a power-sharing government under the 2005 Comprehensive Peace Agreement (CPA); the NCP, which came to power
by military coup in 1989, is the majority partner; the agreement stipulates national elections
for the 2008–2009 time frame.

Independence: January 1, 1956 (from Egypt and U.K.).

Constitution: implemented on June 30, 1998; partially suspended on December 12, 1999
by President Bashir; under the CPA, Interim National Constitution ratified on July 5, 2005;
Constitution of Southern Sudan signed December 2005.

Legislature: bicameral body comprising the National Assembly and Council of States
(replaced unicameral National Assembly of 360 seats); pending elections in 2009 and National
Election Law, the Presidency appointed 450 members to the National Assembly according to
the provisions of the 2005 Comprehensive Peace Agreement: 52 percent NCP; 28 percent

SPLM; 14 percent other Northerners; 6 percent other Southerners. Two representatives from every state constitute the Council of States; terms in each chamber are five years following the first elections.

Political parties: National Congress Party or NCP; Sudan People's Liberation Movement or SPLM; and elements of the National Democratic Alliance or NDA, including factions of the Democratic Union Party and Umma Party.

STATUS AND PROGRESS OF WOMEN

The Inter-Parliamentary Union (IPU) reports that Sudan elected the first woman to parliament in November 1964.[43] The IPU lists Sudan as making progress with the number of women in parliament. In 1995, 26 women served out of 316 seats (8.23 percent) and in 2006, 66 out of 450 (14.67 percent). The improvement was 6.44 percent.[44]

The Sudan *Beijing+10* review reported that there were notable gains for women since the first report, but challenges remain, including follow-up and monitoring of programs, lack of publicizing the objectives of the 10-year strategy, lack of institutional frameworks and mechanisms including adequate resources, reluctance to enlist women in programs, and the infeasibility to implement programs in areas of conflict, drought or floods.[45]

Some fundamental aims were to recognize that gender equality and equity and human dignity are noble values, to follow the values and teachings of the Islamic religion in the matter of equality and equity, to include the goals of community and national society, to use gains already made by women, and to make efforts to eliminate cultural practices harmful to women.[46]

Ultimately, the report's goal is "To promote the advancement of women in terms of their mission and to empower them socially, politically, economically, culturally and technologically as their families' dedicated caregivers and a model to be emulated in a Sudan where justice, equality, peace and security shall prevail."[47]

Sudan's suffrage for women was established in 1964. In 1990, Sudan was one of eight Arab countries that had women ministers. In 2005, Sudan had one woman minister. In the December 2000 elections, 35 women held seats out of 360 (9.7 percent).[48] In 2007, Sudan had not yet ratified the Convention on the Elimination of All Forms of Discrimination (CEDAW).[49]

Tunisian Republic

BACKGROUND[50]

Location: Northern Africa, bordering the Mediterranean Sea, between Algeria and Libya
Population: 10,175,014 (July 2006 est.)
Per Capita Income: $8,600 (2006 est.)

Government type: republic.

Independence: March 20, 1956 (from France).

Constitution: June 1, 1959; amended 1988, 2002.

Legislature: bicameral system consists of the Chamber of Deputies or Majlis al-Nuwaab (189 seats; members elected by popular vote to serve five-year terms) and the Chamber of Advisors (126 seats; 85 members elected by municipal counselors, deputies, mayors, and professional associations and trade unions; 41 members are presidential appointees; members serve six-year terms).

Political parties: Al-Tajdid Movement; Constitutional Democratic Rally Party (Rassemblement Constitutionnel Democratique) or RCD (official ruling party); Green Party for Progress or PVP; Liberal Social Party or PSL; Movement of Socialist Democrats or MDS; Popular Unity Party or PUP; Progressive Democratic Party; Unionist Democratic Union or UDU.

STATUS AND PROGRESS OF WOMEN

The head of the state of Tunisia has supported the process of emancipation of women since the country became independent from France in 1956. A legal framework exists that has advanced women's lives in all areas.[51] In particular, Article 6 of the Tunisian Constitution lays out that "all the citizens have the same rights and the same duties equally and are equal in front of the law."[52] Equality of men and women is also reflected in various codes having to do with nationality, the penal system and labor standards. Tunisia has also ratified many international instruments that protect human rights.

Tunisian law provides equality to access public office. Thus, the number of women participating is increasing at decision-making levels. The Industry and Environment Office (IE) of the United Nations Environment Program's (UNEP) point five of the Presidential Electoral Program (1999–2004) allows the accession of more than 20 percent of women in decision-making jobs and the electoral authorities. Point 16 sets the goal to a minimum of a 30 percent presence of women at responsible and decision-making positions before 2009.[53]

In November 2004, women represented 14.89 percent of the total number of the executive branch, up from 13.6 percent in the preceding government. These members include seven women (up from six women[54]). Two are ministers: women's, family, and children's affairs; and equipment, the habitat and regional planning. Five secretaries of state include: information, internet and free software; social advancement; hospital establishments; women's, family, and children's affairs; and foreign affairs.[55]

In 1959, Tunisia elected its first woman to parliament.[56] In recent times, the proportion of women within the legislative branch has also increased, from 7.4 percent in 1994 to 11.5 percent in 1999 to 22.75 percent in 2004. Parliament numbers 43 women deputies out of a total of 189, up from 21 out of a total of 182 in 1999. A woman occupies the IE position of second vice president of the chamber of deputies and another woman is a president of the standing committees of the chamber. The chamber of advisors numbers 17 women, of which one occupies IE post of second vice president.[57] The Inter-Parliamentary Union lists Tunisia as a country that is making progress. In 1995, 11 women held seats out of 163 (6.75 percent), compared to 2006 when women held 43 out of 189 seats (22.75 percent), reflecting a 16 percent gain.[58]

Tunisia's *Beijing+10* report indicated women are welcome in the ranks of the party in power, the Constitutional Democratic Assembly (RCD), but the seven opposition parties also accept women's participation. In 1992 the RCD established a permanent general secretariat for women's affairs and appointed 28 women deputy general secretaries of coordinating committees in all parts of the country. Women accounted for 26 percent of the membership of the Central Committee of the RCD; 21.25 percent of basic party cells, compared to 2.9 percent in 1988; and 21 percent of local federations, compared to 2.1 percent in 1988.[59]

In 2005, Tunisia demonstrated women have increased their presence in positions in national institutions, as well as the advisory authorities such as the Economic and Social Council. Two women occupy IE posts as advisers to the Presidency of the Republic; and in 2004, for the first time, a woman was a nominee for governor (prefect) and for the town councils and mayors.[60]

In Tunisia's *Beijing+10* report, the country vowed to institutionalize the gender approach in decision making. Until 2006, emphasis will be placed on increasing the number of women in decision-making posts and the number of actions designed to strengthen women's participation; widening the range of application of programs designed to change people's mentalities; and dedication to the principle of gender equality and partnership between men and women.[61]

Western Sahara

BACKGROUND[62]

Location: Northern Africa, bordering the North Atlantic Ocean, between Mauritania and Morocco

Population: 273,008 (July 2006 est.)

Per Capita Income: N/A

Government type: legal status of territory and issue of sovereignty unresolved; territory contested by Morocco and Polisario Front (Popular Front for the Liberation of the Saguia el Hamra and Rio de Oro), which in February 1976 formally proclaimed a government-in-exile of the Sahrawi Arab Democratic Republic (SADR), led by President Mohamed Abdelaziz; territory partitioned between Morocco and Mauritania in April 1976, with Morocco acquiring northern two-thirds; Mauritania, under pressure from Polisario guerrillas, abandoned all claims to its portion in August 1979; Morocco moved to occupy that sector shortly thereafter and has since asserted administrative control; the Polisario's government-in-exile was seated as an Organization of African Unity (OAU) member in 1984; guerrilla activities continued sporadically, until a UN-monitored cease-fire was implemented September 6, 1991.

Independence: sovereignty unresolved.

Constitution: none.

Legislature: none.

Political parties: none.

STATUS AND PROGRESS OF WOMEN

As in many countries where there is or has been conflict, the women of Western Sahara ran things because there was no one but the women to run things. The men were away fighting. As a result, the women are among the most liberated Muslim women in the world. "They don't veil their faces, they wear make-up, they sit in their parliament-in-exile, and they provide 90 percent of the local councilors who run the refugee camps in the Algerian desert. Male Sahrawi leaders say Iran and other Muslim countries have begun to complain about the Sahrawi women's status."[63]

That the Sahrawi women are more liberated than in most predominantly Muslim countries is a status the women believe is worth working to keep. Sahrawi women take an active role in their political struggle. They defend the role of women, the tradition of Sahrawi society. In old Sahrawi tradition, it is women who take responsibility. Women have the roles of ministers and ambassadors, but they are demanding more.[64] The *Contemporary African Database* lists three women who have served or are serving as ministers. The ministries included health and culture and sport.[65]

CENTRAL AFRICA

*Central Africa countries: Cameroon, Central African Republic, Chad,
Republic of the Congo, Equatorial Guinea, Gabon, São Tomé and Príncipe*

Republic of Cameroon

BACKGROUND[1]

Location: Western Africa, bordering the Bight of Biafra, between Equatorial Guinea and Nigeria
Population: 17,340,702
Per Capita Income: $2,400 (2006 est.)

Government type: republic; multiparty presidential regime.

Independence: January 1, 1960 (from French-administered UN trusteeship). The former French Cameroon and part of British Cameroon merged in 1961 to form the present country. Cameroon has generally enjoyed stability, which has permitted the development of agriculture, roads, and railways, as well as a petroleum industry. Despite a slow movement toward democratic reform, political power remains firmly in the hands of an ethnic oligarchy headed by President Paul Biya.

Constitution: May 20, 1972, approved by referendum; adopted June 2, 1972; revised January 1996.

Legislature: unicameral National Assembly or Assemblee Nationale (180 seats; members are elected by direct popular vote to serve five-year terms); note: the president can either lengthen or shorten the term of the legislature.

Elections: last held July 2007 (next to be held in 2012).

Election results: percent of vote by party — N/A; seats by party — RDCP 140, SDF 14, UDC 4, other 22. Note: the constitution calls for an upper chamber for the legislature, to be called a Senate, but it has yet to be established.

Political parties: Cameroonian Democratic Union or UDC; Cameroon People's Democratic Movement or CPDM; Movement for the Defense of the Republic or MDR; Movement for the Liberation and Development of Cameroon or MLDC; Movement for the Youth of Cameroon or MYC; National Union for Democracy and Progress or UNDP; Social Democratic Front or SDF; Union of Peoples of Cameroon or UPC.

STATUS AND PROGRESS OF WOMEN

Cameroon's *Beijing+10* review does not include a specific section on "Women in Power in Decision Making." The report points out that in 1997 by decree the government provides:

"The Ministry of Women's Affairs shall be responsible for drafting and implementing measures relating to respect of women's rights and strengthening guarantees of gender equality in the political, economic, social and cultural spheres."[2]

The Inter-Parliamentary Union (IPU) reports that Cameroon elected the first woman to Parliament in April 1960.[3] The IPU lists Cameroon as having a setback with the number of women in parliament. In 1995, 22 women served out of 180 seats (12.22 percent), and in 2006, 16 out of 180 (8.89 percent). The setback was -3.33 percent.[4] However, in one five-year period "at the legislative and political levels, the number of women members of the National Assembly (total number of deputies: 180) rose from 10 in 1997 to 19 in 2002."[5]

Central African Republic

BACKGROUND[6]

Location: Central Africa, north of Democratic Republic of the Congo
Population: 4,303,356
Per Capita Income: $1,100 (2006 est.)

Government type: republic.

Independence: August 13, 1960 (from France). The former French colony of Ubangi-Shari became the Central African Republic upon independence in 1960. After three tumultuous decades of misrule — mostly by military governments — civilian rule was established in 1993 and lasted for one decade. President Ange-Felix Patasse's civilian government was plagued by unrest, and in March 2003 he was deposed in a military coup led by General Francois Bozize, who established a transitional government. Though the government has the tacit support of civil society groups and the main parties, a wide field of candidates contested the municipal, legislative, and presidential elections held in March and May of 2005 in which General Bozize was affirmed as president. The government still does not fully control the countryside, where pockets of lawlessness persist.

Constitution: ratified by popular referendum December 5, 2004; effective December 27, 2004.

Legislature: unicameral National Assembly or Assemblee Nationale (109 seats; members are elected by popular vote to serve five-year terms).

Elections: last held 13 March 2005 and 8 May 2005 (next to be held 2010).

Election results: percent of vote by party — MLPC 43 percent, RDC 18 percent, MDD 9 percent, FPP 6 percent, PSD 5 percent, ADP 4 percent, PUN 3 percent, FODEM 2 percent, PLD 2 percent, UPR 1 percent, FC 1 percent, independents 6 percent; seats by party — MLPC 47, RDC 20, MDD 8, FPP 7, PSD 6, ADP 5, PUN 3, FODEM 2, PLD 2, UPR 1, FC 1, independents 7.

Political parties: Alliance for Democracy and Progress or ADP ; Central African Democratic Assembly or RDC; Civic Forum or FC; Democratic Forum for Modernity or FODEM; Liberal Democratic Party or PLD; Movement for Democracy and Development or MDD; Movement for the Liberation of the Central African People or MLPC (the party of the deposed president); National Convergence or KNK; Patriotic Front for Progress or FPP; People's Union for the Republic or UPR; National Unity Party or PUN; Social Democratic Party or PSD.

STATUS AND PROGRESS OF WOMEN

The Inter-Parliamentary Union (IPU) reports that Central African Republic elected the first woman to Parliament in July 1987.[7] From January 1975 to April 1976, Elisabeth Domitien served as prime minister.[8] The IPU lists Central African Republic as having made progress with the number of women in parliament. In 1995, three women served out of 85 seats (3.53 percent), and in 2006, 11 out of 105 (10.48 percent). The progress was 6.95 percent.[9]

Political reform and democratization have been underway, but this process has not yet benefited women in terms either of their political representation or of their participation in decision-making, according to Central African Republic's *Beijing+10* review. Discrimination is apparent in the distribution of power and authority. Women are very poorly represented in political and administrative bodies, less than five percent. At the time of the report, the Transitional Government, the National Transition Council and the Monitoring Committee for the National Dialogue together had 17 women members. Before the dissolution of the National Assembly in 2003, ten women held positions in the legislature out of a total of 89 deputies. Women had advanced by three percent between 1990 and 2001.[10]

The Government has a national policy for the advancement of women and a National Plan of Action, but the arrangements for coordination and monitoring of the National Plan's implementation were faced with obstacles and constraints of several kinds, such as its low status and budget constraints.[11]

Republic of Chad

BACKGROUND[12]

Location: Central Africa, south of Libya
Population: 9,944,201 (July 2006 est.)
Per Capita Income: $1,500 (2006 est.)

Government type: republic.

Independence: August 11, 1960 (from France). Chad endured three decades of civil warfare as well as invasions by Libya before a semblance of peace was finally restored in 1990. The government eventually drafted a democratic constitution, and held flawed presidential elections in 1996 and 2001. In 1998, a rebellion broke out in northern Chad, which sporadically flares up despite several peace agreements between the government and the rebels. In 2005 new rebel groups emerged in western Sudan and have made probing attacks into eastern Chad. Power remains in the hands of an ethnic minority. In June 2005, President Idriss Deby held a referendum successfully removing constitutional term limits.

Constitution: passed by referendum March 31, 1996; a June 2005 referendum removed constitutional term limits.

Legislature: bicameral according to constitution, consists of a National Assembly (155 seats; members elected by popular vote to serve four-year terms) and a Senate (not yet created and size unspecified; members to serve six-year terms, one-third of membership renewable every two years).

Elections: National Assembly — last held 21 April 2002 (next to be held by 2007)

Election results: percent of vote by party — N/A; seats by party — MPS 110, RDP 12, FAR 9, RNDP 5, URD 5, UNDR 3, other 11.

Political parties: Federation Action for the Republic or FAR; National Rally for Development and Progress or RNDP; National Union for Democracy and Renewal or UNDR; Party for Liberty and Development or PLD; Patriotic Salvation Movement or MPS; Rally for Democracy and Progress or RDP; Union for Democracy and Republic or UDR; Union for Renewal and Democracy or URD.

STATUS AND PROGRESS OF WOMEN

"Gender and information and communication technologies are new issues in Chad,"[13] began Chad's *Beijing+10* report. At the time of the report, Chad did not have a national gender issues mechanism. However, in 2002, a gender issues project was begun at the Ministry of Social Action and the Family with help from UNFPA to restore balance and parity between the various gender areas.[14]

The Inter-Parliamentary Union (IPU) reports that Chad elected the first woman to Parliament in March 1962.[15] The IPU lists Chad as having a setback with the number of women in parliament. In 1995, nine women served out of 55 seats (16.36 percent), and in 2006, ten out of 155 (6.45 percent). The setback was -9.91 percent.[16]

Republic of the Congo

BACKGROUND[17]

Location: Western Africa, bordering the South Atlantic Ocean, between Angola and Gabon
Population: 3,800,610 note: estimates for this country explicitly take into account the effects of excess mortality due to AIDS; this can result in lower life expectancy, higher infant mortality and death rates, lower population and growth rates, and changes in the distribution of population by age and sex than would otherwise be expected (July 2007 est.)
Per Capita Income: $1,400 (2006 est.)

Government type: republic.

Independence: 15 August 1960 (from France). Upon independence in 1960, the former French region of Middle Congo became the Republic of the Congo. A quarter century of experimentation with Marxism was abandoned in 1990 and a democratically elected government took office in 1992. A brief civil war in 1997 restored former Marxist President Denis Sassou-Nguesso, and ushered in a period of ethnic and political unrest. Southern-based rebel groups agreed to a final peace accord in March 2003, but the calm is tenuous and refugees continue to present a humanitarian crisis.

Constitution: approved by referendum 20 January 2002.

Legislature: bicameral Parliament consists of the Senate (66 seats; members are elected by popular vote to serve five-year terms) and the National Assembly (137 seats; members are elected by popular vote to serve five-year terms).

Elections: Senate — last held 11 July 2002 (next to be held in July 2007); National Assembly — last held 27 May and 26 June 2002 (next to be held May 2007).

2002 election results: Senate — percent of vote by party — N/A; seats by party — FDP 56, other 10; 2007 election results: National Assembly — percent of vote by party — N/A; seats by party — FDP 52, ten parties allied with the FDP — 72, UPADS — 10, other — 1, vacant — 2.[18]

Political parties: Democratic and Patriotic Forces or FDP (Denis Sassou-Nguesso, president — an alliance of Convention for Alternative Democracy, Congolese Labor Party or PCT, Liberal Republican Party, National Union for Democracy and Progress, Patriotic Union for the National Reconstruction, and Union for the National Renewal); Congolese Movement for Democracy and Integral Development or MCDDI (Michel Mampouya); Pan-African Union for Social Development or UPADS (Martin Mberi); Rally for Democracy and Social Progress or RDPS (Jean-Pierre Thystere Tchicaya, president); Rally for Democracy and the Republic or RDR (Raymond Damasge Ngollo); Union for Democracy and Republic or UDR; Union of Democratic Forces or UFD (Sebastian Ebao); many less important parties.

STATUS AND PROGRESS OF WOMEN

The Inter-Parliamentary Union (IPU) reports that the Republic of the Congo elected the first woman to Parliament in December 1963.[19] The IPU lists the Republic of the Congo as having made progress with the number of women in parliament. In 1995, two women served out of 125 seats (1.60 percent) and in 2006, 11 out of 129 (8.53 percent). The progress was 6.93 percent.[20]

Although conflict within the country has slowed progress, the Republic of the Congo's constitution recognizes the principle of equality between men and women. Included in the constitution of 2002 is a provision on the due representation of women in decision-making bodies. Article 8 states: "Women have the same rights as men, and the law shall guarantee their position and their due representation in all political, elective and administrative posts."[21]

The 1992 and 2002 election results show progress. (See table.)

REPUBLIC OF THE CONGO: COMPARISON OF
1992 AND 2002 ELECTION RESULTS[22]

	1992						2002					
	Men		Women		Total		Men		Women		Total	
	#	%	#	%	#	%	#	%	#	%	#	%
Legislature	119	95.96	5	4.04	124	100	117	90.69	12	9.31	129	100
Senate	58	96.66	2	2.34	60	100	51	85.00	9	15.00	60	100

In government between 1997 and 2002 the report found in part, 35 men and five women; in the civil service: 33 men and two women departmental directors; and in the Office of the President: two women advisers out of a total of 40.[23]

Personnel movements in the diplomatic service have caused the departure of one of three women directors since March 2000 (although she was promoted to the rank of first councilor in the Embassy in Ethiopia), so that at the time of the report, two women held the post of director compared to 18 men. The report provided extensive data to demonstrate that women were also under-represented in the various other grades of the diplomatic service, as well.[24]

Several measures to improve the representation of women in decision-making posts were introduced, including: encouraging women's large-scale participation in voting through increasing women's awareness of the problems connected with elections, the production of logos for the women candidates in the elections and support for women candidates; and the financing of women's campaigns. The president, governmental authorities, development partners and civil society have made a concerted effort to secure genuine participation by women in decision making.[25]

Equatorial Guinea

BACKGROUND[26]

Location: Western Africa, bordering the Bight of Biafra, between Cameroon and Gabon
Population: 540,109 (July 2006 est.)
Per Capita Income: $50,200 (2005 est.)

Government type: republic.

Independence: October 12, 1968 (from Spain). Equatorial Guinea gained independence in 1968 after 190 years of Spanish rule. This tiny country, composed of a mainland portion plus five inhabited islands, is one of the smallest on the African continent. President Teodoro Obiang Nguema Mbasogo has ruled the country since 1979 when he seized power in a coup. Although nominally a constitutional democracy since 1991, the 1996 and 2002 presidential elections — as well as the 1999 and 2004 legislative elections — were widely seen as flawed. The president exerts almost total control over the political system and has discouraged political opposition. Equatorial Guinea has experienced rapid economic growth due to the discovery of large offshore oil reserves, and in the last decade has become Sub-Saharan Africa's third largest oil exporter. Despite the country's economic windfall from oil production, resulting in a massive increase in government revenue in recent years, there have been few improvements in the population's living standards.

Constitution: approved by national referendum 17 November 1991; amended January 1995.

Legislature: unicameral House of People's Representatives or Camara de Representantes del Pueblo (100 seats; members directly elected by popular vote to serve five-year terms).

Elections: last held 25 April 2004 (next to be held in 2009).

Election results: percent of vote by party — N/A; seats by party — PDGE 98, CPDS 2. Note: Parliament has little power since the constitution vests all executive authority in the president.

Political parties: Convergence Party for Social Democracy or CPDS; Democratic Party for Equatorial Guinea or PDGE (ruling party); Party for Progress of Equatorial Guinea or PPGE; Popular Action of Equatorial Guinea or APGE; Popular Union or UP.

STATUS AND PROGRESS OF WOMEN

The Inter-Parliamentary Union (IPU) reports that Equatorial Guinea elected the first woman to Parliament in September 1968.[27] The IPU lists Equatorial Guinea as having made progress with the number of women in parliament. In 1995, six women served out of 80 seats (7.50 percent), and in 2006, 18 out of 100 (18.00 percent). The progress was 10.50 percent.[28]

In 2007, seven women hold positions of minister in the Government.[29]

In 2004, the Committee on the Elimination of All Forms of Discrimination against Women (CEDAW) reported approximately 150 women were candidates or delegates in the elections of the House of Representatives and Parliament. The Committee noted that if women accounted for at least 30 percent of the members of the House of Representatives, more attention would be paid to gender issues in the adoption of laws providing for equal rights and opportunities.[30]

The Committee stated, "Radical change cannot be achieved in just a few years, since the entire traditional cultural context has relegated women to a second-class status and a position of inferiority.... There are no obstacles, as such. The real problems are the attitudes, low education levels and high illiteracy rates among the female population. The Government's solution is to educate the younger generation and promote adult literacy."[31] The Ministry of Social Affairs and the Status of Women runs two training centers for adult women.

Constitutional and legal protections for equality are largely ignored, and violence against women is widespread. Traditional practices discriminate against women. Few women have educational opportunities or are able to participate in the formal economy or government.[32] But women's participation in public and political life is increasing.[33]

Gabonese Republic

BACKGROUND[34]

Location: Western Africa, bordering the Atlantic Ocean at the Equator, between Republic of the Congo and Equatorial Guinea

Population: 1,424,906 (July 2006 est.)

Per Capita Income: $7,200 (2006 est.)

Government type: republic; multiparty presidential regime.

Independence: August 17, 1960 (from France). Only two autocratic presidents have ruled Gabon since independence from France in 1960. The current president of Gabon, El Hadj Omar Bongo Ondimba — one of the longest-serving heads of state in the world — has dominated the country's political scene for almost four decades. President Bongo introduced a nominal multiparty system and a new constitution in the early 1990s. However, allegations of electoral fraud during local elections in 2002–03 and the presidential elections in 2005 have exposed the weaknesses of formal political structures in Gabon. Gabon's political opposition remains weak, divided, and financially dependent on the current regime. Despite political conditions, a small population, abundant natural resources, and considerable foreign support have helped make Gabon one of the more prosperous and stable African countries.

Constitution: adopted March 14, 1991.

Legislature: bicameral legislature consists of the Senate (91 seats; members elected by members of municipal councils and departmental assemblies to serve six-year terms) and the National Assembly or Assemblee Nationale (120 seats; members are elected by direct, popular vote to serve five-year terms).

Elections: Senate — last held 26 January and 9 February 2003 (next to be held by January 2009); National Assembly — last held 17 and 24 December 2006 (next to be held December 2011).

Election results: Senate — percent of vote by party — N/A; seats by party — PDG 53, RNB 20, PGP 4, ADERE 3, RDP 1, CLR 1, independents 9; National Assembly — percent of vote by party — N/A; seats by party — PDG 82, RPG 8, UPG 8, UGDD 4, ADERE 3, CLR 2, PGP-Ndaot 2, PSD 2, independents 4, others 5.

Political parties: Circle of Liberal Reformers or CLR ; Congress for Democracy and Justice or CDJ; Democratic and Republican Alliance or ADERE; Gabonese Democratic Party or PDG (former sole party); Gabonese Party for Progress or PGP; Gabonese Union for Democracy and Development or UGDD; National Rally of Woodcutters or RNB; National Rally of Woodcutters-Rally for Gabon or RNB-RPG (Bucherons); People's Unity Party or PUP;

Rally for Democracy and Progress or RDP; Social Democratic Party or PSD; Union for Democracy and Social Integration or UDIS; Union of Gabonese Patriots or UPG.

STATUS AND PROGRESS OF WOMEN

The Inter-Parliamentary Union (IPU) reports that Gabon elected the first woman to Parliament in February 1961.[35] The IPU lists Gabon as having made progress with the number of women in parliament. In 1995, seven women served out of 119 seats (5.88 percent), and in 2006, 11 out of 119 (9.24 percent). The progress was 3.36 percent.[36]

Gabon involved 350 participants in the seminar in which women in decision making was evaluated. The conclusions were published in a book, *Results of ... Women and Decision-making.*[37]

In 2005, the CEDAW reported that, at the political level, there was no discrimination based on gender regarding the participation of women in public life. Important posts were held by women. In 2002, the President of the Republic requested that each electoral list include at least three women eligible for election. In 2003, he required each ministerial department chief to nominate at least four women counselors out of 10.[38]

CEDAW commended the State party for introducing temporary special measures to increase the number of women in public life and decision making. The organization expressed concern at the low level of women's participation, particularly in the National Assembly and the Senate, and at the international level. It recommended, in part, implementation and strengthening of training and awareness-raising programs.[39]

Democratic Republic of São Tomé and Príncipe

BACKGROUND[40]

Location: Western Africa, islands in the Gulf of Guinea, straddling the Equator, west of Gabon

Population: 193,413 (July 2006 est.)

Per Capita Income: $1,200 (2003 est.)

Government type: republic.

Independence: July 12, 1975 (from Portugal). Discovered and claimed by Portugal in the late 15th century, the islands' sugar-based economy gave way to coffee and cocoa in the 19th century — all grown with plantation slave labor, a form of which lingered into the 20th century. Although independence was achieved in 1975, democratic reforms were not instituted until the late 1980s. Though the first free elections were held in 1991, the political environment has been one of continued instability with frequent changes in leadership and coup attempts in 1995 and 2003.

Constitution: approved March 1990, effective September 10, 1990.

Legislature: unicameral National Assembly or Assembleia Nacional (55 seats; members are elected by direct, popular vote to serve four-year terms).

Elections: last held March 26, 2006 (next to be held March 2010).

Election results: percent of vote by party — MDFM-PCD 37.2 percent, MLSTP 28.9 percent, ADI 20.0 percent, NR 4.7 percent, other 9.2 percent; seats by party — MDFM-PCD 23, MLSTP 19, ADI 12, NR 1.

Political parties: Democratic Renovation Party; Force for Change Democratic Movement or MDFM; Independent Democratic Action or ADI; Movement for the Liberation of São Tomé and Príncipe–Social Democratic Party or MLSTP-PSD; Party for Democratic Convergence or PCD; Ue-Kedadji coalition; other small parties.

STATUS AND PROGRESS OF WOMEN

The country has had two women prime ministers, Maria das Neves Ceita Batista de Sousa, who served from October 2002 to September 2004, and Maria do Carmo Trovoada Silveira, from June 2005 to April 2006. A woman was first elected to the legislature in 1975, the first legislature of the sovereign state. A. Graca do Espirito Santo served as a presiding officer of the National Assembly from 1980 to 1985 and 1985 to 1991.[41] The Inter-Parliamentary Union lists the country as one that has made progress in its parliament. In 1995, four women out of 55 members (7.27 percent) held seats, and in 2006, the number had increased to five women out of 55 (9.09 percent), a gain to 1.82 percent.[42]

In the *Beijing+5* report, São Tomé and Príncipe indicated that participation of women in the center of power had been reduced and varied each year depending on mandates in place. They stated that improvement was needed as was the creation of an institutional framework for the promotion of women. Also needed was the development and installation of a national action plan so that the inherent question of women could be addressed in the process of national planning.[43]

In 2000, São Tomé and Príncipe reaffirmed its commitment to the goals and objectives contained in the Beijing Declaration and Platform for Action adopted at the Fourth World Conference on Women in 1995. Alberto Paulino, Minister for Justice and Parliamentary Affairs and Deputy Minister, Office of the Prime Minister, reported that men and women were facing the problems of the changing global economy. The government was more aware that women needed to participate more actively in finding solutions which would enable them to have a greater role in easing their burdens. He said, "Great disparities still exist in the country that attribute 'superiority' to men, but it is undeniable that new vitality has been given to the cause of women."[44] The government had established a structure to govern the role of women.

A commission was set up, several provisions were made and projects designed to facilitate women's participation in decision-making forums in the country. He indicated that more work needed to be done and the government would work to further the empowerment and participation of women, who represent half of the population.[45]

The World Bank's *Country Assessment* of São Tomé and Príncipe in 2004 reported that women have held important decision-making positions at the highest level of government; for example, since October 2002, the Prime Minister was a woman. Women held ministerial positions in health and education, foreign affairs, planning and finance, and justice and public administration. Women held the positions of the governor of the Central Bank and president of the Supreme Court. Women also head some essential positions such as Customs and Social Communication. The World Bank report supports the *Beijing+5* report, saying, "women's participation varies from year to year and from one term of office to another, given the lack of a gender policy providing systematic guidelines governing access of women to decision-making positions."[46]

The following table demonstrates changes over time in women's participation in the main decision-making positions.

SÃO TOMÉ AND PRÍNCIPE: WOMEN'S PARTICIPATION IN POLITICAL OFFICE[47]

Positions	1987			1991			1994			2002/2003		
	Total	Women	%	Total	Women	%	Total	Women	%	Total	Women	%
President, Assembly	1	1	100	1	0	0	1	0	0	1	0	0
Parliamentary Leaders	1	0	0	3	1	33	3	1	33	4	0	0
Ambassadors	5	1	20	5	0	0	5	0	0	5	1	20
Presidents, Trade Unions	1	0	0	1	0	0	2	0	0	2	0	0
Presidents, District Chambers	7	0	0	7	0	0	7	1	14.3	7	1	14.3
Participation in Government	13	1	7.7	14	2	14.3	13	1	7.7	13	5	38.5
Participation in Parliament	55	7	12.7	55	3	5.4	55	5	9.1	55	5	9.1

Source: National Center for Administrative Reform and National Assembly

In spite of the progress at the highest level, participation at the local level needed improvement. In the 1991 and 1994 parliaments, women held the position of parliamentary leader, but from 1994 to 2004, no woman held this position.[48]

A major barrier to women participating in decision-making is the heavy burden of domestic chores, especially among the economically disadvantaged. Preconceptions regarding appropriate social roles for men and women are an additional roadblock.[49]

Even though the constitution and various laws guarantee equality along with the various Conventions that had been ratified, in 2004, no mechanisms had been created to facilitate or monitor their implementation; thus, the principles of these conventions had not yet been translated into practice. The World Bank report indicated, "A certain amount of slackness in the enforcement of laws contributes to a climate of impunity. Moreover, a number of cultural taboos and traditions continue to impede progress by perpetuating phenomena such as early pregnancy, street children, domestic violence, child prostitution etc., that result in discrimination and exclusion."[50]

EAST AFRICA

East Africa countries: Burundi, Comoros,
Democratic Republic of the Congo, Djibouti, Ethiopia, Eritrea, Kenya,
Madagascar, Rwanda, Seychelles, Somalia, Somaliland, Tanzania, Uganda

Republic of Burundi

BACKGROUND[1]

Location: Central Africa, east of Democratic Republic of the Congo
Population: 8,090,068
Per Capita Income: $700 (2006 est.)

Government type: republic.

Independence: July 1, 1962 (from UN trusteeship under Belgian administration). Burundi's first democratically elected president was assassinated in October 1993 after only 100 days in office. This event resulted in ethnic violence between Hutu and Tutsi factions. Over 200,000 Burundians died in the conflict that lasted almost a dozen years. Hundreds of thousands were internally displaced or became refugees in neighboring countries. In 2003, an internationally brokered power-sharing agreement between the Tutsi-dominated government and the Hutu rebels prepared the way for a transition process. The transition government formed an integrated defense force, and in 2005, established a new constitution and elected a majority Hutu government. President Pierre Nkurunziza signed a South African–negotiated cease-fire in September of 2006, but still faces many challenges.

Constitution: February 28, 2005; ratified by popular referendum.

Legislature: bicameral Parliament or Parlement, consists of a National Assembly or Assemblee Nationale (minimum 100 seats — 60 percent Hutu and 40 percent Tutsi with at least 30 percent being women; additional seats appointed by a National Independent Electoral Commission to ensure ethnic representation; members are elected by popular vote to serve five-year terms) and a Senate (54 seats; 34 by indirect vote to serve five-year terms, with remaining seats assigned to ethnic groups and former chiefs of state).

Elections: National Assembly — last held July 4, 2005 (next to be held in 2010); Senate — last held July 29, 2005 (next to be held in 2010).

Election results: National Assembly — percent of vote by party — CNDD-FDD 58.6 percent, FRODEBU 21.7 percent, UPRONA 7.2 percent, CNDD 4.1 percent, MRC-Rurenzangemero 2.1 percent, others 6.2 percent; seats by party — CNDD-FDD 59, FRODEBU 25, UPRONA 10, CNDD 4, MRC-Rurenzangemero 2; Senate — percent of vote by party — N/A; seats by party — CNDD-FDD 30, FRODEBU 3, CNDD 1.

Political parties: The three national, mainstream, governing parties are: Burundi Democratic Front or FRODEBU; National Council for the Defense of Democracy, Front for the Defense of Democracy or CNDD-FDD; Unity for National Progress or UPRONA; note: a multiparty system was introduced after 1998, included are: National Council for the Defense of Democracy or CNDD; National Resistance Movement for the Rehabilitation of the Citizen or MRC-Rurenzangemero; Party for National Redress or PARENA.

STATUS AND PROGRESS OF WOMEN

A woman, Sylvie Kinigi, served as prime minister of Burundi from July 1993 to February 1994. Burundi elected the first woman to parliament in October 1982. In August 2005, Nahayo Immaculée became the first presiding officer of the National Assembly. Burundi has 30.5 percent women with a legislated quota of 30 percent women candidates on party lists. Burundi is a fast-track country, where in a relevantly short space of time, the representation of women has increased dramatically.[2]

Burundi's *National Report on the Solemn Declaration on Equality of Men and Women* indicated support for the principle of parity between men and women as expressed in the international conventions and regional directives and through the country's political decisions and articles in the constitution. Men and women who are 18 years old or older may vote. A minimum of 30 percent of women in the leading institutions is also ensured.[3]

For the first time, Burundi has women in the positions of vice president, president of the national assembly and two deputy presidents of the Senate. The table below represents women's progress in parliament. Percentagewise women's representation falls a little short of doubling since the 2001–2002 sessions.[4]

BURUNDI: RATE OF PARTICIPATION OF THE WOMEN IN THE PARLIAMENT[5]

Year	National Assembly				Senate			
	M	F	TOT	%F	M	F	TOT	%Fe
2001–2002	157	37	194	19	44	10	54	18.5
2003–2004	175	45	220	20.4	44	10	54	18.5
2005	82	36	118	30.5	33	16	49	32.6

In the executive branch, women made their best gains in the office of minister, jumping from four out of 26 (15.3 percent) positions from 2001 to 2003 to seven out of 20 in 2005 (35 percent); and governors of provinces, going from zero out of 17 to four out of 17. Among governors banque central, women maintained their one position out of three.

BURUNDI: RATE OF PARTICIPATION OF THE WOMEN AT THE EXECUTIVE LEVEL[6]

Post	2001–2003				2005			
	M	F	TOT	%Fe	M	F	TOT	%Fe
Minister	22	4	26	15.3	13	7	20	35
Chief of Cabinet	23	3	26	11.5	17	3	20	15
Director General	44	4	48	8.3	44	4	48	8.3
Governor of Province	17	0	17	0	13	4	17	23
Administrator Communal	127	2	129	1.5	112	17	129	13.1
Governor Banque Central	2	1	3	33.3	2	1	3	33.3
Administrator Director General	7	0	7	0	7	0	7	0

Union of the Comoros

BACKGROUND[7]

Location: Southern Africa, group of islands at the northern mouth of the Mozambique Channel, about two-thirds of the way between northern Madagascar and northern Mozambique
Population: 690,948 (July 2006 est.)
Per Capita Income: $600 (2005 est.)
   Government type: republic.
   Independence: July 6, 1975. The Comoros has endured 19 coups or attempted coups since gaining independence from France in 1975. In 1997, the islands of Anjouan and Moheli declared independence from the Comoros. In 1999, military chief Col. Azali seized power. He pledged to resolve the secessionist crisis through a confederal arrangement named the 2000 Fomboni Accord. In December 2001, voters approved a new constitution and presidential elections took place in the spring of 2002. Each island in the archipelago elected its own president and a new union president took office in May 2002.
   Constitution: December 23, 2001.
   Legislature: unicameral Assembly of the Union (33 seats; 15 deputies are selected by the individual islands' local assemblies and 18 by universal suffrage; deputies serve for five years)
   Elections: last held 18 and 25 April 2004 (next to be held in 2009).
   Election results: percent of vote by party — N/A; seats by party — CdIA 12, CRC 6; note: 15 additional seats are filled by deputies from local island assemblies.
   Political parties: Convention for the Renewal of the Comoros; Camp of the Autonomous Islands (a coalition of parties organized by the island Presidents in opposition to the Union President); Front National pour la Justice or FNJ (Islamic party in opposition); Mouvement pour la Democratie et le Progress or MDP-NGDC; Parti Comorien pour la Democratie et le Progress or PCDP; Rassemblement National pour le Development or RND.

STATUS AND PROGRESS OF WOMEN

   The Comoros's *Beijing+10* review reported that in 2004, only one woman held the positions of Secretary General of the government of the union and minister for government of the autonomous island of Anjouan.[8] The United States Department of State reported that in 2003, one woman was in the cabinet, two women held senior government positions: one was the President of the Tribunal of First Instance, and the other was legal counsel to President Azali.[9]
   The Inter-Parliamentary Union (IPU) reports that the Comoros elected the first woman to Parliament in December 1993.[10] The IPU lists the Comoros as showing improvement with the number of women in parliament. In 1995, no women served out of 42 seats (0.00 percent) and in 2006, one out of 33 (3.03 percent). The improvement was 3.03 percent.[11]

Democratic Republic of the Congo

BACKGROUND[12]

Location: Central Africa, northeast of Angola
Population: 62,660,551
Per Capita Income: $700 (2006 est.)
   Government type: republic.

Independence: June 30, 1960 (from Belgium). Established as a Belgian colony in 1908, the Republic of the Congo gained its independence in 1960, but its early years were marred by political and social instability. Col. Joseph Mobutu seized power and declared himself president in a November 1965 coup. He subsequently changed his name — to Mobutu Sese Seko — as well as that of the country — to Zaire. Mobutu retained his position for 32 years through several sham elections, as well as through the use of brutal force. Ethnic strife and civil war, touched off by a massive inflow of refugees in 1994 from fighting in Rwanda and Burundi, led in May 1997 to the toppling of the Mobutu regime by a rebellion backed by Rwanda and Uganda and fronted by Laurent Kabila. He renamed the country the Democratic Republic of the Congo (DRC), but in August 1998 his regime was itself challenged by a second insurrection, again backed by Rwanda and Uganda. Troops from Angola, Chad, Namibia, Sudan, and Zimbabwe intervened to support Kabila's regime. A cease-fire was signed in July 1999 by the DRC, Congolese-armed rebel groups, Angola, Namibia, Rwanda, Uganda, and Zimbabwe, but sporadic fighting continued. Laurent Kabila was assassinated in January 2001 and his son, Joseph Kabila, was named head of state. In October 2002, the new president was successful in negotiating the withdrawal of Rwandan forces occupying eastern Congo; two months later, the Pretoria Accord was signed by all remaining warring parties to end the fighting and establish a government of national unity. A transitional government was set up in July 2003. Joseph Kabila as president and four vice presidents represented the former government, former rebel groups, and the political opposition. The transitional government held a successful constitutional referendum in December 2005 and elections for the presidency, National Assembly, and provincial legislatures in 2006. Kabila was inaugurated president in December 2006. The National Assembly was installed in September 2006. Its president, Vital Kamerhe, was chosen in December. Provincial assemblies were constituted in early 2007, and elected governors and national senators in January 2007.

Constitution: February 18, 2006.

Legislature: bicameral legislature consists of a National Assembly (500 seats; 61 members elected by majority vote in single-member constituencies; 439 members elected by open list proportional-representation in multi-member constituencies; members serve 5-year terms) and a Senate (108 seats; members elected by provincial assemblies to serve 5-year terms).

Elections: National Assembly — last held July 30, 2006 (next to be held in 2011); Senate — last held January 19, 2007 (next to be held by 2012).

Election results: National Assembly — percent of vote by party — N/A; seats by party — PPRD 111, MLC 64, PALU 34, MSR 27, FR 26, RCD 15, Independents 63, others 160 (includes 63 political parties that won 10 or fewer seats); Senate — percent of vote by party — N/A; seats by party — PPRD 22, UPN 14, FR 7, RCD 7, PDC 6, CDC 3, MSR 3, PALU 2, independents 26, others 18 (political parties that won a single seat).

Political parties: Christian Democrat Party or PDC; Congolese Rally for Democracy or RCD; Convention of Christian Democrats or CDC; Forces of Renewal or FR; Movement for the Liberation of the Congo or MLC ; People's Party for Reconstruction and Democracy or PPRD; Social Movement for Renewal or MSR; Unified Lumumbist Party or PALU; Union for Democracy and Social Progress or UDPS; Union of Mobutuist Democrats or UDEMO.

STATUS AND PROGRESS OF WOMEN

The Democratic Republic of Congo's *Beijing+10* report described progress in terms of "Some advances made in this area deserve to be pointed out, although they are still lukewarm." The table below demonstrates what the report sees as the lack of political will to empower women in decision making.

DEMOCRATIC REPUBLIC OF CONGO: INSTITUTIONAL MECHANISMS—
WOMEN AND THE DECISION-MAKING PROCESS[13]

Transitional institutions during 2004	Total figures	Women		Men	
		nos.	%	nos.	%
Presidency	5	0	0	5	100
Government	61	7	11	54	89
Senate	120	3	2.5	117	97.5
National Assembly	500	60	12	440	88
Magistracy	1,800	200	11	1,600	89
Public and mixed economy enterprises	362	23	6	339	94
Diplomacy	311	37	12	274	88
Institutions for support of democracy	5	0	0	5	100
Public administration (General Secretariat)	47	6	13	41	87
Territory Governor	33	11	33	22	67

The Inter-Parliamentary Union (IPU) reports that the Democratic Republic of Congo elected the first woman to Parliament in November 1970.[14] The IPU lists the Democratic Republic of Congo as having made improvement with the number of women in parliament. In 1995, 37 women served out of 738 seats (5.01 percent), and in 2006, 60 out of 500 (12.00 percent). The improvement was 6.99 percent.[15]

The constitution provides for equality in the law, but the report lists some obstacles to gender integration: lack of a coherent policy and support mechanism, negative prejudices based on customs and traditions, low level of women's education, lack of data and information, lack of legal power within marriage, marginalization by male partners and women's lack of self-confidence. The report states that measures to improve include a 30 percent level of women in positions of decision-making and organizing women to get involved in political management.[16]

In conclusion the report states, "As the so-called liberation war raged in 1996, and during the one of 1998, a good number of initiatives relating to the implementation of the gender approach were abandoned."[17]

Republic of Djibouti

BACKGROUND[18]

Location: Eastern Africa, bordering the Gulf of Aden and the Red Sea, between Eritrea and Somalia
Population: 486,530 (July 2006 est.)
Per Capita Income: $1,000 (2005 est.)
Government type: republic.
Independence: June 27, 1977 (from France). The French Territory of the Afars and the Issas became Djibouti in 1977. Hassan Gouled Aptidon installed an authoritarian one-party

state and proceeded to serve as president until 1999. Unrest among the Afars minority during the 1990s led to a civil war that ended in 2001 following the conclusion of a peace accord between Afar rebels and the Issa-dominated government. In 1999, Djibouti's first multi-party presidential elections resulted in the election of Ismail Omar Guelleh; he was re-elected to a second and final term in 2005. Djibouti occupies a strategic geographic location at the mouth of the Red Sea and serves as an important transshipment location for goods entering and leaving the east African highlands. The present leadership favors close ties to France, which maintains a significant military presence in the country, but is also developing stronger ties with the U.S. Djibouti hosts the only U.S. military base in sub–Saharan Africa and is a front-line state in the global war on terrorism.

Constitution: multiparty constitution approved by referendum September 4, 1992.

Legislature: unicameral Chamber of Deputies or Chambre des Deputes (65 seats; members elected by popular vote for five-year terms).

Elections: last held January 10, 2003 (next to be held January 2008).

Election results: percent of vote — RPP 62.2 percent, FRUD 36.9 percent; seats — RPP 65, FRUD 0; note: RPP (the ruling party) dominated the election.

Political parties: Democratic National Party or PND; Democratic Renewal Party or PRD; Djibouti Development Party or PDD; Front pour la Restauration de l'Unite Democratique or FRUD; People's Progress Assembly or RPP (governing party); Peoples Social Democratic Party or PPSD; Republican Alliance for Democracy or ARD; Union for Democracy and Justice or UDJ.

STATUS AND PROGRESS OF WOMEN

The Inter-Parliamentary Union (IPU) reports that Djibouti elected the first woman to Parliament in 2003.[19] The IPU lists Djibouti as having made improvement with the number of women in parliament. In 1995, no women served out of 65 seats (0.00 percent) and in 2006, seven out of 65 (10.77 percent). The improvement was 10.77 percent.[20] The IPU attributes much of Djibouti's progress to the implementation of quotas.[21]

Djibouti's *Beijing+10* report states that in terms of both domestic and international legislation, the conditions for equality between men and women have been established, such as in the constitution. Yet, for a long time, little improvement took place for women. When a woman was appointed to head a ministry (that for the Promotion of Women) in 1999 and seven women deputies (a 10 percent quota) entered the National Assembly in January 2003, "women felt themselves freed from a traditional constraint, which unofficially blocked their access to high-level and symbolic decision-making posts."[22]

The report stated that even though the legal framework and political will were strongly in favor of equal participation, women were still underrepresented in positions of responsibility in ministries such as Justice, Finance, Foreign Affairs, and Defence. In addition, there were no female diplomats or secretary generals in the ministries.[23]

"The level of women's participation in political and decision-making spheres is largely a function of cultural factors,"[24] the report concluded. Thus, Djibouti's strategy to integrate women was to have an act of will (as in the case of the National Assembly quota rule) and give priority to sensitization and training of all social players in order to expedite a change of mindsets.

State of Eritrea

BACKGROUND[25]

Location: Eastern Africa, bordering the Red Sea, between Djibouti and Sudan
Population: 4,786,994 (July 2006 est.)
Per Capita Income: $1,000 (2005 est.)

Government type: transitional government; note: following a successful referendum on independence for the Autonomous Region of Eritrea on April 23–25, 1993, a National Assembly, composed entirely of the People's Front for Democracy and Justice or PFDJ, was established as a transitional legislature; a Constitutional Commission was also established to draft a constitution; Isaias Afworki was elected president by the transitional legislature; the constitution, ratified in May 1997, did not enter into effect, pending parliamentary and presidential elections; parliamentary elections were scheduled for December 2001, but were postponed indefinitely; currently the sole legal party is the People's Front for Democracy and Justice (PFDJ).

Independence: May 24, 1993 (from Ethiopia). Eritrea was awarded to Ethiopia in 1952 as part of a federation. Ethiopia's annexation of Eritrea as a province 10 years later sparked a 30-year struggle for independence that ended in 1991 with Eritrean rebels defeating governmental forces; independence was overwhelmingly approved in a 1993 referendum. A two-and-a-half-year border war with Ethiopia that erupted in 1998 ended under UN auspices in December 2000. Eritrea currently hosts a UN peacekeeping operation that is monitoring a 25 km-wide Temporary Security Zone on the border with Ethiopia. An international commission, organized to resolve the border dispute, posted its findings in 2002. However, both parties have been unable to reach agreement on implementing the decision. In November 2006, the international commission informed Eritrea and Ethiopia they had one year to demarcate the border or the border demarcation would be based on coordinates.

Constitution: a transitional constitution, decreed on May 19, 1993, was replaced by a new constitution adopted on May 23, 1997, but not yet implemented.

Legislature: unicameral National Assembly (150 seats; term limits not established).

Elections: in May 1997, following the adoption of the new constitution, 75 members of the PFDJ Central Committee (the old Central Committee of the EPLF), 60 members of the 527-member Constituent Assembly, that had been established in 1997 to discuss and ratify the new constitution, and 15 representatives of Eritreans living abroad were formed into a Transitional National Assembly to serve as the country's legislative body until countrywide elections to a National Assembly were held; although only 75 of 150 members of the Transitional National Assembly were elected, the constitution stipulates that once past the transition stage, all members of the National Assembly will be elected by secret ballot of all eligible voters; National Assembly elections scheduled for December 2001 were postponed indefinitely.

Political parties: People's Front for Democracy and Justice or PFDJ, the only party recognized by the government; note: a National Assembly committee drafted a law on political parties in January 2001, but the full National Assembly has not yet debated or voted on it.

STATUS AND PROGRESS OF WOMEN

The Inter-Parliamentary Union (IPU) reports that Eritrea elected the first woman to Parliament in February 1994, but states that the constitution adopted in 1997 stipulated all

citizens 18 and over had the right to vote.[26] The IPU lists Eritrea as having made improvement with the number of women in parliament. In 1995, 22 women served out of 105 seats
(20.95 percent), and in 2006, 33 out of 150 (22.00 percent). The improvement was 1.05
percent.[27]

At the time of Eritrea's *Beijing+10* review women made up 22 percent of the National
Assembly members, and between 27 and 37 percent in the six regional assemblies. Out of the
17 central government ministers, 3 were women. At 8.5 percent in diplomatic missions, the
report stated that women's proportion was still very low. However, it represented a slight
growth over that of 1998, which was 5.5 percent.[28]

The table shows slow progress in women's representation in the legislative bodies and
higher government positions. The increases in women's share of regional assemblies (from 20
percent before 1997 to 30.6 percent in the current term) are notable. This discussion does
not include Eritrea's significant improvement in election of women to the magistrate.

ERITREA: WOMEN IN DECISION MAKING
GOVERNMENT POSTS, 1992, 1998 AND 2003[29]

Position	1992			1998			2003		
	Total	No.	%	Total	No.	%	Total	No.	%
National Assembly	105	22	21.0	150	33	22.0	150	33	22.0
Regional Assemblies (1992–1997)			20.0	399	122	30.6	Term continues		
Ministers	13	2	15.4	17	2	11.8	17	3	17.6
Director Generals	4	1	25.0	51	2	3.9	51	3	5.9
Regional Governors	10	0	0.0	6	0	0.0	6	0	0.0
Directors/Division Heads							153	10	6.5
Unit Heads							306	20	6.5
Ambassadors				18	2	11.1	28	1	3.6

Women represented 27.2 percent of all government employees, but their presence was
higher in the junior and clerical jobs rather than senior or professional categories. Women
constituted over 41 percent of all administrative and clerical, and more than 29 percent of
junior professional positions, while their ratio in the professional category was 11.6 percent.

Federal Democratic Republic of Ethiopia

BACKGROUND[30]

Location: Eastern Africa, west of Somalia
Population: 74,777,981
Per Capita Income: $1,000 (2006 est.)
    Government type: federal republic.
    Independence: Ancient Ethiopia is unique among African countries, for the monarchy
maintained its freedom from colonial rule with the exception of the 1936–1941 Italian occu-
pation before and during World War II. In 1974, the Derg, a military junta, deposed Emperor
Haile Selassie, who had ruled since 1930. Ethiopia became a socialist state. A coalition of rebel
forces, the Ethiopian People's Revolutionary Democratic Front (EPRDF) was able to topple

the regime in 1991 because of conditions resulting from bloody coups, uprisings, wide-scale drought, and massive refugee problems. Ethiopia adopted a constitution in 1994, and the first multiparty elections were held in 1995. A peace treaty in December 2000 ended a border war with Eritrea that had erupted late in the 1990's. Final demarcation of the boundary is yet to be decided due to Ethiopian objections to an international commission's finding requiring it to surrender territory considered sensitive to Ethiopia.

Constitution: ratified December 8, 1994; effective August 22, 1995.

Legislature: bicameral Parliament consists of the House of Federation or upper chamber (108 seats; members are chosen by state assemblies to serve five-year terms) and the House of People's Representatives or lower chamber (547 seats; members are directly elected by popular vote from single-member districts to serve five-year terms).

Elections: last held May 15, 2005 (next to be held in 2010).

Election results: percent of vote — N/A; seats by party — EPRDF 327, CUD 109, UEDF 52, SPDP 23, OFDM 11, BGPDUF 8, ANDP 8, independent 1, others 6, undeclared 2.

Political parties: Afar National Democratic Party or ANDP; Benishangul Gumuz People's Democratic Unity Front or BGPDUF; Coalition for Unity and Democratic Party or CUDP; Ethiopian People's Revolutionary Democratic Front or EPRDF (an alliance of Amhara National Democratic Movement or ANDM, Oromo People's Democratic Organization or OPDO, the South Ethiopean People's Democratic Front or SEPDF, and TigrAyan Peoples' Liberation Front or TPLF); Gurage Nationalities' Democratic Movement or GNDM; Oromo Federalist Democratic Movement or OFDM; Somali People's Democratic Party or SPDP; United Ethiopean Democratic Forces or UEDF; dozens of small parties.

STATUS AND PROGRESS OF WOMEN

In October 1957, Ethiopia elected the first woman to parliament and from 1995 to 2000, Almaz Meko served as the presiding officer of the House of the Federation.[31] The IPU lists Ethiopia as making progress with the number of women in parliament. In 1995, 11 women served out of 220 seats (5 percent), and in 2006, 117 out of 546 (21.43 percent). The improvement was 16.43 percent.[32]

Ethiopia, a post-conflict country, in 1993 provided for equal rights of women and men in its constitution. Ethiopia has also ratified the Convention on Elimination of All Forms of Discrimination Against Women (CEDAW).[33] The Ethiopian government has signed the Protocol on the African Charter on Human and Peoples' Rights on the Rights of Women in Africa in June 2004 and the ratification process is underway.[34]

Ethiopia contradicts its constitutional law with other discriminatory measures, in this case within the constitution. Article 35[35] grants rights for women but Article 34 (5) states, "This constitution shall not preclude the adjudication of disputes relating to personal and family laws in accordance with the religious and customary laws, with the consent of the parties to the disputes. Particulars shall be determined by law."[36]

The 1955 Civil Code includes numerous discriminatory provisions regarding women, making them clearly subordinate to men. It renounces religious and customary rules that governed matrimonial and family rights, but the new constitution reinstated them.[37]

Ethiopia's report, *Implementation of the AU Solemn Declaration on Gender Equality* in 2006, stated that its government had been "promoting the mainstreaming of gender in all its development policies and strategies to address gender inequality."[38]

Article 3 of Ethiopia's constitution provides equal opportunity for women to participate in the decision-making process. It gives women the right to vote and be elected. The ruling party required 30 percent of its candidates for the 2005 election be women. As a result, the number of women in parliament increased significantly. In the federal parliament's House of People's Representatives, the number of women increased, with 502 males and 42 females in 2000, and 413 males and 117 females in 2005. In the House of the Federation, similar increases in women members occurred, with 110 males and seven females in 2000, and 91 males and 21 females in 2005. The number of elected women also increased at the regional level.[39]

Ethiopia's Civil Service Reform Programs incorporate affirmative action, stating, "preference shall be given to female candidates who have equal or close scores to that of male candidates."[40]

Women's representation in the executive branch also improved. In 2000, men held 16 positions and women held one, compared to 2005 when men held 20 positions to women's two. In the position of deputy minister/state ministers there were 12 men to 4 women in 2000 and 30 men to five women in 2005.[41]

Republic of Kenya

BACKGROUND[42]

Location: Eastern Africa, bordering the Indian Ocean, between Somalia and Tanzania
Population: 34,707,817
Per Capita Income: $1,200 (2006 est.)
　　Government type: republic.
　　Independence: December 12, 1963 (from U.K.). Jomo Kenyatta, founding president and liberation struggle icon, led Kenya from independence in 1963 until his death in 1978. Daniel Toroitich arap Moi became president in a constitutional succession. The country was a de facto one-party state from 1969 until 1982 when the ruling Kenya African National Union (KANU) made itself the sole legal party in Kenya. In 1991, Moi complied to pressure for political liberalization. The ethnically fractured opposition could not dislodge KANU in elections in 1992 and 1997. Moi stepped down in December 2002 following fair and peaceful elections. Mwai Kibaki, running with the National Rainbow Coalition (NARC), won the presidency. In 2005, Kibaki's NARC coalition splintered over the constitutional review process. Defectors joined with KANU to form a new opposition coalition, the Orange Democratic Movement, which defeated the government's draft constitution in a popular referendum in November 2005.
　　Constitution: December 12, 1963; amended as a republic 1964; reissued with amendments 1979, 1982, 1986, 1988, 1991, 1992, 1997, 2001; note: a new draft constitution was defeated by popular referendum in 2005.
　　Legislature: unicameral National Assembly or Bunge (224 seats; 210 members elected by popular vote to serve five-year terms, 12 so-called nominated members who are appointed by the president but selected by the parties in proportion to their parliamentary vote totals, 2 ex-officio members).
　　Elections: last held December 27, 2002 (next to be held December 2007).
　　Election results: percent of vote by party — N/A; seats by party — NARC 125, KANU 64, FORD-P 14, other 7; ex-officio 2; seats appointed by the president — NARC 7, KANU 4, FORD-P 1.

Political parties: Forum for the Restoration of Democracy-Kenya or FORD-Kenya; Forum for the Restoration of Democracy-People or FORD-People; Kenya African National Union or KANU; National Rainbow Coalition-Kenya or NARC-K; Orange Democratic Movement-Kenya or ODM-Kenya.

STATUS AND PROGRESS OF WOMEN

Kenya elected and nominated the first women parliament members in 1969.[43] The Inter-Parliamentary Union lists Kenya as making progress with the number of women in parliament. In 1995, six women served out of 202 seats (2.97 percent), and in 2006, 16 out of 224 (7.14 percent) served, making an improvement of 4.17 percent.[44]

The United Nations Economic Commission for Africa's (ECA) *Beijing+5* report stated that it was difficult to say which of Kenya's improvements were the direct results of the Beijing Platform because the base year of comparison was 1992 while the Beijing Platform was developed in 1995. Nonetheless, the report noted some positive growth.[45]

In 1995, women in Kenya's parliament had 4.2 percent of the 222 elected seats compared to 3.2 percent in 1991. More women had been nominated, representing 42 percent of total nominations, compared to 1992's eight percent. Women were 23 percent of staff in public administration compared to 21 percent in 1992. The number of women in the judiciary rose from 25 percent in 1992 to 30 percent in 1998. ECA adds, "It is also worth noting that more women judges (commissioners of assizes) have been appointed since May 1999."[46]

The United Nations Economic Commission for Africa (ECA) placed Kenya in the third group, meaning it poorly addresses the needs of women. For example, Kenya reserves only 5 of 220 seats for women in parliament.[47]

Republic of Madagascar

BACKGROUND[48]

Location: Southern Africa, island in the Indian Ocean, east of Mozambique
Population: 18,595,469 (July 2006 est.)
Per Capita Income: $900 (2006 est.)

Government type: republic.

Independence: June 26, 1960 (from France). Formerly an independent kingdom, Madagascar became a French colony in 1896, but regained its independence in 1960. During 1992–93, free presidential and National Assembly elections were held, ending 17 years of single-party rule. In 1997, in the second presidential race, Didier Ratsiraka, the leader during the 1970s and 1980s, was returned to the presidency. The 2001 presidential election was contested between the followers of Didier Ratsiraka and Marc Ravalomanana, nearly causing secession of half of the country. In April 2002, the High Constitutional Court announced Ravalomanana the winner.

Constitution: August 19, 1992, by national referendum.

Legislature: bicameral legislature consists of a National Assembly or Assemblee Nationale (160 seats; members are directly elected by popular vote to serve four-year terms) and a Senate or Senat (100 seats; two-thirds of the seats filled by regional assemblies whose members will be elected by popular vote; the remaining one-third of the seats appointed by the president; all members will serve four-year terms).

Elections: National Assembly — last held December 15, 2002 (next to be held in 2007).

Election results: National Assembly — percent of vote by party — N/A; seats by party — TIM 103, FP 22, AREMA 3, LEADER/Fanilo 2, RPSD 5, others 3, independents 22.

Political parties: Association for the Rebirth of Madagascar or AREMA; Economic Liberalism and Democratic Action for National Recovery or LEADER/Fanilo; Fihaonana Party or FP; I Love Madagascar or TIM; Renewal of the Social Democratic Party or RPSD.

STATUS AND PROGRESS OF WOMEN

Madagascar's *Beijing+10* report indicated that in 2001, participation of women remained weak. The opportunities offered women to participate in political and economic decision-making continued to be limited. Women occupied only eight percent of the parliamentary positions, 28.9 percent of managerial staff and executive staff and a little more than one-third of the technical positions. Women continued to undergo inegalitarian treatment and the political field remained always partial to men (only 5 percent of the seats in the Lower House and 15 percent in the Upper House in 2003 were occupied by women).[49]

Representation of women in positions included executives, but the representation in the various governments did not exceed the threshold of 15 percent. No women served as prime minister, president of the parliament or of the Republic, and no woman as governor/chief of a province. Women are generally found in assistant positions. The report gave several reasons. Men and women admit that the presence on the political scene of women ministers, deputes, mayors, and advisers is important for women to gain equality. They also recognize that men hold the greater number of offices. Women often do not participate because of their work role and lower educational level. Both men and women tend to prefer to elect males to political positions.[50]

The Inter-Parliamentary Union (IPU) reports that Madagascar elected the first woman to Parliament in August 1965.[51] The IPU lists Madagascar as having made improvement with the number of women in parliament. In 1995, five women served out of 138 seats (3.62 percent), and in 2006, 11 out of 160 (6.88 percent). The improvement was 3.26 percent.[52]

Republic of Rwanda

BACKGROUND[53]

Location: Central Africa, east of Democratic Republic of the Congo
Population: 8,648,248
Per Capita Income: $1,600 (2006 est.)

Government type: republic; presidential, multiparty system.

Independence: July 1, 1962 (from Belgium-administered UN trusteeship). Rwanda became a sovereign state when it gained independence in the midst of conflict between ethnic tribes which began three years earlier when the majority ethnic group, the Hutus, overthrew the ruling Tutsi king. Over the next several years, thousands of Tutsis were killed, and some 150,000 driven into exile. The children of these exiles later formed a rebel group, the Rwandan Patriotic Front (RPF), and began a civil war in 1990. The war worsened ethnic tensions, culminating in April 1994 with a genocide that killed approximately 800,000 Tutsis and moderate Hutus. Tutsi rebels defeated the Hutu regime and ended the killing in July 1994, but approximately two million Hutu refugees, fearing Tutsi retribution, fled to neighboring countries. Most of the refugees have returned to Rwanda, but several thousand remain in the Democratic Republic of the Congo and formed an extremist insurgency to retake Rwanda, much as the RPF tried in 1990.

Rwanda held its first local elections in March 1999 and its first post-genocide presidential and legislative elections in August and September 2003. The country continues to struggle to keep peace, but elements threaten that peace: the persistent Hutu insurgency across the border, and Rwandan involvement in two wars in recent years in the Democratic Republic of the Congo.

Constitution: new constitution passed by referendum May 26, 2003.

Legislature: bicameral Parliament consists of Senate (26 seats; 12 members elected by local councils, 8 appointed by the president, 4 by the Political Organizations Forum; 2 represent institutions of higher learning; members serve eight-year terms) and Chamber of Deputies (80 seats; 53 members elected by popular vote, 24 women elected by local bodies, 3 selected by youth and disability organizations, to serve five-year terms).

Elections: Senate — last held N/A, members appointed as part of the transitional government (next to be held in 2011); Chamber of Deputies — last held 29 September 2003 (next to be held in 2008).

Election results: seats by party under the 2003 Constitution — RPF 40, PSD 7, PL 6, additional 27 members indirectly elected.

Political parties: Centrist Democratic Party or PDC; Democratic Popular Union of Rwanda or UDPR; Democratic Republican Movement or MDR (officially banned); Islamic Democratic Party or PDI; Liberal Party or PL; Party for Democratic Renewal (officially banned); Rwandan Patriotic Front or RPF; Social Democratic Party or PSD.

STATUS AND PROGRESS OF WOMEN

Rwanda is truly a success story in empowering women.[54] Not only has Rwanda survived war and genocide, but since 2003, it leads the world with the highest percentage (48.8 percent, lower house and 34.6 percent, Senate) of women elected to parliament.[55] In addition, in 2005, Rwanda led African countries in the proportion of women, also about 49 percent, in parliaments that drastically increased ten years after the Beijing Platform for Action (BPFA).[56] On January 12, 1965, Rwanda formed its first legislature as the present sovereign state and in December 1981, the first woman was elected to the parliament. From July 1993 to April 1994, Rwanda had a woman prime minister, Agathe Uwilingiyimana.[57]

Historically, Rwanda also leads all countries of the world in its progress in the number of women in parliament. In 1995, 12 women held seats out of 70 members (17.14 percent), and in 2006, 39 women out of 80 members (48.75 percent) did so, bringing the increase to 31.61 percent.[58]

Rwanda's *Beijing+10* report indicates that the government made many efforts to ensure women's equality of opportunity to access and fully participate in the structures of decision-making in governmental bodies. The Constitution provides for the minimum rate of representation of women at 30 percent in decision-making bodies. Public awareness campaigns were organized to demonstrate favoring women's participation. Evening training courses at the university were offered.[59]

The official website of the Rwanda government lists eight female ministers.[60]

Republic of Seychelles

BACKGROUND[61]

Location: Archipelago in the Indian Ocean, northeast of Madagascar

Population: 81,541 (July 2006 est.)

Per Capita Income: $7,800 (2002 est.)

Government type: republic.

Independence: June 29, 1976 (from U.K.). Great Britain defeated France for the Seychelles Islands in 1814. After independence in 1976, France-Albert Rene served as president from 1977 to 2004. A new constitution and free elections in 1993 ended socialist rule. Vice President James Michel took over the presidency when Rene stepped down and in July 2006 was elected to a new five-year term.

Constitution: June 18, 1993.

Legislature: unicameral National Assembly or Assemblee Nationale (34 seats — 25 elected by popular vote, 9 allocated on a proportional basis to parties winning at least 10 percent of the vote; members serve five-year terms).

Elections: last held December 4–6, 2002 (next to be held in December 2007).

Election results: percent of vote by party — SPPF 54.3 percent, SNP 42.6 percent, DP 3.1 percent; seats by party — SPPF 23, SNP 11.

Political parties: Democratic Party or DP; Seychelles National Party or SNP (formerly the United Opposition or UO); Seychelles People's Progressive Front or SPPF (the governing party).

STATUS AND PROGRESS OF WOMEN

Seychelles *Beijing+5* report indicates, "Women in Seychelles have from the establishment of our republic, been part of our decision makers."[62] In the same month and year that Seychelles became a sovereign state, it elected its first woman to parliament, and in September 1976, it nominated its first woman for parliament.[63]

The Inter-Parliamentary Union (IPU) lists Seychelles as a country that has made progress in the number of seats held by women. In 1995, women held nine seats out of 33 (27.27 percent), and in 2006, 10 seats out of 34 (29.41 percent).[64] Seychelles holds women in power and decision-making as a high priority. The United Nations Economic Commission for Africa's (ECA) first report in 2001 noted Seychelles is one of the countries that has a high representation of women in the national assembly.[65]

At the time of the *Beijing+10* report, Seychelles reported that no official national gender policy had been adopted and mainstreaming had not yet been fully achieved. Even though no gender policy per se existed, the government was implementing activities relating to gender.[66] The percentage of women in the cabinet, 27 percent, and parliament, 24 percent, remained constant from 1997 to 2002 and compared favorably with regional and national norms. The number of women ministers decreased from three to two in 2004. The number of women parliamentarians showed a slight increase.[67]

Seychelles concluded that the government needs to provide greater economic independence and the facilitative environment for the full participation of women in decision-making which at the political and administrative levels has not been achieved. Other challenges include a need for more qualitative research to understand the underlying causes for the poor representation of women in politics. While women admit having problems reconciling family responsibilities with the heavy demands of public life, more research is needed on how domestic responsibilities are shared between men and women in the home; a need to give women parliamentarians the lobbying and advocacy skills to promote greater gender equality; a need for the media to portray women in politics more positively; and the need for more funding of the Seychelles Women's Commission.[68]

Somalia

BACKGROUND[69]

Location: Eastern Africa, bordering the Gulf of Aden and the Indian Ocean, east of Ethiopia
Population: 8,863,338
Per Capita Income: $600 (2006 est.)

Government type: no permanent national government; transitional, parliamentary federal government.

Independence: July 1, 1960 (British Somaliland, which became independent from the UK on June 26, 1960, and Italian Somaliland, which became independent from the Italian-administered UN trusteeship on July 1, 1960, merged to form the Somali Republic). Britain withdrew from British Somaliland in 1960 in order to allow its protectorate to join with Italian Somaliland and form the new nation of Somalia. In 1969, a coup headed by Mohamed Siad Barre ushered in an authoritarian socialist rule that managed to impose a degree of stability in the country for a couple of decades. After the regime's overthrow early in 1991, Somalia descended into turmoil, factional fighting, and anarchy. In May of 1991, northern clans declared an independent Republic of Somaliland that now includes the administrative regions of Awdal, Woqooyi Galbeed, Togdheer, Sanaag, and Sool. Although not recognized by any government, this entity has maintained a stable existence, aided by the overwhelming dominance of a ruling clan and economic infrastructure left behind by British, Russian, and American military assistance programs. The regions of Bari, Nugaal, and northern Mudug comprise a neighboring self-declared autonomous state of Puntland, which has been self-governing since 1998, but does not aim at independence; it has also made strides toward reconstructing a legitimate, representative government, but has suffered some civil strife. Puntland disputes its border with Somaliland as it also claims portions of eastern Sool and Sanaag. Beginning in 1993, a two-year UN humanitarian effort (primarily in the south) was able to alleviate famine conditions, but when the UN withdrew in 1995, having suffered significant casualties, order still had not been restored. The mandate of the Transitional National Government (TNG), created in August 2000 in Arta, Djibouti, expired in August 2003. A two-year peace process, led by the Government of Kenya under the auspices of the Intergovernmental Authority on Development (IGAD), concluded in October 2004 with the election of Abdullahi Yusuf Ahmed as President of the Transitional Federal Government of Somalia and the formation of a transitional government, known as the Somalia Transitional Federal Institutions (TFIs). The Somalia TFIs include a 275-member parliamentary body, known as the Transitional Federal Assembly (TFA), a transitional Prime Minister, Ali Mohamed Gedi, and a 90-member cabinet. The Transitional Federal Government (TFG) has been deeply divided since just after its creation and until late December 2006 controlled only the town of Baidoa. In June 2006, a loose coalition of clerics, business leaders, and Islamic court militias known as the Supreme Council of Islamic Courts (SCIC) defeated powerful Mogadishu warlords and took control of the capital. The Courts continued to expand, spreading their influence throughout much of southern Somalia and threatening to overthrow the TFG in Baidoa. Ethiopian and TFG forces, concerned over suspected links between some SCIC factions and al-Qaida, in late December 2006 drove the SCIC from power, but the joint forces continue to fight remnants of SCIC militia in the southwestern corner of Somalia near the Kenyan border. The TFG, backed by Ethiopian forces, in late December 2006 moved into Mogadishu, but continues to struggle to exert control over the capital and to prevent the reemergence of warlord rule that typified Mogadishu before the rise of the SCIC.

Constitution: August 25, 1979; presidential approval September 23, 1979; note: the formation of transitional governing institutions, known as the Transitional Federal Government, is currently ongoing.

Legislature: unicameral National Assembly; note: fledgling parliament; a 275-member Transitional Federal Assembly; the new parliament consists of 61 seats assigned to each of four large clan groups (Darod, Digil-Mirifle, Dir, and Hawiye) with the remaining 31 seats divided between minority clans.

Political parties: none.

STATUS AND PROGRESS OF WOMEN

The Inter-Parliamentary Union (IPU) reports that Somalia elected the first woman to Parliament in December 1979.[70] The legal status of women is dictated by the pre-war civil and criminal code, but these laws have not been enforced for a decade. The constitution prohibits discrimination on the basis of gender. Some Muslims have been resistant to women entering the public sphere.[71]

Like many countries where conflict is evident, Somalian women have played a role in the peace and rebuilding efforts. In 2000, in the transition government, women held 25 seats out of 245 in the Transitional National Assembly (TNA). The Transitional National Government has consistently had two female ministers since its creation in 2000, despite having been reformed twice.[72]

Traditionally, women cannot represent clans and are not even considered clan members, which limits their participation in political discussions. In 2003, this exclusion provided greater opportunities to engage in cross-clan coalition building. For example, at the Arta Conference, women from different clans came together to form the sixth clan so women could participate formally in the peace negotiations. The significance lies in that the women called for women's rights to be included in all stages of the peace process.[73]

In October 2004, the United Nations Secretary-General reported that the Transitional Federal Parliament did not meet the requisite 12 percent quota for women. Only 23 out of the total 275 seats were filled by women, whereas 33 should have been occupied by women in accordance with the transitional federal charter.[74] A ministry for gender and family affairs was established in 2004. Somalia is not a signatory to the Convention on the Elimination of Discrimination against Women (CEDAW).[75]

Republic of Somaliland

BACKGROUND[76]

Location: shares borders with Republic of Djibouti to the west, Federal Republic of Ethiopia to the south and Somalia to the east. Somaliland has a coastal line to the north of the country which extends 460 miles along the Red Sea.

Population: 3,500,000

Per Capita Income: N/A

Government type: republic.

Independence: On May 18, 1991, the people of Somaliland declared independence from Somalia. However, it is not recognized by any other country or international organization, although it has working arrangements with an increasing number.

Constitution: adopted on May 31, 2001.

Legislature: The country has a republican form of government. The legislative assembly is composed of two chambers — an elected elder's chamber, and a house of representatives. An elected president and an elected vice president head the government. The president nominates the cabinet, which is approved by the legislature.

Political parties: Peace, Unity, and Development Party (Kulmiye Nabad, Midnimo iyo horumar, also known as Solidarity / The Gathering / Union and Development), For Justice and Development (Ururka Caddaalada iyo Daryeelka, also known as the Justice and Welfare Party), for Unity, Democracy, and Independence (Ururka dimuqraadiga ummadda bahaw-day, also known as Allied People's Democratic Party / United Democratic People's Party / National Alliance Democratic Party / Pillar). The party chairman is Dahir Riyale Kahin, who is the current President of Somaliland.

ADDED INFORMATION

"Though not internationally recognized, Somaliland has a working political system, government institutions, a police force and its own currency. The territory has lobbied hard to win support for its claim to be a sovereign state,"[77] states the BBC country profile. In an interview, Edna Adan Ismail, who served as Minister of Foreign Affairs in Somaliland from June 2003 to August 2006, explains that Somaliland is fully sovereign and an independent nation:

> Somaliland is the former British Somaliland Protectorate that was never a colony. Even prior to independence from Britain on the 26th of June, 1960, it had retained its sovereignty and had been running its own internal affairs and thus never lost its traditional capability to settle internal disputes and inter-clan affairs.
> After independence from Britain, it also gained its place in history and became the first fully sovereign and the only independent Somali nation. Through royal proclamation, Britain notified the United Nations that it had handed over Somaliland to its inhabitants and to the Somaliland Parliament that was constituted one year earlier as well as to its head of government, the Honorable Mohamed Haji Ibrahim Egal (who was my first husband when we married in 1963 after he had resigned from the Somalia government and was head of the Opposition).
> During the years prior to Independence, all Somalis had wanted to form the Greater Somalia after all of them became independent. Somaliland and then later Somalia became the first to become independent and united on the 1st of July, 1960.
> Regretfully, from the start, the union never worked between the former English-speaking and the former Italian-speaking Somali nations that were also inhabited by different Somali clans with different culture, traditions, and native languages.[78]

I asked Ismail, "Do you believe that Somaliland will be able to sustain its independence from Somalia?" She replied:

> Most definitely, yes.
> While there has been nothing but confusion in Somalia since 1991, Somaliland has been running its own affairs quite well for the past 16 years after it defeated the troops of Somalia and closed its borders with Somalia. Prior to this, because of the 10-year civil war between Somalia

and Somaliland between 1982 and 1991, Somalilanders had been left to fend for themselves and therefore have over a quarter of a century of experience in running Somaliland on a self-help basis and without international recognition.

It may be relevant to know that Somaliland has made better progress and has had better stability than many other African countries that enjoy international recognition and access to international political and financial support.

Because of the lack of recognition, Somaliland is not able to make full use of its abundant natural resources and makes do with whatever it can generate through trade and commerce and with help from its people in the diaspora.

Finally, Somaliland has a bigger land-mass and a larger population than over 26 African countries, therefore size does not matter.[79]

But according to Ismail there are nations that trade with Somaliland and give de facto recognition to the country, such as Yemen, Saudi Arabia, United Arab Emirates, Djibouti, Ethiopia, Kenya and Somalia. Further, she explains, "The Somaliland currency is used in the 5th Region of Ethiopia, parts of Somalia, and occasionally in Djibouti. Somaliland also has its own passport used for travel to UK, Germany, Belgium, USA, Korea, South Africa, Mozambique, Ethiopia, Kenya, Nigeria, Djibouti, Rwanda, Uganda and Zambia."[80]

Ismail explains that Somaliland has authorized offices for its representatives in "the United Kingdom and this office has direct access to the British Foreign and Commonwealth Office and also issues visas; Washington D.C. and has direct access to the State Department. It does not issue visas, but provides a letter of facilitation for visas upon arrival in Somaliland; for the EU and Belgium is based in Brussels; Italy; Addis Ababa and this office also issues visas and is the biggest; Djibouti and it also issues visas; and Pretoria. Somaliland has honorary representatives in Saudi Arabia, India, Ceylon, Kenya, Mozambique, China, France, Switzerland, Norway, Sweden, Germany, Nigeria and Canada."[81]

A briefing paper that Ismail prepared while Minister of Foreign Affairs states:

On the 30th of September 2005, we held our first Democratic Parliamentary Elections, thus completing our long and difficult transition from a traditional, clan-based political system to a stable multi-party democracy in Somaliland. The good relations we enjoy with neighboring states are the cornerstones of our foreign policy, which envisions a more stable and prosperous Horn of Africa.[82]

The paper emphasizes that above all, Somaliland is building a society founded on peace, justice, and the rule of law. Somaliland has specific accomplishments:

In December 2002, we held our first local government elections, followed in April 2003 by the first presidential elections where three political parties, UDUB, UCID and KULMIYE peacefully contested the seat of the president of Somaliland and that of the vice president. On the 14th of May, 2003, the National Electoral Commission and the Supreme Court of Somaliland confirmed the simple majority of the UDUB party, after which President Dahir Rayale Kahin and Vice President Ahmed Yussuf Yassin were sworn in office for a five-year term.[83]

THE STATUS AND PROGRESS OF WOMEN

Outside the family level, women have traditionally been omitted from the decision-making level. According to Amina Mohamed Warsame, women were not represented in the governing bodies and this total absence and exclusion of women from decision making in top leadership positions has negative consequences for them.[84]

After the national conference in Hargeisa in 1997, in which some women participated, the possibility of entering positions that influence public decision making appeared to move in the right direction. Warsame's study concluded that "Somaliland women are becoming more aware of their political rights and are beginning to question the commonly held perception that only men have a right to reach decisions on their behalf."[85]

From my research, I learned that Edna Adan Ismail served as Minister of Foreign Affairs in Somaliland from June 2003 to August 2006 and Minister of Family Welfare and Social Development from August 2002 to June 2003. Ismail says of the number of women who serve: "In May 2003, I was made Foreign Minister for Somaliland and during that time, I was the only woman cabinet minister in the government and there were no women members of parliament or women members of the senate. The parliament has 62 members and the senate also has 62 members and all are men. When I was moved to become the Minister of Foreign Affairs, Mrs. Fatima Sudi became the Minister of Family Welfare and Social Development and still holds that position. She is now the only woman in the cabinet. Until I left politics in August 2006, we were two women in the cabinet, and now there is only one in a cabinet of over 40 men consisting of ministers, vice-ministers, and ministers of state. During December 2005 General Elections, seven women stood for election to the parliament and only two women got elected."[86]

Warsame's study also advocated that women will not be a part of the political decision-making process unless the Somaliland government assumes the major responsibility of including them in the top decision-making positions. Affirmative-action policies and quota requirements may override clan biases.[87]

Bashir Goth agrees that government's role must expand: "Although Somaliland's present government has set the tone for women's participation in politics by giving them several Ministerial posts, the reality is that our women are still underrepresented in every realm of the political spectrum. It is not healthy to see only two or three faces of women in a cabinet of almost 50 Ministers and no women representation at all in the two houses of parliament."[88]

United Republic of Tanzania

BACKGROUND[89]

Location: Eastern Africa, bordering the Indian Ocean, between Kenya and Mozambique
Population: 37,445,392
Per Capita Income: $800 (2006 est.)

Government type: republic.

Independence: April 26, 1964; Tanganyika became independent December 9, 1961 (from U.K.-administered UN trusteeship); Zanzibar became independent December 19, 1963 (from U.K.); Tanganyika united with Zanzibar April 26, 1964, to form the United Republic of Tanganyika and Zanzibar; renamed United Republic of Tanzania, October 29, 1964. One-party rule ended in 1995 when for the first time since the 1970s democratic elections were held. Zanzibar's semi-autonomous status and popular opposition have led to two contentious elections since 1995, both of which the ruling party won.

Constitution: April 25, 1977; major revisions October 1984.

Legislature: unicameral National Assembly or Bunge (323 seats—232 elected by popular vote, 75 allocated to women nominated by the president, 5 to members of the Zanzibar House of Representatives, and 1 to the attorney general; members serve five-year terms); note: in addition to enacting laws that apply to the entire United Republic of Tanzania, the

Assembly enacts laws that apply only to the mainland; Zanzibar has its own House of Representatives to make laws especially for Zanzibar (the Zanzibar House of Representatives has 50 seats, directly elected by universal suffrage to serve five-year terms).

Elections: last held December 14, 2005 (next to be held in December 2010).

Election results: National Assembly — percent of vote by party — N/A; seats by party — CCM 206, CUF 19, CHADEMA 5, other 2, women appointed by the president 37, Zanzibar representatives 5; Zanzibar House of Representatives — percent of vote by party — N/A; seats by party — CCM 30, CUF 19; 1 seat was nullified with a special election to take place soon.

Political parties: Chama Cha Demokrasia na Maendeleo (Party of Democracy and Development) or CHADEMA; Chama Cha Mapinduzi or CCM (Revolutionary Party); Civic United Front or CUF; Democratic Party (unregistered); Tanzania Labor Party or TLP; United Democratic Party or UDP.

STATUS AND PROGRESS OF WOMEN

Tanzania's Constitution at Articles 66(1)(b) and 78(1) promote women's representation in the National Assembly through allocation in that seats are to be reserved over and above the elected seats, up to 30 percent additional for women. In the 2000 elections, 20 percent of the total constituency seats were reserved and in 2005, the number increased to 75 (30 percent). In 2000, these reserved seats were allocated to each political party in proportion to the seats the party won in the election.[90]

At the time of the *Beijing+5* report, Tanzania had introduced affirmative action and quotas.[91] Three of six areas of critical concern included in the report were women's empowerment and decision making; institutional capacity and gender mainstreaming; and advocacy for women and gender advancement. Substantial achievements in gender mainstreaming are reflected in: parliament's having 16 percent women (the constitution required 15 percent); and the Ministries of Community Development, Women's Affairs and Children, and Manpower Development. Although the number of women in senior positions needed to increase, women in positions at the local and district level had increased. Financing was listed as the major obstacle. Tanzania was reviewing its constitution and other laws so that they might be more gender sensitive.[92]

In 2003, the United States Agency for International Development (USAID) found that the national government had an extremely high level of awareness and commitment to addressing gender inequalities. Tanzania's vision 2025 sets as its goal: "...racial and gender imbalances will have been redressed.... [A]ll social relations and processes which manifest and breed inequality, in all aspects of the society ... will have been reformed."[93] In addition, the Ministry for Gender and Community Development was reorganized and worked to place and/or support positions of gender expertise within selected ministries and to organize and operate a centralized national database on gender.

In 2006, the Inter-Parliamentary Union listed Tanzania as a country that made progress in the number of women in parliament. In 1995, 28 women held seats out of 249 (11.24 percent), and in 2006, 97 women held seats out of 319 (30.41 percent).[94]

The Tanzanian government has had activity to promote women's participation in decision making. The government has changed regulations and upholds affirmative action. In 1996, Cabinet Decision no. 23 endorsed for implementation the increase of women at all decision-making levels. The government worked to increase women's participation to 30 percent. In 2000, the parliament passed a bill to increase the seats on the local level to 33 percent of seats for women and in the Union Parliament to 20 percent of the seats. In the 2000 general elections, women's right to vote and the right to stand for election equal to that of men was successfully practiced.[95]

Of national significance, in 2004, the Pan African Parliament elected Gertrude Ibengwe Mongella of Tanzania as president, making her the head of state and chief of government of the African Union.[96]

Republic of Uganda

BACKGROUND[97]

Location: Eastern Africa, west of Kenya
Population: 28,195,754
Per Capita Income: $1,800 (2006 est.)

Government type: republic.

Independence: October 9, 1962 (from U.K.). The first two Ugandan regimes were marked by violence. The first, the Idi Amin government (1971–1979), banned women's organizations in 1973. The second, the Obote regime (1980–1985), did not include the representation of women in parliament or local councils. Since 1986, Yoweri Museveni has ruled and has brought relative stability and economic growth. During the 1990s, the government put into effect non-party presidential and legislative elections.

Constitution: October 8, 1995; in 2005 the constitution was amended, removing presidential term limits and legalizing a multiparty political system.

Legislature: unicameral National Assembly (332 members — 215 directly elected by popular vote, 104 nominated by legally established special interest groups [women 79, army 10, disabled 5, youth 5, labor 5], 13 ex-officio members; members serve five-year terms).

Elections: last held February 23, 2006 (next to be held in 2011).

Election results: percent of vote by party — N/A; seats by party — NRM 191, FDC 37, UPC 9, DP 8, CD 1, JEEMA 1, Independents 36, other 49.

Political parties: Conservative Party or CP; Democratic Party or DP; Forum for Democratic Change or FDC; Justice Forum or JEEMA; National Democrats Forum; National Resistance Movement or NRM; Ugandan People's Congress or UPC; note: a national referendum in July 2005 opened the way for Uganda's transition to a multiparty political system.

STATUS AND PROGRESS OF WOMEN

The United Nations Economic Commission for Africa's (ECA) first report in 2001, noted Uganda had six women cabinet members and 11 women out of 35 state ministers even though women in power and decision-making is not a priority area. Uganda's constitution provides for affirmative action and the country is committed to the quota system.[98]

In spite of the country's unsettled beginning the first legislature of the sovereign State elected the first woman to Parliament in April 1962, according to the Inter-Parliamentary Union (IPU).[99] In 2006, IPU lists Uganda as a country that has made progress in the number of women in parliament. In 1995, 47 women held positions out of 270 members (17.41 percent) of Uganda's unicameral National Assembly, and in 2006, women held 73 out of 305 (23.93 percent), an increase of 6.52 percent.[100]

ECA's Governance report noted that the adoption of a new constitution in 1995 improved women's empowerment. Women were involved in drawing up the constitution and the Constituent Assembly had one female representative for each district and two women out of 21 members served on the Constitutional Commission.[101] A post-conflict country, Uganda in 1995 provided equal rights for women and men in its constitution. Uganda has also ratified the Convention on Elimination of All Forms of Discrimination Against Women (CEDAW). In 1998, the ruling party had reserved for women 30 percent of the seats in assemblies on all levels of government.[102]

Uganda's *Beijing+10* report indicates the following framework to increase women's participation in decision making: the 1993 Decentralization Policy, 1997 Local Government Act, 1997 National Gender Policy, 1999 National Action Plan on Women, 2001 Presidential Election Manifesto, 1999 Poverty Eradication Action Plan and the Plan for Modernization of Agriculture. The National Gender Policy is in place and the key players in implementing it include the National Machinery (an institutional governmental and sometimes parliamentary structure set up to promote women's advancement and to ensure the full enjoyment by women of their human rights[103]), Ministry of Finance, Planning and Economic Development and various implementing institutions.

WEST AFRICA

West Africa countries: Benin, Burkina Faso, Cape Verde,
Côte d'Ivoire, the Gambia, Ghana, Guinea, Guinea-Bissau,
Liberia, Mali, Niger, Nigeria, Senegal, Sierra Leone, Togo

Republic of Benin

BACKGROUND[1]

Location: Western Africa, bordering the Bight of Benin, between Nigeria and Togo
Population: 7,862,944
Per Capita Income: $1,100 (2006 est.)

Government type: republic.

Independence: August 1, 1960 (from France). Present-day Benin was the site of Dahomey, a prominent West African kingdom that rose in the 15th century. The territory became a French colony in 1872 and achieved independence on August 1, 1960, as the Republic of Benin. A succession of military governments ended in 1972 with the rise to power of Mathieu Kerekou and the establishment of a government based on Marxist-Leninist principles. A move to representative government began in 1989. Two years later, free elections ushered in former Prime Minister Nicephore Soglo as president, marking the first successful transfer of power in Africa from a dictatorship to a democracy. Kerekou was returned to power by elections held in 1996 and 2001, though some irregularities were alleged. Kerekou stepped down at the end of his second term in 2006 and was succeeded by Thomas Yayi Boni, a political outsider and independent.

Constitution: adopted by referendum December 2, 1990.

Legislature: unicameral National Assembly or Assemblee Nationale (83 seats; members are elected by direct popular vote to serve four-year terms).

Elections: last held March 25, 2007 (next to be held by March 2011).

Election results: percent of vote by party — N/A; seats by party — FCBE 35, ADD 20, PRD 10, other and independents 18.

Political parties: Alliance for Dynamic Democracy or ADD; Alliance of Progress Forces or AFP; African Movement for Democracy and Progress or MADEP; Democratic Renewal Party or PRD; Force Cowrie for an Emerging Benin or FCBE; Impulse for Progress and Democracy or IPD; Key Force or FC; Movement for Development and Solidarity or MDS; Movement for Development by the Culture-Salute Party-Congress of People for Progress Alliance or Alliance MDC-PS-CPP; New Alliance or NA; Rally for Democracy and Progress or RDP; Renaissance Party du Benin or RB; The Star Alliance (Alliance Étoile); Union of Tomorrow's Benin or UBF; note: approximately 20 additional minor parties.

STATUS AND PROGRESS OF WOMEN

In 2005, the Committee on the Elimination of Discrimination against Women reported that the Committee on Constitutional, legislative and regulatory measures provided for Beninese women to be represented in the political, economic and social life of the country, and the seventh section of the Government's program of action for 2001–2006, entitled "gender promotion," included specific objectives for the advancement of women. Although the laws exist, the Committee believed the status of implementation was in need of acceleration.[2]

The Committee also expressed concern about the low level of representation of women in public and political life and in decision-making positions. An absence exists of proactive measures to increase women's participation in political and public life. Further the Committee expressed concern regarding "the State party's position that the use of temporary special measures such as quotas might be considered to be in violation of the principle of equality between women and men of the country's constitution."[3] The Committee recommended full implementation of general recommendations on the participation of women in public life. In addition to increase of women in political and public life and in decision-making positions, Benin should institute quotas, training and awareness-raising programs and establish goals.

The Inter-Parliamentary Union (IPU) reports that Benin elected the first woman to Parliament in November 1979.[4] The IPU lists Benin as having setbacks with the number of women in parliament. In 1995, 5 women served out of 64 seats (7.81 percent), and in 2006, 6 out of 83 (7.23 percent). The setback was -0.58 percent.[5]

The percentage of women in decision-making positions in ministries and government bodies is low. Representation is highest in the Ministry of Health (35 percent). In the Ministry of Rural Development, women comprise 7.3 percent. Overall, women hold 2.5 percent of the highest positions and comprise less than 19 percent of higher-level administrative and management staff in public office.[6]

Burkina Faso

BACKGROUND[7]

Location: Western Africa, north of Ghana
Population: 13,902,972
Per Capita Income: $1,300 (2006 est.)
   Government type: parliamentary republic.
   Independence: August 5, 1960 (from France). Burkina Faso (formerly Upper Volta) suffered repeated military coups during the 1970s and 1980s, followed by multiparty elections in the early 1990s. Current President Blaise Compaore came to power in a 1987 military coup and has won every election since then. Burkina Faso's high population density and limited natural resources result in poor economic prospects for the majority of its citizens. Recent unrest in Côte d'Ivoire and northern Ghana has hindered the ability of several hundred thousand seasonal Burkinabe farm workers to find employment in neighboring countries.

Constitution: June 2, 1991, approved by referendum; June 11, 1991, formally adopted; last amended January 2002.

Legislature: unicameral National Assembly or Assemblee Nationale (111 seats; members are elected by popular vote to serve five-year terms).

Elections: National Assembly election last held May 2007 (next to be held in May 2012).

Election results: percent of vote by party — N/A; seats by party — CDP 73, RDA-ADF 14, UPR 5, UNIR-MS 4, CFD-B 3 and other 12.

Political parties: African Democratic Rally-Alliance for Democracy and Federation or ADF-RDA; Confederation for Federation and Democracy or CFD; Congress for Democracy and Progress or CDP; Movement for Tolerance and Progress or MTP ; Party for African Independence or PAI; Party for Democracy and Progress/Socialist Party or PDP/PS; Rally of Ecologists of Burkina Faso or RDEB; Republican Party for Integration and Solidarity or PARIS; Union for Rebirth–Sankarist Movement or UNIR-MS; Union for the Republic or UPR.

STATUS AND PROGRESS OF WOMEN

The Inter-Parliamentary Union (IPU) reports that Burkina Faso elected the first woman to Parliament in April 1978.[8] The IPU lists Burkina Faso as having improved with the number of women in parliament. In 1995, four women served out of 107 seats (3.74 percent), and in 2006, 13 out of 111 (11.71 percent). The improvement was 7.97 percent.[9]

The Committee on the Elimination of Discrimination against Women reported that Brukina Faso had made efforts to increase the level of representation of women in elective bodies. In 1995, 152 women were elected in communal elections as compared with 1,546 men. In 2000, 232 women were elected as compared with 860 men. In 1992, four women served in the National Assembly; in 2002 (the current term in the report), 13 women served, compared with 98 men. No temporary special measures or obligatory quotas have been used to achieve equal representation of women and men in political and public life.[10]

The Committee recommended that political parties should allocate at least 30 percent of seats in governing bodies to women. The Constitution and the Electoral Code guarantee women's rights to be elected and lead political parties. Civil society is firmly committed to supporting women who aspire to hold elected office. In the 2002 legislative elections, associations and non-governmental organizations (NGOs) supported women from political parties who were registered on the electoral lists.[11]

Republic of Cape Verde

BACKGROUND[12]

Location: Western Africa, group of islands in the North Atlantic Ocean, west of Senegal
Population: 420,979 (July 2006 est.)
Per Capita Income: $6,000 (2006 est.)

Government type: republic.

Independence: July 5, 1975 (from Portugal). The uninhabited islands were discovered and colonized by the Portuguese in the 15th century; Cape Verde subsequently became a trading center for African slaves and later an important coaling and resupply stop for whaling and transatlantic shipping. Following independence in 1975, and a tentative interest in unification with Guinea-Bissau, a one-party system was established and maintained until multiparty elections were held in 1990. Cape Verde continues to exhibit one of Africa's most stable democratic governments. Repeated droughts during the second half of the 20th century caused significant hardship and prompted heavy emigration. As a result, Cape Verde's expatriate population is greater than its domestic one. Most Cape Verdeans have both African and Portuguese antecedents.

Constitution: new constitution came into force September 25, 1992; a major revision on November 23, 1995, substantially increased the powers of the president; a 1999 revision created the position of national ombudsman (Provedor de Justica).

Legislature: unicameral National Assembly or Assembleia Nacional (72 seats; members are elected by popular vote to serve five-year terms).

Elections: last held January 22, 2006 (next to be held in January 2011).

Election results: percent of vote by party — PAICV 52.3 percent, MPD 44 percent, UCID 2.7 percent; seats by party — PAICV 41, MPD 29, ADM 2.

Political parties: African Party for Independence of Cape Verde or PAICV; Democratic Alliance for Change or ADM(a coalition of PCD, PTS, and UCID); Democratic Christian Party or PDC; Democratic Renovation Party or PRD; Democratic and Independent Cape Verdean Union or UCID; Movement for Democracy or MPD; Party for Democratic Convergence or PCD; Party of Work and Solidarity or PTS; Social Democratic Party or PSD.

STATUS AND PROGRESS OF WOMEN

The Inter-Parliamentary Union (IPU) reports that Cape Verde elected the first woman to Parliament in July 1975.[13] The IPU lists Cape Verde as having improved with the number of women in parliament. In 1995, six women served out of 79 seats (7.59 percent), and in 2006, 11 out of 72 (15.28 percent). The improvement was 7.69 percent.[14]

The Committee on the Elimination of Discrimination against Women (CEDAW) welcomed the increasing participation of women in some appointed bodies, for example, the judiciary (46.9 percent). The Committee was concerned that participation in elected bodies remained low. The electoral code provides for mechanisms to promote the participation of women in political and public life, but no regulation on the implementation of such mechanisms exists. The Committee urges the acceleration and increase of representation of women in elected and appointed bodies, including through the preparation of necessary regulations to put in place the mechanism and put into place necessary temporary measures. The Committee requested the State party to conduct awareness-raising activities and to encourage men to undertake their fair share of domestic responsibilities so that women can devote time to public and political life.[15]

In 2006, the CEDAW urged the government to expand the participation of women in political life, since it was below 20 percent. The Committee recommended that government should also consider financial incentives and directives specifying the placement of female candidates on election ballots to raise the number of women in political parties.[16]

Cape Verde's report to CEDAW stated that the status of the country's women has long been inferior to that of men, but successive governments have been concerned about the issues relating to discrimination against women. The law guarantees women equal rights and dignity with men. Since 1999, electoral subsidies have been provided to political parties or coalitions and to lists put forward by citizens' groups, at least 25 percent of whose successful candidates for municipal election are women. The State also awards an electoral subsidy in national elections. At the time of this report in 2006, three women were ministers, of Justice, Education and Human Resource Development, and Environment, Agriculture and Fisheries. There were eight women members of the National Assembly.[17]

Cape Verde indicated that women did take part in campaigns, but there were instances of violence during some elections. Maintaining the 25 percent participation rate was not only a matter of numbers, but of maintaining standards. Sometimes women did not understand quota issues and education was needed as to why quotas were needed. Education was also needed about the culture of debate and of asserting oneself. But the real challenge was making time in the busy lives of women.[18]

Since its establishment in 1994, the Institute on the Status of Women has been seeking to attract greater attention to women's issues. In 1996, the National Action Plan for the Advancement of Women was adopted and introduced gender mainstreaming. In 2000 and 2001, the Cabinet of the Prime Minister, the Institute on the Status of Women and the United Nations Population Fund (UNFPA) worked on a program for introduction of the gender perspective into development programs.[19]

Republic of Côte d'Ivoire

BACKGROUND[20]

Location: Western Africa, bordering the North Atlantic Ocean, between Ghana and Liberia
Population: 17,654,843
Per Capita Income: $1,600 (2006 est.)

Government type: republic; multiparty presidential regime established 1960; note: the government is currently operating under a power-sharing agreement mandated by international mediators.

Independence: August 7, 1960 (from France). Close ties to France since independence in 1960, the development of cocoa production for export, and foreign investment made Côte d'Ivoire one of the most prosperous of the tropical African states, but did not protect it from political turmoil. In December 1999, a military coup — the first ever in Côte d'Ivoire's history — overthrew the government. Junta leader Robert Guei blatantly rigged elections held in late 2000 and declared himself the winner. Popular protest forced him to step aside and brought runner-up Laurent Gbagbo into power. Ivorian dissidents and disaffected members of the military launched a failed coup attempt in September 2002. Rebel forces claimed the northern half of the country, and in January 2003 were granted ministerial positions in a unity government under the auspices of the Linas-Marcoussis Peace Accord. President Gbagbo and rebel forces resumed implementation of the peace accord in December 2003 after a three-month stalemate, but issues that sparked the civil war, such as land reform and grounds for citizenship, remain unresolved. The central government has yet to exert control over the northern regions and tensions remain high between Gbagbo and opposition leaders. Several thousand French and West African troops remain in Côte d'Ivoire to maintain peace and facilitate the disarmament, demobilization, and rehabilitation process.

Constitution: approved by referendum, July 23, 2000.

Legislature: unicameral National Assembly or Assemblee Nationale (225 seats; members are elected in single- and multi-district elections by direct popular vote to serve five-year terms).

Elections: elections last held December 10, 2000, with by-elections on January 14, 2001 (next to be held by October 2007, after the government postponed the elections in 2005 and 2006).

Election results: percent of vote by party — N/A; seats by party — FPI 96, PDCI-RDA 94, RDR 5, PIT 4, other 2, independents 22, vacant 2; note: a Senate that was scheduled to be created in the October 2006 elections never took place.

Political parties: Citizen's Democratic Union or UDCY; Democratic Party of Côte d'Ivoire–African Democratic Rally or PDCI-RDA; Ivorian Popular Front or FPI; Ivorian Worker's Party or PIT; Opposition Movement of the Future or MFA; Rally of the Republicans or RDR; Union for Democracy and Peace in Côte d'Ivoire or UDPCI; over 20 smaller parties.

STATUS AND PROGRESS OF WOMEN

The Inter-Parliamentary Union (IPU) reports that Côte d'Ivoire elected the first woman to Parliament in November 1965.[21] The IPU lists Côte d'Ivoire as having a setback with the number of women in parliament. In 1995, eight women served out of 75 seats (10.67 percent), and in 2006, 19 out of 223 (8.52 percent). The setback was -2.15 percent.[22]

Government policy encourages full participation by women in social and economic life.[23] The United States Department of State's 2005 report indicates that women held 19 of 225 seats in the National Assembly. A woman served as the first vice president of the National Assembly. Women held four of the 31 ministerial positions in the cabinet. Of the 41 supreme court justices, 4 were women. Henriette Dagri Diabate served as Secretary General of the RDR, the party's second-ranking position. Women's organizations campaigned against the legal texts and procedures that discriminated against them. The Coalition of Women Leaders continued its efforts to promote greater participation of women in decision-making.[24]

UNDP's 2006–2007 report noted that the country was in a difficult period, but that the period is also one of hope. So that peace, the development and social cohesion are durable, they must be built on solid bases. These bases are social justice, equality between the areas and the genders.[25]

Republic of The Gambia

BACKGROUND[26]

Location: Western Africa, bordering the North Atlantic Ocean and Senegal
Population: 1,641,564 (July 2006 est.)
Per Capita Income: $2,000 (2006 est.)
Government type: republic.
Independence: February 18, 1965 (from U.K.). Geographically surrounded by Senegal, The Gambia formed a short-lived federation of Senegambia between 1982 and 1989. In 1991 the two nations signed a friendship and cooperation treaty, but tensions have flared up intermittently since then. Yahya A.J.J. Jammeh led a military coup in 1994 that overthrew the president and banned political activity. A new constitution and presidential elections in 1996, followed by parliamentary balloting in 1997, completed a nominal return to civilian rule. Jammeh has been elected president in all subsequent elections, including most recently in late 2006.

Constitution: April 24, 1970; suspended July 1994; rewritten and approved by national referendum August 8, 1996; reestablished January 1997.

Legislature: unicameral National Assembly (53 seats; 48 elected by popular vote, 5 appointed by the president; members serve five-year terms).

Elections: last held January 25, 2007 (next to be held 2012).

Election results: percent of vote by party — N/A; seats by party — APRC 47, UDP 4, NADD 1, independent 1.

Political parties: Alliance for Patriotic Reorientation and Construction or APRC (the ruling party); Gambia People's Democratic Party or GPDP; National Alliance for Democracy and Development or NADD; National Convention Party or NCP; National Reconciliation Party or NRP; People's Democratic Organization for Independence and Socialism or PDOIS; United Democratic Party or UDP.

STATUS AND PROGRESS OF WOMEN

In 2006, Belinda Bidwell became the first woman to hold the position of president of the National Assembly.[27] Fatoumata Jahumpa-Ceesay became president of the assembly in January 2007.[28] In 2002, women held seven (13.21 percent) and in 2007, they held five (9.43 percent) out of the 53-member assembly.[29]

The Gambia elected the first woman parliament member in May 1982.[30] Other women have served in the National Assembly. Nyimasatta Sanneh-Bojang was the first woman elected to Parliament. Other women include Louise Antoinette Njie and Cecilia Cole.[31]

The Gambia's National Women's Council and Bureau were established in 1980 to ensure policy and programs' responsiveness to gender roles and needs and to ensure equity and gender balance. In 1994, to increase women's leadership in the development process, the government appointed four female ministers: education, youth sports and culture, information and tourism as well as health, social welfare and women's affairs.[32]

In 2007, women hold seven Cabinet positions: vice president; minister of trade, industry and employment; minister of information technology; minister of tourism; minister of education; secretary general, office of the president; and secretary to the cabinet. The official designation for ministers is secretary of state.[33]

The Gambia has made progress especially in the legislative area; for example, there are differences between its 1970 constitution and the one adopted in 1997. Among other advancements for women, for the first time in Gambian law, a definition of discrimination was extended to include "on the basis of gender."[34]

The Gambia has ratified the various international conventions, but has yet to integrate those provisions into some of its law. Although the constitution has some positive antidiscriminatory law, it "also explicitly proclaims the need to preserve traditions and customs," and on this basis, The Gambia has "issued significant reservations to most of the international and regional conventions which it has ratified."[35] For example, all discriminations related to Islamic law are applied to Gambian women, such as polygamy, inequality in regard to succession, divorce at the instigation of the husband except in certain specific cases, and the testimony of two women being equal to that of one man.[36]

In 2005, Mrs. Isatou Njie-Saidy, Vice President and Secretary of State (Minister) for Women's Affairs, agreed with the Committee on the Elimination of Discrimination against Women's (CEDAW) assessment of The Gambia's progress: "In spite of the momentum gained in addressing gender equality, equity and women's empowerment, a number of challenges remain, key among them being socio-cultural practices and attitudes inimical to the welfare of women and girls, inadequate donor and local resources, and high debt service."[37]

Nonetheless, in 1999, the National Assembly approved the document "National Policy in Favor of the Advancement of Women." The government's document "2020 Vision" also recognized the need to eliminate all forms of discrimination against women and gradually to make its laws and legislative acts compatible with the CEDAW.[38]

In spite of The Gambia's progress, the CEDAW notes Gambian society is still largely conservative with regard to the status of women and that the distribution of social roles and power between the genders has not changed. The CEDAW adds that women have assumed government positions, but that has not actually changed the division of power between the sexes.[39]

Although 69 percent of The Gambia's population live in abject poverty,[40] the country continues to make strong efforts in parity between men and women in high offices.

Republic of Ghana

BACKGROUND[41]

Location: Western Africa, bordering the Gulf of Guinea, between Côte d'Ivoire and Togo
Population: 22,409,572
Per Capita Income: $2,600 (2006 est.)

Government type: constitutional democracy.

Independence: March 6, 1957 (from U.K.). Formed from the merger of the British colony of the Gold Coast and the Togoland trust territory, Ghana in 1957 became the first sub–Saharan country in colonial Africa to gain its independence. A long series of coups resulted in the suspension of Ghana's third constitution in 1981 and a ban on political parties. A new constitution, restoring multiparty politics, was approved in 1992. Lt. Jerry Rawlings, head of state since 1981, won presidential elections in 1992 and 1996, but was constitutionally prevented from running for a third term in 2000. John Kufuor, who defeated former Vice President John Atta-Mills in a free and fair election, succeeded him.

Constitution: approved April 28, 1992.

Legislature: unicameral Parliament (230 seats; note: increased from 200 seats in last election; members are elected by direct, popular vote to serve four-year terms).

Elections: last held December 7, 2004 (next to be held December 2008).

Election results: percent of vote by party — N/A; seats by party — NPP 128, NDC 94, PNC 4, CPP 3, independent 1.

Political parties: Convention People's Party or CPP; Democratic Freedom Party or DFP; Every Ghanaian Living Everywhere or EGLE; Great Consolidated Popular Party or GCPP; National Democratic Congress or NDC; New Patriotic Party or NPP; People's National Convention or PNC; Reform Party; United Renaissance Party or URP.

STATUS AND PROGRESS OF WOMEN

The Inter-Parliamentary Union (IPU) reports that Ghana nominated the first woman to Parliament in August 1960 and elected the first woman to Parliament in September 1969.[42] The IPU lists Ghana as having improved with the number of women in parliament. In 1995,

16 women served out of 200 seats (8.00 percent), and in 2006, 25 out of 230 (10.87 percent). The improvement was 2.87 percent.[43]

Ghana's *Beijing+10* review indicated that since their *Beijing+5* review the category of women's access to decision making, among others, had gained importance.[44]

Ghana reported that women still lag behind men in participation in leadership, as the table shows.

GHANA: NUMBER OF PEOPLE IN KEY POSITIONS IN THE PUBLIC SECTOR, 1997–2000 AND 2000–2004[45]

| POSITIONS | 1997–2000 | | | | | 2000–2004 | | | | |
	Total	Male	%	Female	%	Total	Male	%	Female	%
Parliament Members	200	183	91.5	17	8.5	200	181	90.5	19	9.5
Cabinet Ministers	19	18	94.7	1	5.3	20	18	94.7	2	10.0
Regional Ministers	10	8	80.0	2	20.0	10	10	100.0	0	0.0

Appointment of women to selected key positions is quite low, as reported in the table below, according to the report.

GHANA: APPOINTMENTS TO KEY POSITIONS, 2004[46]

SECTOR	Total	Female	%	Male	%
Cabinet Ministers	20	2	10.0	18	90.0
Ministers of State	33	2	6.1	31	93.9
Deputy Ministers	31	5	16.1	26	83.9
Members of Parliament	200	19	9.5	181	90.5
Ambassadors	45	4	9.0	41	91.0
Chief Directors of Ministries	11	2	18.2	9	81.8
Heads of Armed Forces	4	0	0.0	4	100.0
Regional Ministers	10	0	0.0	10	100.0

To address the challenges, Ghana had a number of strategies. Affirmative action has been initiated to attain a 40 percent quota (not reached at the time of the report) for women's participation in public, advisory bodies and programs. Training and economic support for women was needed. Ghana reported an absence of a legal framework to validate and enforce affirmative action policy; a lack of qualified women, but an unwillingness on the part of qualified women and an incomplete development of a databank as some of the challenges.[47]

Republic of Guinea

BACKGROUND[48]

Location: Western Africa, bordering the North Atlantic Ocean, between Guinea-Bissau and Sierra Leone
Population: 9,690,222 (July 2006 est.)
Per Capita Income: $2,000 (2006 est.)
   Government type: republic.

Independence: October 2, 1958 (from France). Guinea has had only two presidents since gaining its independence from France in 1958. Lansana Conte came to power in 1984 when the military seized the government after the death of the first president, Sekou Toure. Guinea did not hold democratic elections until 1993 when Gen. Conte (head of the military government) was elected president of the civilian government. He was reelected in 1998 and again in 2003. Guinea has maintained its internal stability despite spillover effects from conflict in Sierra Leone and Liberia. As those countries have rebuilt, Guinea's own vulnerability to political and economic crisis has increased. In 2006, declining economic conditions and popular dissatisfaction with corruption and bad governance prompted two massive strikes that sparked urban unrest in many Guinean cities.

Constitution: December 23, 1990 (Loi Fundamentale).

Legislature: unicameral People's National Assembly or Assemblee Nationale Populaire (114 seats; members are elected by direct, popular vote to serve five-year terms).

Elections: last held June 30, 2002 (next to be held in 2007).

Election results: percent of vote by party — PUP 61.6 percent, UPR 26.6 percent, other 11.8 percent; seats by party — PUP 85, UPR 20, other 9.

Political parties: Democratic Party of Guinea-African Democratic Rally or PDG-RDA; Dyama; National Union for Progress or UPN ; Party for Unity and Progress or PUP (the governing party); People's Party of Guinea or PPG; Rally for the Guinean People or RPG; Union of Democratic Forces of Guinea or UFDG; Union of Republican Forces or UFR; Union for Progress of Guinea or UPG; Union for Progress and Renewal or UPR.

Status and Progress of Women

The Inter-Parliamentary Union (IPU) reports that Guinea elected the first woman to Parliament in September 1963.[49] The IPU lists Guinea as having improved with the number of women in parliament. In 1995, eight women served out of 114 seats (7.02 percent), and in 2006, 22 out of 114 (19.30 percent). The improvement was 12.28 percent.[50]

Guinea's *Beijing+10* report indicated women in the following appointive and elective posts: Government: five women ministers out of 31; National Assembly: 22 women members out of 114; Supreme Court: three women members out of 11; Economic and Social Council: 12 women members out of 45; National Communications Council: no women out of nine members; and Governors: no women out of eight.[51]

The report states that, while "in principle and in official talk women are not subject to any discrimination, when it comes to access to responsibility and decision-making power the reality shows that only very few women effectively enjoy this right."[52] The country's new approach facilitated the access of ever-increasing numbers of women to senior administrative and political posts; for example, the number of women ministers in the government has risen from four before 2004 to five in 2004, and their representation in the National Assembly increased in 2003 from 11 to 22 out of 114 deputies. In 2002, women won about 5.8 percent of the seats in the elections to the Legislature. Two women are ambassadors, there is but no woman secretary-general of a ministry (out of 32).

The constraints found in the category of women and decision-making were also considered challenges. They included women's lack of access; high rate of illiteracy; social constraints; lack of solidarity among women; women's lowly positions on electoral lists; lack of identity documents for participating in elections; inadequate training in civic affairs; and women's lack of interest in political issues and self-confidence. Although institutional mechanisms were in place for women to advance, they, too, were challenged, by means such as lack of resources for implementation and shortage of personnel and failure to fill vacancies related to the National Policy for the Advancement of Women.[53]

Republic of Guinea-Bissau

BACKGROUND[54]

Location: Western Africa, bordering the North Atlantic Ocean, between Guinea and Senegal
Population: 1,442,029 (July 2006 est.)
Per Capita Income: $900 (2006 est.)

Government type: republic.

Independence: September 24, 1973 (unilaterally declared by Guinea-Bissau); September 10, 1974 (recognized by Portugal). Since independence from Portugal, the country has experienced considerable political and military upheaval. In 1980, a military coup established as president authoritarian dictator Joao Bernardo "Nino" Vieira. Despite setting a path to a market economy and multiparty system, Vieira's regime suppressed political opposition and purged political rivals. Several coup attempts through the 1980s and early 1990s failed to unseat him. In 1994, Vieira was elected president in the country's first free elections. Starting in 1998, a military mutiny and resulting civil war led to Vieira's removal in May 1999. In February 2000, a transitional government turned over power to opposition leader Kumba Yala, after he was elected president in transparent polling. In September 2003, Yala was ousted by the military in a bloodless coup, and businessman Henrique Rosa became interim president. In 2005, former President Vieira was re-elected. He pledged to pursue economic development and national reconciliation.

Constitution: May 16 1984; amended May 1991, December 1991, February 1993, June 1993, and in 1996.

Legislature: unicameral National People's Assembly or Assembleia Nacional Popular (100 seats; members are elected by popular vote to serve a maximum of four years).

Elections: last held March 28, 2004 (next to be held in 2008).

Election results: percent of vote by party — PAIGC 31.5 percent, PRS 24.8 percent, PUSD 16.1 percent, UE 4.1 percent, APU 1.3 percent, 13 other parties 22.2 percent; seats by party — PAIGC 45, PRS 35, PUSD 17, UE 2, APU 1.

Political parties: African Party for the Independence of Guinea-Bissau and Cape Verde or PAIGC; Party for Social Renewal or PRS; Democratic Social Front or FDS; Electoral Union or UE; Guinea-Bissau Civic Forum/Social Democracy or FCGSD; Guinea-Bissau Democratic Party or PDG; Guinea-Bissau Socialist Democratic Party or PDSG; Labor and Solidarity Party or PST; Party for Democratic Convergence or PCD; Party for Renewal and Progress or PRP; Progress Party or PP ; Union for Change or UM; Union of Guinean Patriots or UPG; United Platform or UP (coalition formed by PCD, FDS, FLING, and RGB-MB); United Popular Alliance or APU; United Social Democratic Party or PUSD.

STATUS AND PROGRESS OF WOMEN

The Inter-Parliamentary Union (IPU) reports that Guinea-Bissau had an acting female president, Carmen Periera, from May 14 to 16, 1984. The country nominated the first woman to parliament in October 1972 and elected the first woman in March 1984.[55] The IPU lists Guinea-Bissau as having made improvement with the number of women in parliament. In 1995, 10 women served out of 100 seats (10.0 percent), and in 2006, 14 out of 100 (14.0 percent). The improvement was 4.00 percent.[56]

Discrimination against women is prohibited by law, traditional and Islamic laws do not govern the status of women, and men and women are treated equally under the law.[57] According to a June 2004 report of the Secretary-General to the Security Council, women made significant advances in politics in the May 2004 elections in Guinea-Bissau. A woman was elected as President of the Supreme Court, five women were appointed as ministers and two women were appointed to the Bureau of the National Popular Assembly.[58]

Republic of Liberia

BACKGROUND[59]

Location: Western Africa, bordering the North Atlantic Ocean, between Côte d'Ivoire and Sierra Leone
Population: 3,042,004 (July 2006 est.)
Per Capita Income: $1,000 (2006 est.)
    Government type: republic.
    Independence: From American Colonization Society, July 26, 1847. Settlement of freed slaves from the U.S. in what is today Liberia began in 1822; by 1847, the Americo-Liberians were able to establish a republic. William Tubman, president from 1944 to 1971, did much to promote foreign investment and to bridge the economic, social, and political gaps between the descendents of the original settlers and the inhabitants of the interior. In 1980, a military coup led by Samuel Doe ushered in a decade of authoritarian rule. In December 1989, Charles Taylor launched a rebellion against Doe's regime that led to a prolonged civil war in which Doe himself was killed. A period of relative peace in 1997 allowed for elections that brought Taylor to power, but major fighting resumed in 2000. An August 2003 peace agreement ended the war and prompted the resignation of former president Charles Taylor, who was exiled to Nigeria. After two years of rule by a transitional government, democratic elections in late 2005 brought President Ellen Johnson-Sirleaf to power. The UN Mission in Liberia (UNMIL), which maintains a strong presence throughout the country, completed a disarmament program for former combatants in late 2004, but the security situation is still volatile and the process of rebuilding the social and economic structure of this war-torn country remains sluggish.
    Constitution: January 6, 1986.
    Legislature: bicameral National Assembly consists of the Senate (30 seats — number of seats changed in October 11, 2005 elections; members elected by popular vote to serve nine-year terms) and the House of Representatives (64 seats; members elected by popular vote to serve six-year terms).
    Elections: Senate — last held October 11, 2005 (next to be held in 2011); House of Representatives — last held October 11, 2005 (next to be held in 2011).
    Election results: Senate — percent of vote by party — N/A; seats by party — COTOL 7, NPP 4, CDC 3, LP 3, UP 3, APD 3, other 7; House of Representatives — percent of vote by party — N/A; seats by party — CDC 15, LP 9, UP 8, COTOL 8, APD 5, NPP 4, other 15.

Political parties: Alliance for Peace and Democracy or APD; Coalition for the Transformation of Liberia or COTOL; Congress for Democratic Change or CDC; Liberian Action Party or LAP; Liberty Party or LP; National Patriotic Party or NPP; Unity Party or UP.

STATUS AND PROGRESS OF WOMEN

Liberia has a history of women serving in government. But in 2006, President Johnson-Sirleaf commended women in top positions in her government for performing up to her expectations since she took office in January 2006. She commended the ministerial positions of Justice, Commerce, Youth and Sport, and Finance. She urged women in government to work hard, and stated that "the success of her government will be the success of all women in the country and the world at large."[60]

Women hold approximately 35 percent of Liberia's cabinet positions including the ministries of gender and development, finance, youth and sports, justice, commerce. Other positions in which women also serve include the director of police, commissioner of the bureau of immigration and naturalization, deputy minister of internal affairs, deputy minister of labor, and deputy minister of finance.[61]

In 2006, United States Ambassador to the United Nations, John R. Bolton, said of Johnson-Sirleaf, "In her short time in office, we are impressed with the courage and determination she has already shown in addressing Liberia's challenges, especially in such areas as economic and civil service reform."[62]

In 2007, one of Johnson-Sirleaf's concerns is that aid to Liberia is taking second place to the assistance being given to countries which the West fears Islamic extremists are harbored. She said, "It will be catastrophic if aid is to be reduced."[63] Liberia remains volatile after the civil war. *The Independent* describes Liberia thus: "Towns are filled with young, unemployed ex-fighters which the UN describes as 'a very serious source of tension.' Poverty is everywhere."[64]

Civil war left Liberia's population traumatized and its infrastructure looted and burnt to the ground. Liberia's democracy is fragile, and the country's recovery is at risk due to violence, insecurity and poverty.[65]

The Inter-Parliamentary Union (IPU) reported Liberia as a country that had made progress in the number of women in national parliaments. In 1995, the lower chamber of parliament had two women out of 35 seats (5.71 percent) and in 2006, that number increased to eight women out of 64 seats (12.50 percent).[66] In addition, Liberia had an elected woman president, Ruth Perry, from November 1996 to August 1998.[67]

In 1944, Liberian women were given the right to vote, but statements at the Fourth World Conference on Women at Beijing in 1995 and the 1999 assessment of Liberia's progress documented "the under-representation of women in decision-making roles."[68] The 1999 report indicated that women held two percent of ministerial positions, five percent of legislative seats and one percent of other executive positions. Liberia ratified important policy frameworks in 1998, the Beijing Platform for Action, the United Nations Convention on the Elimination of All Forms of Discrimination Against Women (CEDAW) and in 2000 the UN Security Council Resolution 1325.[69]

In spite of the disastrous effects of a 14-year-long civil war, Liberia's "women have been involved on all sides prior to widespread fighting, throughout the contemporary conflict and in the early stages of a peace process today."[70] In September 2004, a group of women presented parliamentary Speaker George Dweh with a resolution calling for electoral law reform. The reform required that every qualified political party earmark a minimum of 30 percent seats for women in their candidates' list. It also required setting aside a minimum of 30 percent representation for women in decision-making positions within their parties. Unfortunately, the National Transitional Legislative Assembly rejected the women's resolution in its reform. In addition, in the election prior to Johnson-Sirleaf's winning, 14 percent of political party and independent candidates were women. Of the 22 presidential candidates, two were female.[71]

President Johnson-Sirleaf is widely admired, at home and abroad. In spite of the country's heavy debt, she has kept corruption at bay by dismissing officials and demanding transparency in contracts. She has appointed experienced women to run the top ministries of finance, justice and commerce.[72]

Republic of Mali

BACKGROUND[73]

Location: Western Africa, southwest of Algeria
Population: 11,716,829 (July 2006 est.)
Per Capita Income: $1,200 (2006 est.)
   Government type: republic.
   Independence: September 22, 1960 (from France). The Sudanese Republic and Senegal became independent of France in 1960 as the Mali Federation. When Senegal withdrew after only a few months, what formerly made up the Sudanese Republic was renamed Mali. Rule by dictatorship was brought to a close in 1991 by a coup that ushered in democratic government. President Alpha Konare won Mali's first democratic presidential election in 1992 and was reelected in 1997. In keeping with Mali's two-term constitutional limit, Konare stepped down in 2002 and was succeeded by Amadou Toure.
   Constitution: adopted January 12, 1992.
   Legislature: unicameral National Assembly or Assemblee Nationale (147 seats; members are elected by popular vote to serve five-year terms).
   Elections: last held July 1 and 22, 2007 (next to be held in July 2012).
   Election results: percent of vote by party — N/A; seats by party — ADP coalition 113 (including ADEMA 51, URD 34, MPR 8, CNID 7, UDD 3, and other 10), FDR coalition 15 (including RPM 11, PARENA 4), SADI 4, independent 15.
   Political parties: Alliance for Democracy and Progress or ADP (a coalition of 14 political parties including ADEMA and URD formed in December 2006 to support the presidential candidacy of Amadou Toure); Alliance for Democracy or ADEMA; Convergence 2007; Hope 2002 (a coalition of CNID, MPR, RDT, and RPM); National Congress for Democratic Initiative or CNID; Party for Democracy and Progress or PDP; Party for National Renewal or PARENA; Patriotic Movement for Renewal or MPR; Rally for Democracy and Labor or RDT; Rally for Mali or RPM; Sudanese Union/African Democratic Rally or US/RDA; Union for Democracy and Development or UDD; Union for Republic and Democracy or URD.

STATUS AND PROGRESS OF WOMEN

Mali has endured droughts, rebellions, a coup and 23 years of military dictatorship[74] under Mussa Traore. He ruled Mali as an authoritarian African state. No rule of law existed. It was a one-party state, and the party controlled all institutions. Civil society organizations, such as trade unions or women's organizations, were all connected to the one party. In spite of the state practices, in 1974, Mali had a constitution which claimed to protect human rights. In 1982, the government ratified the African Charter on Human and Peoples' Rights.[75] In 1992, Mali had its first democratically-elected president and now has a civilian government.[76]

Mali has the Two-Round System (TRS), a plurality/majority election system. Its quota type is the Political Party Quota for Electoral Candidates, and in the 2006 election, 15 women were elected to the parliament of 147 (10.2 percent).[77] In 2004, one-third of Mali's ministers were women.[78] In 1960, Mali elected its first woman to parliament.[79]

In February 2007, Kalifa Gadiaga, Information Specialist at the United States Embassy in Bamako, Mali, reports, "five women are serving in a government of 28 members. They are: Soumare Aminata Sidibé, Minister of State Properties and Lands, Sylla Fanta, Minister of Justice, Diallo M'Bodji Sène, Minister for the Promotion of Women and Children, Maiga Zenab Mint Youba, Minister of Health, and BA Hawa Keita, Minister of Employment and Professional Training. This government normally continues until the end of April, because the first round of presidential elections is set for April 29 and the second round for the 3rd week of June. Normally after the elections, there will be another government."[80]

The Association for the Progress and the Defense of Women's rights (APDF) was founded in 1991 in Mali.[81] APDF lists the campaign of training and information of women in civic, political education, especially for the women candidates, as one of its many accomplishments.[82] APDF also works to "implement the provisions of the Beijing Platform for Action."[83]

Mali has ratified the United Nations Convention on the Elimination of All Forms of Discrimination Against Women and the African Charter of Human and Peoples' Rights and its additional protocol. Yet, there is a low rate of representation of women in decision-making positions in government, the National Assembly and central services.[84]

In Mali's 2005 report, a ten-year plan for a program for education includes gender advancement recommendations. The political will of the Mali government to make the advancement of women one of its priorities was demonstrated by the establishment of the Ministry for the Advancement of Women, Children and the Family in September 1997. In addition, a policy has been developed, composed of the Plan of Action for the Advancement of Women 1996–2000, and was reviewed in light of the conclusions at the fourth World Conference on Women held at Beijing in 1995; and the Strategic Plan 2002–2006, which is consistent with the strategic priorities selected by the Strategic Framework to Combat Poverty.[85]

Republic of Niger

BACKGROUND[86]

Location: Western Africa, southeast of Algeria
Population: 12,525,094 (July 2006 est.)
Per Capita Income: $1,000 (2006 est.)

Government type: republic.

Independence: August 3, 1960 (from France). Until 1981, Niger had single-party and military rule under General Ali Saibou. In 1993, multiparty elections resulted in a democratic government. In 1996 Colonel Ibrahim Bare led a coup. In 1999 Bare was killed in a coup by military officers who restored democratic rule and held elections that resulted in the election of Mamadou Tandja in December. In 2004, Tandja was reelected. Niger is one of the poorest countries in the world with minimal government services and insufficient funds to develop its resource base. Mostly an agrarian and subsistence-based economy, Niger is often plagued with extended droughts.

Constitution: adopted July 18, 1999.

Legislature: unicameral National Assembly (113 seats; note: expanded from 83 seats; members elected by popular vote for five-year terms).

Elections: last held December 4, 2004 (next to be held December 2009).

Election results: percent of vote by party — N/A; seats by party — MNSD 47, CDS 22, PNDS 25, RSD 7, RDP 6, ANDP 5, PSDN 1.

Political parties: Democratic and Social Convention-Rahama or CDS-Rahama; National Movement for a Developing Society-Nassara or MNSD-Nassara; Niger Social Democratic Party or PSDN; Nigerien Alliance for Democracy and Social Progress-Zaman Lahiya or ANDP-Zaman Lahiya; Nigerien Party for Autonomy or PNA-Alouma'a; Nigerien Party for Democracy and Socialism or PNDS-Tarrayya; Nigerien Progressive Party or PPN-RDA; Rally for Democracy and Progress or RDP-jama'a; Social and Democratic Rally or RSD-Gaskiyya.

STATUS AND PROGRESS OF WOMEN

The United States Department of State reports that traditionally, women play a subordinate role in Niger's politics. The societal practice of husbands' voting their wives' proxy ballots effectively disenfranchises many women. This practice was used widely in the 1999 presidential and National Assembly elections. The percentage of women in government and politics does not correspond to their percentage of the population. One woman won a seat in the 83-seat National Assembly; there are 2 female ministers in the government. The mayor of the city of Agadez, the capital of a district that includes one-third of the country, is a woman. The National Assembly passed a law in 2000 mandating that women would receive 25 percent of government positions, but by year's end, women still did not fill that percentage of government positions.[87]

In spite of this report, in December of 1989, Niger elected the first woman to parliament.[88] In 1996, Niger had 14.3 percent women in its ministerial positions and 10 percent in subministerial offices.[89] The Inter-Parliamentary Union lists Niger as making progress with the number of women in parliament. In 1995, three women served out of 83 seats (3.61 percent), and in 2006, 14 out of 113 (12.39 percent) served making an improvement of 8.78 percent.[90]

In June 2006, Niger's parliament voted down Africa's Maputo Protocol on women's rights, an accord intending to ensure women's equality in all spheres of life. In 2005, Niger had six female ministers in the cabinet.[91]

Niger's report to the Convention on the Elimination of All Forms of Discrimination Against Women (CEDAW) in 2001 said that Niger had ratified several international instruments. Historically, among those instruments, the Convention on the Political Rights of Women was adopted on December 20, 1952, and ratified on December 7, 1964.[92]

To guarantee that women were more involved in decision-making bodies, the Government adopted Act No. 2000–2008, which introduced a quota system of 10 percent for the National Assembly and 25 percent each for government; diplomatic missions; central and decentralized administration; and state companies. Recent developments include the stipulation that during local legislative elections, the lists submitted by each political party or group of political parties or group of independent candidates must include candidates of both genders, with the proportion of elected candidates of either gender not to be less than 10 percent; the establishment of the National Institute for Monitoring the Advancement of Women; and the creation of the post of gender adviser to the President and the Prime Minister.[93]

The constitution and Electoral Code provide that both genders can vote and stand for elections. The weight of social expectations outweighs the permission of the egalitarian legal provisions. Women hardly participate in politics even though the Niger Women's Union was formed in 1961, and in 1975, the Niger Women's Association replaced the Union.[94]

Niger reported on women in government from 1958 to 2000. No women held positions of minister until 1987 to 1989, when one woman served. From 1989 to 1990 and from 1990 to 1993, two women each term held offices; from 1993 to 1996, five women; from 1996 to 1997 and from 1997 to 1999, four women each term, and from April to December 1999 and January 2000, one woman served. On the international level, only three out of nine ambassadors are women.[95]

Although women comprise large percentages of the membership of political parties, they are shut out of the party leadership and have no say in decisions. Their function is usually to boost the careers of men.[96]

Federal Republic of Nigeria

BACKGROUND[97]

Location: Western Africa, bordering the Gulf of Guinea, between Benin and Cameroon
Population: 131,859,731
Per Capita Income: $1,400 (2006 est.)

Government type: federal republic.

Independence: October 1, 1960 (from U.K.). In 1999, after almost 16 years of military rule, a new constitution was adopted. A peaceful transition to civilian government was completed. President Olusegun Obasanjo was elected by popular vote in 1999 and in 2003. Long-standing ethnic and religious tensions and past mismanagement of funds are challenges. Nigeria is currently in its longest period of civilian rule since independence. The general elections in April 2007 would mark the first civilian-to-civilian transfer of power in Nigeria's history.

Constitution: adopted May 5, 1999; effective May 29, 1999.

Legislature: bicameral National Assembly consists of Senate (109 seats — 3 from each state plus 1 from Abuja; members elected by popular vote to serve four-year terms) and House of Representatives (360 seats; members elected by popular vote to serve four-year terms).

Elections: Senate — last held April 21, 2007; House of Representatives — last held April 21, 2007 (next for both to be held April 2011).

Election results: Senate — percent of vote by party — official results not yet posted; House of Representatives — official results not yet posted.

Political parties: Action Congress or AC; Alliance for Democracy or AD; All Nigeria Peoples' Party or ANPP; All Progressives Grand Alliance or APGA; Democratic People's Party or DPP; Fresh Democratic Party; Movement for the Restoration and Defense of Democracy or MRDD; National Democratic Party or NDP; Peoples Democratic Party or PDP; Peoples

Redemption Party or PRP; Peoples Salvation Party or PSP; United Nigeria Peoples Party or UNPP.

STATUS AND PROGRESS OF WOMEN

Nigeria's *Beijing+5* report indicated efforts to involve women in power and decision-making capacities through such activities as workshops, conferences, seminars, rallies, dialogue with political presidential aspirants, strengthening women education centers and promotion of political women in nongovernmental organization's formation.[98]

In addition, Nigeria strengthened its institutional mechanism for mainstreaming gender by establishing: a network on gender studies to standardize curriculum in gender at higher institutions and universities; a gender unit at federal and state ministries and a data unit; state ministries of women affairs and social development; and standardization of a national gender training manual.[99]

Nigeria's *Beijing+10* report indicated that despite the acceptance of the need for gender balance in decision-making bodies, "a gap between de jure and de facto equality still persists," and the country had a long way to go to meet the 30 percent quota.[100] Still, token representation existed, indicating a gradual improvement over a period of about 20 years. In 1985, there was one woman out of 95 senators, and in 1999, there were three women out of 109 senators (2.8 percent) and 12 women members of the House of Representatives out of 360 (3.3 percent). In 2003, the number of women senators remained the same, three out of 109, but in the House of Representatives, the number increased to 23 women out of 360 members (6.4 percent).[101]

In other elected and appointed positions in 2003, results for national women office holders were: six ministers, nine presidential assistants, two presidential advisers, five ambassadors, two deputy governors out of 36, and 38 women in the 36 state Houses of Assembly.[102]

Institutional mechanisms for advancement of women included the Federal Ministry of Women's Affairs and the National Centre for Women's Development. Some constraints include inadequate financial and human resources, insufficient data, absence of a gender policy and noninvolvement of women. Constraints to increasing women's participation include the absence of a 30 percent affirmative action policy; lack of female solidarity; social, economic and religious barriers and a patriarchal system.[103]

The United Nations Economic Commission for Africa's (ECA) first report in 2001 assessed a lack of progress in Nigeria in meeting the goals of the Beijing conference. On the national level, a proposed 30 percent women's quota in the democratic constitution did not pass. The three main political parties in their manifestos did not commit to quotas. The president's pledge for affirmative action was not reflected in his appointments; for example, of the 46 ministers, five were women (10.8 percent). Approximately 106 ambassadors were nominated, of which seven were women (6.6 percent).[104]

At the state and local levels, of the 23 local government chairpersons in Rivers State, there were no women. The report describes the state's situation: "The State Governor is a man and there are no women in the 32-member State Assembly. The National Assembly has 16 members representing Rivers State, none of whom is a woman. The two ministers and one special adviser from Rivers State are men. At the State level, of the 16 commissioners and about five special advisors, only three are women.[105]

In 2005, along with some other countries, the ECA placed Nigeria in the third group, one that poorly addresses the needs of women. Nigeria reserved no seats for women at the state or national level. Out of its 36 states, there is no female governor. From 1999 to 2003,

Nigeria had one female deputy governor, Kofoworola Bucknor from Lagos State, in the fourth republic. Prolonged differences with the state governor forced her to resign.[106]

Republic of Senegal

BACKGROUND[107]

Location: Western Africa, bordering the North Atlantic Ocean, between Guinea-Bissau and Mauritania

Population: 11,987,121 (July 2006 est.)

Per Capita Income: $1,800 (2006 est.)

Government type: republic.

Independence: April 4, 1960 (from France); note: complete independence achieved upon dissolution of federation with Mali on August 20, 1960. The Socialist Party ruled until current President Abdoulaye Wade was elected in 2000. Senegal and the Gambia joined to form the nominal confederation of Senegambia in 1982, but the integration of the two countries was never carried out, and the union was dissolved in 1989. Occasionally since 1982, a southern separatist group clashes with government forces, but Senegal continues as one of the most stable democracies in Africa. The country has a long history of participating in international peacekeeping.

Constitution: adopted January 7, 2001.

Legislature: unicameral National Assembly or Assemblee Nationale (120 seats; members are elected by direct, popular vote to serve five-year terms); note: the former National Assembly had 120 seats, but deputies in late 2006 voted to expand the number of seats to 140.

Elections: last held June 3, 2007 (next to be held 2012); note: the National Assembly in December 2005 voted to postpone legislative elections originally scheduled for 2006; parliamentary elections were rescheduled to coincide with the February 25, 2007, presidential elections later rescheduled for June 3, 2007, and boycotted; Senate — last held August 19, 2007 (next to be held — N/A).

Election results: National Assembly percent of vote by party — N/A; seats by party — SOPI Coalition 131, other 19; Senate results — percent of vote by party — N/A; seats by party — PDS 34, AJ/PADS 1, 65 to be appointed by the president.

Political parties: African Party of Independence; And-Jef/African Party for Democracy and Socialism (also known as AJ/PADS); Alliance of Forces of Progress or AFP; Democratic and Patriotic Convention or CDP (also known as Garab-Gi); Democratic League-Labor Party Movement or LD-MPT; Front for Socialism and Democracy or FSD; Gainde Centrist Bloc or BGC; Independence and Labor Party or PIT; Jef-Jel; National Democratic Rally or RND; People's Labor Party or PTP; Reform Party or PR; Rewmi; Senegalese Democratic Party or PDS; Socialist Party or PS; SOPI Coalition (a coalition led by the PDS); Union for Democratic Renewal or URD.

STATUS AND PROGRESS OF WOMEN

In 1960, Senegal formed its first legislature as a sovereign state and in December of 1963, elected the first woman to parliament.[108] The Inter-Parliamentary Union lists Senegal as having made progress in the number of women who hold seats. In 1995, 14 women out of 120 members (11.67 percent) held seats, and in 2006, 23 women out of 120 members (19.17 per-cent) demonstrating an increase of 7.50 percent.[109]

The United Nations Economic Commission for Africa (ECA) reports that Senegal is tak-ing positive action to involve women in government. Constitutional reform created a Min-istry for Women's Affairs. In 1997, the government drafted a National Action Plan for Women. After the 1998 elections, Senegal adopted an affirmative action policy. Political parties agreed to a 25 percent quota for women in party positions and as candidates. As a result, a woman is a founder, the first secretary of the Parti Pour la Renaissance Africaine party.[110]

Senegal's report, the *Solemn Declaration* on the equality between men and women, con-cluded that the country followed through on all of the international protocols. In spite of the strength of constraints that are deeply anchored in tradition, the head of the state and gov-ernment have evidenced real political good will for the equality of women.[111]

In spite of the government's good will, the application of the principle of parity is not yet effective. To realize Senegal as a state without discrimination, the report estimates, it will take from 2007 to 2016. However, the government is addressing discrimination to help women access positions of decision-making. In 2006, women occupy positions that they had not since independence. These positions include: in government: nine women ministers out of 40, including one Minister of State (22.5 percent); advisers of the President: 20 percent are women; advisers of the Prime Minister: 26 percent of the national Parliament are women: 23 women were appointed out of 120 (19 percent); and the Council of the Republic for the Eco-nomic and Social Affairs: 31 women out of 110 (28 percent).[112]

Senegal's women ambassadors hold 15 percent of the positions; three women out of 35 hold territorial Command: one woman associated with the governor, one woman Prefect, one woman associated with the Prefect, for a potential of 101 stations in the governances and pre-fectures the regional Councils; 61 out of 470 women are regional advisers (13 percent); a woman president of regional council on 11 town councils; 1133 women out of 4216 advisers (27 per-cent) and six women mayors out of 103 (5.8 percent) rural Councils; 1043 out of 9092 advis-ers are women (11.5 percent), a woman is a president of rural council (Chefferie) of villages; three out of 14,000 villages are directed by women.[113]

Until 2006, military and paramilitary bodies were exclusively reserved to men. These positions are now open.[114]

Republic of Sierra Leone

BACKGROUND[115]

Location: Western Africa, bordering the North Atlantic Ocean, between Guinea and Liberia
Population: 6,005,250 (July 2006 est.)
Per Capita Income: $900 (2006 est.)

Government type: constitutional democracy.

Independence: April 27, 1961 (from U.K.). The government is slowly reestablishing its authority after the 1991–2002 civil war that resulted in tens of thousands of deaths and the displacement of more than two million people representing about one-third of the popula-tion. The last UN peacekeepers withdrew in December 2005, leaving full responsibility for security with domestic forces. A new civilian UN mission, the UN Integrated Office in Sierra Leone (UNIOSIL), was established to support the government's efforts to consolidate peace.

The most pressing long-term threat to stability in Sierra Leone is the potential for political insecurity surrounding July 2007 elections.

Constitution: October 1, 1991; subsequently amended several times.

Legislature: unicameral Parliament (124 seats — 112 elected by popular vote, 12 filled by paramount chiefs elected in separate elections; members serve five-year terms).

Elections: last held August 11, 2007 (next to be held in 2012).

Election results: percent of vote by party — N/A; seats by party — APC 59, SLPP 43, PMDC 10.

Political parties: All People's Congress or APC; Peace and Liberation Party or PLP; People's Movement for Democratic Change or PMDC; Sierra Leone People's Party or SLPP; numerous others.

STATUS AND PROGRESS OF WOMEN

"Sierra Leone adopted the Beijing Platform for Action in 1995, but there were few institutional structures, generally disjointed, to address the situation,"[116] stated Mrs. Shirley Y. Gbujama, Minister of Social Welfare, Gender and Children's Affairs in 2000. The Ministry of Gender and Children's Affairs was established in 1996 with the first democratically elected government after more than two decades. Among other duties, this ministry would develop strategies for international agencies which address the issues covered under the twelve areas of concern. Other institutional structures were established and women organized through nongovernmental structures.

To address women's participation in power and decision making, the government appointed women to the Ministries of Gender and Children's Affairs, Foreign Affairs and International Cooperation, Housing and Country Planning and the Ministry of Development and Economic Planning. A woman was appointed head of the National Commission for Democracy and Human Rights, and another was appointed as chairperson as the Mining and General Services. The number of women also increased in junior ministerial positions. Although "men continued to dominate parliamentary representations with 92.2 percent, women's representation at 7.8 percent marks a modest improvement, when compared with the situation before Beijing."[117]

The Inter-Parliamentary Union (IPU) lists Sierra Leone as having made improvement with the number of women in parliament. In 1995, five women served out of 80 seats (6.25 percent), and in 2006, 18 out of 124 (14.52 percent). The improvement was 8.27 percent.[118]

In 2000, Gbujama stated, "In spite of all the difficulties and problems that have abounded throughout the five-year period since Beijing, it is evident that whatever we have achieved was done through sustained action; in only short peaceful periods which amount to not more than two and a half years."[119]

Togolese Republic

BACKGROUND[120]

Location: Western Africa, bordering the Bight of Benin, between Benin and Ghana
Population: 5,548,702
Per Capita Income: $1,700 (2006 est.)

Government type: republic under transition to multiparty democratic rule.

Independence: April 27, 1960 (from French-administered UN trusteeship). French Togoland became Togo in 1960. Gen. Gnassingbe Eyadema, installed as military ruler in 1967, continued to rule well into the 21st century. Despite the facade of multiparty elections instituted in the early 1990s, the government continued to be dominated by President Eyadema, whose Rally of the Togolese People (RPT) party has maintained power almost continuously since 1967. Togo has come under fire from international organizations for human rights abuses and is plagued by political unrest. While most bilateral and multilateral aid to Togo remains frozen, the EU initiated a partial resumption of cooperation and development aid to Togo in late 2004 based upon commitments by Togo to expand opportunities for political opposition and liberalize portions of the economy. Upon his death in February 2005, President Eyadema was succeeded by his son Faure Gnassingbe. The succession, supported by the military and in contravention of the nation's constitution, was challenged by popular protest and a threat of sanctions from regional leaders. Gnassingbe succumbed to pressure and in April 2005 held elections that legitimized his succession. Legislative elections were scheduled for June 2007.

Constitution: multiparty draft constitution approved by High Council of the Republic, July 1, 1992; adopted by public referendum September 1992.

Legislature: unicameral National Assembly (81 seats; members are elected by popular vote to serve five-year terms).

Elections: last held 27 October 2002 (were to be held August 5, 2007, but have been delayed until an indefinite date).

Election results: percent of vote by party — N/A; seats by party — RPT 72, RSDD 3, UDPS 2, Juvento 2, MOCEP 1, independents 1; note: two opposition parties boycotted the election, the Union of the Forces for Change and the Action Committee for Renewal.

Political parties: Action Committee for Renewal or CAR; Democratic Convention of African Peoples or CDPA; Democratic Party for Renewal or PDR; Juvento; Movement of the Believers of Peace and Equality or MOCEP; Pan-African Patriotic Convergence or CPP; Rally for the Support for Development and Democracy or RSDD; Rally of the Togolese People or RPT; Socialist Pact for Renewal or PSR; Union for Democracy and Social Progress or UDPS; Union of Forces for a Change or UFC.

STATUS AND PROGRESS OF WOMEN

The Inter-Parliamentary Union (IPU) reports that Togo elected the first woman to parliament in April 1961.[121] The IPU lists Togo as having made improvement with the number of women in parliament. In 1995, one woman served out of 81 seats (1.23 percent), and in 2006, six out of 81 (7.41 percent). The improvement was 6.18 percent.[122]

Togo's *Beijing+10* report stated, "Ten years after Beijing, Togo can point to considerable progress in a number of strategic and developmental respects. But, owing to the country's permanent state of crisis, much remains to be done."[123] One of the areas the report believed to be a challenge was the involvement of women in the management of public affairs. Togo acknowledged that women have political rights, skills and know-how, "but it must be said that women remain under-represented at the upper levels of power and decision-making: in the Executive, the Legislature and the Judiciary and in the control of information."[124]

The report stated that following Beijing and the review and appraisal (*Beijing+5*), the ministry responsible requested other ministries to establish focal points for gender and the advancement of women with a view to maximizing the impact of the programs and other measures for women. No practical action had yet been taken to carry out this request.[125]

Although the constitution provides for the equality of all citizens, male and female, without any discrimination, the reality is quite different. Women remain a minority in decision-making bodies. In 2003, in the government, five women out of 25 were ministers, and in the National Assembly, five women out of 81 were deputies.[126]

Togo has the national mechanism for the advancement of women established by decree in 1977; it was amended in 1992, creating the Directorate for the Advancement of Women, which was restored to the status of General Directorate by in 1994. The directorate considered creating focal points for the integration of women at decision-making levels in all the ministerial departments, but this approach was met with some resistance. In 1996, a national policy for the advancement of women was considered, but not developed. In 1998, a project began with NGOs to combat inequalities. A committee was set up to monitor progress of the Beijing Platform. Specifically, for the area of women and decision-making, the report recommended the adoption of a graduated quota as a means of securing due representation of women in decision-making bodies at all levels.[127]

SOUTHERN AFRICA

*Southern Africa countries: Angola, Botswana,
Lesotho, Malawi, Mauritius, Mozambique, Namibia,
South Africa, Swaziland, Zambia, Zimbabwe*

Republic of Angola

BACKGROUND[1]

Location: Southern Africa, bordering the South Atlantic Ocean, between Namibia and Democratic Republic of the Congo
Population: 12,127,071 (July 2006 est.)
Per Capita Income: $4,300 (2006 est.)
   Government type: republic; multiparty presidential regime.
   Independence: November 11, 1975 (from Portugal). Angola is rebuilding after the end
of a 27-year civil war in 2002. Fighting between the Popular Movement for the Liberation
of Angola (MPLA) and the National Union for the Total Independence of Angola (UNITA)
followed independence. In 1992 Angola held national elections, but UNITA renewed fighting after the MPLA defeated it at the polls. Estimates are that 1.5 million lives may have been
lost and four million people displaced during the quarter century of fighting. The death of
UNITA leader Jonas Savimbi in 2002 ended UNITA's insurgency. While the MPLA leader,
President Jose Eduardo Dos Santos, had pledged to hold legislative elections in 2007, he has
since announced that legislative elections will be held in 2008, with presidential elections
planned for 2009. A specific election timetable has yet to be established.
   Constitution: adopted by People's Assembly, August 25, 1992.
   Legislature: unicameral National Assembly or Assembleia Nacional (220 seats; members
elected by proportional vote to serve four-year terms).
   Elections: last held September 29–30, 1992 (next to be held September 2008).
   Election results: percent of vote by party — MPLA 54 percent, UNITA 34 percent, other
12 percent; seats by party — MPLA 129, UNITA 70, PRS 6, FNLA 5, PLD 3, other 7.
   Political parties: Liberal Democratic Party or PLD; National Front for the Liberation of
Angola or FNLA; National Union for the Total Independence of Angola or UNITA (largest
opposition party); Popular Movement for the Liberation of Angola or MPLA (ruling party
in power since 1975); Social Renewal Party or PRS. About a dozen minor parties participated
in the 1992 elections but only won a few seats; they and the other 115 smaller parties have
little influence in the National Assembly.

STATUS AND PROGRESS OF WOMEN

Angola has a history of women in leadership positions dating back to antiquity; for example, Queen Nzingha, who lived from 1583 to 1663, was a "brilliant military strategist, charismatic leader, and a true Warrior Queen."[2]

Angola elected the first woman to Parliament in November 1980.[3] The IPU lists Angola as making progress with the number of women in parliament. In 1995, 21 women served out of 220 seats (9.55 percent), and in 2006, 33 out of 220 (15 percent). The improvement was 5.45 percent.[4]

The United Nations Commission for Africa's (ECA) *Beijing+5* report found Angola had introduced affirmative action and quotas. The country had also appointed women as Cabinet Ministers of Petroleum and Fisheries.[5]

In 1998, the ECA reported that Angola's 1992 election was significant. Mrs. Analia de Victoria Periara was one of 13 candidates that ran for president. Her party, the Liberal Democratic Party, gained 29 percent of the vote for the presidency. It also gained 2.3 percent of the votes for the legislature, resulting in 3 seats in parliament.[6]

Angola noted in its *Beijing+10* report that legislation assures women equality, but they ascend to power on a smaller scale. Illiteracy and lack of economic power limit women's access. A reduction of the number of women in parliament, government, magistracy and public functions demonstrates that women had not been considered appropriately in the proposals of political parties to assure women positions in decision making. In the 2004, in the National Assembly, 36 women held positions (16.4 percent) out of 220 seats, compared to 184 men (83.6 percent). Only one political party proposed a woman candidate to the presidency of the Republic.[7]

In 1996, the percentage of women in government positions was 20 percent. Out of 31 ministers, four (12.9 percent) were women; of 42 vice ministers, six (14.3 percent) were women. In 2000, out of 29 ministers, 26 were men and three (10.3 percent) were women, representing a drop of 2.6 percent of women. Vice ministers' positions consisted of 40 men and five women (11.1 percent), representing a drop of 3.2 percent of women.[8] In July 2006, Angola had two female ministers, Mrs. Ana Dias Lourenço, the Minister of Planning, and Mrs. Candida Ce leste da Silva, the Minister of the Family and the Promotion of Women.[9]

Angola's country report indicated that work in gender equity suffered mainly from the country's political military situation, which placed it in a permanent state of emergency, population movement and nonallocation of financial resources. In spite of the country's condition, some improvements occurred in the position of women at top political levels.[10]

Republic of Botswana

BACKGROUND[11]

Location: Southern Africa, north of South Africa
Population: 1,639,833
Per Capita Income: $11,400 (2006 est.)
 Government type: parliamentary republic.
 Independence: September 30, 1966 (from U.K.). Formerly the British protectorate of Bechuanaland, Botswana adopted its new name upon independence. The country has a thriving economy due to four decades of uninterrupted civilian leadership, progressive social

policies, and significant capital investment. Mineral extraction, mainly diamond mining, is the primary economic activity. Tourism is growing because of conservation practices and extensive nature preserves. Botswana has one of the world's highest known rates of HIV/AIDS infection, but it also has one of Africa's most progressive and comprehensive programs to combat it.

Constitution: March 1965; effective September 30, 1966.

Legislature: bicameral Parliament consists of the House of Chiefs (a largely advisory 15-member body with 8 permanent members consisting of the chiefs of the principal tribes, and 7 non-permanent members serving 5-year terms, consisting of 4 elected subchiefs and 3 members selected by the other 12 members) and the National Assembly (63 seats, 57 members are directly elected by popular vote, 4 are appointed by the majority party, and 2, the President and Attorney General, serve as ex-officio members; members serve five-year terms).

Elections: National Assembly elections last held October 30, 2004 (next to be held October 2009).

Election results: percent of vote by party — BDP 51.7 percent, BNF 26.1 percent, BCP 16.6 percent, other 5 percent; seats by party — BDP 44, BNF 12, BCP 1.

Political parties: Botswana Alliance Movement or BAM; Botswana Congress Party or BCP; Botswana Democratic Party or BDP; Botswana National Front or BNF; Botswana Peoples Party or BPP; MELS Movement of Botswana or MELS; New Democratic Front or NDF; a number of minor parties joined forces in 1999 to form the BAM but did not win any parliamentary seats. These parties include the United Action Party; the Independence Freedom Party or IFP; the Botswana Progressive Union.

STATUS AND PROGRESS OF WOMEN

The Inter-Parliamentary Union (IPU) reports that Botswana elected the first woman to parliament in October 1979.[12] The IPU lists Botswana as making progress with the number of women in parliament. In 1995, four women served out of 47 seats (8.51 percent), and in 2006, seven out of 63 (11.11 percent). The improvement was 2.60 percent.[13]

The United Nations Economic Commission for Africa's (ECA) *Beijing+5* report believed that Botswana's public perception of gender equality and advancement of women had significantly improved. Even so, as a result of Botswana's previous election, parliament consisted of 40 men and four women and the cabinet consisted of 13 men and three women. Public service positions were no exception to these ratios.[14]

In spite of the improvement of the status of women in Botswana, discriminatory laws and practices continue even though the constitution provides for gender equality. Botswana's national machinery is new and lacks adequate finances and staff with the required skills. The tendency is to view women's issues as the exclusive responsibility of the National Women's Machinery while other departments view those issues as secondary responsibilities.[15]

Botswana's *Beijing+10* report indicated improvement had occurred since the *Beijing+5* report. A major achievement in implementing the National Plan of Action for gender equality and advancement of women was the adoption of two very important documents in 1996: the National Policy on Women in Development, and ratification of the UN Convention on the Elimination of All Forms of Discrimination Against Women (CEDAW). In addition, in 1996–97, the National Women's Machinery was upgraded to a government department, Women's Affairs.[16]

BOTSWANA: GENDER REPRESENTATION
PARLIAMENT AND CABINET, 1994, 1997[17]

Institution	1994			1999		
	M	F	F%	M	F	F%
Parliament	40	4	9	36	8	18.2
Cabinet	13	2	13	13	4	23.5

Major challenges listed were the prevailing gender stereotypes and the absence of a comprehensive affirmative action plan. Botswana's goal for the elections in 2004 was to achieve 30 percent representation of women.

The following tables give a picture of the representation of women in decision-making positions in political parties.

BOTSWANA: REPRESENTATION IN
PARTY CENTRAL COMMITTEE BY GENDER, 1999[18]

Party	M	F	F%
Congress Party (BCP)	12	7	37
Democratic Party (BDP)	12	6	33
National Front (BNF)	21	3	13
TOTAL	45	16	26

BOTSWANA: PARLIAMENTARY CANDIDATES
BY GENDER PER POLITICAL PARTY, 1999 ELECTIONS[19]

	Party	Total	M	F	F%
Candidates	BCP	40	37	3	8
	BDP	40	34	6	15
	BNF	40	39	1	3
TOTAL		120	110	10	8

Kingdom of Lesotho

BACKGROUND[20]

Location: Southern Africa, an enclave of South Africa
Population: 2,022,331
Per Capita Income: $2,600 (2006 est.)

Government type: parliamentary constitutional monarchy.

Independence: October 4, 1966 (from U.K.). Basutoland was renamed the Kingdom of Lesotho when it became independent. The Basuto National Party ruled for the first two decades. King Moshoeshoe was exiled in 1990, returned in 1992, and was reinstated in 1995. Constitutional government was restored in 1993 after seven years of military rule. In 1998, violent protests and a military mutiny following a contentious election brought about a short but bloody intervention by the military forces of South Africa and Botswana under the auspices of the Southern African Development Community. Constitutional reforms have since restored political stability and in 2002, peaceful parliamentary elections took place.

Constitution: April 2, 1993.

Legislature: bicameral Parliament consists of the Senate (33 members; 22 principal chiefs and 11 other members appointed by the ruling party) and the Assembly (120 seats, 80 by direct popular vote and 40 by proportional vote; members elected by popular vote for five-year terms); note: number of seats in the Assembly rose from 80 to 120 in the May 2002 election.

Elections: last held February 17, 2007 (next to be held in 2012).

Election results: percent of vote by party — N/A; seats by party — LCD 61, NIP 21, ABC 17, LWP 10, ACP 4, BNP 3, other 4.

Political parties: Alliance of Congress Parties or ACP; All Basotho Convention or ABC; Basotholand African Congress or BAC; Basotho Congress Party or BCP; Basotho National Party or BNP; Kopanang Basotho Party or KPB; Lesotho Congress for Democracy or LCD (the governing party); Lesotho Education Party or LEP; Lesotho Workers Party or LWP; Marematlou Freedom Party or MFP; National Independent Party or NIP; New Lesotho Freedom Party or NLFP; Popular Front for Democracy or PFD; Sefate Democratic Union or SDU; Social Democratic Party of SDP.

STATUS AND PROGRESS OF WOMEN

In 1965, one year before Lesotho became a sovereign state, it nominated its first woman to parliament, and in 1993, elected its first woman to parliament. Since November 1999, a woman, Ntlhoi Motsamai, has been the presiding officer of the National Assembly.[21] The Inter-Parliamentary Union lists Lesotho as making progress with the number of women in parliament. In 1995, three women served out of 65 seats (4.62 percent), and in 2006, 14 out of 120 (11.67 percent) served, making an improvement of 7.05 percent.[22] Queen Regent "MaMohato Tabitha" Masentle Lerotholi served twice, in 1970 and again in 1996.[23]

Lesotho's government is a democratic system with the rule of law, regular free and fair elections, and a balance of power. The government consists of a Constitutional Monarch, the Executive, the Legislature and the Judiciary. Politics are male-dominated. Parliaments have had a minimum representation of women since gaining independence in 1966.[24]

"Backed by a democratic mandate, Chapter II and III of the Constitution, the government is challenged by gender inequities and inequalities," Lesotho reported to the African Union in 2006.[25] The government adopted a Gender and Development Policy in 2003 to address the many challenges. The policy specified one of the objectives was to promote equal opportunities and participation in politics and decision-making.

Although women do participate in the political process, the number of women in the central committees of political parties is low. Parties do not address issues related to women nor do they encourage women to participate. Of 17 members in the ruling party, the Lesotho Congress for Democracy, women are seven (41 percent), compared to 10 (59 percent) men. In the main opposition party, the Basutoland National Party, women total six (32 percent) out of 19, compared to 13 (68 percent) men.[26] By 2005, the ruling party had put into effect a policy requiring a minimum of 30 percent of the positions in the central committee to be women.[27]

The 2005 National Assembly had the largest representation of women since the first parliament in 1966, and the speaker is female. Its membership is comprised of 17 (14 percent) women out of 120, compared to 103 (86 percent) men. In the Senate, 11 (33 percent) members of 33 (with one post vacancy) are women, compared to 21 (64 percent) men.[28] Progress in 2005 evidenced in the promotion of a female assistant minister to minister, increasing the total number of female ministers to six compared to 11 males.[29]

In 2003, the Electoral Institute of Southern Africa (EISA) recommended that lack of parity be resolved through institutionalizing the inequity and inequality by reforming the standing orders and increasing the number of women in parliament through quota as well as other societal gender sensitization efforts. The 2002 general elections registration recorded 57 percent women and 43 percent men voting population. But in reality, women were faced with more challenges due to socialization, lack of control of resources and gender roles.[30]

In spite of setting up a structure whereby gender equity and equality can be attained, the report acknowledged one of four challenges will be equal participation of women and men in the 2007 national elections.[31]

Republic of Malawi

BACKGROUND[32]

Location: Southern Africa, east of Zambia
Population: 13,013,926
Per Capita Income: $600 (2006 est.)

Government type: multiparty democracy.

Independence: July 6, 1964 (from U.K.). Malawi was established in 1891 as the British protectorate of Nyasaland. The country became independent in 1964. President Hastings Kamuzu Banda led the country for three decades with one-party rule. In 1994, Malawi held multiparty elections under a provisional constitution which came into full effect in 1995. The current President, Bingu wa Mutharika, was elected in May 2004 following Banda's failed attempt to amend the constitution to permit another term. Consequently, Mutharika struggled to assert his authority against Banda. Mutharika left the political party on whose ticket he was elected and started his own party, the Democratic Progressive Party (DPP). Although Mutharika wages anti-corruption campaigns, increasing corruption, population growth, increasing pressure on agricultural lands, and the spread of HIV/AIDS are major problems for the country.

Constitution: May 18, 1994.

Legislature: unicameral National Assembly (193 seats; members elected by popular vote to serve five-year terms).

Elections: last held May 20, 2004 (next to be held May 2009).

Election results: percent of vote by party — N/A; seats by party — UDF 74, MCP 60, Independents 24, RP 16, others 18, vacancies 1.

Political parties: Alliance for Democracy or AFORD; Congress for National Unity or CONU; Democratic Progressive Party or DPP; Malawi Congress Party or MCP; Malawi Democratic Party or MDP; Malawi Forum for Unity and Development or MAFUNDE; Mgwirizano Coalition or MC (coalition of MAFUNDE, MDP, MGODE, NUP, PETRA, PPM, RP); Movement for Genuine Democratic Change or MGODE; National Democratic Alliance or NDA; National Unity Party or NUP; People's Progressive Movement or PPM; People's Transformation Movement or PETRA; Republican Party or RP; United Democratic Front or UDF.

STATUS AND PROGRESS OF WOMEN

The same year Malawi became a sovereign state, it elected its first woman to parliament.[33] The Inter-Parliamentary Union lists Malawi as making progress with the number of women in parliament. In 1995, ten women served out of 177 seats (5.65 percent), and in 2006, 26 out of 191 (13.61 percent) served, making an improvement of 7.96 percent.[34]

The United Nations Economic Commission for Africa's (ECA) *Beijing+5* report found Malawi's national machinery worked very hard to put more women in positions of power in the 1999 elections. Organizations that helped included the Women's Voice, the Association of Malawian Professional Women, the National Democratic Institute and the Parliamentary Women's Caucus. These organizations emphasized civic and voter education that targeted women. Their efforts resulted in 16 women entering the 193-seat National Assembly compared to the previous nine women out of 177 seats after the 1994 general elections. ECA states that Malawi still fell short of the target of 30 percent of seats for women.[35] In 2002, Malawi had 17 women in parliament out of 106 (16.0 percent) and in 2004, the number of women increased to 27.[36]

The United Nations Development Program (UNDP) civic education project in Malawi contends their efforts have resulted in a 60 percent increase in women's participation in decision-making positions, especially in the boards of parastatals (state-related enterprises). A number of women became chairpersons. Progress is slower in the civil service.[37]

At the time of Malawi's *Beijing+10* report, major progress was limited to formulation of policies, programs and strategies at the national level. Institutional development and strengthening at both national and district levels was still in process. These aspects were largely responsible for the constraints experienced.[38]

The Malawi government developed and implemented a National Platform for Action in 1997. This platform is described as "a powerful agenda for the empowerment of women."[39] The plan requires the integration of gender perspectives in all policies and programs. Other measures ensuring parity are the National Gender Policy and the 1995 Constitution.

Statistics at the time of the report show a generally low participation of women in government structures. From 1994 to 2004, women held high-level cabinet positions only in the year of 2004, 19 in all. In other cabinet positions and parliament women gained positions as follows:

MALAWI: WOMEN IN THE CABINET AND PARLIAMENT, 1994–2004

	1994			1999			2004		
	Total	Women	%	Total	Women	%	Total	Women	%
Cabinet	22	2	9	46	8	17	27	6	22.2
Parliament	171	9	5.2	193	17	8.8	186	27	14.5[40]

Malawi has made great effort in gender mainstreaming, but the report indicated there were constraints. These challenges include: the constitution did not provide a quota system; sabbatical leave was not provided for women who wish to join politics; operational legislation to the constitutional provision on women's rights as in the Bill of Rights is not enacted; and change is needed in attitudes about women's being qualified. Malawi wrote that the way forward included continuing the many things the government was already doing, such as gender mainstreaming; gender planning and budget guidelines; gender auditing tools to monitor progress; implementation of the national, regional and international instruments; and providing support mechanisms for women in decision-making positions through training.[41]

Republic of Mauritius

BACKGROUND[42]

Location: Southern Africa, island in the Indian Ocean, east of Madagascar
Population: 1,240,827 (July 2006 est.)
Per Capita Income: $13,500 (2006 est.)

Government type: parliamentary democracy.

Independence: March 12, 1968 (from U.K.). Arab and Malay sailors knew about the Southern African island of Mauritius in the 10th century. The Portuguese explored the island in 1505, after which the Dutch, French, and British held the island until independence was attained in 1968. A stable democracy with regular free elections and a positive human rights record, Mauritius has attracted considerable foreign investment and has earned one of Africa's highest per capita incomes.

Constitution: March 12, 1968; amended March 12, 1992.

Legislature: unicameral National Assembly (70 seats; 62 elected by popular vote, 8 appointed by the election commission to give representation to various ethnic minorities; members serve five-year terms).

Elections: last held on July 3, 2005 (next to be held in 2010).

Election results: percent of vote by party — N/A; seats by party — AS 38, MSM/MMM 22, OPR 2; appointed seats — AS 4, MSM/MMM 2, OPR 2.

Political parties: Alliance Sociale or AS; Hizbullah; Mauritian Labor Party or MLP; Mauritian Militant Movement or MMM (in coalition with MSM); Mauritian Social Democrat Party or PMSD; Militant Socialist Movement or MSM (the governing party); Rodrigues Movement or MR; Rodrigues Peoples Organization or OPR.

STATUS AND PROGRESS OF WOMEN

Mauritius elected its first woman to parliament in June 1975.[43] The Inter-Parliamentary Union lists Mauritius as making progress with the number of women in parliament. In 1995, two women served out of 70 seats (2.86 percent), and in 2006, 12 out of 70 (17.14 percent) served, making an improvement of 14.28 percent.[44]

The Ministry of Women's Rights, Child Development and Family Welfare was created in 1982, but it wasn't until 1992 that Mauritius became a republic. The head of state is the president. The amended constitution stated that political power remained with parliament. The unicameral National Assembly is composed of up to 70 deputies.[45] Although the Sex Discrimination Act had been in effect since 2002, in 1995, the constitution was amended to add a guarantee of nondiscrimination in terms of gender, by adding the word "sex" in the definition of discriminatory practices had been included.[46]

Men and women may vote at the age of eighteen and can be elected as members of the Legislative Assembly. Very few women stand as candidates in the legislative, municipal and village elections. Although recommendations were that political parties should provide extra help and support to female candidates, no improvement has occurred in women's participation in political and public life.[47]

But women are not totally absent from positions. The elections of July 2005 brought an increase in the number of women holding elected offices. Women are two out of 20 ministers (10 percent), the Ministry of Women's Rights, Child Development, Family Welfare and Consumer Protection and the Ministry of Social Security, National Solidarity, Senior Citizens Welfare and Reform Institution. In parliament, women held 12 out of 70 memberships (17.1 percent), compared to only four in the previous election.[48] Of urban councillors, women held 16 out of 116 positions (13.8 percent), and of rural councillors, women held 89 out of 1488 (6.0 percent) positions. In the public sector Mauritius had already achieved the required increase, and in the judiciary, the country had affirmative action to have a more equitable representation.[49]

Republic of Mozambique

BACKGROUND

Location: Southeastern Africa, bordering the Mozambique Channel, between South Africa and Tanzania

Population: 19,686,505

Per Capita Income: $1,500 (2006 est.)

Government type: republic.

Independence: June 25, 1975 (from Portugal). Almost five centuries as a Portuguese colony came to a close with independence in 1975. Large-scale emigration by whites, economic dependence on South Africa, a severe drought, and a prolonged civil war hindered the country's development. The ruling Front for the Liberation of Mozambique (FRELIMO) party formally abandoned Marxism in 1989, and a new constitution the following year provided for multiparty elections and a free market economy. A UN-negotiated peace agreement between FRELIMO and rebel Mozambique National Resistance (RENAMO) forces ended the fighting in 1992. In December 2004, Mozambique underwent a delicate transition as Joaquim Chissano stepped down after 18 years in office. His newly elected successor, Armando Emilio Guebuza, has promised to continue the sound economic policies that have encouraged foreign investment.

Constitution: November 30, 1990.

Legislature: unicameral Assembly of the Republic or Assembleia da Republica (250 seats; members are directly elected by popular vote on a secret ballot to serve five-year terms).

Elections: last held December 1–2, 2004 (next to be held December 2009).

Election results: percent of vote by party — FRELIMO 62 percent, RENAMO 29.7 percent; seats by party — FRELIMO 160, RENAMO 90.

Political parties: Front for the Liberation of Mozambique (Frente de Liberatacao de Mocambique) or FRELIMO; Mozambique National Resistance-Electoral Union (Resistencia Nacional Mocambicana-Uniao Eleitoral) or RENAMO-UE.

STATUS AND PROGRESS OF WOMEN

In December 1977, Mozambique elected the first woman to parliament. In February 2004, the country elected Luisa Diogo prime minister.[50] The Inter-Parliamentary Union lists

Mozambique as making progress with the number of women in parliament. In 1995, 63 women served out of 250 seats (25.20 percent), and in 2006, 87 out of 250 (34.80 percent) served, making an improvement of 9.60 percent.[51] Mozambique has a 34.8 percent voluntary party quota.[52]

Although a post-conflict country, in 1990 the country provided for equal rights of women and men in its constitution. Mozambique has also ratified the Convention on Elimination of All Forms of Discrimination Against Women (CEDAW). In 1998, the ruling party had reserved for women 30 percent of the seats in assemblies on all levels of government.[53] The United Nations Commission for Africa (ECA) report found Mozambique had introduced affirmative action and quotas.[54]

Mozambique's *Beijing+10* report indicated institutional progress: in 2000, the Ministry of Women and Social Welfare Coordination, and in 2001, a National Directorate for Women, were founded; in 2002, a National Plan for the Advancement of Women, and in 2003, the Gender National Strategic Policy, were drafted.[55]

At the time of the report, Mozambique had eight women in central executive power: three ministers, representing 25.3 percent of the total universe of the 42 cabinet members. Some women were in positions traditionally reserved for men such as Planning and Finance and Mineral Resources and Energy. For the first time in the country's history, a woman is a prime minister. Women represented 31.2 percent of the total members of parliament.[56]

Reasons for lack of participation of women included low schooling level; cultural barriers; attitudes and traditional practices limiting women to domestic activities; communications; and gender stereotyping.[57]

Republic of Namibia

BACKGROUND[58]

Location: Southern Africa, bordering the South Atlantic Ocean, between Angola and South Africa

Population: 2,044,147

Per Capita Income: $7,400 (2006 est.)

Government type: republic.

Independence: March 21, 1990 (from South African mandate). South Africa occupied the German colony of South-West Africa during World War I, and as a mandate, administered it until after World War II, when it annexed the territory. The area was named Namibia after the Marxist South-West Africa People's Organization (SWAPO) guerrilla group launched a war of independence in 1966. In 1988 South Africa agreed to end its administration in accordance with a UN peace plan. Namibia won its independence in 1990 and has been governed by SWAPO since. Sam Nujoma led the country during its first 14 years of self-rule. In November 2004, Hifikepunye Pohamba was elected president in a landslide victory.

Constitution: ratified February 9, 1990; effective March 12, 1990.

Legislature: bicameral legislature consists of the National Council (26 seats; 2 members are chosen from each regional council to serve six-year terms) and the National Assembly (72 seats; members are elected by popular vote to serve five-year terms).

Elections: National Council — elections for regional councils, to determine members of the National Council, held November 29–30, 2004 (next to be held November 2010); National Assembly — last held November 15–16, 2004 (next to be held November 2009).

Election results: National Council — percent of vote by party — SWAPO 89.7 percent, UDF 4.7 percent, NUDO 2.8 percent, DTA 1.9 percent; seats by party — SWAPO 24, UDF 1, DTA 1; National Assembly — percent of vote by party — SWAPO 76.1 percent, COD 7.3 percent, DTA 5.1 percent, NUDO 4.2 percent, UDF 3.6 percent, RP 1.9 percent, MAG 0.8 percent, other 1.0 percent; seats by party — SWAPO 55, COD 5, DTA 4, NUDO 3, UDF 3, RP 1, MAG 1; note: the National Council is primarily an advisory body.

Political parties: Congress of Democrats or COD; Democratic Turnhalle Alliance of Namibia or DTA; Monitor Action Group or MAG; National Democratic Movement for Change or NamDMC; National Unity Democratic Organization or NUDO; Republican Party or RP; South West Africa National Union or SWANU; South West Africa People's Organization or SWAPO; United Democratic Front or UDF.

STATUS AND PROGRESS OF WOMEN

Namibia's constitution upholds the equality of men and women and prohibits gender discrimination. Affirmative action policies are in effect. After Namibia gained independence in 1990, efforts were made to make all laws gender sensitive and a Law Reform and Development Commission was established.[59] The Inter-Parliamentary Union reports that Namibia elected the first woman to Parliament in November 1989.[60] The IPU lists Namibia as making progress with the number of women in parliament. In 1995, 13 women served out of 72 seats (18.06 percent), and in 2006, 21 out of 78 (26.92 percent). The improvement was 8.87 percent.[61]

Electoral law requires that 25 percent of local government candidates be women. The United Nations Economic Commission for Africa (ECA) reported in 2005 that in the 1992 and 1998 elections women won 32 percent and 40 percent of the seats. The Married Persons Equality Act passed in 1996, making spouses equal before the law. Men were no longer heads of households and married women could have their own bank accounts.[62]

ECA's earlier report stated, "After Namibia's elections in 1998, 15 women out of ... 78 legislators ... were elected, amounting to about 19.2 percent. While this signified a reduction from the previous elections there was, however, some improvement at the local level. Namibia has implemented quotas for its 11 local councils at the regional and local levels. In the 1998 election, 158 or 40 percent of the 397 filled seats were taken by women."[63] Namibia's country report to the African Union in 2006 stated that Namibia adopted its National Gender Policy in 1997 and a National Gender Plan of Action in 1998. These two national documents addressed ten critical areas of concern of which gender power and decision making was one.[64]

The distribution of women in Namibia's positions was: one out of 13 regional governors, 136 of 329 local counselors, five out of 28 mayors and 16 out of 27 deputy mayors. Further, Namibia set up a gender and development distribution center and began to develop a directory of women in decision-making. The country also had introduced quotas.[65]

Further, the country is faced with a dependence on donors due to its lack of human, material and financial shortages; the need for research to make informed decisions; the prevalence of HIV/AIDS; a lack of a specific gender budget; and accessible credit systems for women.[66]

In 2005, women represented a low of 23 percent in parliament, but a high of 46 percent in civil service. National gender policy calls for the Department of Women's Affairs to oversee gender equality in all aspects of public life. In 1997, Namibia ratified the Convention on the Elimination of All Forms of Discrimination Against Women.[67]

In 2006, Namibia reported, "there has been an increase in the number of women members of parliament, from 20 percent to 27 percent. This has been largely contributed by the increase in the number of women members of the National Council from two during the previous elections to seven currently. It is important also to note that there have been major new developments with the new parliament — the appointment of a woman Deputy Prime Minister, Deputy-Speaker of the National Assembly, Minister of Justice and Attorney-General, the Minister of Finance and the Deputy Chairperson of the National Council."[68]

Likewise, Namibia has experienced greater improvements at regional and local levels with the increase in the number of women regional councilors from 5 to 13, and governors from one to three. Women in local authority increased from 42 percent to 45 percent. Local government is Namibia's only area that has gone far beyond the Southern African Development Community (SADC) minimum target of 30 percent women representation by 2005.[69]

In addition, the Namibia Defence Force (NDF) has been very successful in implementing the United Nations Resolution 1325. NDF has deployed women in peacekeeping operations. The number of women has steadily increased in the last four years.[70]

In spite of Namibia's great strides, the African Development Bank report of 2006 stated that women remain underrepresented in decision-making positions and challenges remain to women's greater participation in governance and decision-making.[71]

Republic of South Africa

BACKGROUND[72]

Location: Southern Africa, at the southern tip of the continent of Africa
Population: 44,187,637
Per Capita Income: $13,000 (2006 est.)
Government type: republic.
Independence: May 31, 1910 (from U.K.). The British took over the Cape of Good Hope area in 1806. Many Dutch settlers, known as the Boers, migrated north and established republics. The discovery of diamonds in 1867 and gold in 1886 stimulated wealth and immigration, but increased the subjugation of natives. The Boers were defeated in the Boer War (1899–1902). The resulting Union of South Africa operated under a policy of apartheid, the separate development of the races. In the 1990s, apartheid politically ended and brought black majority rule. South Africa became a republic in 1961 following an October 1960 referendum.
Constitution: December 1996; certified and signed and entered into effect on February 4, 1997; it is being implemented in phases.
Legislature: bicameral Parliament consisting of the National Assembly (400 seats; members are elected by popular vote under a system of proportional representation to serve five-year terms) and the National Council of Provinces (90 seats; 10 members elected by each of the nine provincial legislatures for five-year terms; has special powers to protect regional interests, including the safeguarding of cultural and linguistic traditions among ethnic minorities); note: following the implementation of the new constitution on February 4, 1997, the former Senate was disbanded and replaced by the National Council of Provinces with essentially no change in membership and party affiliations, although the new institution's responsibilities have been changed somewhat by the new constitution.

Elections: National Assembly and National Council of Provinces — last held April 14, 2004 (next to be held 2009).

Election results: National Assembly — percent of vote by party — ANC 69.7 percent, DA 12.4 percent, IFP 7 percent, UDM 2.3 percent, NNP 1.7 percent, ACDP 1.6 percent, other 5.3 percent; seats by party — ANC 279, DA 50, IFP 28, UDM 9, NNP 7, ACDP 6, other 21; National Council of Provinces — percent of vote by party — N/A; seats by party — N/A.

Political parties: African Christian Democratic Party or ACDP; African National Congress or ANC; Democratic Alliance or DA; Freedom Front Plus or FF+; Inkatha Freedom Party or IFP; Pan-Africanist Congress or PAC; United Democratic Movement or UDM.

STATUS AND PROGRESS OF WOMEN

South Africa elected its first woman to parliament in 1933. The following women have served as presiding officers within parliament or one of its chambers: Baleka Mbete, National Assembly since 2004; N. Pandore, National Council of Provinces from 1999 to 2004; and F.N. Ginwala, National Assembly from 1994 to 1999 and 1999 to 2004.[73] South Africa had women presiding officers in both houses in May 2000 and July 1995, and in one of their houses in January 2005 and January 2006.[74] The Inter-Parliamentary Union lists South Africa as a country that has made progress in that in 1995, 100 women held seats out 400 members (25 percent), and in 2006, 131 women out of 400 (32.75 percent), making a 7.75 percent increase.[75] South Africa is a post-conflict country whose representation of women increased dramatically from 2.7 percent to 25 percent in one election. In 2005, women represented 32.8 percent of the voluntary party quotas.[76]

The United Nations Economic Commission for Africa's (ECA) first report in 2001 found that South Africa had developed a national plan of action to implement the Beijing and Dakar platforms. South Africa's constitution provides for affirmative action to increase the number of women in positions. The country also had introduced quotas. In the area of political participation, the country showed 20 percent of parliamentary seats and 50 percent of local governing council seats were reserved for women.[77]

In 1990, South Africa provided for equal rights of women and men in its constitution. The country has also ratified the Convention on Elimination of All Forms of Discrimination Against Women (CEDAW).[78]

At the time of the *Beijing+5* report, South Africa had the highest representation of women in the national assembly on the continent; 19 percent of local government elected representatives in the 1995 elections were women and 14 percent of positions at the executive level were held by women; and 13 percent of foreign heads of mission were women.[79]

At the time of the *Beijing+10* report, less than one-third (31.03 percent) of the national departments complied with the Gender Policy Framework for Women's Empowerment and Gender Equality. In the cabinet, women represented nine out of 27 ministers (33 percent). Women advanced significantly on the national level. The greatest improvement was on the parliamentary level even though no South African law specified a quota for women in parliament or the cabinet; the report indicates that the lack of such a law is a concern and a need exists to strengthen the capacity of the state to deliver. Women also face the challenges of HIV/AIDS; socialization of children into unequal gender roles; patriarchy; polygyny; aspects of discrimination in religion and law; distortion of culture; virginity testing, female genital mutilation and issues related to succession and inheritance.[80]

During the post-apartheid period, South Africa's world ranking in women in parliament significantly increased from 141st to seventh. The former speaker was a woman. Many government bodies have been created to promote and monitor gender equality within its institutions, such as the Office on the Status of Women in the office of the president, the Commission on Gender Equality, and the Standing Committee on the Quality of Life and Status of Women in parliament.[81]

ECA's 2005 *Governance Report* revealed a positive number of women in government positions. The executive branch has women in charge in of the ministries of foreign affairs, land affairs, health and minerals and energy. Women hold 137 seats of the approximately 350 members of the National Assembly. Women hold nine chairs of committees, 15 whips and two presiding officers. Eighteen women are representatives on the National Council of Provinces, nine ministers in the provincial cabinets, and six deputies.[82]

South Africa's report on its implementation of the *Solemn Declaration on Gender Equality in Africa* stated: "In 2005, South Africa appointed its first female deputy president. Therefore, overall, there is a 43.33 percent representation of women in the cabinet. There are three women appointed as office-bearers of the National Assembly, namely the speaker, the deputy speaker and the house chairperson. They constitute 37.5 percent of office bearers in the National Assembly. The deputy chairperson and the chairperson of committees for the National Council of Provinces (NCOP) are women. They constitute 33.33 percent of the office bearers in the NCOP. Twenty-nine (28.15 percent) women were appointed as ambassadors, high commissioners and consul-generals in 2006."[83]

Kingdom of Swaziland

BACKGROUND[84]

Location: Southern Africa, between Mozambique and South Africa
Population: 1,136,334
Per Capita Income: $5,500 (2006 est.)

Government type: monarchy.

Independence: September 6, 1968 (from U.K.). The British granted autonomy for the Swazis of southern Africa in the late 19th century and in 1968 independence was granted. Student and labor unrest during the 1990s forced King Mswati III, the world's last absolute monarch, to allow political reform and greater democracy. In recent years, he has lapsed on these promises. Swaziland recently surpassed Botswana as the country with the world's highest known rates of HIV/AIDS infection.

Constitution: signed by the King in July 2005; went into effect in February 2006.

Legislature: bicameral Parliament or Libandla, a legislative body, consists of the Senate (30 seats; 10 appointed by the House of Assembly and 20 appointed by the monarch; members serve five-year terms) and the House of Assembly (65 seats; 10 appointed by the monarch and 55 elected by popular vote; members serve five-year terms).

Elections: House of Assembly — last held October 18, 2003 (next to be held October 2008).

Election results: House of Assembly — balloting is done on a nonparty basis; candidates for election are nominated by the local council of each constituency and for each constituency the three candidates with the most votes in the first round of voting are narrowed to a single winner by a second round.

Political parties: The status of political parties, previously banned, is unclear under the new 2006 Constitution and currently being debated; the following are considered political associations: African United Democratic Party or AUDP; Imbokodvo National Movement or INM; Ngwane National Liberatory Congress or NNLC; People's United Democratic Movement or PUDEMO.

STATUS AND PROGRESS OF WOMEN

The United Nations Economic Commission for Africa's (ECA) *Beijing+5* report saw slight improvement in women's participation in decision-making in Swaziland. Power-sharing sensitization campaigns progressed.[85] Obstacles encountered included the patriarchal structure of society, socialization and culture, and a lack of support systems, research, policy and quota systems. Swaziland advocated a 30 percent commitment in women's participation by 2005 and to host the global network of women in politics.[86]

Swaziland's *Beijing+10* report states, "In Swaziland, women are generally underrepresented in positions of power and decision-making."[87] However, the Gender Coordination Unit conducted training of trainers on women in politics and decision making.

In 1972, Swaziland nominated and elected the first women to parliament.[88] The Inter-Parliamentary Union lists Swaziland as a country that has made progress in representation of women in parliament. In 1995, two women held seats out of 65 (3.08 percent), and in 2006, seven women did so out of 65 (10.77 percent), showing an increase of 7.69 percent.[89] The IPU lists two women in the section Queens/Grand Duchesses: Dzeliwe Shongwe, who served as a Queen Regent from August 1982 to August 1983; and Ntombi Thwala, who served from August 1983 to March 1986.[90] Ntombi replaced Dzeliwe as a Queen Regent. When Ntombi's son became king in 1986, she became the Indovukazi (Queen Mother) and joint head of state.[91]

In 2004, three women held positions on the 16-member cabinet. Overall representation for women came to 19 percent. The deputy speaker in the House of Assembly was a woman and the deputy president in the Senate was a woman.[92]

A draft constitution worked to increase women's participation even though the prevailing social and cultural practices acted as constraints. Sensitizing society on the importance of this issue was a challenge, as was the intensification of voter and civic education with the aim of influencing the 2008 elections. A Women's Parliamentary Caucus was suggested along with promoting networking and lobbying for affirmative action. The government's Gender Coordination Unit and various profiles and proposals on gender for possible donors demonstrates good-faith efforts. The work is challenged by lack of staffing, capacity, financial resources and coordination.[93]

The government of Swaziland evaluates gender progress thus: "Gender in Swaziland is no longer an issue. In Swaziland, women are well represented in parliament and in the public service and the private sector. There has been enough sensitization on this subject, and Government created a unit in the Ministry of Home Affairs to sensitize the populace on gender issues."[94]

Republic of Zambia

BACKGROUND[95]

Location: Southern Africa, east of Angola
Population: 11,502,010
Per Capita Income: $1,000 (2006 est.)
    Government type: republic.

Independence: October 24, 1964 (from U.K.). The territory of Northern Rhodesia was administered by the [British] South Africa Company from 1891 until it was taken over by the U.K. in 1923. The name was changed to Zambia upon independence. In the 1980s and 1990s, declining copper prices and a prolonged drought hurt the economy. Elections in 1991 brought an end to one-party rule, but the subsequent vote in 1996 saw blatant harassment of opposition parties. The election in 2001 was marked by administrative problems. Three parties filed a legal petition challenging the election of ruling party candidate Levy Mwanawasa. The new president established an anticorruption task force in 2002, but the government has yet to make a prosecution. The Zambian leader was reelected in 2006 in a free and fair election.

Constitution: August 24, 1991; amended in 1996 to establish presidential term limits.

Legislature: unicameral National Assembly (158 seats; 150 members are elected by popular vote, eight members are appointed by the president to serve five-year terms).

Elections: last held September 28, 2006 (next to be held in 2011).

Election results: percent of vote by party — N/A; seats by party — MMD 72, PF 44, UDA 27, ULP 2, NDF 1, independents 2; seats not determined 2.

Political parties: All Peoples Congress Party; Forum for Democracy and Development or FDD; Heritage Party or HP; Liberal Progressive Front or LPF; Movement for Multiparty Democracy or MMD; Patriotic Front or PF; Party of Unity for Democracy and Development or PUDD; Reform Party; United Liberal Party; United National Independence Party or UNIP; United Party for National Development or UPND; Zambia Democratic Congress or ZADECO; Zambian Republican Party or ZRP.

STATUS AND PROGRESS OF WOMEN

The Inter-Parliamentary Union reports that Zambia elected and nominated the first women to Parliament in January 1964.[96] The IPU lists Zambia as making progress with the number of women in parliament. In 1995, ten women served out of 150 seats (6.67 percent), and in 2006, 20 out of 158 (12.66 percent). The improvement was 5.99 percent.[97]

Although Zambia's *Beijing+10* review stated that the country had not yet reached the 30 percent target of women in decision-making positions, Zambia had been making steady progress. Women NGOs had intensified their efforts by conducting training. The resulting reality was that women's interests "may not be properly represented in organizations where the majority are overwhelmingly men."[98]

In spite of the government's efforts, women have not effectively participated in the decision-making process. Women are underrepresented at all levels of government. There has been a steady increase of women in parliament since 1988, but their numbers remain low. In 1991, women held 6.7 percent of parliament seats, and in 2004, they held 12 percent.[99]

Zambia reported five women out of 20 cabinet ministers (25 percent), the deputy level women represented 8.9 percent, and permanent secretaries, 19 percent.[100]

ZAMBIA: PERCENTAGE OF WOMEN IN DECISION-MAKING
POSITIONS FOR SELECTED POSITIONS, 1997–2003[101]

Positions	1997	1998	1999	2000	2001	2002	2003
Parliament	10.1	10.1	10.1	10.1	12.0	12.0	12.0
Cabinet	4.2	4.2	4.2	4.2	15.0	19.2	25.0
Deputy Ministers	9.8	7.3	7.3	7.3	8.6	8.6	9.8

Constraints Zambia encountered included illiteracy; gender-biased cultural beliefs and behaviors; women's lack of resources, primarily financial; lack of support from political parties and electoral processes; and poor media coverage.[102]

At the time of the report, Zambia undertook the following measures to enhance the participation of women in decision-making: Strategic Plan of Action for the National Gender Policy, formulation of the Electoral Reforms Technical Committee to review the Electoral Act, creation of the Committee on Legal Affairs, Governance, Human Rights and Gender, establishment of a special program at the University of Zambia, and sensitization programs that target women and political parties.[103]

To further enhance the participation of women, Zambia recommended the following measures be undertaken by government and stakeholders: incorporate gender in concerns in the constitution; engender the electoral process; and put in place affirmative action measures and adopt into national law all conventions and international instruments.[104]

Republic of Zimbabwe

BACKGROUND[105]

Location: Southern Africa, between South Africa and Zambia
Population: 12,236,805
Per Capita Income: $2,000 (2006 est.)
Government type: parliamentary democracy.
Independence: April 18, 1980 (from U.K.). The United Kingdom annexed Southern Rhodesia from the [British] South Africa Company in 1923. The constitution in 1961 favored whites in power. The U.K. did not recognize the government declaration of independence in 1965. Instead, the U.K. demanded more complete voting rights for the black African majority in the country (then called Rhodesia). The country gained its independence as Zimbabwe in 1980.
Constitution: December 1979.
Legislature: bicameral Parliament consists of a House of Assembly (150 seats; 120 elected by popular vote for five-year terms, 12 nominated by the president, 10 occupied by traditional chiefs chosen by their peers, and eight occupied by provincial governors appointed by the president) and a Senate (66 seats; 50 elected by popular vote for a five-year term, six nominated by the president, 10 nominated by the Council of Chiefs).
Elections: House of Assembly last held March 31, 2005 (next to be held in 2010), Senate last held November 26, 2005 (next to be held in 2010).
Election results: House of Assembly — percent of vote by party — ZANU-PF 59.6 percent, MDC 39.5 percent, other 0.9 percent; seats by party — ZANU-PF 78, MDC 41, independents 1; Senate — percent of vote by party — ZANU-PF 73.7 percent, MDC 20.3 percent, other 4.4 percent, independents 1.6 percent; seats by party — ZANU-PF 43, MDC 7.
Political parties: African National Party or ANP; Movement for Democratic Change or MDC; Peace Action is Freedom for All or PAFA; United Parties; United People's Party; Zimbabwe African National Union-Ndonga or ZANU-Ndonga; Zimbabwe African National Union-Patriotic Front or ZANU-PF; Zimbabwe African Peoples Union or ZAPU; Zimbabwe Youth in Alliance or ZIYA.

STATUS AND PROGRESS OF WOMEN

Before Zimbabwe gained independence, gender parity in decision-making was never on the agenda, and women were not organized. All elections since 1985 have been marred by violence.[106] Zimbabwe's 1996 report to the Convention on the Elimination of All Forms of Discrimination against Women (CEDAW) stated that no legal barrier existed to women's participation in public and political life. The Constitution and Electoral Act of 1990 enables women to vote and stand for election. The Sex Discrimination Removal Act of 1980 allows women to hold public office and participate in public functions. Women do not become candidates as often as men and frequently women vote for men. Custom and tradition limit women's participation.[107]

In March 1980, Zimbabwe's first women were elected and nominated to Parliament, and in November 2005, Edna Madzongwe became the presiding officer of the Senate.[108] From 1980 to 1995, total membership of women in parliament steadily increased with percentages almost doubling from 7.9 to 14. (See the table below.) From 1990 to 1995, 17 women held seats in parliament out of 150.[109] The Inter-Parliamentary Union shows slightly higher figures, but those figures do not alter the fact that Zimbabwe's parliament shows progress in its lower house, House of Assembly, in that in 1995, 22 women held seats out of 150 (14.67 percent), which increased to 24 seats out of 150 (16 percent) in 2006.[110] The *Beijing+10* report indicated that the proportion fell to 11 percent in the fourth parliament (2000–2005). The target set by the Southern African Development Community (SADC) was to reach 30 percent by 2005.[111]

ZIMBABWE: PARTICIPATION IN LEGISLATIVE BODIES, 1980–1995[112]

	1980–1984	1985–1990	1990–1995
HOUSE OF ASSEMBLY	100	150	150
Men	92	133	129
Women	8	17	21
Percent Women	8.0	11.3	14
SENATE	40	—	—
Men	37	—	—
Women	3	—	—
Percent Women	7.5	—	—
TOTAL PARLIAMENTARIANS	140	150	150
Men	129	133	129
Women	11	17	21
Percent Women	7.9	11.3	14

In the executive offices, progress is mixed. Ministers, including Ministers of State, show two women and 25 men in 1985, three to 29 in 1990 and two to 21 in 1995. Deputy Ministers show two women to 14 men in 1985, six to 67 in 1990 and four to 11 in 1995. Governor/Resident Ministers show no women and seven men in 1985, and one woman and 7 men in 1990 and 1995.[113]

Participation in political party decision-making bodies reveal that from 1985 to 1989 in the Politburo one woman out of a total of 15 served; from 1990 to 1994, two out of 16, and in 1994, 3 women out of 24 served. On the Central Committee 24 women served out of a total of 90 members from 1985 to 1989, no data were listed for the period 1990 to 1994, and 31 women out of 180 served in 1994.[114]

On the international level, women have held high posts, but in limited numbers. In 1995, four women out of a total of 33 had served as an ambassador or high commissioner; four out of 28 as ministers/counselors; four out of 30 as counselors; and six out of 52 as deputy ambassadors.[115]

In spite of progress, participation of women at the national level, in government or in political parties, remains a challenge, according to Netsai Mushonga. Male leadership determines the agenda of political parties. Many political parties are male-dominated and have policies that accommodate women, making them cosmetic. In 2005, one of the parties announced that women would stand for election in 30 percent of the constituencies. Male leadership carefully handpicked the women who were assigned to constituencies where that political party had traditionally lost.[116]

The result is that women occupy 11 percent of the positions in parliament. In the senate, women hold a better proportion of 20 percent. Mushonga adds, "the ruling party (ZANU-PF) has a quota system for women. None of the opposition political parties have a gender policy or quota system for women."[117]

At the time of the *Beijing+5* report, Zimbabwe had introduced affirmative action and quotas.[118] It had also set up a Gender Issues Department in 1997. That year it also launched a program to increase women's participation in decision making. The government initiated a National Gender policy as well. Funding from the National Machinery was at first limited, but later it helped fund a project called Gender Awareness to equip leaders to involve women in development issues.[119]

The Zimbabwe Women's Resource Centre and Network (ZWRCN) is a non-governmental organization. In 1999, the organization's Gender Budgeting Initiative (GBI) began an effort "to analyze national and local budgets for their differential impact (in terms of benefits and burden) on women, men, boys and girls and proposing interventions to promote gender equality. Gender budgeting is thus an analysis of any form of public expenditure or method of raising revenue from a gender perspective."[120]

Zimbabwe's *Beijing+10* built on the previous report and the government drew up the National Plan of Action. The Women's Parliamentary Caucus had been established and in 1997 the Women in Politics and Decision Making Project began. Zimbabwe is a signatory to a number of regional and international conventions: Convention on the Elimination of All Forms of Discrimination Against Women (CEDAW), Convention on Civil and Political Rights (CCPR), Beijing Declaration and Platform for Action, SADC Declaration on Gender and Development and its Addendum on the Prevention and Eradication of Violence Against Women and Children, and the African Union Protocol on the rights of women in Africa (2004).[121]

Zimbabwe's *Beijing+10* report stated that although government had made substantial efforts, "the number of women in politics and decision making positions has continued to decline over the years."[122] The government instituted an affirmative action (UNICEF 1995) whose target was to have women hold at least 30 percent of all public service senior posts by the year 2000. The results of that effort are shown in the table below.

ZIMBABWE: PERSONS IN EXECUTIVE OFFICE BY GENDER AND YEAR[123]

	1990		1995		2003	
	Female	Male	Female	Male	Female	Male
Ministers	3	29	2	21	4	24
Deputy Ministers	6	67	4	11	1	11
Governor/Resident Ministers	1	7	7	1	1	7

Women held 22 percent of senior civil service positions in 1997, and in 2002, they held 30 percent. The target is to reach 50 percent by 2015.[124]

In 2005, Advocacy Officer Judith Chiyangwa, Southern African Development Community Declaration on Gender and Development, the Women in Politics Support Unit, said, "A lot of work still needs to be done to increase the participation of women in politics and decision making."[125] Chiyangwa noted that the Zimbabwe's government had made efforts in increasing women's participation in politics and in decision-making positions, in particular the promotion of Mrs. Joyce Mujuru to vice president. Noted also was the increase in the number of women voted into parliament from 16 in the previous election to 21. This increase still fell short of the 30 percent target.

Zimbabwe's *Beijing+10* report would agree with Chiyangwa's conclusions in that it saw as a major challenge how to institute the quota system. The report acknowledged that existing discriminatory practices and the mindset of women to vote for men needed changing. In addition, family responsibility, lack of income, education, and self-confidence, and the inability to control their sexuality and reproductive roles prevent women from attaining high positions.[126]

Conclusion: Leadership, Power and Decision Making

> *These fundamental and demonstrable games [of the ongoing struggle of women getting into politics] notwithstanding, remain in Liberia and other parts of the world and continue to remain on the fringes of governance structures.... We are aware as a result of our fortitude and struggle [in Liberia] there are fortresses of political resistance to this new force of women leadership but we are certain that the wind of change that has hit the west coast of Africa will blow strongly.*
>
> — *Ellen Johnson-Sirleaf, president of Liberia*[1]

Women Heads of State Face Challenges and Structural Limitations

Sylvia Tamale concludes that, although change is taking place, "Eliminating hostility to women in senior political positions will be a painstakingly slow process, but inspiration can be taken from the new breeze that is blowing across our fair continent."[2]

Women sometimes have a tough time getting to the senior positions. The void at top levels of decision making is caused by challenges facing women related to political participation, reports the Inter-Parliamentary Union.[3] The search is for answers to questions like: Do women rule differently from men? What are the challenges that face women leaders? Is there more opportunity for women heads of state?[4]

These questions have a combination of answers. Structural limitations inhibit women who seek high office: sexism, discrimination, patriarchal privilege and gender-based hierarchies. To overcome these structural limitations, according to Peggy Antrobus, first, women who work in these organizations can transform them by challenging sexism and discrimination at the risk of job, status or popularity. Second, women workers and their supporters must recognize potential in women who are beginning to question patriarchal privilege and challenge gender-based hierarchies. Third, in order to promote transformational leadership within organizations, strategies such as alliance and coalition building are needed.[5]

Challenges in the 21st Century

Women in leadership positions is not a social transformation, but is in keeping with ancient history's legacy. The challenge for women in office is to be motivated to change the rules rather than play by the rules. According to Aruna Rao and David Kelleher, this challenge must be met if we are to transform our institutions to reflect and promote gender equality.[6] Yet, a challenge also exists for women who wish to be elected or appointed officials. The Inter-Parliamentary Union reports there has been incremental change overall, but there has been a slight decrease of elected heads of state and government.[7]

THE ISSUE OF POWER

In 21st-century Africa, the issues of power and women's role must be addressed. Who controls power? Who decides to share power? Who wields power?[8] Caroline Sweetman points out that because women make up half the human race, half of the leaders of humanity should be female on the ground of equity alone.[9]

Redistributing assets to women remains critical. Women have less political and social power and usually have lower incomes and less access to resources and opportunities. The United Nations Development Program's *Human Development Report 2005* noted, "Nowhere are power inequalities and their consequences more clearly displayed than for women."[10]

The World Bank's 2006 *World Development Report* states that needed actions include: "redistributing access to capital, perhaps by promoting micro-credit, strengthening women's land rights or access to jobs and welfare programs, changing affirmative action programs to break down stereotyping and improving access to the justice system."[11] Ernest Harsch believes that government policies are essential, but just as important is women's strong commitment to organize themselves to advance that is taking place all across Africa.

Statistics bear out the need for the redistribution. Paul Vallely reports, "Women work two-thirds of Africa's working hours, and produce 70 percent of its food, yet earn only 10 percent of its income, and own less than one percent of its property."[12]

MEDIA REPRESENTATION OF WOMEN

Writers' presentation of women suggests a "revaluedcultural" weapons approach. Abioseh Michael Porter, for example, describes fiction writer Chinua Achebe's[13] *Anthills of the Savannah* as a long-overdue nod to women, especially to their extraordinary, even if often unacknowledged, roles in the shaping of Africa.[14] Porter also points out the importance of linguistics in shaping views. Language manipulators, he writes, are often exploitative. Interpreters in Ahmadou Kourouma's[15] *Monnè, outrages et défis* scheme with colonialists, linguistically and otherwise, in the various forms of exploitation and degradation of the African people, especially women.[16]

Porter suggests that the authors he evaluates, Achebe and Kourouma among others, indicate concrete ways in which readers of West African literature might approach the new millennium with "revaluedcultural" weapons.[17]

My exploration of country reports reflects the literature. Poverty, media, land rights, affirmative action, health and parity issues, are all addressed by African countries in both the *Beijing+5* and *+10* reports. In countries where conflict is current or recent, the reports found that women are sometimes shut out of politics even though the law provides for equality, as happened to the women who participated in Namibia's political campaign of 1986 that led to independence.[18]

WOMEN AND CONFLICT

"Conflict has characterized the recent history of far too many African countries,"[19] writes Meredeth Turshen. Ten countries fought wars of liberation and 21 countries, including some that also engaged in wars of liberation, have engaged in civil wars. Many politically weak governments stay in power by increasing militarization, states Turshen.

War breaks down the patriarchal structure of society that devalued women. In doing so, it provides an opportunity for positive change in gender relations. Women can often enter previously barred positions because men are away fighting or due to their death.[20] But when and if men return, women are not always allowed into positions.

One role women have entered is that of peacemaking, but they have had to struggle to do so. The contributions of women peacemakers in Africa for the most part are unnoticed, writes Michael Fleshman. Governments and rebel movements dismiss women's efforts because they view war and peace to be men's work. Women are often relegated to the role of victim. He says, "women have had to fight their own battles for a seat at the peace table."[21] The only way to make certain that African women become equal partners in peace is to support their struggles for full participation in national political, economic and social life, he concludes.

The objective expressed by the NGO Akina Mama wa Afrika (AMwA) is a phenomenal ideal. When fully realized, female leaders will have created and sustained feminist space, and will thus have transformed feminism in government in Africa. The AMwA group believes their form of leadership is not based on power, but rather is "a process of inspiring ourselves and others towards the achievement of a vision, which transforms women's lives. Within this context, women should be seeking the kind of leadership which can dismantle all forms of patriarchal injustice and oppression."[22] Women are crucial on the individual and collective level, but empowerment is achieved through collective action and mobilization based on common concerns. This is not possible without creating opportunities for individuals and groups of women, "to be informed enough and angry enough to challenge the status quo and demand ... a better world."[23] So, AMwA is interested in producing leaders who are practical and serve all classes, and who do not seek their personal advancement at the expense at others. To accomplish these goals, AMwA must build a critical mass of feminist women leaders who can take Africa into the 21st century with a new agenda grounded in social justice, good governance and accountability.

QUOTAS AND AFFIRMATIVE ACTION

In 2004, Akwe Amosu and Ofeibea Quist-Arcton reported that quotas and affirmative action were still needed in Africa.[24] More than 20 countries either had legislated quotas or political parties that had voluntarily adopted them. These measures have contributed directly to the increased number of women who have accessed the legislature.[25] Electoral systems matter.[26] Gender quotas can help assure women will hold office.[27] The IPU believes that the incremental change in the past decades are the result of electoral quotas, political party commitment and will and "sustained mobilization and emphasis placed on achieving gender equality by the international community."[28] Although there are more arguments in favor of quotas and affirmative action than against, some improvements are still needed.

Conclusion

Country reports reveal that most African countries have gained independence relatively recently. When you think about their accomplishments in so short a period of time, you see that a tremendous amount of progress has occurred. Another amazing fact is that countries that have experienced conflict are also making good progress.

The United Nations Economic Commission for Africa's *Beijing+10* report stated, "Commitment to good governance has become one of the hallmarks of the last decade."[29] Some positive trends include the consolidation of democracy in South Africa after apartheid; the increasing number of countries where democratic elections took place peacefully; the creation of mechanisms for accountability such as the African Peer Review Mechanism within the New Partnership for Africa's Development (NEPAD); the marked increase in the proportion of women in parliaments in some countries, equal to or surpassing the targets set in the Beijing Platform for Action (Rwanda, 48.8 percent; South Africa, 32.8 percent; Mozambique, 30 percent; Seychelles, 29.4 percent; Namibia, 26.4 percent; and Uganda, 24.7 percent). Women are being elected to powerful positions in government.[30]

The Economic Commission for Africa noted improvements needed: "Although there has been an increase in the numbers of women in legislative bodies, generally women continue to be under-represented in all structures of power and decision-making. They are subjected to cultural attitudes that do not recognize the right of women to lead."[31] The ECA added that policies in place may promote gender equality in appointments to decision-making positions, but implementation lags far behind. Furthermore, women are often appointed to head ministries that are considered traditionally female such as health, education, social services, gender and human resources, rather than the traditionally male areas such as science and technology, justice, defense, finance and foreign trade.

The Commission stated, "While it is a matter of social justice that women should take their rightful places in decision-making structures, the challenge is to ensure that both men and women who enter into positions of power and decision-making prioritize the need for gender sensitive policies and programs, and use their positions to bring about gender equality in development."[32]

Noteworthy are Aili Mari Tripp's preliminary observations on the implications of the challenges to neopatrimonial rule brought by the women's movements in Africa. Because of these movements, women's organizations have set in motion societal transformation, even though more change is still needed.[33] Part of that transformation is increasing the ability of women to access high-level positions.

Women in political leadership are in keeping with Africa's ancient history, but the 21st century requires more change. Women are in social transformation to produce that change. All across Africa exciting change is occurring for women. The Beijing Platform country reports evidence the change as well as the need for improvement, as do the women political leaders who guide the change.

Appendix: Women
in Parliaments

WORLD CLASSIFICATION AS OF FEBRUARY 28, 2007

Rank	Country	LOWER OR SINGLE HOUSE				UPPER HOUSE OR SENATE			
		Elections	Seats*	Women	%W	Elections	Seats*	Women	%W
1	Rwanda	09 2003	80	39	48.8	09 2003	26	9	34.6
2	Sweden	09 2006	349	165	47.3	—	—	—	—
3	Costa Rica	02 2006	57	22	38.6	—	—	—	—
4	Finland	03 2003	200	76	38.0	—	—	—	—
5	Norway	09 2005	169	64	37.9	—	—	—	—
6	Denmark	02 2005	179	66	36.9	—	—	—	—
7	Netherlands	11 2006	150	55	36.7	06 2003	75	22	29.3
8	Cuba	01 2003	609	219	36.0	—	—	—	—
"	Spain	03 2004	350	126	36.0	03 2004	259	60	23.2
9	Argentina	10 2005	257	90	35.0	10 2005	72	31	43.1
10	Mozambique	12 2004	250	87	34.8	—	—	—	—
11	Belgium	05 2003	150	52	34.7	05 2003	71	27	38.0
12	Iceland	05 2003	63	21	33.3	—	—	—	—
13	South Africa†	04 2004	400	131	32.8	04 2004	54	18	33.3
14	Austria	10 2006	183	59	32.2	N/A	62	17	27.4
"	New Zealand	09 2005	121	39	32.2	—	—	—	—
15	Germany	09 2005	614	194	31.6	N/A	69	15	21.7
16	Burundi	07 2005	118	36	30.5	07 2005	49	17	34.7
17	Tanzania	12 2005	319	97	30.4	—	—	—	—
18	Uganda	02 2006	332	99	29.8	—	—	—	—
19	Seychelles	12 2002	34	10	29.4	—	—	—	—
20	Peru	04 2006	120	35	29.2	—	—	—	—
21	Belarus	10 2004	110	32	29.1	11 2004	58	18	31.0

*Figures correspond to the number of seats currently filled in Parliament.

†South Africa: The figures on the distribution of seats do not include the 36 special rotating delegates appointed on an ad hoc basis, and all percentages given are therefore calculated on the basis of the 54 permanent seats.

| Rank | Country | LOWER OR SINGLE HOUSE | | | | UPPER HOUSE OR SENATE | | | |
		Elections	Seats*	Women	%W	Elections	Seats*	Women	%W
22	Guyana	08 2006	69	20	29.0	—	—	—	—
23	Andorra	04 2005	28	8	28.6	—	—	—	—
24	Macedonia (F.Y.R.)	07 2006	120	34	28.3	—	—	—	—
25	Afghanistan	09 2005	249	68	27.3	09 2005	102	23	22.5
"	Viet Nam	05 2002	498	136	27.3	—	—	—	—
26	Namibia	11 2004	78	21	26.9	11 2004	26	7	26.9
27	Grenada	11 2003	15	4	26.7	11 2003	13	4	30.8
28	Iraq	12 2005	275	70	25.5	—	—	—	—
"	Suri-name	05 2005	51	13	25.5	—	—	—	—
29	East Timor	08 2001	87	22	25.3	—	—	—	—
30	Lao P.D.R.	04 2006	115	29	25.2	—	—	—	—
31	Ecuador	10 2006	100	25	25.0	—	—	—	—
"	Switzerland	10 2003	200	50	25.0	10 2003	46	11	23.9
32	Lithuania	10 2004	141	35	24.8	—	—	—	—
33	Australia	10 2004	150	37	24.7	10 2004	76	27	35.5
34	Singapore	05 2006	94	23	24.5	—	—	—	—
35	Liechtenstein	03 2005	25	6	24.0	—	—	—	—
36	Lesotho	02 2007	119	28	23.5	N/A	33	12	36.4
37	Honduras	11 2005	128	30	23.4	—	—	—	—
38	Luxembourg	06 2004	60	14	23.3	—	—	—	—
39	Tunisia	10 2004	189	43	22.8	07 2005	112	15	13.4
40	Mexico	07 2006	500	113	22.6	07 2006	128	22	17.2
41	United Arab Em.	12 2006	40	9	22.5	—	—	—	—
42	Bulgaria	06 2005	240	53	22.1	—	—	—	—
43	Eritrea	02 1994	150	33	22.0	—	—	—	—
44	Ethiopia	05 2005	529	116	21.9	10 2005	112	21	18.8
45	Moldova	03 2005	101	22	21.8	—	—	—	—
46	Croatia	11 2003	152	33	21.7	—	—	—	—
47	Pakistan	10 2002	342	73	21.3	03 2006	100	17	17.0
"	Portugal	02 2005	230	49	21.3	—	—	—	—
48	Canada	01 2006	308	64	20.8	N/A	100	35	35.0
"	Monaco	02 2003	24	5	20.8	—	—	—	—
49	Poland	09 2005	460	94	20.4	09 2005	100	13	13.0
"	Serbia	01 2007	250	51	20.4	—	—	—	—
50	China	02 2003	2980	604	20.3	—	—	—	—
51	North Korea	08 2003	687	138	20.1	—	—	—	—
52	Bahamas	05 2002	40	8	20.0	05 2002	16	7	43.8
"	Slovakia	06 2006	150	30	20.0	—	—	—	—
53	Dominican Rep.	05 2006	178	35	19.7	05 2006	32	1	3.1

Rank	Country	LOWER OR SINGLE HOUSE				UPPER HOUSE OR SENATE			
		Elections	Seats*	Women	%W	Elections	Seats*	Women	%W
"	United Kingdom	05 2005	646	127	19.7	N/A	751	142	18.9
54	Trinidad and T.	10 2002	36	7	19.4	10 2002	31	10	32.3
55	Guinea	06 2002	114	22	19.3	—	—	—	—
56	Senegal	04 2001	120	23	19.2	—	—	—	—
57	Latvia	10 2006	100	19	19.0	—	—	—	—
58	Estonia	03 2003	101	19	18.8	—	—	—	—
59	Saint Vincent & the Grenadines	12 2005	22	4	18.2	—	—	—	—
60	Equat. Guinea	04 2004	100	18	18.0	—	—	—	—
"	Venezuela	12 2005	167	30	18.0	—	—	—	—
61	Mauritania	11 2006	95	17	17.9	01 2007	53	9	17.0
62	Sudan	08 2005	450	80	17.8	08 2005	50	2	4.0
63	Tajikistan	02 2005	63	11	17.5	03 2005	34	8	23.5
"	Uzbekistan	12 2004	120	21	17.5	01 2005	100	15	15.0
64	Italy	04 2006	630	109	17.3	04 2006	322	44	13.7
"	Nepal	01 2007	329	57	17.3	—	—	—	—
65	Mauritius	07 2005	70	12	17.1	—	—	—	—
66	Bolivia	12 2005	130	22	16.9	12 2005	27	1	3.7
67	El Salvador	03 2006	84	14	16.7	—	—	—	—
"	Panama	05 2004	78	13	16.7	—	—	—	—
"	Zimbabwe	03 2005	150	25	16.7	11 2005	66	23	34.8
68	United States	11 2006	435	71	16.3	11 2006	100	16	16.0
69	Turkmenistan	12 2004	50	8	16.0	—	—	—	—
70	Czech Republic	06 2006	200	31	15.5	10 2006	81	12	14.8
71	Cape Verde	01 2006	72	11	15.3	—	—	—	—
"	Philippines	05 2004	236	36	15.3	05 2004	24	4	16.7
72	Nicaragua	11 2006	92	14	15.2	—	—	—	—
73	Bangladesh*	10 2001	345	52	15.1	—	—	—	—
74	Angola	09 1992	220	33	15.0	—	—	—	—
"	Chile	12 2005	120	18	15.0	12 2005	38	2	5.3
75	Zambia	09 2006	157	23	14.6	—	—	—	—
76	Sierra Leone	05 2002	124	18	14.5	—	—	—	—
77	Bosnia & Herz.	10 2006	42	6	14.3	10 2002	15	1	6.7
"	Cyprus	05 2006	56	8	14.3	—	—	—	—
78	Israel	03 2006	120	17	14.2	—	—	—	—
79	Guinea-Bissau	03 2004	100	14	14.0	—	—	—	—
80	Malawi	04 2004	191	26	13.6	—	—	—	—

*Bangladesh: In 2004, the number of seats in parliament was raised from 300 to 345, with the addition of 45 reserved seats for women. These reserved seats were filled in September and October 2005, being allocated to political parties in proportion to their share of the national vote received in the 2001 election.

Rank	Country	LOWER OR SINGLE HOUSE				UPPER HOUSE OR SENATE			
		Elections	Seats*	Women	%W	Elections	Seats*	Women	%W
81	South Korea	04 2004	299	40	13.4	—	—	—	—
82	Barbados	05 2003	30	4	13.3	05 2003	21	5	23.8
"	Ireland	05 2002	166	22	13.3	07 2002	60	10	16.7
83	Greece	03 2004	300	39	13.0	—	—	—	—
84	Dominica	05 2005	31	4	12.9	—	—	—	—
85	Gabon	12 2006	120	15	12.5	02 2003	91	14	15.4
"	Liberia	10 2005	64	8	12.5	10 2005	30	5	16.7
86	Niger	11 2004	113	14	12.4	—	—	—	—
87	France	06 2002	574	70	12.2	09 2004	331	56	16.9
"	Slovenia	10 2004	90	11	12.2	12 2002	40	3	7.5
88	Maldives	01 2005	50	6	12.0	—	—	—	—
"	Syria	03 2003	250	30	12.0	—	—	—	—
89	Burkina Faso	05 2002	111	13	11.7	—	—	—	—
"	Jamaica	10 2002	60	7	11.7	10 2002	21	4	19.0
"	San Marino	06 2006	60	7	11.7	—	—	—	—
90	Azerbaijan	11 2005	124	14	11.3	—	—	—	—
"	Indonesia	04 2004	550	62	11.3	—	—	—	—
91	Romania	11 2004	331	37	11.2	11 2004	137	13	9.5
92	Botswana	10 2004	63	7	11.1	—	—	—	—
"	Uruguay	10 2004	99	11	11.1	10 2004	31	3	9.7
93	Ghana	12 2004	230	25	10.9	—	—	—	—
94	Djibouti	01 2003	65	7	10.8	—	—	—	—
"	Morocco	09 2002	325	35	10.8	09 2006	270	3	1.1
"	Swaziland	10 2003	65	7	10.8	10 2003	30	9	30.0
95	Antigua & Barb.	03 2004	19	2	10.5	03 2004	17	3	17.6
"	Central Afr. Rep.	05 2005	105	11	10.5	—	—	—	—
96	Hungary	04 2006	386	40	10.4	—	—	—	—
"	Kazakhstan	09 2004	77	8	10.4	09 2004	39	2	5.1
97	Mali	07 2002	147	15	10.2	—	—	—	—
98	Paraguay	04 2003	80	8	10.0	04 2003	45	4	8.9
99	Cambodia	07 2003	123	12	9.8	01 2006	61	9	14.8
"	Russia	12 2003	447	44	9.8	N/A	178	6	3.4
100	The Gambia	01 2007	53	5	9.4	—	—	—	—
"	Georgia	03 2004	235	22	9.4	—	—	—	—
"	Japan	09 2005	480	45	9.4	07 2004	242	35	14.5
101	Malta	04 2003	65	6	9.2	—	—	—	—
102	Malaysia	03 2004	219	20	9.1	03 2004	70	18	25.7
103	Cameroon	06 2002	180	16	8.9	—	—	—	—
104	Brazil	10 2006	513	45	8.8	10 2006	81	10	12.3

Rank	Country	LOWER OR SINGLE HOUSE				UPPER HOUSE OR SENATE			
		Elections	Seats*	Women	%W	Elections	Seats*	Women	%W
105	Thailand	10 2006	242	21	8.7	—	—	—	—
"	Ukraine	03 2006	450	39	8.7	—	—	—	—
106	Montenegro	09 2006	81	7	8.6	—	—	—	—
"	Togo	10 2002	81	7	8.6	—	—	—	—
107	Congo	05 2002	129	11	8.5	10 2005	60	8	13.3
"	Côte d'Ivoire	12 2000	223	19	8.5	—	—	—	—
108	Colombia	03 2006	166	14	8.4	03 2006	102	12	11.8
"	Dem. Rep. Congo	07 2006	500	42	8.4	01 2007	108	5	4.6
109	India	04 2004	545	45	8.3	07 2006	242	26	10.7
110	Guatemala	11 2003	158	13	8.2	—	—	—	—
111	Somalia	08 2004	269	21	7.8	—	—	—	—
112	Libya	03 2006	468	36	7.7	—	—	—	—
113	Kenya	12 2002	219	16	7.3	—	—	—	—
"	São Tomé & Pr.	03 2006	55	4	7.3	—	—	—	—
114	Benin	03 2003	83	6	7.2	—	—	—	—
115	Albania	07 2005	140	10	7.1	—	—	—	—
"	Kiribati	05 2003	42	3	7.1	—	—	—	—
116	Madagascar	12 2002	160	11	6.9	03 2001	90	10	11.1
117	Belize	03 2003	30	2	6.7	03 2003	12	3	25.0
118	Mongolia	06 2004	76	5	6.6	—	—	—	—
119	Chad	04 2002	155	10	6.5	—	—	—	—
120	Algeria	05 2002	389	24	6.2	12 2006	144	4	2.8
121	Nigeria	04 2003	360	22	6.1	04 2003	109	4	3.7
"	Samoa	03 2006	49	3	6.1	—	—	—	—
122	Saint Lucia*	12 2006	18	1	5.6	01 2007	11	2	18.2
123	Jordan	06 2003	110	6	5.5	11 2005	55	7	12.7
124	Armenia	05 2003	131	7	5.3	—	—	—	—
125	Sri Lanka	04 2004	225	11	4.9	—	—	—	—
126	Lebanon	05 2005	128	6	4.7	—	—	—	—
127	Turkey	11 2002	550	24	4.4	—	—	—	—
128	Haiti	02 2006	98	4	4.1	02 2006	30	4	13.3
"	Iran	02 2004	290	12	4.1	—	—	—	—
129	Vanuatu	07 2004	52	2	3.8	—	—	—	—
130	Tonga	03 2005	30	1	3.3	—	—	—	—
131	Comoros	04 2004	33	1	3.0	—	—	—	—
"	Marshall Islands	11 2003	33	1	3.0	—	—	—	—
132	Bhutan	N/A	150	4	2.7	—	—	—	—

Saint Lucia: No woman was elected in the 2006 elections. However, one woman was appointed Speaker of the House and therefore became a member of the House.

Rank	Country	LOWER OR SINGLE HOUSE				UPPER HOUSE OR SENATE			
		Elections	Seats*	Women	%W	Elections	Seats*	Women	%W
133	Bahrain	11 2006	40	1	2.5	12 2006	40	10	25.0
134	Oman	10 2003	83	2	2.4	N/A	58	9	15.5
135	Egypt	11 2005	442	9	2.0	05 2004	264	18	6.8
136	Kuwait*	06 2006	65	1	1.5	—	—	—	—
137	Papua New Guinea	06 2002	109	1	0.9	—	—	—	—
138	Yemen	04 2003	301	1	0.3	04 2001	111	2	1.8
139	Kyrgyzstan	02 2005	72	0	0.0	—	—	—	—
"	Micronesia	03 2005	14	0	0.0	—	—	—	—
"	Nauru	10 2004	18	0	0.0	—	—	—	—
"	Palau	11 2004	16	0	0.0	11 2004	9	0	0.0
"	Qatar	06 2005	35	0	0.0	—	—	—	—
"	Saint Kitts & N.	10 2004	15	0	0.0	—	—	—	—
"	Saudi Arabia	04 2005	150	0	0.0	—	—	—	—
"	Solomon Islands	04 2006	50	0	0.0	—	—	—	—
"	Tuvalu	08 2006	15	0	0.0	—	—	—	—

Source: Reprinted with permission from the Inter-Parliamentary Union. Accessed March 16, 2007, *http://www.ipu.org/wmn-e/classif.htm.*

Kuwait: No woman candidate was elected in the 2006 elections. One woman was appointed to the 16-member cabinet. As cabinet ministers also sit in parliament, there is therefore one woman out of a total of 65 members.

Abbreviations and Glossary

ADB African Development Bank

ADF African Development Fund

AMwA Akina Mama wa Afrika is an international, pan–African, non-governmental development organization for African women based in the U.K. with an Africa regional office in Kampala, Uganda.

ANC African National Congress

AU African Union

Bretton Woods A no longer existing international system of monetary management that established the rules for commercial and financial relations among the world's major industrial states; this system was the first example of a fully negotiated monetary order intended to govern monetary relations among independent nation-states.

CEDAW Convention of the Elimination of All Forms of Discrimination Against Women/Committee on the Elimination of All Forms of Discrimination Against Women

FEMNET African Women's Development and Communication Network

FPTP First Past the Post, a plurality/majority election system: "The simplest form of plurality/majority electoral system, using *single-member districts* and *candidate-centered* voting; the winning candidate is the one who gains more votes than any other candidate, even if this is not an absolute majority of valid votes"*

IDEA International Institute for Democracy and Electoral Assistance, an intergovernmental organization which supports sustainable democracy worldwide

IRIN Integrated Regional Information Networks, United Nations

List PR List Proportional Representation, a proportional representation election system: "A system in which each participant party or grouping presents a list of candidates for an *electoral district*, voters vote for a party, and parties receive seats in proportion to their overall share of the vote; winning candidates are taken from the lists"*

MDG Millennium Development Goals

NAFDAC National Agency for Food and Drug Administration and Control (in Nigeria)

National Machinery An institutional governmental and sometimes a parliamentary structure set up to promote women's advancement and to ensure the full enjoyment by women of their human rights

*International IDEA and Stockholm University, Electoral System Design: the New IDEA Handbook, 2005–2006, ix, 177–180, 182. Sept. 25, 2006, http://www.idea.int/publications/esd/index.cfm.

NEPAD New Partnership for Africa's Development

NHDR National Human Development Reports, United Nations

MK uMkhonto we Sizwe, the armed wing of the African National Congress (ANC)

MMP Mixed Member Proportional, a mixed systems election system: "A *mixed system* in which all the voters use the first *electoral system*, usually a *plurality/majority system*, to elect some of the representatives to an elected body; the remaining seats are then allocated to parties and groupings using the second *electoral system*, normally *List PR*, so as to compensate for disproportionality in their representation in the results from the first *electoral system*"*

N no provisions for direct elections

Parallel Parallel Systems, a mixed election system: "A *mixed system* in which the choices expressed by the voters are used to elect representatives through two different systems, usually one *plurality/majority* system and one *proportional representation* system, but where no account is taken of the seats allocated under the first system in calculating the results in the second system"*

NGO non-governmental organization

parastatal government related enterprise State owned

PBV Party Block Vote, a plurality/majority election system: "A *plurality/majority* system using *multi-member districts* in which voters cast a single *party-centered* vote for a party of choice, and do not choose between candidates; the party with most votes will win every seat in the *electoral district*"*

PR Proportional Representation election system

SACP South African Communist Party

SADC Southern African Development Community

TRS The Two-Round System, a plurality/majority election system: "A *plurality/majority* system in which a second election is held if no candidate achieves a given level of votes, most commonly an absolute majority (50 percent plus one), in the first election round; [this system] may take a majority-plurality form, in which it is possible for more than two candidates to contest the second round"*

UN United Nations

UNDP United Nations Development Program

WHO/EMRO World Health Organization Eastern Mediterranean Regional Office

---

*International IDEA and Stockholm University, Electoral System Design: the New IDEA Handbook, *2005–2006, ix, 177–180, 182. Sept. 25, 2006, http://www.idea.int/publications/esd/index.cfm.*

Chapter Notes

Preface

1. Agence France Presse, "Women Leaders Take Hold on Power Across the Globe," Jan. 16, 2006, Paris.

2. Women's eNews, *Africa's Rising Leaders*, Sept. 26, 2005. May 11, 2006, http://www.womensenews.org/article.cfm/dyn/aid/2461/.

3. E. Wamala, A.R. Byaruhanga, A.T. Dalfovo, J.K. Kigongo, S.A. Mwanahewa and G. Tusabe, eds., "Cultural Elements in Social Reconstruction in Africa," in E. Wamala et al. ed., *Social Reconstruction in Africa Ugandan Philosophical Studies, Cultural Heritage and Contemporary Change, Africa* 4, II, ch. 5, Mar. 27, 2003. June 3, 2006, http://www.crvp.org/book/Series02/II-4/chapter_v.htm.

4. United Nations, Division for the Advancement of Women, Department of Economic and Social Affairs, *Platform for Action Fourth World Conference on Women*, Beijing, China, Sept. 1995. Jan, 3, 2007, http://www.un.org/womenwatch/daw/beijing/platform/index.html.

5. United Nations, Division for the Advancement of Women, Department of Economic and Social Affairs, "Replies to Questionnaire on the Implementation of the Beijing Platform for Action," revised on 24 May 2002. Mar. 16, 2007, http://www.un.org/womenwatch/daw/followup/countrylist.htm; United Nations, Division for the Advancement of Women, Department of Economic and Social Affairs, "Member States Responses to the Questionnaire," Apr. 30, 2004. Mar. 16, 2007, http://www.un.org/womenwatch/daw/Review/english/responses.htm.

6. Femmes Africa Solidarité, *African Women Pioneers*, U.N. Liaison Office, N.Y., a work in progress. Aug. 29, 2006 http://www.fasngo.org/en/whatnew/african%20women%20pioneers.pdf.

7. "Stade Aline Sitoe Diatta," *Wikipedia*, Dec. 25, 2006. Jan. 17, 2007, http://en.wikipedia.org/wiki/Stade_Aline_Sitoe_Diatta.

Part I

Chapter 1

1. African Unification Front, "AU President Gertrude Mongella: Biographical Brief," n.d. Apr. 5, 2007, http://www.africanfront.com/2004-m.php.

2. Inter-Parliamentary Union, *Women in Politics: 60 Years in Retrospect* (data valid as at 1 February 2006),

"Women Heads of State: A General Overview" and "A Chronology of Women Heads of State or Government," Data Sheet No. 4. May 20, 2006, http://www.ipu.org/PDF/publications/wmninfokit06_en.pdf.

3. Worldwide Guide to Women in Leadership, May 8, 2006. May 9, 2006, http://www.guide2womenleaders.com/index.html.

4. Worldwide Guide to Women in Leadership.

5. Inter-Parliamentary Union: guide2womenleaders.com, "Women in Government: Expert Cites Progress," *USA Today*, Jan. 23, 2006, 6A.

6. Worldwide Guide to Women in Leadership.

7. Worldwide Guide to Women in Leadership.

8. Inter-Parliamentary Union: guide2womenleaders.com.

9. Worldwide Guide to Women in Leadership.

10. Inter-Parliamentary Union: guide2womenleaders.com.

11. Irwin Arieff, "UN Assembly's First Muslim Leader Vows Reform," *Reuters*, Sept. 12, 2006. Sept. 12, 2006, Reuters.com.

12. U.N. Foundation, "Ban Chooses Tanzanian Woman as UN No. 2," *UN Wire*, E-mail News Covering the UN and the World, Jan. 8, 2007.

13. Inter-Parliamentary Union: guide2womenleaders.com.

14. Inter-Parliamentary Union, *Women in Politics*, 6.

15. Inter-Parliamentary Union, *Women in Politics*, Data Sheet No. 5.

16. Maulana Karenga, "A New President and Promise for Liberia: Searching for Signs and Wonders," *Los Angeles Sentinel*, Jan. 26, 2006, A-7. June 22, 2006, http://www.us-organization.org/position/documents/ANewPresidentandPromiseforLiberia.pdf.

17. Worldwide Guide to Women in Leadership.

18. "Egypt: Rulers, Kings and Pharaohs of Ancient Egypt: Cleopatra VII and Ptolemy XIII Cleopatra VII: Ptolemaic Dynasty," InterCity Oz, Inc., 1996. May 11, 2006, http://touregypt.net/cleopatr.htm.

19. Worldwide Guide to Women in Leadership, "African Female Leaders," Mar. 2, 2006. May 8, 2006, http://www.guide2womenleaders.com/womeninpower/Africa.htm.

20. Inter-Parliamentary Union, *Women in Politics*, "A Chronology of Women: Heads of State or Government," Data Sheet No. 4.

21. Inter-Parliamentary Union, *Women in Politics*, "A Chronology of Women: Heads of State or Government," Data Sheet No. 4.

22. Inter-Parliamentary Union, *Women in Politics*,

"A Chronology of Women: Heads of State or Government," Data Sheet No. 4.

23. Lesotho, Government Official Website, "The Lesotho Monarchy: Her Majesty Queen 'Masenate Mohato Seeiso," June 27, 2006. June 28, 2006, http://www.lesotho.gov.ls/articles/2004/King_Birth_2004/queen.html.

24. Women World Leaders: 1945–2005, "Reigning Queens 1945–2005," Mar. 16, 2006. July 1, 2006, http://www.terra.es/personal2/monolith/00women1.htm.

25. Inter-Parliamentary Union, *Women in Politics*, "A Chronology of Women: Heads of State or Government," Data Sheet No. 4.

26. Swaziland, Government, "The Kings Office: Kings of the Kingdom," n.d. June 28, 2006, http://www.gov.sz/home.asp?pid=900.

27. Worldwide Guide to Women in Leadership, "Reigning Queens and Empresses from 1900," Mar. 2, 2006. July 28, 2005, http://www.guide2womenleaders.com/queens_and_empresses.htm.

28. Worldwide Guide to Women in Leadership, "Angola Heads of State," Nov. 18, 2004. June 25, 2006, http://www.guide2womenleaders.com/Angola_Heads.htm.

29. Agence France Presse, "Women Leaders Take Hold on Power Across the Globe," Paris, Jan. 16, 2006.

30. Inter-Parliamentary Union, *Women in Politics*, "Women Heads of State or Government: A General Overview."

31. "Maria do Carmo Silveira, Former Prime Minister of São Tomé and Príncipe," *Africa Centre, London: Contemporary Africa Database*: People: Positions; Selected Works, Sept. 26, 2006. Oct. 23, 2006, http://people.africadatabase.org/en/person/18507.html.

32. Women World Leaders, "Previous Women Heads of State or Government," Jan. 15, 2006. July 2, 2006, http://www.geocities.com/capitolHill/Lobby/4642/.

33. Worldwide Guide to Women in Leadership, "Benin Heads of State," Mar. 14, 2005. June 25, 2006, http://www.guide2womenleaders.com/Benin_Heads.htm.

34. Inter-Parliamentary Union, *Women in Politics*, "A Chronology of Women: Heads of State or Government," Data Sheet No. 4.

35. Women World Leaders, "Women Vice Presidents," Jan. 15, 2006. July 2, 2006, http://www.geocities.com/capitolHill/Lobby/4642/.

36. Inter-Parliamentary Union, "Women Speakers of National Parliaments: History and the Present," Feb. 28, 2007. Mar. 15, 2007, http://www.ipu.org/wmn-e/speakers.htm.

37. Inter-Parliamentary Union, "Women Speakers of National Parliaments.

38. Gretchen Bauer and Hannah E. Britton, "Women in African Parliaments: A Continental Shift?" in Gretchen Bauer and Hannah E. Britton, eds., *Women in African Parliaments*, Boulder, Colo.: Lynne Rienner Publishers, 2006, 1–2.

39. Bauer and Britton, in Bauer and Britton, eds., 2.

40. United Nations Economic Commission for Africa (UNECA), Sub-regional Offices, 2000. Mar. 16, 2007, http://www.uneca.org/eca_programmes/srdc/index.htm.

41. Bauer and Britton, in Bauer and Britton, eds., 1.

42. Bauer and Britton, in Bauer and Britton, eds., 1.

43. Women's eNews, *Africa's Rising Leaders*, Sept. 26, 2005. May 11, 2006, http://www.womensenews.org/article.cfm/dyn/aid/2461/.

44. Worldwide Guide to Women in Leadership, "Women Presidential Candidates," May 4, 2006. May 9, 2006, http://www.guide2womenleaders.com/woman_presidential_candidates.htm.

45. Worldwide Guide to Women in Leadership, "Women Presidential Candidates."

46. Worldwide Guide to Women in Leadership, "Women Presidential Candidates."

47. Worldwide Guide to Women in Leadership, "Women Ambassadors," Feb. 23, 2006. May 9, 2006, http://www.guide2womenleaders.com/woman_ambassadors.htm.

48. Worldwide Guide to Women in Leadership, "Women Ambassadors."

49. Worldwide Guide to Women in Leadership, "Women Ambassadors."

50. Worldwide Guide to Women in Leadership, "Women Ambassadors."

51. Worldwide Guide to Women in Leadership, "Women Ambassadors."

52. Worldwide Guide to Women in Leadership, "Women Ambassadors."

53. Worldwide Guide to Women in Leadership, "Women Ambassadors."

54. Worldwide Guide to Women in Leadership, "Women Ambassadors."

55. Bike Agozino, "What Women's Studies Offer Men: Entremesa Discussion," *West Africa Review* 2, no. 1 (Aug. 2000). May 12, 2006, http://www.westafricareview.com/vol2.1/agozino.html; Sarah Childs, "The Complicated Relationship between Sex, Gender and the Substantive Representation of Women," *European Journal of Women's Studies* 13, no. 1 (2006):7–21.

56. L. Muthoni Wanyeki, Executive Director, African Women's Development and Communication Network (FEMNET), email interview, Aug. 23, 2006.

57. Wanyeki.

58. International IDEA and Stockholm University, *Women in Parliament: Beyond Numbers: A Revised Edit*, 2005, 13. Sept. 25, 2006, http://www.idea.int/publications/wip2/index.cfm.

59. Julie Ballington, "Conclusion: Women's Political Participation and Quotas in Africa," in Julie Ballington, ed., *The Implementation of Quotas: African Experiences, Quota Report Series No. 3*, Stockholm, Sweden: International Institute for Democracy and Electoral Assistance (IDEA), Nov. 2004, 128. *See also* at http://www.quotaproject.org/publications/Quotas_Africa.pdf, Sept. 23, 2006.

Chapter 2

1. International IDEA and Stockholm University, *Women in Parliament: Beyond Numbers: A Revised Edit*, 2005, 13. Sept. 25, 2006,http://www.idea.int/publications/wip2/index.cfm.

2. Nadezhda Shvedova, "Obstacles to Women's Participation in Parliament," International IDEA and Stockholm University, *Women in Parliament: Beyond Numbers: A Revised Edit*, 2005, 48. Sept. 25, 2006, http://www.idea.int/publications/wip2/index.cfm.

3. Shvedova, 48.

4. Shvedova, 49.

5. Karen Fogg, "Preface," in Julie Ballington, ed., *The Implementation of Quotas: African Experiences, Quota Report Series No. 3*, Stockholm, Sweden: International Institute for Democracy and Electoral Assistance (IDEA), Nov. 2004, 3. Sept. 23, 2006, http://www.quotaproject.org/publications/Quotas_ Africa. pdf.

6. Fogg, "Preface," in Ballington, ed., 3.

7. Aili Mari Tripp, "Women in Movement: Transformations in African Political Landscapes," *International Feminist Journal of Politics* 5, no. 2, (July 2003): 233.

8. Tripp, 233.

9. Tripp, 233.

10. Tripp, 233.

11. Tripp, 233.

12. Slvia Tamale, "'Point of Order, Mr. Speaker': African Women Claiming Their Space in Parliament," in Caroline Sweetman, ed., *Women and Leadership*. Oxfam Focus on Gender Series, Dorset, U.K.: Oxfam, 2000, 8.

13. Tamale in Sweetman, ed., 8.

14. Femmes Africa Solidarité, *African Women Pioneers*, U.N. Liaison Office, N.Y., a work in progress. Aug. 29, 2006 http://www.fasngo.org/en/whatnew/ african%20women%20pioneers.pdf.

15. L. Muthoni Wanyeki, Executive Director, African Women's Development and Communication Network (FEMNET), email interview, Aug. 23, 2006.

16. Gumisai Mutume, "African Women Are Ready to Lead: But Social Beliefs and Attitudes Hinder Their Quest," *Africa Renewal* 20, no. 2 (July 2006):6. Mar. 17, 2007, http://www.un.org/ecosocdev/geninfo/afrec/ vol20no2/AR-20no2-english.pdf.

17. Mutume, "African Women Are Ready to Lead," 6.

18. Mutume, "African Women Are Ready to Lead," 7.

19. Barbara Nelson and Najma Chowdhury, eds., *Women and Politics Worldwide*, New Haven: Yale University, 1994 in Alida Brill, "Introduction," in Alida Brill, ed., *A Rising Public Voice: Women in Politics Worldwide*, New York: The Feminist Press at the City University of New York, 1995, 2.

20. Miki Caul Kittilson, *Challenging Parties, Changing Parliaments: Women and Elected Office in Contemporary Western Europe*, Columbus: Ohio State University Press, 2006, 2, 140.

21. Kittilson, 2, 158.

22. Alida Brill, "Introduction," in Brill, ed., 2.

23. Thenjiwe Mtintso, "From Prison Cell to Parliament," in Brill, ed., 105; "Thenjiwe Mtintso," African National Congress, Biographies of ANC Leaders, Sept. 11, 2006. Sept. 13, 2006; http://www.anc.org.za/peo ple/mtintso_t.html.

24. Mtintso, in Brill, ed., 107.

25. Mtintso, in Brill, ed., 110.

26. Mtintso, in Brill, ed., 111–112.

27. Mtintso, in Brill, ed., 112.

28. Mtintso, in Brill, ed., 115.

29. Mtintso, in Brill, ed., 116.

30. Kavita Datta and Cathy McIlwaine, "'Empowered Leaders'? Perspectives on Women Heading Households in Latin America and Southern Africa," in Sweetman, ed., 41, 42.

31. Datta and McIlwaine, in Sweetman, ed., 44.

32. Datta and McIlwaine, in Sweetman, ed., 45.

33. Datta and McIlwaine, in Sweetman, ed., 45, 46.

34. Datta and McIlwaine, in Sweetman, ed., 47.

35. Datta and McIlwaine, in Sweetman, ed., 40, 41.

36. Datta and McIlwaine, in Sweetman, ed., 47.

37. Jane Thompson Stephens, *The Rhetoric of Women's Leadership*, Dissertation, Greensboro, N.C.: University of North Carolina at Greensboro, 2000, 5–6, 11.

38. Stephens, 11.

39. Stephens, 11.

40. Stephens, 11, 158.

41. Stephens, 12.

42. Rosemarie Skaine, *Female Genital Mutilation: Legal, Cultural and Medical Issues*, Jefferson, N.C.: McFarland, 2005, 165.

43. Stephens, 56.

44. Stephens, 59.

45. Stephens, 136.

46. Stephens, 135.

47. Stephens, 97, 158.

48. Nkiru Nzegwu, "African Women and the Fire Dance," *West Africa Review* 2, no. 1 (Aug. 2000). May 12, 2006, http://www.westafricareview.com/vol2.1/nzeg wu2.html.

49. Nzegwu.

50. Nzegwu.

51. Nzegwu.

52. Nzegwu.

53. Nzegwu.

54. Nzegwu.

55. Abantu for Development, "African Women and Governance: Towards Action for Women's Participation in Decision-Making," London: Abantu Publications, 1995, 4.

56. Madonna Owusuah Larbi, "New Gender Perspectives for the Millennium: Challenges and Successful Models of North-South Collaboration," *West Africa Review* 2, no. 1 (Aug. 2000). May 12, 2006, http://www. westafricareview.com/vol2.1/larbi.html.

57. Bike Agozino, "What Women's Studies Offer Men: Entremesa Discussion," *West Africa Review* 2, no. 1 (Aug. 2000). May 12, 2006, http://www.westafricare view.com/vol2.1/agozino.html.

58. Rob Crilly, "Liberian Leader Wants Closer Relationship with U.S.," *USA Today*, Jan. 23, 2006, 6A.

59. Stephens, 11.

60. Nzegwu.

61. Larbi.

62. Larbi.

63. Discover France, "Burkina Faso (Upper Volta)," n.d. Aug. 5, 2006, http://www.discoverfrance.net/ Colonies/Burkina_Faso.shtml.

64. Naomi Chazan, "The New Politics of Participation in Tropical Africa," *Comparative Politics* 14, no. 2 (Jan. 1982): 180.

65. Chazan, 180, 183, 185.

66. Abantu for Development, 1.

67. Akwe Amosu and Ofeibea Quist-Arcton, "Women in Politics," *BBC Focus on Africa* 17, no. 1 (2006): 22.

68. Amosu and Quist-Arcton, 20.

69. Amosu and Quist-Arcton, 22.

70. Amosu and Quist-Arcton, 22.

71. Wanyeki, email interview, Aug. 23, 2006.

72. Mutume, "African Women Are Ready to Lead," 9.

73. Wanyeki, email interview, Aug. 23, 2006.

74. Gumisai Mutume, "Women Break into African Politics Quota Systems Allow More Women to Gain Elected Office." *Africa Recovery* 18, no. 1 (April 2004): 4. May 15, 2006, http://www.un.org/ecosocdev/gen info/afrec/vol18no1/181women.htm.

75. Fogg, "Preface," in Julie Ballington, ed., 3.

76. Drude Dahlerup, "Quotas — a Key to Equality?" *Quota Database, International IDEA and Stockholm University Global Database of Quotas for Women*, 2006. Sept. 24, 2006, http://www.quotaproject.org/about_research.cfm.

77. Julie Ballington, "Conclusion: Women's Political Participation and Quotas in Africa," in Ballington, ed., 124.

78. Ballington, "Conclusion," in Ballington, ed., 124

79. Mutume, "African Women Are Ready to Lead," 9.

80. Mutume, "Women Break into African Politics," 4.

81. Wanyeki, email interview, Aug. 23, 2006.

82. Mutume, "African Women Are Ready to Lead," 8.

83. Inter-Parliamentary Union, "Women in National Parliaments: World Classification," Feb. 28, 2007. Mar, 18, 2007, http://www.ipu.org/wmn-e/class if.htm; Inter-Parliamentary Union, "Women in National Parliaments: World Averages," Feb. 28, 2007. Mar. 18, 2007, http://www.ipu.org/wmn-e/world.htm.

84. Gretchen Bauer and Hannah E. Britton, "Women in African Parliaments: A Continental Shift?" in Gretchen Bauer and Hannah E. Britton, eds., *Women in African Parliaments*, Boulder, Colo.: Lynne Rienner Publishers, 2006, 11–12.

85. Sweetman, ed., "Editorial," 2.

86. Sweetman, ed., "Editorial," 3, 6.

87. Amy S. Patterson, "A Reappraisal of Democracy in Civil Society: Evidence from Rural Senegal," *Journal of Modern Africa Studies* 36 (1998): 423.

88. Abantu for Development, 41p.

89. Note: For a complete listing of nongovernmental women's organizations (NGOs) by country, see United Nations, "Networking: Directory of African NGOs," n.d. Mar. 18, 2007, http://www.un.org/africa/osaa/ngodirectory/index.htm.

90. FEMNET, "About FEMNET: Vision and Mission," Aug. 16, 2006. Aug. 16, 2006, http://www.fem net.or.ke/subsection.asp?ID=2.

91. Wanyeki, email interview, Aug. 23, 2006.

92. Wanyeki, email interview, Aug. 23, 2006.

93. Wanyeki, email interview, Aug. 23, 2006.

94. Wanyeki, email interview, Aug. 23, 2006.

Chapter 3

1. United Nations, Division for the Advancement of Women, Department of Economic and Social Affairs, *Platform for Action Fourth World Conference on Women*. Beijing, China, Sept. 1995. Jan, 3, 2007, http://www.un.org/womenwatch/daw/beijing/platform/decision.html.

2. Emevwo Biakolo, Maitseo Bolaane and Michelle Commeyras, "Women in Conversation with an African Man on Gender Issues," *JOUVERT: A Journal of Post-Colonial Studies* 5, no. 2 (Winter 2001). May 12, 2006, http://social.chass.ncsu.edu/jouvert/v5i2/comey.htm.

3. United Nations, *Report of the Secretary-General on the Work of the Organization*, General Assembly, 60th Session, Sup. no. 1 (A/60/1), 2005, 22, no. 106. Aug.

17, 2006, http://daccessdds.un.org/doc/UNDOC/GEN /N05/453/25/PDF/N0545325. pdf?OpenElement.

4. AfricaFocus, "PanAfrica; Africa: Women's Rights Petition," *Bulletin*, June 30, 2004. Aug. 18, 2006, http://www.africafocus.org/docs04/wom0406.php.

5. AfricaFocus.

6. Pambazuka News, "Victory for Women's Rights in Africa!" 2006. Aug. 18, 2006, http://www.pamba zuka.org/en/petition/index.php.

7. Equality Now — SOAWR Secretariat, email from Faiza Jama Mohamed, Africa Regional Director, Aug. 21, 2006; See also Equality Now, "Protocol on the Rights of Women in Africa," n.d. Aug. 19, 2006, http://www.equalitynow.org/english/campaigns/african-proto col/african-protocol_en.html.

8. Inter-Parliamentary Union (IPU), *Women in Politics: 60 Years in Retrospect* (data valid as at 1 February 2006), "The Participation of Women and Men in Decision-Making," Data Sheet No. 6, 7. May 20, 2006, http://www.ipu.org/PDF/publications/wmninfokit06 _en.pdf.

9. IPU, 7.

10. IPU, 7.

11. IPU, 7.

12. IPU, 7.

13. IPU, 7.

14. IPU, 6.

15. Gilda Louis Sheppard, "Leadership Roles and Perspectives Among Ghanaian Women," The Union Institute: Dissertation, Jan. 1999, Abstract.

16. Sara Hlupekile Longwe, "Towards Realistic Strategies for Women's Political Empowerment in Africa," in Caroline Sweetman, ed., *Women and Leadership*, Oxfam Focus on Gender Series, Dorset, UK: Oxfam, 2000. 30.

17. Longwe in Sweetman, ed., 30.

18. Longwe in Sweetman, ed., 30.

19. Peggy Antrobus, "Transformational Leadership: Advancing the Agenda for Gender Justice," in Sweetman, ed., 52.

20. Antrobus in Sweetman, ed., 56.

21. Antrobus in Sweetman, ed., 56.

22. Antrobus in Sweetman, ed., 56.

23. Julia Preece, "Education for Transformative Leadership in Southern Africa," *Journal of Transformative Education* 1, no. 3 (2003): Abstract.

24. Aruna Rao and David Kelleher, "Leadership for Social Transformation: Some Ideas and Questions on Institutions and Feminist Leadership," in Sweetman, ed., 74.

25. Rao and Kelleher, in Sweetman, ed., 75.

26. Peter M. Blau and Marshall W. Meyers, *Bureaucracy in Modern Society*, New York: Random House, 1971, 72 in Rosemarie Skaine, *A Study of Perceptions of Inequity Among Merit System Employees at the University of Northern Iowa*, Thesis, University of Northern Iowa, Aug. 1977, 60.

27. Shireen Hassim, "The Virtuous Circle of Representation: Women in African Parliaments," in Gretchen Bauer and Hannah E. Britton, eds., *Women in African Parliaments*, Boulder, Colo.: Lynne Rienner Publishers, 2006, 184.

28. Hassim, in Bauer and Britton, eds., 184.

29. Hassim, in Bauer and Britton, eds., 184, 185.

30. L. Muthoni Wanyeki, "Femme Globale: Gender Perspectives in the 21st Century: Women Contesting

the Information Society: from Beijing to Geneva, Tunis and Beyond," staff paper, FEMNET, n.d., 1. Aug. 16, 2006, http://www.femnet.or.ke/publications.asp?docu menttype*id=3*.

31. Wanyeki, 2.
32. Wanyeki, 2.
33. United Nations, Information Service, "Challenges of Development Require Not Only Leadership, Resources, but A Legal Response, Secretary-General Says," SG/SM/8597, Feb. 5, 2003. Aug. 25, 2006. http://www.unis.unvienna.org/unis/pressrels/2003/sgs m8597.html.
34. United Nations Information Service, "Challenges."
35. Takyiwaa Manuh, "Women in Africa's Development: Overcoming Obstacles, Pushing for Progress," *Africa Recovery* Briefing Paper, No. 11, April 1998. Aug. 25, 2006, http://www.un.org/ecosocdev/geninfo/afrec/ bpaper/maineng.htm.
36. Manuh.
37. Manuh.

Chapter 4

1. Wangari Maathai, "Women, Information, and the Future: The Women of Kenya and the Green Belt Movement," in Alida Brill (ed.), *A Rising Public Voice: Women in Politics Worldwide*, New York: The Feminist Press at the City University of New York, 1995, 241.
2. Jane Musoke-Nteyafas, "Meet Ellen Johnson-Sirleaf First African Woman President," AfroToronto. com, Nov. 28, 2005. Oct. 7, 2006, http://www.afro toronto.com/Articles/Nov05/JohnsonSirleaf.html.
3. Embassy of Liberia, Washington D.C., "Profile of Her Excellency Ellen Johnson-Sirleaf President of the Republic of Liberia," 2004. Oct. 5, 2006, http:// www.embassyofliberia.org/biography.htm.
4. Femmes Africa Solidarité, *Celebrating with Her Excellency Madam Ellen Johnson-Sirleaf President of Liberia*, U.N. Liaison Office, N.Y., n.d., 2. Oct. 1, 2006, http://www.fasngo.org/en/network/index.htm.
5. Femmes Africa Solidarité, *Celebrating*; Musoke-Nteyafas.
6. Musoke-Nteyafas.
7. Femmes Africa Solidarité, *Celebrating*.
8. BBC News, "African First for Liberian Leader," Jan. 16, 2006, Africa. Oct. 1, 2006, http://news.bbc.co. uk/2/hi/africa/4615764.stm.
9. President Ellen Johnson-Sirleaf, "Inaugural Speech," Monrovia, Liberia, Jan. 16, 2006. Oct. 5, 2006, http://www.embassyofliberia.org/news/Inaugural % Speech.htm.
10. Laura Bush, "Ellen Johnson-Sirleaf Africa's First Female President," Time.com, Apr. 30, 2006. Oct. 4, 2006, http://www.time.com/time/magazine/article/ 0,9171,1187159,00.html.
11. Agenda for Africa, "Person of the Month — Dec 2005A." Oct. 1, 2006, http://www.agendaafrica.com/ site/en/newsletters/potm/dec2005.html.
12. Embassy of Liberia, "Profile"; Alistair Boddy-Evans, "Biography: Ellen Johnson-Sirleaf, Liberia's 'Iron Lady,'" About: African History, 2006. Oct. 7, 2006, http://africanhistory.about.com/od/liberia/p/Sirleaf. htm.
13. Boddy-Evans.

14. President Ellen Johnson-Sirleaf, Speech to the U.S. Congress, U.S. Joint Session of Congress, Washington D.C, March 15, 2006. Oct. 5, 2006, http://www.embassyofliberia.org/news/item_congress speech.html.
15. Agenda for Africa.
16. Embassy of Liberia, "Profile."
17. Agenda for Africa.
18. Agenda for Africa.
19. Embassy of Liberia, "Profile."
20. Embassy of Liberia, Washington D.C., "President Ellen Johnson-Sirleaf and First Lady Laura Bush Receive IRI-2006 Freedom Award," Sept. 22, 2006. Oct. 5, 2006, http://www.embassyofliberia.org/news/ item_iriaward.html.
21. Embassy of Liberia, "Profile."
22. Ernest Harsch, "Liberian Woman Breaks the 'Glass Ceiling': Ambitious Agenda for President Ellen Johnson-Sirleaf," *Africa Renewal* 19, no. 4 (Jan. 2005): 4. Oct. 8, 2006, http://www.un.org/ecosocdev/geninfo/ afrec/vol19no4/194sirleaf.htm.
23. David Harris, "Ellen Johnson-Sirleaf: Profiles President of Liberia," Africa Centre, London: *Contemporary Africa Database*: People, Ellen Johnson-Sirleaf main page, Sept. 26, 2006. Oct. 9, 2006, http://peo ple.africadatabase.org/en/profile/2655.html.
24. Johnson-Sirleaf, "Speech to the U.S. Congress."
25. Harsch, 4.
26. Harris.
27. Harris.
28. Harsch, 4.
29. Harris.
30. Her Excellency Ellen Johnson-Sirleaf, "Statement," 61st Regular Session of the United Nations General Assembly, New York, Sept. 19, 2006. Oct. 5, 2006, http://www.un.org/webcast/ga/61/pdfs/liberia-e.pdf.
31. Johnson-Sirleaf, "Speech to the U.S. Congress."
32. BBC News, "African First for Liberian Leader."
33. Mojúbàolú Olúfúnké Okome, "Ellen Sirleaf-Johnson: A Tribute," *JENDA: A Journal of Culture and African Women Studies* Issue 7 (2005). Oct. 14, 2006, http://www.jendajournal.com/issue7/okome.html.
34. Femmes Africa Solidarité, "Gertrude Mongella," Leadership Bank, Leadership Profile, 2006. Nov. 8, 2006, http://www.fasngo.org/en/presentation/leadbank /people/gertrudemong.htm.
35. Mathaba News Service, "Africa's First Lady," Comment, posted Jan. 2006. Nov. 8, 2006, http://www .mathaba.net/0_index.shtml?x=504287.
36. Femmes Africa Solidarité, "Beijing Conference Chairperson: Ms. Gertrude Mongella, Teacher and Politician, Tanzania," 2006. Nov. 8, 2006, http://www. fasngo.org/en/presentation/leadbank/index.htm.
37. Femmes Africa Solidarité, "Beijing Conference Chairperson."
38. Femmes Africa Solidarité, "Beijing Conference Chairperson."
39. Femmes Africa Solidarité, "Gertrude Mongella."
40. Pan-African Parliament, Profile of the Bureau: Profiles of the Members of the Pan-African Parliament Bureau, "The President Hon. Dr. Gertrude Ibengwe Mongella," 2005. Nov. 8, 2006, http://www.pan-african-parliament.org/profbureau.htm.
41. Pan-African Parliament, Profile, "Gertrude Ibengwe Mongella."
42. Femmes Africa Solidarité, "Gertrude Mongella";

Pan-African Parliament, Profile, "Gertrude Ibengwe Mongella."

43. Pan-African Parliament, Profile, "Gertrude Ibengwe Mongella."

44. Pan-African Parliament, Profile, "Gertrude Ibengwe Mongella."

45. Pan-African Parliament, Profile, "Gertrude Ibengwe Mongella."

46. African Unification Front, "Continental Parliament Elects Gertrude Mongella the Leader of Africa," Mar. 18, 2004. Nov. 8, 2006, http://www.africanfront.com/2004-l.php.

47. Femmes Africa Solidarité, "Gertrude Mongella."

48. "Women Who Lead Their Governments," *Toronto Star*, News, A12, Mar. 5, 2006; "Mozambican Liberation Front," *Wikipedia*, Dec. 4, 2006. Dec. 5, 2006, http://en.wikipedia.org/wiki/FRELIMO.

49. Elizabeth MacDonald and Chana R. Schoenberge, "Special Report: The 100 Most Powerful Women: #96 Luisa Diogo, Mozambique," Forbes.com, Aug. 31, 2006. Oct. 27, 2006, http://www.forbes.com/lists/2006/11/06women_Luisa-Diogo_ZTLN.html.

50. Mark Malloch Brown, "Luisa Diogo Advocate for Africa," *Time 100*, Apr. 26, 2004. Oct. 27, 2006, http://www.time.com/time/magazine/article/0,9171,993968,00.*html*; Encyclopedia of World Biography, "Luisa Diogo Biography," Notable Biographies, Ca-Ge, 2006. Oct. 27, 2006, http://www.notablebiographies.com/news/Ca-Ge/Diogo-Luisa.html.

51. Brown.

52. Encyclopedia of World Biography, "Luisa Diogo Biography;" NNDB, "Luisa Diogo," 2006. Oct. 27, 2006, http://www.nndb.com/people/093/000044958/.

53. Encyclopedia of World Biography, "Luisa Diogo Biography."

54. Encyclopedia of World Biography, "Luisa Diogo Biography."

55. Encyclopedia of World Biography, "Luisa Diogo Biography."

56. Paul Fauvet, "Mozambique's Diogo Sworn in as New PM," IOL, Feb. 22, 2004. Oct. 27, 2006, http://www.iol.co.za/index.php?click_id=84&art_id=qwl077443643261S530&set_id=1.

57. MacDonald and Schoenberge, "#96 Luisa Diogo, Mozambique."

58. "Maria do Carmo Silveira, Former Prime Minister of São Tomé and Príncipe," Africa Centre, London: *Contemporary Africa Database: People*: Positions; Selected Works, Sept. 26, 2006. Oct. 23, 2006, http://people.africadatabase.org/en/person/18507.html.

59. United Nations, Peace Women, Women's International League for Peace and Freedom (WILPF), "The Select Club of Women in Power," n.d. Oct. 25, 2006, http://www.peacewomen.org/news/International/Nov05/Select_Club.htm.

60. Agence France Presse, "Women, Power and Africa: Liberia's Sirleaf Joins Select Few," Paris, Jan. 15, 2006.

61. United Nations, "The Select Club of Women in Power."

62. Agence France Presse, "Women, Power and Africa."

63. Answers.com, "Maria do Carmo Silveira," n.d. Oct. 23, 2006, http://www.answers.com/topic/maria-do-carmo-silveira.

64. "Maria do Carmo Silveira," *Contemporary Africa Database*; United Nations, "The Select Club of Women in Power."

65. United Nations, International Women's Day: Women in Decision Making: Meeting Challenges, Creating Change, "Baleka Mbete," Mar. 8, 2006. Nov. 5, 2006, http://www.un.org/events/women/iwd/2006/mbete.htm.

66. South African Parliament, Office of the Speaker, "Baleka Mbete, Ms.," n.d. Nov. 4, 2006, http://parliament.gov.za/pls/portal/web_app.utl_output_doc?p_table=people&p_doc_col=bio&p_mime_col=mime_type&p_id=2166.

67. South African Parliament, "Baleka Mbete, Ms."

68. European Union Parliamentary Support Program, "A Poetic Politician," *PSP*, Newsletter, ed. 7, Jan.–March, 2000, 3. Nov. 7, 2006, http://www.parliament.gov.za/eupsp/newsletters/07-00.html; South African Parliament, "Baleka Mbete, Ms."; Wikipedia.org, "Keorapetse Kgositsile," *Wikipedia*, 2006. Nov. 4, 2006, http://www.search.com/reference/Keorapetse_Kgositsile.

69. European Union Parliamentary Support Programme, "A Poetic Politician."

70. South African Parliament, "Baleka Mbete, Ms."; United Nations, International Women's Day, "Baleka Mbete."

71. South African Parliament, "Baleka Mbete, Ms."; United Nations, International Women's Day, "Baleka Mbete."

72. South African Parliament, "Baleka Mbete, Ms."

73. United Nations, International Women's Day, "Baleka Mbete."

74. European Union Parliamentary Support Programme, "A Poetic Politician."

75. European Union Parliamentary Support Programme, "Style Praised," *PSP*, Newsletter, ed. 8, April–May, 2000. Nov. 7, 2006, http://www.parliament.gov.za/eupsp/newsletters/08-00.html#focus.

76. Ilse Fredericks, Bienne Huisman and Sivuyile Mbambato, "Movers and Shakers Strut Their Stuff," *Sunday Times* (South Africa), Feb. 13, 2005, Sec: Human Interest, 3.

77. European Union Parliamentary Support Programme, "A Poetic Politician."

78. European Union Parliamentary Support Programme, "A Poetic Politician."

79. European Union Parliamentary Support Programme, "A Poetic Politician."

80. Judith February, "Parliament. Parts of it were EXCELLENT," Financial Mail (South Africa), Dec. 3, 2004.

81. Baleka Mbete, "Address by the Speaker of the National Assembly of the Parliament of the RSA," National Assembly of Parliament of the Republic of the Côte d'Ivoire, Aug. 14, 2006. Nov. 4, 2006, http://www.parliament.gov.za/pls/portal/web_app.utl_output_doc?p_table=press_releases&p_doc_col=press_release&p_mime_col=mime_type&p_id=638993.

82. BuaNews, "South Africa; Mbeki Commits to Sustaining Women's Emancipation," *Africa News*, Aug. 9, 2006.

83. Audrey Edwards, "The Leaders of the Movement—Women's Role in Ending Apartheid in South Africa—South Africa Reborn," *Essence*, Oct, 1997. Nov. 6, 2006, http://www.findarticles.com/p/articles/mi_m1264/is_n6_v28/ai_19801496.

84. Progressiveafricans, "Fatoumata Jahumpa-Ceesay Is New Speaker of National Assembly," Gambia News Site, Feb. 5, 2007. Feb. 5, 2007, http://state housenews. info/index.php?option=com_content&task =view&id=137&Itemid=9.

85. "Citation, Hon. (Mrs.) Fatoumata Jahumpa-Ceesay, Parliamentarian Par Excellence," email attachment to the author by The Gambian Embassy in the United States, Feb. 7, 2007.

86. Sulayman Joof, "Fatou Jahumpa-Ceesay: an Amazone Queen," Gambia News Site, Feb. 6, 2007. Feb. 15, 2007, http://statehousenews.info/index.php? option= com_content&task=view&id=139&Itemid=9.

87. "Citation, Hon. (Mrs.) Fatoumata Jahumpa-Ceesay."

88. "Citation, Hon. (Mrs.) Fatoumata Jahumpa-Ceesay."

89. "Citation, Hon. (Mrs.) Fatoumata Jahumpa-Ceesay."

90. "Citation, Hon. (Mrs.) Fatoumata Jahumpa-Ceesay."

91. "Citation, Hon. (Mrs.) Fatoumata Jahumpa-Ceesay."

92. "Citation, Hon. (Mrs.) Fatoumata Jahumpa-Ceesay."

93. "Citation, Hon. (Mrs.) Fatoumata Jahumpa-Ceesay."

94. Ethirajan Anbarasan, "Wangari Muta Maathai: Kenya's Green Militant," *UNESCO Courier*, Dec. 1999. May 13, 2006, http://www.unesco.org/courier/1999_12/ uk/dires/intro.htm.

95. Elizabeth MacDonald and Chana R. Schoenberge, "Special Report: The 100 Most Powerful Women," "#68 Wangari Maathai Nobel Laureate, Deputy Minister of Environment: Kenya," Forbes.com, Jul. 28, 2005. Sept. 1, 2006, http://www.forbes.com/ lists/2005/11/BDLL.html.

96. MacDonald and Schoenberge, "#68 Wangari Maathai."

97. Anbarasan, "Wangari Muta Maathai."

98. Green Belt Movement, "Curriculum Vitae," 2006. Oct. 22, 2006, http://greenbeltmovement.org/w. php?id=47.

99. Green Belt Movement, "About Wangari Maathai: Summary Biography of Professor Wangari Maathai," n.d. Oct. 20, 2006, http://greenbeltmovement.org/w. php?id=3.

100. Green Belt Movement, "About Wangari Maathai."

101. BBC News, "The Green Belt Movement: Profile: Wangari Maathai," Oct. 10, 2004. Oct. 20, 2006, http://greenbeltmovement.org/a.php?id=18.

102. BBC News, "The Green Belt Movement."

103. Anbarasan, "Wangari Muta Maathai."

104. Maathai in Brill, ed., 240.

105. Maathai in Brill, ed., 240.

106. Maathai in Brill, ed., 245.

107. Maathai in Brill, ed., 245.

108. Anbarasan, "Wangari Muta Maathai."

109. MacDonald and Schoenberge, "#68 Wangari Maathai."

110. Green Belt Movement, "Nobel Citation," 2004. Oct. 22, 2006, http://greenbeltmovement.org/ w.php?id=45.

111. Green Belt Movement, "Curriculum Vitae."

112. Green Belt Movement, "Curriculum Vitae."

113. Maathai in Brill, ed., 245.

114. Farkhonda Hassan, "Bióloga and Egyptian Química," n.d. Nov. 30, 2006, translated version of http://www.ikuska.com/Africa/Historia/biografias/ biografias_g1.htm.

115. Global Alliance, "Prominent Women: Farkhonda M. Hassan, Ph.D.," 2006. Nov. 30, 2006, http://www.globalalliancesmet.org/prom_hassan.html; National Council for Women, "The Secretary General Farkhonda Hassan Member of Parliament Biography," 2005. Dec. 8, 2006, http://www.ncwegypt.com/ english/coun_sec.jsp.

116. National Council for Women, "The Secretary General."

117. "Egypt: Getting Tougher on Women's Rights," *Al-Ahram Weekly*, no. 527 (Mar. 29–Apr. 4, 2001). Nov. 30, 2006, http://weekly.ahram.org.eg/2001/527/ eg13.htm.

118. Global Alliance, "Prominent Women."

119. "Egypt: Getting Tougher on Women's Rights."

120. Allan Burch, Biography for Farkhonda Hassan in Farkhonda Hassan, "Essays on Science and Society: Islamic Women in Science," *Science* 290, no. 5489 (Oct. 6, 2000): 55. Nov. 30, 2006, http://www.sciencemag.org/cgi/content/full/290/5489/55; National Council for Women, "The Secretary General."

121. National Council for Women, "The Secretary General."

122. Burch, "Essays on Science and Society." American University in Cairo, "2004–2005 Catalog," Appendix: Personnel and Enrollment, Faculty Register. Dec. 1, 2006, http://www.aucegypt.edu/catalog 04/appendix/facreg/*facreg.htm*; National Council for Women, "The Secretary General."

123. *Chem@AUC*, "Retirement...," American University in Cairo: Chemistry Department Newsletter, no. 4 (June 2004), 2. Nov. 30, 2006, http://www.aucegypt.edu/academic/chemistry/newsletters/2004.pdf.

124. American University in Cairo, "2004–2005 Catalog."

125. *Chem@AUC*, "Retirement... ."

126. Judith Miller, "Egypt Acts to Shield Nature from Modern Life's Ravages," *New York Times*, Jul. 29, 1983, Cairo, Friday, Late City Final Ed., A3.

127. Miller, "Egypt Acts to Shield Nature."

128. "Egypt: Getting Tougher on Women's Rights."

129. "Gender Insensitive Policies Keep African Women Marginalized," Panafrican News Agency (PANA) Daily Newswire, Oct. 9, 2004.

130. United Nations, Integrated Regional Information Networks, "Egypt; Activists Call Appointments of Women, Minorities 'Fig-Leaf,'" *Africa News*, Dec. 14, 2005.

131. United Nations, "Egypt; Activists."

132. "Memory of a Murdered President Disarms Egypt's Virgin Policemen; Conference Notebook: Robert Fisk Finds the Authorities Adopting a Creative Attitude to the Security Question," *The Independent* (London), Sept. 5, 1994, Sec.: International News Page, 7.

133. National Council for Women, "The Secretary General."

134. "Dr. Ngozi Okonjo-Iweala," Africa Centre, London: *Contemporary Africa Database*: Positions, Sept. 26, 2006. Oct. 31, 2006, http://people.africadatabase. org/en/person/16262.html; Elizabeth MacDonald and Chana R. Schoenberge, "Special Report: The 100 Most

Powerful Women: #62 Ngozi Okonjo-Iweala, Nigeria" Forbes.com, Aug. 31, 2006. Oct. 31, 2006, http://www. forbes.com/lists/2006/11/06women_Ngozi — Okonjo-Iweala_H2RN.html; United Nations, Office for the Coordination of Humanitarian Affairs, "Minister's Departure Spawns Fears That Anti-graft Fight Waning," IRINnews.org, Aug. 11, 2006. Oct. 31, 2006, http://www.irinnews.org/report. asp?ReportID=55081 &SelectRegion=West_Africa&SelectCountry=NIGE RIA.

135. MacDonald and Schoenberge, "#62 Ngozi Okonjo-Iweala."

136. "Dr. Ngozi Okonjo-Iweala," *Contemporary Africa Database*; MacDonald and Schoenberge, "#62 Ngozi Okonjo-Iweala"; United Nations, "Minister's Departure."

137. Michael Okoye, "The Blessing," KWENU! Our culture, our future, Abuja, Nigeria, May 25, 2006. Nov. 1, 2006, http://www.kwenu.com/publications/okoye/the_blessing.htm.

138. "Dr. Ngozi Okonjo-Iweala, *Contemporary Africa Database*.

139. Vital Voices, "2006 Global Leadership Awards and Benefit: Women Changing Our World," Apr. 27, 2006. Nov. 1, 2006, http://www.vitalvoices.org/desk topdefault.aspx?page_id=372.

140. BBC, "Profile: Nigeria's Respected Finance Minister," Apr. 24 2006. Oct. 31, 2006, http://odili.net /news/source/2006/apr/24/85.html; Columbia University, "World Leaders Forum: Ngozi Okonjo-Iweala," 2006. Oct. 31, 2006, http://www.worldleaders.colum bia.edu/bio_okonjo-iweala.html.

141. MacDonald and Schoenberge, "#62 Ngozi Okonjo-Iweala."

142. MacDonald and Schoenberge, "#62 Ngozi Okonjo-Iweala"; United Nations, "Minister's Departure."

143. United Nations, "Minister's Departure."

144. Nora Boustany, "Rebuilding a Life and Then a Country," *Washington Post*, May 10, 2006, A21. Oct. 31, 2006, http://www.washingtonpost.com/wp-dyn/content/ article/2006/05/09/AR2006050901831.html.

145. allAfrica.com, "Nigeria: Honoured Offshore, Ignored At Home," Oct. 22, 2006. Oct. 31, 2006, http://allafrica.com/stories/200610230442.html.

146. United Nations, "Minister's Departure."

147. Nora Boustany, "Rebuilding a Life and Then a Country."

148. Nora Boustany, "Rebuilding a Life and Then a Country."

149. allAfrica.com, "Nigeria: Honoured Offshore."

150. Ann McFerran, "I Keep My Ego in My Handbag," *Guardian*, Aug. 1, 2005. Oct. 31, 2006, http://www.guardian.co.uk/g2/story/0,3604,1540043,00.html.

151. McFerran, "I Keep My Ego in My Handbag."

152. allAfrica.com, "Nigeria: Honoured Offshore"; Columbia University, "World Leaders Forum."

153. BBC, "Profile: Nigeria's Respected Finance Minister."

154. McFerran, "I Keep My Ego in My Handbag."

155. Edna Adan Ismail, Curriculum Vita, Aug. 1, 2006.

156. Edna Adan Ismail, email interview from Hargeisa, Somaliland, Jan. 12, 2007.

157. Ismail, email interview, Jan. 12, 2007.

158. Ismail, email interview, Jan. 12, 2007.

159. Lawrence V. Conway (President, Medical Mission Hall of Fame Foundation, Medical College of Ohio), Letter to Edna Adan Ismail, Oct. 1, 2006.

160. "About Amanitare," n.d. Jan. 22, 2007, http://www.rainbo.org/amanitare/about.html.

161. Ismail, Curriculum Vita, Aug. 1, 2006.

162. Ismail, Curriculum Vita.

163. Ismail, Curriculum Vita.

164. Ismail, Curriculum Vita.

165. Ismail, Curriculum Vita.

166. Ismail, Curriculum Vita.

167. Ismail, Curriculum Vita.

168. Ismail, Curriculum Vita.

169. Ismail, Curriculum Vita.

170. Ismail, Curriculum Vita.

171. Anita le Roux, "Addressing the Problem of the Drug Qat," Institute for Human Rights and Criminal Justice Studies, ICC, Durban, Dec. 3–7, 2001, 2. Mar. 19, 2007, http://www.crimeinstitute.ac.za/2ndconf/papers/le_roux.pdf.

172. Ismail, email interview, Jan. 12, 2007.

173. Ismail, email interview, Jan. 12, 2007.

174. *Note: Photograph of Senator Nyiramirimo located at*: Republic of Rwanda: Senate, Members, "Dr. Nyiramirimo, Odette," 2007. Mar. 31, 2007, http://www.rwandaparliament.gov.rw/SE/uk/compo/index.htm.

175. Republic of Rwanda: Senate, Members, "Dr. Nyiramirimo, Odette"; Marc Lacey, "Women's Voices Rise as Rwanda Reinvents Itself," *New York Times*, Feb. 26, 2005. Nov. 16, 2006, http://www.genocidewatch.org/rwandawomensvoicesriseasrwandareinventsitself 26feb05.htm.

176. Philip Gourevitch, *We Wish to Inform You That Tomorrow We Will Be Killed with our Families: Stories from Rwanda*, 1st ed., New York: Farrar, Straus, and Giroux, 1998, 66, 67.

177. Gourevitch, *We Wish to Inform You*, 70.

178. Republic of Rwanda: Senate, Members, "Dr. Nyiramirimo"; Gourevitch, *We Wish to Inform You*, 70.

179. "Odette Nyiramilimo," *Wikipedia*, Oct. 25, 2006. Nov. 17, 2006, http://en.wikipedia.org/wiki/Odette_Nyiramilimo.

180. Gourevitch, *We Wish to Inform You*, 63.

181. Gourevitch, *We Wish to Inform You*, 66–67.

182. "Odette Nyiramilimo," *Wikipedia*; Gourevitch, *We Wish to Inform You*, 236.

183. Gourevitch, *We Wish to Inform You*, 236.

184. Gourevitch, *We Wish to Inform You*, 72–73, 101, 102.

185. "Juvénal Habyarimana," *Wikipedia*, Nov. 25, 2006. Nov. 26, 2006, http://en.wikipedia.org/wiki/Juv%C3%A9nal_Habyarimana.

186. United Nations High Commissioner for Refugees (UNHCR), "Rwanda: The Heart of Darkness Revisited," *Refugees Magazine*, I. 135 (June 2004). Nov. 16, 2006, http://www.unhcr.org/publ/PUBL/4100cd 774.html.

187. Gourevitch, *We Wish to Inform You*, 112, 118, 120.

188. Gourevitch, *We Wish to Inform You*, 133.

189. United Nations Integrated Regional Information Networks, "Rwanda; Government Puts Genocide Victims At 1.07 Million," *Africa News*, Dec. 19, 2001.

190. Frontline, "The Triumph of Evil: Interviews: Philip Gourevitch," PBS, WGBH, 1995–2006. Nov.

17, 2006, http://www.pbs.org/wgbh/pages/frontline/shows/evil/ interviews/gourevitch.html.

191. Frontline, "The Triumph of Evil."

192. United Nations, "Rwanda: The Heart of Darkness Revisited."

193. United Nations, "Rwanda: The Heart of Darkness Revisited."

194. United Nations, "Rwanda: The Heart of Darkness Revisited."

195. Lacey, "Women's Voices Rise as Rwanda Reinvents Itself"; "Paul Kagame," *Wikipedia*, Dec. 6, 2006. http://en.wikipedia.org/wiki/Paul_Kagame.

196. Inter-Parliamentary Union, "Women in National Parliaments: World Averages," Feb. 28, 2007. Mar. 19, 2007, http://www.ipu.org/wmn-e/classif.htm.

197. Lacey, "Women's Voices Rise as Rwanda Reinvents Itself."

198. Lacey, "Women's Voices Rise as Rwanda Reinvents Itself."

199. Lacey, "Women's Voices Rise as Rwanda Reinvents Itself."

200. *New Times*, "Rwanda; Senator Castigates Rusesbagina," *Africa News*, May 15, 2006; *New Times*, "Rwanda; Rusesabagina Dodges Radio Talk Show," *Africa News*, Feb. 6, 2006; *New Times*, "Rwanda; Senator Castigates Rusesabagina," *Africa News*, May 15, 2006.

201. Edwin Musoni, "Rwanda to Participate in Global Population Forum," *The New Times* (Kigali), Nov. 20, 2006. Nov. 27, 2006, http://allafrica.com/stories/200611200295.html.

202. Musoni, "Rwanda to Participate in Global Population Forum."

Part II

Introduction

1. "Mrs. Mubarak Proposes a New International Forum for Women," Mrs. Suzanne Mubarak Address, June 7, 2000. April 2, 2007, http://www.presidency.gov.eg/html/s_7-June2000_speech.htm.

2. Josephine Ouedraogo, "Presentation on the African Gender and Development Index (AGDI)," Beijing+10 in Africa, News and Information, U.N. Economic Commission for Africa (ECA), Oct. 6–14, 2004. Dec. 10, 2006, http://www.uneca.org/fr/Beijing/Speech_JO_AGDI.htm.

3. Josephine Ouedraogo, "Consolidate Progress Achieved by Women to Better Meet Development Challenges," Beijing+10 in Africa, News and Information, U.N. Economic Commission for Africa (ECA), Apr. 7, 2004. Dec. 10, 2006, http://www.uneca.org/fr/Beijing/interview%20JO.htm.

4. United Nations, Economic Commission for Africa (ECA), *African Women's Report 1998, Post-Conflict Reconstruction in Africa: A Gender Perspective*, Addis Ababa, Ethiopia, 1999, 43, 45. Dec. 21, 2006, www.uneca.org/acgd/Publications/en_awr98.pdf.

5. United Nations, Economic and Social Commission for Western Asia (ESCWA), *Women in Decision-Making in the Arab Region*, EGM/EPWD/2005/OP.1, Dec. 12, 2005, 3, 4. Mar. 23, 2007, http://www.un.org/womenwatch/daw/egm/eql-men/docs/OP.1_ESCWA.pdf.

6. United Nations, ESCWA, *Women in ... the Arab Region*, 4.

7. United Nations, ESCWA, *Women in ... the Arab Region*, 4.

8. United Nations, ESCWA, *Women in ... the Arab Region*, 4.

9. United Nations, *Beijing Declaration and Platform for Action*, Fourth World Conference on Women, Sept. 15 1995, A/CONF.177/20 (1995) and A/CONF.177/20/Add.1 (1995), University of Minn., Human Rights Library. Dec. 12, 2006, http://www1.umn.edu/humanrts/instree/e5dplw.htm.

10. United Nations, Economic Commission for Africa (ECA), *5 Years After Beijing: What Efforts in Favor of African Women? Assessing Political Empowerment of Women*, Addis Ababa, Ethiopia, Sept. 2001. Dec. 10, 2006, http://www.uneca.org/ fr/acgd/en/1024x768/en_12areas/en_politic/en_0109_political.pdf.

11. United Nations, Economic Commission for Africa (ECA), *Promoting Gender Equality and Women's Empowerment in Africa: Questioning the Achievements and Confronting the Challenges Ten Years After Beijing*, Addis Ababa, Ethiopia, Feb. 2005. Dec. 10, 2006, www.uneca.org/acgd/Publications/Gender_Equality.pdf.

12. United Nations, ECA, *5 Years After Beijing*, ii, 16.

13. United Nations, ECA, *5 Years After Beijing*, ii.

14. United Nations, ECA, *5 Years After Beijing*, 1, 11.

15. United Nations, ECA, *Ten Years After Beijing*, 18.

16. United Nations, ECA, *Ten Years After Beijing*, 19.

17. United Nations, ECA, *Ten Years After Beijing*, 19.

18. United Nations, ECA, *Ten Years After Beijing*, 19–20.

19. United Nations, ECA, *Ten Years After Beijing*, 36–37.

20. United Nations, Economic Commission for Africa (ECA), *African Governance Report 2005*, Addis Ababa, Ethiopia, Nov. 2005, 29. Dec. 12, 2006, http://www.uneca.org/agr/agren.pdf.

21. United Nations, ECA, *African Governance Report 2005*, 30–31, Fig. 1.10.

22. United Nations, ECA, *African Governance Report 2005*, 33.

23. Ouedraogo, "Presentation."

24. Ouedraogo, "Presentation."

25. United Nations Economic Commission for Africa (ECA), "*The African Gender and Development Index*," Addis Ababa, Ethiopia, Sept. 2004. Dec. 27, 2006, http://www.uneca.org/eca_programmes/acgd/publications/AGDI_book_final.pdf.

26. Tacko Ndiaye (Economic Affairs Officer, United Nations Economic Commission for Africa, Addis Ababa, Ethiopia), email to author, Dec. 27, 2006.

North Africa

1. United States, Central Intelligence Agency (CIA), "The World Fact Book," Algeria, Mar. 8, 2007. Mar. 10, 2007 and Oct. 4, 2007, https://www.cia.gov/cia/publications/factbook/geos/ag.html.

2. Inter-Parliamentary Union (IPU), *Women in Politics: 60 Years in Retrospect* (data valid as at 1 February 2006), Historical Table, Data Sheet No. 1, 1. May 20, 2006, http://www.ipu.org/PDF/publications/wmninfokit06_en.pdf.

3. IPU, *Women in Politics: 60 Years in Retrospect*, Progress and Setbacks, Data Sheet No. 2, 4.

4. Algeria, People's Democratic Republic of Algeria, Ministry Delegated to the Minister for Health, the Population and the Hospital Reform, Responsible for the Family and the Female Condition, *National Report on the Solemn Declaration on Equality of Men and Women C.U.A.*, Sec. 5, June 2006. Dec. 31, 2006, http://www.africa-union.org/root/au/Conferences/Past/2006/October/WG/Report-Algeria.doc. Translated from French to English by Alta Vista, Babel Fish Translation, http://babelfish.altavista.com/, Jan. 3, 2007.

5. Algeria, *National Report on the Solemn Declaration*, Sec. 5. Translated from French to English by Alta Vista, Babel Fish.

6. Algeria, *Algeria: Reply to the Questionnaire to Governments on Implementation of the Beijing Platform for Action (1995) and the Outcome of the Twenty-Third Special Session of the General Assembly (2000)*, 2004:14. Mar. 15, 2007, http://www.un.org/womenwatch/daw/Review/responses/ALGERIA-English.pdf.

7. Algeria, "The Institutions of the Government of Algeria," 2006. Jan. 4, 2007, http://www.elmouradia.dz/francais/institution/gov/GOV.htm.

8. Algeria, *Algeria: Reply to the Questionnaire*, 3.

9. United States, CIA, "The World Fact Book," Egypt, Mar. 8, 2007. Mar. 10, 2007, https://www.cia.gov/cia/publications/factbook/geos/eg.html.

10. United States, CIA, "The World Fact Book," Egypt.

11. IPU, *Women in Politics: 60 Years in Retrospect*, Progress and Setbacks, Historical Table, Data Sheet No. 1, 2.

12. United Nations, ECA, *5 Years After Beijing*, 16.

13. IPU, *Women in Politics: 60 Years in Retrospect*, Progress and Setbacks, Data Sheet No. 2, 4.

14. Egypt, National Council for Women, *Egypt, Beijing+10* report, n.d., 2, 3. Mar. 14, 2007, http://www.un.org/womenwatch/daw/Review/responses/EGYPT-English.pdf; Egypt, National Council for Women, 2007. Mar. 24, 2007, http://www.ncwegypt.com/english/index.jsp.

15. Egypt, National Council of Women, *Beijing+10*, 3.

16. Egypt, National Council of Women, *Beijing+10*, 13.

17. Egypt, National Council of Women, *Beijing+10*, 12. 13.

18. Egypt, National Council of Women, *Beijing+10*, 13.

19. Egypt, National Council of Women, *Beijing+10*, 13.

20. United States, CIA, "The World Fact Book," Libya, Mar. 15, 2007. Mar. 23, 2007, https://www.cia.gov/cia/publications/factbook/geos/ly.html.

21. United Nations, Division for the Advancement of Women, "Fact Sheet on Women in Government," January 1996. Mar. 9, 2007, http://www.un.org/womenwatch/daw/public/percent.htm.

22. "Libya: Women," *Africa Centre, Contemporary Africa Database*, London, Sept. 26, 2006. Mar. 23, 2007, http://people.africadatabase.org/en/n/cty/fem/28/.

23. United Nations, *Network: Women's Newsletter*, vol. 5. no. 1, March 2001. March 23, 2007, http://www.un.org/womenwatch/osagi/network/mar2001.htm.

24. Libya, *Reply to Questionnaire on the Implementation of the Beijing Platform for Action* (Arabic) 2000. Mar. 23, 2007, http://www.un.org/womenwatch/daw/followup/responses/Libya.pdf; United Nations, Division for the Advancement of Women, Department of Economic and Social Affairs, "Member States Responses to the Questionnaire," Apr. 30, 2004. Mar. 16, 2007, http://www.un.org/womenwatch/daw/Review/english/responses.htm.

25. United Nations, ESCWA, *Women in ... the Arab Region*, 4, 5, 6.

26. United States, CIA, "The World Fact Book," Mauritania, Mar. 11, 2007. Mar. 8, 2007, https://www.cia.gov/cia/publications/factbook/geos/mr.html.

27. Women's Learning Partnership, "Mauritania: Women's Status at a Glance," 2007. Mar. 12, 2007, http://www.learningpartnership.org/partners/mauritania.

28. IPU, *Women in Politics: 60 Years in Retrospect*, Historical Table, Data Sheet No. 1, 3.

29. Mauritania, Islamic Republic of Mauritania, Secretary of State for the Condition of Women, *Evaluation of the Institution of the Recommendations of the Plan of Action of Beijing: Beijing+10*, April 2004, 31, 32. Mar. 11, 2007, http://www.un.org/womenwatch/daw/Review/responses/MAURITANIA-English.pdf.

30. Mohamed Khayar, "Electoral Changes in Mauritania Yield Victory for Women," Feb. 14, 2007. Mar. 12, 2007, http://www.magharebia.com/cocoon/awi/print/en_GB/features/awi/features/2007/02/14/feature-02.

31. Mauritania, *Beijing+10*, 29.

32. Mauritania, *Beijing+10*, 31.

33. United States, CIA, "The World Fact Book," Morocco, Mar. 15, 2007. Mar. 23, 2007, https://www.cia.gov/cia/publications/factbook/geos/mo.html.

34. IPU, *Women in Politics: 60 Years in Retrospect*, Historical Table, Data Sheet No. 1, 4.

35. IPU, *Women in Politics: 60 Years in Retrospect*, Progress and Setbacks, Data Sheet No. 2, 1.

36. IPU, *Women in Politics: 60 Years in Retrospect*, Participation of Women and Men, Data Sheet No. 6, 3.

37. Morocco, *National Report Beijing+10*, n.d., 3. Mar. 23, 2007, http://www.un.org/womenwatch/daw/Review/responses/MOROCCO-English.pdf.

38. Morocco, *Beijing+10*, 2.

39. Morocco, *Beijing+10*, 22.

40. Morocco, *Beijing+10*, 22.

41. Morocco, *Beijing+10*, 30.

42. United States, CIA, "The World Fact Book," Sudan, Mar. 15, 2007. Mar. 23, 2007, https://www.cia.gov/cia/publications/factbook/geos/su.html.

43. IPU, *Women in Politics: 60 Years in Retrospect*, Historical Table, Data Sheet No. 1, 5.

44. IPU, *Women in Politics: 60 Years in Retrospect*, Progress and Setbacks, Data Sheet No. 2, 2.

45. Sudan, Ministry of Welfare and Social Development, General Directorate for Women and the Family, *Quarter-Century Strategy for the Advancement of Women 2003–2027*, Sept. 2002, 2, 3. Mar. 23, 2007, http://www.un.org/womenwatch/daw/Review/responses/SUDAN-English.pdf.

46. Sudan, *Quarter-Century Strategy*, 3, 4.

47. Sudan, *Quarter-Century Strategy*, 5.

48. United Nations, ESCWA, *Women in ... the Arab Region*, 4, 5, 6.

49. United Nations, Division for the Advancement

of Women, Department of Economic and Social Affairs, Convention on the Elimination of All Forms of Discrimination (CEDAW), "Country Reports," Aug. 31, 2006. Mar. 23, 2007, http://www.un.org/womenwatch/daw/cedaw/reports.htm#s.

50. United States, CIA, "The World Fact Book," Tunisia, Mar. 15, 2007. Mar. 23, 2007, https://www.cia.gov/cia/publications/factbook/geos/ts.html.

51. Tunisia, Republic of Tunisia, Ministry for Women's, Family, and Children's Affairs and the People, Initial Report of Tunisia, *Solemn Declaration on the Equality Between Men and Women in Africa*, Introduction, June 2006. Dec. 30, 2006, http://www.africa-union.org/root/au/Conferences/Past/2006/October/WG/Report-Tunisia.doc. Translated from French to English by Alta Vista, Babel Fish Translation, http://babelfish.altavista.com/, Jan. 7, 2007.

52. Tunisia, *Solemn Declaration*, Sec. 5.

53. Tunisia, *Solemn Declaration*, Sec. 5.

54. Tunisia, Tunisian Republic Ministry of Women's, Family and Children's Affairs Board of General Communications and Information, *Reply of Tunisia to the Questionnaire to Governments on Implementation of the Beijing Platform for Action* (1995) *and the Outcome of the Twenty-third Special Session of the General Assembly* (2000), Tunis, May 2005, 9. Mar. 2, 2007, http://www.un.org/womenwatch/daw/Review/responses/TUNISIA-English.pdf.

55. Tunisia, *Solemn Declaration*, Sec. 5.

56. IPU, *Women in Politics: 60 Years in Retrospect*, Historical Table, Data Sheet No. 1, 5.

57. Tunisia, *Solemn Declaration*, Sec. 5.

58. IPU, *Women in Politics: 60 Years in Retrospect*, Progress and Setbacks, Data Sheet No. 2, 1.

59. Tunisia, *Reply to Beijing and General Assembly*, 25–26.

60. Tunisia, *Solemn Declaration*, Sec. 5.

61. Tunisia, *Reply to Beijing and General Assembly*, 39.

62. United States, CIA, "The World Fact Book," Western Sahara, Mar. 15, 2007. Mar. 24, 2007, https://www.cia.gov/cia/publications/factbook/geos/wi.html#Govt.

63. Rod Usher, "A World Where Muslim Women Wear the Pants," Peace Women, Women's International League for Peace and Freedom, n.d. Mar. 24, 2007, http://www.peacewomen.org/news/WesternSahara/newsarchive/pants.html.

64. Pascale Harter, "Sahara Women Relish Their Rights," BBC News, Oct. 30, 2003. Mar. 24, 2007, http://news.bbc.co.uk/2/hi/africa/3227997.stm.

65. "Western Sahara," People, Women in Western Sahara, *Africa Centre. Contemporary Africa Database*, London, Sept. 26, 2006. Mar. 24, 2007, http://people.africadatabase.org/en/n/cty/fem/51/.

Central Africa

1. United States, Central Intelligence Agency (CIA), "The World Fact Book," Republic of Cameroon, Mar. 15 and Oct. 4, 2007. Mar. 26 and Oct. 11, 2007, https://www.cia.gov/cia/publications/factbook/geos/cm.html#Govt.

2. Cameroon, Ministry of Women's Affairs, *Replies to Questionnaire on the Implementation Of the Dakar and Beijing Platforms*, n.d., 2. Apr. 1, 2007, http://www.un.org/womenwatch/daw/Review/responses/CAMEROON-English.pdf.

3. Inter-Parliamentary Union (IPU), *Women in Politics: 60 Years in Retrospect* (data valid as at 1 February 2006), Historical Table, Data Sheet No. 1, 1. May 20, 2006, http://www.ipu.org/PDF/publications/wmninfokit06_en.pdf.

4. IPU, *Women in Politics: 60 Years in Retrospect*, Progress and Setbacks, Data Sheet No. 2, 4.

5. Cameroon, *Replies to Dakar and Beijing Platforms*, n.d., 3.

6. United States, CIA, "The World Fact Book," Central African Republic, Mar. 15, 2007. Mar. 26, 2007, https://www.cia.gov/cia/publications/factbook/geos/ct.html#People.

7. IPU, *Women in Politics: 60 Years in Retrospect*), Historical Table, Data Sheet No. 1, 1.

8. IPU, *Women in Politics: 60 Years in Retrospect*, A Chronology of Women, Data Sheet No. 4, Women Prime Ministers.

9. IPU, *Women in Politics: 60 Years in Retrospect*, Progress and Setbacks, Data Sheet No. 2, 2.

10. Central African Republic, Ministry of the Family, Central African Republic Social Affairs and National Solidarity, Cabinet, *Implementation of The Beijing Platform for Action (1995) and The Outcome of the 23rd Special Session ff the General Assembly (2000) in the Central African Republic*, n.d., 7, 8. Apr. 2, 2007, http://www.un.org/womenwatch/daw/Review/responses/CENTRAL-AFRICAN-REPUBLIC-English.pdf.

11. Central African Republic, *Beijing and General Assembly*, 18, 20.

12. United States, CIA, "The World Fact Book," Chad, Mar. 15, 2007. Mar. 26 and Oct. 24, 2007, https://www.cia.gov/cia/publications/factbook/geos/cd.html#Geo.

13. Chad, Republic of Chad, Ministry of Social Action and the Family, N'Djamena, *Reply to Questionnaires on Gender and Information and Communication Technologies in Chad*, May 14, 2004, 1. Apr. 1, 2007, http://www.un.org/womenwatch/daw/Review/responses/CHAD-English.pdf.

14. Chad, *Reply Gender and Information and Communication Technologies*, 2.

15. IPU, *Women in Politics: 60 Years in Retrospect*, Historical Table, Data Sheet No. 1, 2.

16. IPU, *Women in Politics: 60 Years in Retrospect*, Progress and Setbacks, Data Sheet No. 2, 4.

17. United States, Central Intelligence Agency (CIA), "The World Fact Book," Republic of the Congo, Mar. 15, Aug. 27 and Oct. 4, 2007. Mar. 26, Aug. 27 and Oct. 11, 2007, https://www.cia.gov/cia/publications/factbook/geos/cg.html#Intro.

18. Phuong Tran, "Republic of Congo's Ruling Coalition Wins Election Amidst Accusations of Fraud," Voice of America, Dakar, Aug. 10, 2007. Aug. 27, 2007, http://www.voanews.com:80/english/2007-08-10-voa44.cfm.

19. Inter-Parliamentary Union. *Women in Politics: 60 Years in Retrospect* (data valid as at 1 February 2006), Historical Table, Data Sheet No. 1, 2. May 20, 2006, http://www.ipu.org/PDF/publications/wmninfokit06_en.pdf.

20. Inter-Parliamentary Union, *Women in Politics: 60 Years in Retrospect* (data valid as at 1 February 2006),

Progress and Setbacks, Data Sheet No. 2, 2. May 20, 2006, http://www.ipu.org/PDF/publications/wmninfokit 06_en.pdf.

21. Congo, Republic of the Congo, Ministry of Agriculture, Livestock, Fisheries and the Advancement of Women, Secretary of State, Cabinet, *Reply to the Questionnaire Concerning the Report of the Congo on Implementation of the Dakar Plan of Action and Beijing +10*, n.d., 5. Apr. 1, 2007, http://www.un.org/women watch/daw/Review/responses/CONGO-English.pdf.

22. Congo, *Dakar and Beijing +10*, 5.

23. Congo, *Dakar and Beijing +10*, 15.

24. Congo, *Dakar and Beijing +10*, 16, 17.

25. Congo, *Dakar and Beijing +10*, 14, 17.

26. United States, CIA, "The World Fact Book," Equatorial Guinea, Mar. 15, 2007. Mar. 26, 2007, https://www.cia.gov/cia/publications/factbook/geos/ek.html.

27. IPU, *Women in Politics: 60 Years in Retrospect*, Historical Table, Data Sheet No. 1, 2.

28. IPU, *Women in Politics: 60 Years in Retrospect*, Progress and Setbacks, Data Sheet No. 2, 2.

29. Equatorial Guinea, "Government," Apr. 2, 2007. Apr. 2, 2007, http://guinea-equatorial.com/gov. asp.

30. United Nations, Committee on the Elimination of Discrimination against Women (CEDAW), *Responses to the List of Issues and Questions for Consideration of the Combined Second, Third, Fourth and Fifth Periodic Reports, Equatorial Guinea*, CEDAW/PSWG/2004/II/CRP.2/Add.2, Apr. 1, 2004, 4. Apr. 1, 2007, http://www.un.org/womenwatch/daw/cedaw/cedaw31/EqGuinea-crp2add2-e.pdf.

31. United Nations, CEDAW, *Responses of the Combined Second, Third, Fourth and Fifth Periodic Reports, Equatorial Guinea*, 6.

32. "Equatorial Guinea," 2006. Mar. 30, 2007, http://www.freedomhouse.org/uploads/WoW/2006/EquatorialGuinea2006.pdf.

33. AFROL Gender Profiles: Equatorial Guinea, Apr. 2, 2007. Apr. 2, 2007, http://www.afrol.com/Categories/Women/profiles/equatorialguinea_women.htm.

34. United States, CIA, "The World Fact Book," Gabon, Mar. 15, 2007. Mar. 26, 2007, https://www.cia.gov/cia/publications/factbook/geos/gb.html#People.

35. IPU, *Women in Politics: 60 Years in Retrospect*, Historical Table, Data Sheet No. 1, 2.

36. IPU, *Women in Politics: 60 Years in Retrospect*, Progress and Setbacks, Data Sheet No. 2, 3.

37. Gabon, Republique Gabonaise, Ministere de LaFamille, de la Protection de L'enfance et de la Promotion de la Femme, *Rapport Sur L'Evaluation Decennale De La Mise En Ceuvres Des Plates-Formes D'Actions De Dakar Et De Beijing*, Feb. 2004, 9. Apr, 2, 2007, http://www.un.org/womenwatch/daw/Review/responses/GABON-French.pdf. Translated from French to English by Alta Vista, Babel Fish Translation, http://babelfish.altavista.com/, Apr, 2, 2007.

38. United Nations, CEDAW, *Concluding Comments: Gabon*, CEDAW/C/GAB/CC/2-5, February 15, 2005, 2. Apr. 2, 2007, http://www.un.org/women watch/daw/cedaw/cedaw32/conclude-comments/Gabon/CEDA W-CC-GAB-0523904e.pdf.

39. United Nations, CEDAW, *Concluding Comments: Gabon*, 6.

40. United States, CIA, "The World Fact Book," São Tomé & Príncipe, Mar. 8, 2007. Mar. 12, 2007, https://www.cia.gov/cia/publications/factbook/geos/tp.html.

41. IPU, *Women in Politics: 60 Years in Retrospect*, 4.

42. IPU, *Women in Politics: 60 Years in Retrospect*, Progress and Setbacks of Women in National Parliaments Between 01.07.1995 and 01.02.2006, Data Sheet No. 2.

43. São Tomé & Príncipe, *Reply to Questionnaire on the Implementation of the Beijing Platform for Action*, Aug. 18, 2000, 15, 19. Feb. 28, 2007, http://www.un.org/womenwatch/daw/followup/countrylist.htm. Translated from French to English by Alta Vista, Babel Fish Translation, http://babelfish.altavista.com/, Feb. 28, 2007.

44. United Nations, "General Assembly Reaffirms Commitment to 1995 Beijing Conference Goals, as 'Women 2000' Special Session Concludes at Headquarters," Press Release GA/9725, June 10, 2000. Feb. 28, 2007, http://www.un.org/News/Press/docs/2000/2000 0610.ga9725.doc.html.

45. United Nations, "General Assembly Reaffirms Commitment."

46. World Bank, *São Tomé and Príncipe Country Gender Assessment*, Draft for Review Only, Report No. xxxxx-STP, Human Development II, Country Department 15, Africa Region June 7, 2004, 28. Feb. 28, 2007, http://siteresources.worldbank.org/EXTAFRREGTOP GENDER/Resources/SaoTomeCGA.pdf.

47. World Bank, *São Tomé and Príncipe Country Gender Assessment*, 28, 29.

48. World Bank, *Gender Assessment*, 29.

49. World Bank, *Gender Assessment*, 29.

50. World Bank, *Gender Assessment*, 31.

East Africa

1. United States, Central Intelligence Agency (CIA), "The World Fact Book," Burundi, Mar. 8, 2007. Mar. 10, 2007, http://www.cia.gov/cia/publications/factbook/geos/by.html.

2. Inter-Parliamentary Union (IPU), *Women in Politics: 60 Years in Retrospect* (data valid as at 1 February 2006), Historical Table, Data Sheet No. 1, 1; Participation of Women and Men in Decision Making, Data Sheet No. 6, 4. May 20, 2006, http://www.ipu.org/PDF/publications/wmninfokit06_en.pdf.

3. Burundi, Embassy of the Republic of Burundi, Addis Abeba, *Republique du Burundi Declaration Solennelle Sur L'egalite Entre Les Hommes et Les Femmes en Afrique: Rapport Initial*, Article 5. The Principle of the Parity Between the Men and the Women, Bujumbura, Sept. 2006. Translated from French to English by Alta Vista, Babel Fish Translation, http://babelfish.altavista.com/, Dec. 31, 2006. Dec. 31, 2006, http://www.africa-union.org/root/ua/Conferences/novembre/GE/2-3% 20oct/Report-Burundi.doc.

4. Burundi, *Declaration Solennelle Sur L'egalite*, Article 5.

5. Burundi, *Declaration*, Article 5.

6. Burundi, *Declaration*, Article 5.

7. United States, CIA, "The World Fact Book," Comoros, Mar. 15, 2007. Mar. 26, 2007, https://www.cia.gov/cia/publications/factbook/geos/cn.html.

8. Comores, Union of Comores, Ministere Des Affaires Sociales et Des Reformes Administratives,

Direction Nationale De La Promotion De La Femme et de Groupe Vulnerable, Direction de la Promotion de la Femme, *Rapport D'Evaluation National De La Plate-Forme D'Action De Beijing (Beijing+10)*, April 2004. Mar. 29, 2007, http://www.un.org/women-watch/daw/Review/responses/COMOROS-French. pdf. Translated from French to English by Alta Vista, Babel Fish Translation, http://babelfish.altavista.com/, Mar. 29, 2007.

9. United States, Department of State, Bureau of Democracy, Human Rights, and Labor, "Comoros, Country Reports on Human Rights Practices," Feb. 25, 2004. Mar. 29, 2007, http://www.state.gov/g/drl/rls/hrrpt/ 2003/27720.htm.

10. IPU, *Women in Politics: 60 Years in Retrospect*, Historical Table, Data Sheet No. 1, 2.

11. IPU, *Women in Politics: 60 Years in Retrospect*, Progress and Setbacks, Data Sheet No. 2, 3.

12. United States, CIA, "The World Fact Book," Democratic Republic of Congo, Mar. 15, 2007. Mar. 26 and Oct. 4, 2007, https://www.cia.gov/cia/publica tions/factbook/geos/cg.html.

13. Democratic Republic of Congo, Ministry of the Condition of Women and the Family, *National Report of the Democratic Republic of Congo on the Review and Evaluation of the Beijing+10 Plan of Action*, Feb. 2004, 21–22. Mar. 29, 2007, http://www.un.org/women watch/daw/Review/responses/DEMREPOFTHE CONGO-English.pdf.

14. IPU, *Women in Politics: 60 Years in Retrospect*, Historical Table, Data Sheet No. 1, 2.

15. IPU, *Women in Politics: 60 Years in Retrospect*, Progress and Setbacks, Data Sheet No. 2, 2.

16. Democratic Republic of Congo, *Beijing+10*, 22–23, 29.

17. Democratic Republic of Congo, *Beijing+10*, 30.

18. United States, CIA, "The World Fact Book," Djibouti, Mar. 15, 2007. Mar. 26, 2007, https://www. cia.gov/cia/publications/factbook/geos/dj.html.

19. IPU, *Women in Politics: 60 Years in Retrospect*, Historical Table, Data Sheet No. 1, 2.

20. IPU, *Women in Politics: 60 Years in Retrospect*, Progress and Setbacks, Data Sheet No. 2, 1.

21. IPU, *Women in Politics: 60 Years in Retrospect*, Participation of Women and Men, Data Sheet No. 6, 3.

22. Djibouti, Republic of Djibouti, Office of the Prime Minister, Ministry for the Promotion of Women, Family Well-Being, and Social Affairs, *National Ten-year Evaluation Report on Implementation of the Beijing Platform for Action*, June 2004, 16. Mar. 30, 2007, http://www.un.org/womenwatch/daw/Review/responses /DJIBOUTI-English.pdf.

23. Djibouti, *Ten-year Report*, 17.

24. Djibouti, *Ten-year Report*, 17.

25. United States, CIA, "The World Fact Book," Eritrea, Mar. 15, 2007. Mar. 26, 2007, https://www.cia. gov/cia/publications/factbook/geos/er.html.

26. IPU, *Women in Politics: 60 Years in Retrospect*, Historical Table, Data Sheet No. 1, 2, n. 4, 6.

27. IPU, *Women in Politics: 60 Years in Retrospect*, Progress and Setbacks, Data Sheet No. 2, 3.

28. Eritrea, *Implementation of the Beijing Platform for Action and The Outcome of the Twenty-Third Special Session of the General Assembly*, Mar. 2004, 6. Mar. 30, 2007, http://www.un.org/womenwatch/daw/Review/responses/ERITREA-ENGLISH.pdf.

29. Eritrea, *Beijing and General Assembly*, Mar. 2004, 7, 8.

30. United States, CIA, "The World Fact Book," Ethiopia, Mar. 8, 2007. Mar. 10, 2007, https://www.cia.gov/cia/publications/factbook/geos/et.html.

31. IPU, *Women in Politics: 60 Years in Retrospect*, Historical Table, Data Sheet No. 1, 2.

32. IPU, *Women in Politics: 60 Years in Retrospect*, Progress and Setbacks, Data Sheet No. 2, 1.

33. United Nations, Economic Commission for Africa (ECA), *African Women's Report 1998, Post-Conflict Reconstruction in Africa: A Gender Perspective*, Addis Ababa, Ethiopia, 1999, 43. Dec. 21, 2006, www. uneca.org/acgd/Publications/en_awr98.pdf.

34. Ethiopia, "*Report of the Federal Democratic Republic of Ethiopia on the Implementation of the Au Solemn Declaration on Gender Equality in Africa*, The Protocol[s], Aug. 2006. Dec. 26, 2006, http://www.africa-union.org/root/au/Conferences/Past/2006/Octo ber/WG/Report-Ethiopia.doc.

35. Ethiopia, *Solemn Declaration*, Introduction.

36. United Nations, ECA, *Post-Conflict Reconstruction*, 44.

37. United Nations, ECA, *Post-Conflict Reconstruction*, 44.

38. Ethiopia, *Solemn Declaration*, Introduction.

39. Ethiopia, *Solemn Declaration*, Gender Parity; Federal Parliament.

40. Ethiopia, *Solemn Declaration*, Gender Parity.

41. Ethiopia, *Solemn Declaration*, Executive Branch.

42. United States, CIA, "The World Fact Book," Lesotho, Mar. 11, 2007. Mar. 8, 2007, https://www.cia. gov/cia/publications/factbook/geos/ke.html.

43. IPU, *Women in Politics: 60 Years in Retrospect*, Historical Table, Data Sheet No. 1, 3.

44. IPU, *Women in Politics: 60 Years in Retrospect*, Progress and Setbacks, Data Sheet No. 2, 3.

45. United Nations, Economic Commission for Africa (ECA), *5 Years After Beijing: What Efforts in Favor of African Women? Assessing Political Empower-ment of Women*, Addis Ababa, Ethiopia, Sept. 2001, 14. Dec. 10, 2006, http://www.uneca. org/fr/acgd/en/1024 sx768/en_12areas/en_politic/en_0109_political.pdf.

46. United Nations, ECA, *5 Years After Beijing*, 14.

47. United Nations, Economic Commission for Africa (ECA), *African Governance Report 2005*, Addis Ababa, Ethiopia, Nov. 2005, 32–33. Dec. 12, 2006, http://www.uneca.org/agr2005/.

48. United States, CIA, "The World Fact Book," Madagascar, Mar. 15, 2007. Mar. 26, 2007, https://www.cia.gov/cia/publications/factbook/geos/ma.html.

49. Madagascar, Republic of Madagascar, Ministere de la Population de la Protection Sociale et des Loisirs, *Rapport National Sur L'Evaluation Decennale De Mise En Application Du Plan D'ActionDE Beijing — Madagascar*, June 2004, 11. Mar. 30, 2007, http://www.un.org/womenwatch/daw/Review/responses/MADAGASCAR -French.pdf. Translated from French to English by Alta Vista, Babel Fish Translation, http://babelfish.altavista. com/, Mar. 30, 2007.

50. Madagascar, *Rapport Beijing — Madagascar*, 11.

51. IPU, *Women in Politics: 60 Years in Retrospect*, Historical Table, Data Sheet No. 1, 3.

52. IPU, *Women in Politics: 60 Years in Retrospect*, Progress and Setbacks, Data Sheet No. 2, 3.

53. United States, CIA, "The World Fact Book,"

Rwanda, Feb. 8, 2007. Mar. 6, 2007, https://www.cia.
gov/cia/publications/factbook/geos/rw.html.

54. Gumisai Mutume, "Women Break into African
Politics Quota Systems Allow More Women to Gain
Elected Office," *Africa Recovery* 18 no. 1 (April 2004):4.
May 15 2006 http://www.un.org/ecosocdev/geninfo/
afrec/vol18no1/181women.htm.

55. Gretchen Bauer and Hannah E. Britton,
"Women in African Parliaments: A Continental Shift?"
in Gretchen Bauer and Hannah E. Britton (eds.),
Women in African Parliaments, Boulder, Colo.: Lynne
Rienner Publishers, 2006, 1; IPU, "Women in National
Parliaments: World Classification," Feb. 28, 2007,
http://www.ipu.org/wmn-e/classif.htm.

56. United Nations, ECA, *10 Years After Beijing*, 19.

57. IPU, *Women in Politics: 60 Years in Retrospect*,
Historical Table, Data Sheet No. 1, 4.

58. IPU, *Women in Politics: 60 Years in Retrospect*,
Progress and Setbacks, Data Sheet No. 2, 1.

59. Rwanda, Ministere du Genre et De La Promotion De La Familie and Secretariat Executif Permanent
De Suivi De Beijing, *Rapport D'Evaluation Decennale
De La Mise en Oeuvre Du Programme D'Action De Beijing*, 1995–2004, 18. Mar. 6, 2007, http://www.un.org/
womenwatch/daw/Review/responses/RWANDA-
French.pdf. Translated from French to English by Alta
Vista, Babel Fish Translation, http://babelfish.altavista.
com/, Mar. 6, 2007.

60. Republic of Rwanda, Government, 2007. Mar.
31, 2007, http://www.gov.rw/government/governmentf.
html.

61. United States, CIA, "The World Fact Book,"
Seychelles, Feb. 8, 2007. Feb. 25, 2007, https://www.
cia.gov/cia/publications/factbook/geos/se.html.

62. Seychelles, Ministry of Social Affairs and Manpower Development, *Country Report: Implementation
of the Beijing Platform for Action*, June 1999, 10. Mar. 6,
2007, http://www.un.org/womenwatch/daw/followup/
responses/Seychelles.pdf.

63. IPU, *Women in Politics: 60 Years in Retrospect*,
Historical Table, Data Sheet No. 1, 5.

64. IPU, *Women in Politics: 60 Years in Retrospect*,
Progress and Setbacks, Data Sheet No. 2, 3.

65. United Nations, ECA, *5 Years After Beijing*, 14.

66. Seychelles, *Country Report [Beijing+10]*, n.d., 1.
Mar. 6, 2007, http://www.un. org/womenwatch/daw/
Review/responses/SEYCHELLES-English.pdf.

67. Seychelles, *Country Report [Beijing+10]*, 8.

68. Seychelles, *Country Report [Beijing+10]*, 9, 10.

69. United States, CIA, "The World Fact Book,"
Somalia, Mar. 15, 2007. Mar. 26, 2007, https://www.
cia.gov/cia/publications/factbook/geos/so.html.

70. IPU, *Women in Politics: 60 Years in Retrospect*,
Historical Table, Data Sheet No. 1, 5.

71. United Nations, Development Programs, Program on Governance in the Arab Region, *The Gender
and Citizenship Initiative: Country Profiles: Somalia*, n.d.
Mar. 30, 2007, http://gender.pogar.org/countries/gen-
der.asp?cid=17.

72. United Nations, Arab Region, *Gender and Citizenship Initiative: Somalia*.

73. United Nations, Office for the Coordination of
Humanitarian Affairs, "Somalia: Women Peace Delegates Lobby for Their Rights," Mar. 28, 2003. Mar. 30,
2007, http://www.irinnews.org/report.aspx?reportid=
42312.

74. United Nations, Security Council, *Report of the
Secretary-General on the Situation in Somalia*, S/2004/
804, Oct. 8, 2004, no. 10, 2. Mar. 30, 2007, http://
www.womenwarpeace.org/somalia/docs/sgreptosc8oct
04.pdf.

75. United Nations, Office for the Coordination of
Humanitarian Affairs, "The Somali Democratic Republic Humanitarian Country Profile," Mar. 2007. Mar.
30, 2007, http://www.irinnews.org/country.aspx?Coun
tryCode=SO&RegionCode=HOA.

76. Somaliland Republic, Country Profile, Somaliland Net, Mar. 30, 2007. Mar. 30, 2007, http://www.
somalilandnet.com/slandhome.shtml; Somaliland, *Wikipedia*, Mar. 27, 2007, Mar. 31, 2007, http://en.wiki
pedia.org/wiki/Somaliland; Somaliland, Constitution,
Somaliland Forum, May 31, 2001. Mar. 31, 2007, http:
//www.somalilandforum.com/somaliland/constitution/
revised_constitution.htm.

77. BBC News, "Regions and Territories: Somaliland," World, Africa, Aug. 22, 2006. Jan. 26, 2007, http:
//news.bbc.co.uk/1/hi/world/africa/country_profiles/
3794847.stm.

78. Edna Adan Ismail, email interview from Hargeisa, Somaliland, Jan. 12, 2007.

79. Ismail, email interview, Jan. 12, 2007.

80. Ismail, email interview, Jan. 12, 2007.

81. Ismail, email interview, Jan. 12, 2007.

82. Somaliland Republic, Ministry of Foreign Affairs,
Edna Adan Ismail, Minister, "Paper, Somaliland's Case,"
term June 2003 to August 2006.

83. Somaliland Republic, Ismail, Minister, "Paper,
Somaliland's Case."

84. Amina Mohamed Warsame, "Assessment of Potential Women Leaders in Somaliland," paper presented
to the 2nd Post-War Reconstruction Strategies Conference, Institute for Practical Research and Training,
Somaliland Women's Research and Action Group, Hargeisa, July 20–25, last Update, Aug. 12, 2006. Jan. 27,
2007, http://www.iprt.org/Amina%20Mohamed%20
Warsame.htm.

85. Warsame, "Assessment of Potential Women
Leaders in Somaliland."

86. Ismail, email interview, Jan. 12, 2007; and Edna
Adan Ismail follow-up email, Feb. 1, 2007.

87. Warsame, "Assessment of Potential Women
Leaders in Somaliland."

88. Bashir Goth, "Somaliland Women: Oppressed
Breadwinners and Silent Peace-makers," Al-Jazeerah,
editorials, March 16, 2005. Jan. 27, 2007, http://www.
aljazeerah.info/Opinion%20editorials/2005%20Opin
ion%20Editorials/March/16%20o/Somaliland%20Wo
men%20Oppressed%20breadwinners%20and%20silen
t%20peacemakers%20BY%20Bashir%20Goth.htm.

89. "Parliament of Tanzania, 2003–2007," www.
bunge.go.tz/bunge/Structure.asp. Accessed August 24,
2007; CIA, Factbook, Tanzania, Oct. 4, 2007.

90. Southern Africa, Electoral Institute of Southern
Africa (EISA), *Election Observer Mission Report, Tanzania Presidential, National Assembly and Local Government Elections*, No. 20, Sec. 3.3. Women and Political
Representation, Dec. 14, 2005, 22. Mar. 5, 2007, http:
//www.eisa.org.za/PDF/tzomr2005.pdf.

91. United Nations, ECA, *5 Years After Beijing*, 19.

92. Tanzania, *Response to UN Questionnaire to
Governments on Implementation of the Beijing Platform
for Action*, n.d., 2, 3, 5, 6, 7. Mar. 4, 2007, http://

www.un.org/womenwatch/daw/followup/responses/
Tanzania.pdf.

93. United States, Agency for International Development (USAID), Gender Assessment for USAID/
Tanzania, Sept. 2003, 38. Mar. 4, 2007, http://www.
usaid.gov/our_work/cross-cutting_programs/wid/pubs
/ga_tanzania.pdf.

94. IPU, *Women in Politics: 60 Years in Retrospect*,
Progress and Setbacks, Data Sheet No. 2, 1.

95. Tanzania, National Website, "Gender," n.d.
Mar. 4, 2007, http://www.tanzania.go.tz/gender.html#
Women%20Political%20Empowerment%20and%20
Decision%20Making.

96. Mathaba News Service, "Africa's First Lady,"
Comment, posted Jan. 2006. Nov. 8, 2006, http://www
.mathaba.net/0_index.shtml?x=504287.

97. United States, CIA, "The World Fact Book,"
Uganda, Feb. 8, 2007. Feb. 25, 2007, https://www.cia.
gov/cia/publications/factbook/geos/ga.html; United
Nations, ECA, *African Governance Report 2005*, 31.

98. United Nations, ECA, *5 Years After Beijing*, 14,
18, 21.

99. IPU, *Women in Politics: 60 Years in Retrospect*,
Historical Table, Data Sheet No. 1, 5.

100. IPU, *Women in Politics: 60 Years in Retrospect*,
Progress and Setbacks, Data Sheet No. 2, 2.

101. United Nations, ECA, "*African Governance
Report 2005*," 31.

102. United Nations, ECA, *Post-Conflict Reconstruction*, 43, 44.

103. Giorgia Testolin, "Handbook on National
Machinery to Promote Gender Equality and Action
Plans: Guidelines for Establishing and Implementing
National Machinery to Promote Equality, with Examples of Good Practice," Council of Europe, Strasbourg,
May 2001 EG (2001) no. 7, 6. Mar. 5, 2007, http://
www.humanrights.coe.int/equality/Eng/WordDocs/eg
(2001)7%20Handbook%20on%20National%20Machinery.doc.

West Africa

1. United States, Central Intelligence Agency
(CIA), "The World Fact Book," Benin, Mar. 15, 2007.
Mar. 26 and Oct. 4, 2007, https://www.cia.gov/cia/
publications/factbook/geos/bn.html.

2. United Nations, Committee on the Elimination
of Discrimination against Women (CEDAW), *Concluding Comments: Benin*, CEDAW/C/BEN/CO/1-3, July
22, 2005, 1, 2, 3. Apr. 2, 2007, http://www.un.org/
womenwatch/daw/cedaw/cedaw33/conclude/benin/05
45054E.pdf.

3. United Nations, CEDAW, *Concluding Comments: Benin*, 4, 5.

4. Inter-Parliamentary Union (IPU), *Women in
Politics: 60 Years in Retrospect* (data valid as at 1 February 2006), Historical Table, Data Sheet No. 1, 1. May
20, 2006, http://www.ipu.org/PDF/publications/wmn
infokit06_en.*pdf*.

5. IPU, *Women in Politics: 60 Years in Retrospect*,
Progress and Setbacks, Data Sheet No. 2, 4.

6. United Nations, Food and Agriculture Organization (FAO), Corporate Document Repository, Sustainable Development Department, "Sharing of Power
and Decision-making," *Fact sheet: Benin—Women,*

Agriculture and Rural Development, n.d. Apr. 3, 2007,
http://www.fao.org/docrep/V7948e/v7948e02.htm.

7. United States, CIA, "The World Fact Book,"
Burkina Faso, Mar. 15, 2007. Mar. 26 and Oct. 4, 2007,
https://www.cia.gov/cia/publications/factbook/geos/uv
.html.

8. IPU, *Women in Politics: 60 Years in Retrospect*,
Historical Table, Data Sheet No. 1, 1.

9. IPU, *Women in Politics: 60 Years in Retrospect*,
Progress and Setbacks, Data Sheet No. 2, 2.

10. United Nations, CEDAW, *Responses to the List
of Issues and Questions for Consideration of the Combined
Fourth and Fifth Periodic Report Burkina Faso*, CEDAW/
PSWG/2005/II/CRP.2/Add.2, April 15, 2005, 12. Apr.
3, 2007, http://www.un.org/womenwatch/daw/cedaw/
cedaw33/responses/bfa/BFA-E.pdf.

11. United Nations, CEDAW, *Responses Burkina
Faso*, 12.

12. United States, CIA, "The World Fact Book,"
Cape Verde, Mar. 15, 2007. Mar. 26, 2007, https://
www.cia.gov/cia/publications/factbook/geos/cv.html#
Govt.

13. IPU, *Women in Politics: 60 Years in Retrospect*,
Historical Table, Data Sheet No. 1, 1.

14. IPU, *Women in Politics: 60 Years in Retrospect*,
Progress and Setbacks, Data Sheet No. 2, 2.

15. United Nations, CEDAW, *Concluding Comments:
Cape Verde*, CEDAW/C/CPV/ CO/6, August 25, 2006,
4, 5. Apr. 2, 2007, http://www.un.org/womenwatch/
daw/cedaw/cedaw36/cc/Cape%20Verde%2025Aug.
pdf.

16. United Nations, CEDAW, "Women's Antidiscrimination Committee Chides Delegation of Cape
Verde over Lateness in Submitting First Report Experts
Praise Female Gains in Education, Judicial, Diplomatic
Fields," General Assembly, WOM/1584, August 18,
2006. Apr. 3, 2007, http://www.un.org/News/Press/
docs/2006/wom1584.doc.htm.

17. United Nations, CEDAW, "Women's Antidiscrimination Committee."

18. United Nations, CEDAW, "Women's Antidiscrimination Committee."

19. United Nations, CEDAW, "Women's Antidiscrimination Committee."

20. United States, CIA), "The World Fact Book,"
Côte d'Ivoire, Mar. 15, 2007. Mar. 26 and Oct. 4, 2007,
https://www.cia.gov/cia/publications/factbook/geos/iv.
html.

21. IPU, *Women in Politics: 60 Years in Retrospect*,
Historical Table, Data Sheet No. 1, 2.

22. IPU, *Women in Politics: 60 Years in Retrospect*,
Progress and Setbacks, Data Sheet No. 2, 4.

23. AFROL Gender Profiles: Côte d'Ivoire, Apr. 4,
2007. Apr. 4, 2007, http://www.afrol.com/Categories/
Women/profiles/civ_women.htm.

24. United States, Department of State, Bureau of
Democracy, Human Rights, and Labor. "Côte d'Ivoire,
Country Reports on Human Rights Practices," Mar. 8,
2006. Apr. 4, 2007, http://www.state.gov/g/drl/rls/
hrrpt/2005/61565.ht*m*.

25. United Nations, Development Programs, *Cadre
D'Orientation Pour L'Integration Du Genre Dans Les Programmes Post-Crise Du Systeme Des Nations Unies en
Côte d'ivore 2006–2007*, Jan. 2006, 42. Apr. 4, 2007,
http://www.ci.undp.org/uploadoc/Rapport.pdf. Translated from French to English by Alta Vista, Babel Fish

Translation, http://babelfish.altavista.com/, Apr. 4, 2007.

26. U.S. CIA, "The World Fact Book," The Gambia, Feb. 8, 2007. Feb. 15, 2007, https://www.cia.gov/cia/publications/factbook/geos/ga.html.

27. "Gambian Parliament Picks First Female Speaker," *Xinhua General News Service* (Dakar), Apr. 22, 2006, World News; Political.

28. IPU, "Gambia (The): General Information About the Parliamentary Chamber or Unicameral Parliament," Jan. 25, 2007. Feb. 13, 2007, http://www.ipu.org/parline-e/reports/2117_A.htm.

29. IPU, "Gambia (The): General Information," 2002. May 16, 2006, http://www.ipu.org/english/parline/reports/2117.htm; IPU, "Gambia (The): General Information About the Parliamentary Chamber or Unicameral Parliament," Jan. 25, 2007. Feb. 13, 2007, http://www.ipu.org/parline-e/reports/2117_A.htm.

30. IPU, *Women in Politics: 60 Years in Retrospect*, Historical Table, Data Sheet No. 1, 2.

31. Progressiveafricans, "Fatoumata Jahumpa-Ceesay Is New Speaker of National Assembly," Gambia News Site, Feb. 5, 2007. Feb. 5, 2007, http://statehousenews.info/index.php?option=com_content&task=view&id=137&Itemid=9.

32. Gambia (The): Mrs. Fatoumata C. M. Tambajang, Minister of Health, Social Welfare and Women's Affairs of the Republic of The Gambia, "Statement," International Conference on Population and Development, Cairo, Sept. 5–13, 1994. Mar. 11, 2007, http://www.un.org/popin/icpd/conference/gov/940913142831.html.

33. Tijan Masanneh-Ceesay, servant of the people, Embassy of The Gambia in the United States, email to author, Feb. 4 and 8, 2007.

34. United Nations, CEDAW, "Women's Anti-discrimination Committee Urges Gambia to Revise Discriminatory Laws Based on Religious, Cultural Practices," 697th and 698th meetings, press release, WOM/1517, July 15, 2005. Feb. 14, 2007, http://www.un.org/News/Press/docs/2005/wom1517.doc.htm.

35. United Nations, CEDAW, International Federation of Human Rights (FIDH), "Note on the Situation of Women in Gambia," 33rd session, New York, July 5–22, 2005, 7. Feb. 14, 2007, http://www.fidh.org/IMG/pdf/gm_cedaw2005a.pdf.

36. United Nations, CEDAW, FIDH, "Note on the Situation of Women in Gambia," 8.

37. Gambia (The), Mrs. Isatou Njie-Saidy, Vice President and Secretary of State (Minister) for Women's Affairs of the Republic of The Gambia, "Statement," 49th Session, Commission on the Status of Women on the Review of the Implementation of the Beijing Platform of Action, New York, Mar. 1, 2005. Feb. 15, 2007, http://un.cti.depaul.edu/Countries/Gambia/110971048 4/20050301-49thCSW.pdf.

38. United Nations, CEDAW, FIDH, "Note on the Situation of Women in Gambia," 8.

39. United Nations, CEDAW, FIDH, "Note on the Situation of Women in Gambia," 4, 5.

40. Anna Loum, "Gambia: Hon. Halifa Sallah Counters Hon. Bala Gaye On Budget," Gambianow.com's *Gambia News*, Dec. 23, 2006. Feb. 15, 2007, http://www.gambianow.com/news/News/Gambia_news _Hon_Halifa_Sallah_Counters_Hon_Bala_Gaye_On_ Budget.html.

41. United States, CIA, "The World Fact Book," Ghana, Mar. 15, 2007. Mar. 26, 2007, https://www.cia.gov/cia/publications/factbook/geos/gh.html.

42. IPU, *Women in Politics: 60 Years in Retrospect*, Historical Table, Data Sheet No. 1, 2.

43. IPU, *Women in Politics: 60 Years in Retrospect*, Progress and Setbacks, Data Sheet No. 2, 3.

44. Ghana, Ministry of Women and Children's Affairs, *Ghana's second Progress Report on the Implementation of the African and Beijing Platform of Action and Review Report for Beijing+10*, Sept. 2004, 1.3 on 3. Apr. 4, 2007, http://www.un. org/womenwatch/daw/Review/responses/GHANA-English.pdf.

45. Ghana, *Beijing+10*, 2.6 on 33.

46. Ghana, *Beijing+10*, Sept. 2004, 2.6 on 33, 34.

47. Ghana, *Beijing+10*, 2.6 on 36, 37.

48. United States, CIA, "The World Fact Book," Guinea, Mar. 15, 2007. Mar. 26, 2007, https://www.cia.gov/cia/publications/factbook/geos/gv.html#Econ.

49. IPU, *Women in Politics: 60 Years in Retrospect*, Historical Table, Data Sheet No. 1, 1.

50. IPU, *Women in Politics: 60 Years in Retrospect*, Progress and Setbacks, Data Sheet No. 2, 1.

51. Guinea, Republic of Guinea, Ministry of Social Affairs and the Advancement of Women and Children, National Office for the Advancement of Women, *Reply to the United Nations Questionnaire on the Major Achievements and the Challenges Encountered in the Implementation of the Beijing Platform for Action (September 1995) and the Outcome Documents of The Twentieth Special Session of The General Assembly (June 2000)*, April 2004, 5. Apr. 4, 2007, http://www.un.org/women watch/daw/Review/responses/GUINEA-English.pdf.

52. Guinea, *Beijing and General Assembly*, 16.

53. Guinea, *Beijing and General Assembly*, 26.

54. United States, Central Intelligence Agency (CIA), "The World Fact Book," Guinea-Bissau, Mar. 15, 2007. Mar. 26, 2007, https://www.cia.gov/cia/publications/factbook/geos/pu.html#Govt.

55. Inter-Parliamentary Union (IPU), *Women in Politics: 60 Years in Retrospect* (data valid as at 1 February 2006), Historical Table, Data Sheet No. 1, 2. May 20, 2006, http://www.ipu.org/PDF/publications/wmninfokit06_en.pdf.

56. IPU, *Women in Politics: 60 Years in Retrospect*, Progress and Setbacks, Data Sheet No. 2, 3.

57. "Guinea-Bissau Country Report," Human Rights Violations, including Violence Against Women, Women WarPeace.org, January 25, 2007. Mar. 28, 2007, http://www.womenwarpeace.org/guineabissau/guinea_bissau.htm#impact.

58. United Nations, Security Council, *Report of the Secretary-General on developments in Guinea-Bissau and on the activities of the United Nations Peace-building Support Office in that Country*, S/2004/456, June 4, 2004, 4. Mar. 28, 2007, http://www.womenwarpeace.org/guineabissau/docs/sgreptosc4jun04.pdf.

59. United States, CIA, "The World Fact Book," Liberia, Feb. 8, 2007. Mar. 1, 2007, https://www.cia.gov/cia/publications/factbook/geos/li.html#Military.

60. Michael Kpayili, "Liberia: President Sirleaf Commends Women in Gov't," LiberianTimes.com, Oct. 2, 2006. Jan. 31, 2007, http://www.theliberiantimes.com/article_2006_10_2_5852.shtml.

61. Kpayili.

62. United Nations, Bolton, John R., "Statement on

the Situation in Liberia," USUN Press Release #57 (06), Mar. 17, 2006. July 13, 2006, http://www.un.int/usa/06_057.htm.

63. "Assistance for Africa: 'Don't turn your back on my country.'" *The Independent*, Jan. 3, 2007. Jan. 6, 2007, http://news.independent.co.uk/world/africa/article2121705.ece.

64. Assistance for Africa.

65. Assistance for Africa.

66. IPU, *Women in Politics: 60 Years in Retrospect*, Data Sheet No. 2, 2.

67. IPU, *Women in Politics: 60 Years in Retrospect*, Data Sheet No. 4.

68. African Women and Peace Support Group, *Liberian Women Peacemakers: Fighting for the Right to Be Seen, Heard, and Counted*, Trenton, N.J., Africa World Press, 2004, 54, 55.

69. African Women and Peace Support Group, 55.

70. United Nations, Development Fund for Women, "Liberia," WomenWarPeace.org, n.d., Feb. 20, 2007, http://www.womenwarpeace.org/liberia/liberia.htm.

71. United Nations, Development Fund for Women, "Liberia."

72. Assistance for Africa.

73. United States, CIA, "The World Fact Book," Mali, Feb. 8 and Oct. 4, 2007. Mar. 1 and Oct. 4, 2007, https://www.cia.gov/cia/publications/factbook/geos/ml.html.

74. BBC News, "Country Profile: Mali," Africa, Jan. 2, 2007. Feb. 20, 2007, http://news.bbc.co.uk/2/hi/africa/country_profiles/1021454.stm.

75. "Status of Human Rights Organizations in Sub-Saharan Africa Mali," Human Rights Library, University of Minnesota, n.d. Feb. 21, 2007, http://www1.umn.edu/humanrts/africa/mali.htm.

76. BBC News, "Country Profile: Mali."

77. International IDEA and Stockholm University, "Country Overview," *Quota Database: Global Database of Quotas for Women*, 2006. Feb. 20, 2007, http://www.quotaproject.org/country.cfm?SortOrder=Country.

78. Vital Voices, "Women's Global Progress Watch: Strides and Setbacks for Women's Global Leadership," Strides in Political Life, Summer 2004. Feb. 20, 2007, http://www.vitalvoices.org/desktopdefault.aspx?page_id=66.

79. IPU, *Women in Politics: 60 Years in Retrospect*, Historical Table, Data Sheet No. 1, 3.

80. Mali, Kalifa Gadiaga, Information Specialist at the United States Embassy in Bamako, Mali, Email to author, Feb. 22, 2007.

81. Madonna Owusuah Larbi, "New Gender Perspectives for the Millennium: Challenges and Successful Models of North-South Collaboration," *West Africa Review* 2, no. 1 (Aug. 2000). May 12, 2006, http://www.westafricareview.com/vol2.1/larbi.html.

82. Association for the Progress and the Defense of Women's rights (APDF), "Principal Activities/Achievements," Mali, translated by Google, n.d. Feb. 21, 2007, http://translate.google.com/translate?hl=en&sl=fr&u=http://www. justicemali.org/apdf.htm&sa=X&oi=translate&resnum=1&ct=result&prev=/search%3Fq%3DAPDF%2BMali%26hl%3Den.

83. Larbi.

84. Mali, *Report of Mali to the Sixth Forum on Governance in Africa*, Kigali, Rwanda, (Nov. 2005), 17, 19.

Feb. 21, 2007, http://www.undp.org/agf/papers/Mali%20Report%20on%20APRM%20for%20AGF%20VI%20(English).pdf.

85. Mali, *Report of Mali to the Sixth Forum on Governance in Africa*, 28.

86. United States, CIA, "The World Fact Book," Niger, Feb. 8, 2007. Mar. 7, 2007, https://www.cia.gov/cia/publications/factbook/geos/ng.html.

87. United States, Department of State, Bureau of Democracy, Human Rights, and Labor, Niger, Country Reports on Human Rights Practices," Mar. 4, 2002. Mar. 9, 2007, http://www.state.gov/g/drl/rls/hrrpt/2001/af/8396.*htm*.

88. IPU, *Women in Politics: 60 Years in Retrospect*, Historical Table, Data Sheet No. 1, 4.

89. United Nations, Division for the Advancement of Women, "Fact Sheet on Women in Government," Jan. 1996. Mar. 9, 2007, http://www.un.org/womenwatch/daw/public/percent.htm.

90. IPU, *Women in Politics: 60 Years in Retrospect*, Data Sheet No. 2, 2.

91. United Nations, Office for the Coordination of Humanitarian Affairs, "Niger: Humanitarian Country Profile," IRIN (Integrated Regional Information Networks), Feb. 2007. Mar. 9, 2007, http://www.irinnews.org/country.aspx? CountryCode=NE&RegionCode=WA.

92. Niger, *Initial and second report of the Niger on the Convention on the Elimination of All Forms of Discrimination against Women*, Final Document, June 2001, 11. Mar. 9, 2007, http://daccessdds.un.org/doc/UNDOC/GEN/N05/619/38/PDF/N0561938.pdf?OpenElement.

93. Niger, *Report the Convention on the Elimination of All Forms of Discrimination against Women*, 26, 65, 66.

94. Niger, *Report the Convention on the Elimination of All Forms of Discrimination against Women*, 30, 31.

95. Niger, *Report the Convention on the Elimination of All Forms of Discrimination against Women*, 32, 34.

96. Niger, *Report the Convention on the Elimination of All Forms of Discrimination against Women*, 33.

97. United States, CIA, "The World Fact Book," Nigeria, Feb. 8, 2007. Mar. 7 and Oct. 4, 2007, https://www.cia.gov/cia/publications/factbook/geos/ni.html#Govt.

98. Nigeria, Permanent Mission of Nigeria to the United Nations, *Reply from the Government of the Federal Republic of Nigeria to the Questionnaire on the Implementation of the Beijing Platform for Action*, n.d., 28–30. Mar. 7, 2007, http://www.un.org/womenwatch/daw/followup/responses/Nigeria.pdf.

99. Nigeria, Permanent Mission, *Reply Implementation Beijing Platform*, 31–32. Mar. 7, 2007, http://www.un.org/womenwatch/daw/followup/responses/Nigeria.pdf.

100. Nigeria, Federal Ministry of Women Affairs, *National Report on Progress Made in Implementation of the Beijing Platform for Action (Beijing+10)*, August 2004, 13. Mar. 7, 2007, *http://www.un.org/womenwatch/daw/Review/responses/* NIGERIA-English.pdf.

101. Nigeria, Federal Ministry of Women Affairs, *Progress Made (Beijing+10)*, 14.

102. Nigeria, Federal Ministry of Women Affairs, *Progress Made (Beijing+10)*, 14.

103. Nigeria, Federal Ministry of Women Affairs, *Progress Made (Beijing+10)*, 15, 16.

104. United Nations, Economic Commission for Africa (ECA), *5 Years After Beijing: What Efforts in Favor of African Women? Assessing Political Empowerment of Women*, Addis Ababa, Ethiopia, Sept. 2001, 17. Dec. 10, 2006, http://www.uneca. org/fr/acgd/en/1024 x768/en_12areas/en_politic/en_0109_political.pdf.

105. United Nations, ECA, *5 Years After Beijing*, 17.

106. United Nations, Economic Commission for Africa (ECA), *African Governance Report 2005*, Addis Ababa, Ethiopia, Nov. 2005, 33. Dec. 12, 2006, http://www.uneca.org/agr2005/.

107. United States, CIA, "The World Fact Book," Senegal, Feb. 8, 2007. Mar. 7 and Oct. 4, 2007, https://www.cia.gov/cia/publications/factbook/geos/sg.html#Econ.

108. IPU, *Women in Politics: 60 Years in Retrospect*, Historical Table, Data Sheet No. 1, 4.

109. IPU, *Women in Politics: 60 Years in Retrospect*, Progress and Setbacks, Data Sheet No. 2, 2.

110. United Nations, ECA, *African Governance Report 2005*, 32.

111. Senegal, Republic of Senegal, *Solemn Declaration on the Equality Between the Men and the Women in Africa*, Conclusion, 2006. Dec. 30, 2006, http://www.africa-union.org/root/au/Conferences/Past/2006/October/WG/Report-Senegal.doc. Translated from French to English by Alta Vista, Babel Fish Translation, http://babelfish.altavista.com/, Jan. 5, 2007.

112. Senegal, *Solemn Declaration*, Principle of Parity, 2006, 10.

113. Senegal, *Solemn Declaration*, Principle of Parity, 2006, 10.

114. Senegal, *Solemn Declaration*, Principle of Parity, 2006, 10.

115. United States, CIA, "The World Fact Book," Sierra Leone, Mar. 15, 2007. Mar. 26 and Oct. 4, 2007, https://www.cia.gov/cia/publications/factbook/geos/sl.html#Intro.

116. Sierra Leone, Shirley Y. Gbujama, Minister of Social Welfare, Gender and Children's Affairs, Permanent Mission of the Republic of Sierra Leone to the United Nations, "Statement," 23rd Special Session, United Nations General Assembly, Women 2000: Gender Equality, Development and Peace for the 21st Century, June 9, 2000. Mar. 28, 2007, http://www.un.org/womenwatch/daw/followup/beijing+5stat/statments/sleone9.htm.

117. Sierra Leone, Gbujama.

118. IPU, *Women in Politics: 60 Years in Retrospect*, Progress and Setbacks, Data Sheet No. 2, 2.

119. Sierra Leone, Gbujama.

120. United States, CIA, "The World Fact Book," Togo, Mar. 15, 2007. Mar. 26 and Oct. 4, 2007, https://www.cia.gov/cia/publications/factbook/geos/to.html#People.

121. IPU, *Women in Politics: 60 Years in Retrospect*, Historical Table, Data Sheet No. 1, 5.

122. IPU, *Women in Politics: 60 Years in Retrospect*, Progress and Setbacks, Data Sheet No. 2, 2.

123. Togo, Ministry for Social Affairs, the Togolese Republic, The Advancement of Women and the Protection of Children, *Evaluation of the Implementation of The Beijing Platform for Action Beijing+10*, National Report, April 2004, 3. Mar. 28, 2007, http://www.un.org/womenwatch/daw/Review/responses/TOGO-English.pdf.

124. Togo, *Evaluation Beijing+10*, 5.

125. Togo, *Evaluation Beijing+10*, 5.

126. Togo, *Evaluation Beijing+10*, 17.

127. Togo, *Evaluation Beijing+10*, 24, 26, 27, 28.

Southern Africa

1. United States, Central Intelligence Agency (CIA), "The World Fact Book," Angola, Mar. 8, 2007. Mar. 10, 2007, https://www.cia.gov/cia/publications/factbook/geos/ao.html.

2. Know Your Black History.com, "Queen Nzingha of Angola (1583–1663)," Profiles & Facts, 2005. Dec. 21, 2006, http://www.knowyourblackhistory.com/queen-nzingha.html.

3. Inter-Parliamentary Union (IPU), *Women in Politics: 60 Years in Retrospect* (data valid as at 1 February 2006), Historical Table, Data Sheet No. 1, 1. May 20, 2006, http://www.ipu.org/PDF/publications/wmninfo kit06_en.pdf.

4. IPU, *Women in Politics: 60 Years in Retrospect*, Progress and Setbacks, Data Sheet No. 2, 2.

5. United Nations, Economic Commission for Africa (ECA), *5 Years After Beijing: What Efforts in Favor of African Women? Assessing Political Empowerment of Women*, Addis Ababa, Ethiopia, Sept. 2001, 16, 19. Dec. 19, 2006, http://www.uneca.org/fr/acgd/en/1024x768/en_12areas/en_politic/en_0109_political.pdf.

6. United Nations, Economic Commission for Africa (ECA), *African Women's Report 1998, Post-Conflict Reconstruction in Africa: A Gender Perspective*, Addis Ababa, Ethiopia, 1999, 45. Dec. 21, 2006, www.uneca.org/acgd/Publications/en_awr98.pdf.

7. Angola, Republic of Angola, *National Report Beijing+10*, Oct. 18, 2004:33. Mar. 15, 2007, http://www.un.org/womenwatch/daw/Review/responses/ANGOLA-English.pdf.

8. Angola, *National Report Beijing+10*, 34.

9. Angola Permanent Mission to U.N., "Government Officials in Angola." July 8, 2006. http://un.cti.depaul.edu/Countries/Angola/1142406404/GOVERNMENT%20OFFICIALSRev.pdf.

10. Angola. *National Report Beijing+10*, 51.

11. United States, CIA, "The World Fact Book," Botswana, Mar. 8, 2007. Mar. 10, 2007, https://www.cia.gov/cia/publications/factbook/geos/bc.html.

12. IPU, *Women in Politics: 60 Years in Retrospect*, Historical Table, Data Sheet No. 1, 1.

13. IPU, *Women in Politics: 60 Years in Retrospect*, Progress and Setbacks, Data Sheet No. 2, 3.

14. United Nations, ECA, *5 Years After Beijing*, 13.

15. United Nations, ECA, *5 Years After Beijing*, 13.

16. Botswana, Ministry of Labour and Home Affairs, Women's Affairs Department, *Botswana's Response to the Questionnaire to Governments on Implementation of the Beijing Platform for Action (1995) and the Outcome of the Twenty-Third* Special Session of The General Assembly (2000): 2. Mar. 14, 2007, http://www.un.org/womenwatch/daw/Review/responses/BOTSWANA-English.pdf.

17. Botswana, *Response to Beijing Platform and the General Assembly*, 7.

18. Botswana, *Response to Beijing Platform and the General Assembly*, 7.

19. Botswana, *Response to Beijing Platform and the General Assembly*, 8.

20. United States, CIA, "The World Fact Book," Lesotho, Mar. 11, 2007. Mar. 8, 2007, https://www.cia.gov/cia/publications/factbook/geos/lt.html.

21. IPU, *Women in Politics: 60 Years in Retrospect*, Historical Table, Data Sheet No. 1, 3.

22. IPU, *Women in Politics: 60 Years in Retrospect*, Progress and Setbacks, Data Sheet No. 2, 2.

23. IPU, *Women in Politics: 60 Years in Retrospect*, A Chronology of Women: Heads of State, Data Sheet No. 4.

24. Lesotho, *Lesotho, African Union Solemn Declaration on Gender Equality in Africa*, June 2006, Sec. 5, Gender Parity Principle. Dec. 26, 2006, http://www.africa-union.org/root/au/Conferences/Past/2006/October/WG/Report-Lesotho.doc.

25. Lesotho, *Solemn Declaration*, Introduction.

26. Lesotho, *Solemn Declaration*, Sec. 5, Gender Parity Principle.

27. Lesotho, *Solemn Declaration*, Sec. 5, Gender Parity Principle.

28. Lesotho, *Solemn Declaration*, Sec. 5, Gender Parity Principle.

29. Lesotho, *Solemn Declaration*, Sec. 5, Gender Parity Principle.

30. Lesotho, *Solemn Declaration*, Sec. 5, Gender Parity Principle.

31. Lesotho, *Solemn Declaration*, Challenges.

32. United States, Central Intelligence CIA, "The World Fact Book," Malawi, Mar. 10, 2007. Mar. 8, 2007, https://www.cia.gov/cia/publications/factbook/geos/mi.html.

33. IPU, *Women in Politics: 60 Years in Retrospect*, Historical Table, Data Sheet No. 1, 3.

34. IPU, *Women in Politics: 60 Years in Retrospect*, Progress and Setbacks, Data Sheet No. 2, 2.

35. United Nations, ECA, *5 Years After Beijing*, 12.

36. Malawi, Ministry of Gender and Community Services, *Progress on the Beijing+10 Report*, Feb. 2004, 40. Mar. 10, 2007, http://www.un.org/womenwatch/daw/Review/responses/MALAWI-English.pdf.

37. United Nations, ECA, *5 Years After Beijing*, 12.

38. Malawi, *Progress on the Beijing+10 Report*, 2.

39. Malawi, *Progress on the Beijing+10 Report*, 36.

40. Malawi, *Progress on the Beijing+10 Report*, 37.

41. Malawi, *Progress on the Beijing+10 Report*, 67, 68.

42. United States, CIA, "The World Fact Book," Mauritius, Mar. 8, 2007. Mar. 10, 2007, https://www.cia.gov/cia/publications/factbook/geos/mp.html.

43. IPU, *Women in Politics: 60 Years in Retrospect*, Historical Table, Data Sheet No. 1, 3.

44. IPU, *Women in Politics: 60 Years in Retrospect*, Progress and Setbacks, Data Sheet No. 2, 1.

45. Mauritius, *Mauritius Country Report on the Solemn Declaration on Gender Equality in Africa*, 2006, Introduction on Background. Dec. 26, 2006, http://www.africa-union.org/root/ua/Conferences/novembre/GE/2-3%20oct/Report-Mauritius.doc.

46. Mauritius, *Solemn Declaration*, Sec. 5.

47. Mauritius, *Solemn Declaration*, Introduction on Background.

48. Mauritius, *Solemn Declaration*, Introduction on Background.

49. Mauritius, *Solemn Declaration*, Sec. 5.

50. IPU, *Women in Politics: 60 Years in Retrospect*, Historical Table, Data Sheet No. 1, 4; United States, CIA, "The World Fact Book," Mozambique, Mar. 8, 2007. Mar. 10, 2007, https://www.cia.gov/cia/publications/factbook/geos/mz.html.

51. IPU, *Women in Politics: 60 Years in Retrospect*, Progress and Setbacks, Data Sheet No. 2, 2.

52. IPU, *Women in Politics: 60 Years in Retrospect*, Participation of Women and Men in Decision-Making, Data Sheet No. 6, 4.

53. United States, CIA, Mozambique; United Nations, ECA, *African Women's Report 1998*, 43, 44.

54. United Nations, ECA, *5 Years After Beijing*, 16, 19.

55. Mozambique, *Mozambique Beijing+10 Report*, Summarized Version, Oct. 19, 2004, 1,2. Mar. 10, 2007, http://www.un.org/womenwatch/daw/Review/responses/MOZAMBIQUE-English.pdf.

56. Mozambique, *Mozambique Beijing+10*, 12.

57. Mozambique, *Mozambique Beijing+10*, 13.

58. United States, CIA, "The World Fact Book," Namibia, Mar. 8, 2007. Mar. 10, 2007, https://www.cia.gov/cia/publications/factbook/geos/wa.html.

59. United Nations, ECA, *African Governance Report 2005*, 32.

60. IPU, *Women in Politics: 60 Years in Retrospect*, Historical Table, Data Sheet No. 1, 4.

61. IPU, *Women in Politics: 60 Years in Retrospect*, Progress and Setbacks, Data Sheet No. 2, 2.

62. United Nations, ECA, *African Governance Report 2005*, 33, Box 1.2.

63. United Nations, ECA, *5 Years After Beijing*, 11–12.

64. UNECA, *Beijing+5* (2000); Namibia, Ministry of Gender Equality and Child Welfare, "Namibia's Country Report on the African Union Solemn Declaration on Gender Equality in Africa," 2006, Dec. 26, 2006, http://www.africa-union.org/root/au/Conferences/Past/2006/ October/WG/Report-Namibia.doc.

65. United Nations, ECA, *5 Years After Beijing*, 12, 19.

66. United Nations, ECA, *5 Years After Beijing*, 12.

67. United Nations, ECA, *African Governance Report 2005*, 32.

68. Namibia, *Solemn Declaration*, Women in Cabinet and Parliament.

69. Namibia, *Solemn Declaration*, Women in Cabinet and Parliament.

70. Namibia, *Solemn Declaration*, Sec. 2.

71. Namibia, *Solemn Declaration*, Women in Politics and Decision Making.

72. United States, CIA, "The World Fact Book," South Africa, Feb. 8, 2007. Mar. 6, 2007, https://www.cia.gov/cia/publications/factbook/geos/sf.html.

73. IPU, *Women in Politics: 60 Years in Retrospect*, Historical Table, Data Sheet No. 1, 5.

74. IPU, *Women in Politics: 60 Years in Retrospect*, An Overview of Women in Parliament, Data Sheet No. 5.

75. IPU, *Women in Politics: 60 Years in Retrospect*, Progress and Setbacks, Data Sheet No. 2, 2.

76. IPU, *Women in Politics: 60 Years in Retrospect*, Participation of Women and Men in Decision Making: the Parliamentary Dimension, Data Sheet No. 6, 4.

77. United Nations, ECA, *5 Years After Beijing*, 18, 19.

78. United Nations, ECA, *African Women's Report 1998*, 43, 44.

79. United Nations, ECA, *5 Years After Beijing*, 11.

80. South Africa, Presidency, Office of the Status of Women, *Global Report to Inform the Following Reports: Beijing Platform for Action, Dakar Platform for Action, Commonwealth 7WAMM, CEDAW, National Report on Ten Years of Freedom*, Oct. 19, 2004, 21, 26, 30, 31, 77. Mar. 6, 2007, http://www.un.org/womenwatch/daw/Review/responses/SOUTHAFRICA-English.pdf.

81. United Nations, ECA, *African Governance Report 2005*, 31, 32.

82. United Nations, ECA, *African Governance Report 2005*, 31, 32.

83. South Africa, *Solemn Declaration*, Sec. 5: Gender Parity at National and Local Levels.

84. United States, Central Intelligence Agency, "The World Fact Book," Feb. 8, 2007. Mar. 4, 2007, https://www.cia.gov/cia/publications/factbook/geos/wz.html.

85. United Nations, ECA, *5 Years After Beijing*, 13.

86. Swaziland, "Questionnaire [Beijing+5]," n.d., 8. Mar. 4, 2007, http://www.un.org/womenwatch/daw/followup/responses/Swaziland.pdf.

87. Swaziland, Ministry of Home Affairs Gender Coordination Unit, *Swaziland Country Report: Sub-Regional Review on Implementation of the Beijing Platform for Action (1995) and the Outcome of the 23rd Special Session of the General Assembly (2000)*, Zambia, April 26–29, 2004, 8. Mar. 4, 2007, http://www.un.org/womenwatch/daw/Review/responses/SWAZILAND-English.pdf.

88. IPU, *Women in Politics: 60 Years in Retrospect*, Historical Table, Data Sheet No. 1, 5.

89. IPU, *Women in Politics: 60 Years in Retrospect*, Progress and Setbacks, Data Sheet No. 2, 2.

90. IPU, *Women in Politics: 60 Years in Retrospect*; Queens/Grand Duchesses, Data Sheet No. 4.

91. Wikipedia.org, "Ntombi of Swaziland," *Wikipedia*, Aug. 2006. Mar. 4, 2007, http://en.wikipedia.org/wiki/Ntombi_of_Swaziland.

92. Swaziland, *Review of Beijing Platform and General Assembly*, 8.

93. Swaziland, *Review of Beijing Platform and General Assembly*, 9, 10.

94. Swaziland, Government, Prime Minister's Office, "Responses to Questionnaire from Swazi TV," PM interview with Swazi TV, n.d. Mar. 4, 2007, http://www.gov.sz/home.asp?pid=4040.

95. United States, CIA, "The World Fact Book," Zambia, Mar. 15, 2007. Mar. 25, 2007, https://www.cia.gov/cia/publications/factbook/geos/za.html#Geo.

96. IPU, *Women in Politics: 60 Years in Retrospect*, Historical Table, Data Sheet No. 1, 6.

97. IPU, *Women in Politics: 60 Years in Retrospect*, Progress and Setbacks, Data Sheet No. 2, 2.

98. Zambia, Republic of Zambia, Gender in Development Division, Cabinet Office, *Zambia's Progress Report on the Implementation of the Beijing Platform for Action 2000_2004*, Draft, Mar. 2004, 4. Mar. 25, 2007, http://www.un.org/womenwatch/daw/Review/responses/ZAMBIA-English.pdf.

99. Zambia, *Progress Report Beijing Platform for Action 2000— 2004*, 27, 28.

100. Zambia, *Progress Report Beijing Platform for Action 2000— 2004*, 28.

101. Zambia, *Progress Report Beijing Platform for Action 2000— 2004*, 28.

102. Zambia, *Progress Report Beijing Platform for Action 2000— 2004*, 30.

103. Zambia, *Progress Report Beijing Platform for Action 2000— 2004*, 29.

104. Zambia, *Progress Report Beijing Platform for Action 2000— 2004*, 29–31.

105. United States, CIA, "The World Fact Book," Zimbabwe, Feb. 8, 2007. Feb. 24, 2007, https://www.cia.gov/cia/publications/factbook/geos/zi.html.

106. Netsai Mushonga, "Democracy in the Eyes of Women in Zimbabwe," *Fellowship*, November/December 2006. Feb. 23, 2007, http://www.forusa.org/fellowship/nov-dec06/NetsaiMushonga.html.

107. United Nations, Committee on Elimination of Discrimination against Women (CEDAW), *Initial Report of States Parties: Zimbabwe*, July 20, 1996, 23–24. Feb. 24, 2007, http://daccessdds.un.org/doc/UNDOC/GEN/N96/311/56/IMG/ N9631156.pdf?OpenElement.

108. IPU, *Women in Politics: 60 Years in Retrospect*, Historical Table, Data Sheet No. 1, 6.

109. United Nations, CEDAW, *Initial Report of States Parties: Zimbabwe*, 24.

110. IPU, *Women in Politics: 60 Years in Retrospect*, Data Sheet No. 2.

111. Zimbabwe, *Progress Report on The Implementation of The Platform for Action*, 1995–2003, 11. Feb. 25, 2007, http://www.un.org/womenwatch/daw/Review/responses/ZIMBABWE-English.pdf.

112. United Nations, CEDAW, *Initial Report of States Parties: Zimbabwe*, 25.

113. United Nations, CEDAW, *Initial Report of States Parties: Zimbabwe*, 25.

114. United Nations, CEDAW, *Initial Report of States Parties: Zimbabwe*, 25.

115. United Nations, CEDAW, *Initial Report of States Parties: Zimbabwe*, 27.

116. Netsai Mushonga, "Democracy in the Eyes of Women in Zimbabwe," *Fellowship*, November/December 2006. Feb. 23, 2007, http://www.forusa.org/fellowship/nov-dec06/NetsaiMushonga.html.

117. Mushonga.

118. United Nations, ECA, *5 Years After Beijing*, 19.

119. Zimbabwe, "*Progress Report on the Platform for Action*," 4, 9, 21.

120. Zimbabwe Women's Resource Centre and Network (ZWRCN), "About ZWRCN," 2002. Feb. 23, 2007, http://www.zwrcn.org.zw/about.htm.

121. Zimbabwe, "*Progress Report on the Platform for Action*," 2, 7, 10.

122. Zimbabwe, "*Progress Report on the Platform for Action*," 10.

123. Zimbabwe, "*Progress Report on the Platform for Action*," 11.

124. Zimbabwe, "*Progress Report on the Platform for Action*," 11.

125. "Zimbabwe's Women Call for Leadership Positions," People's Daily Online, Apr. 15, 2005. Feb. 23, 2007, http://english.people.com.cn/200504/15/eng20050415_181143.html.

126. Zimbabwe, "*Progress Report on the Platform for Action*," 13.

Conclusion

1. International IDEA, "President Johnson-Sirleaf Opens International IDEA Seminar on 'Women in

Parliament,'" West Africa Office, Sept. 28, 2006. Oct. 12, 2006, http://www.idea.int/gender/wip_seminar.cfm.

2. Sylvia Tamale, "'Point of Order, Mr. Speaker': African Women Claiming Their Space in Parliament," in Caroline Sweetman, ed., *Women and Leadership*, Oxfam Focus on Gender Series, Dorset, UK: Oxfam, 2000, 14.

3. Inter-Parliamentary Union, *Women in Politics: 60 Years in Retrospect*, "The Participation of Women and Men," Data Sheet No. 6 (data valid as at 1 February 2006),6. May 20, 2006, http://www.ipu.org/PDF/publications/wmninfokit06_en. pdf. 6.

4. Inter-Parliamentary Union: guide2womenleaders.com, "Women in Government: Expert Cites Progress," *USA Today*, Jan. 23, 2006, 6A.

5. Peggy Antrobus, "Transformational Leadership: Advancing the Agenda for Gender Justice," in Sweetman, ed., 55.

6. Aruna Rao and David Kelleher, "Leadership for Social Transformation: Some Ideas and Questions on Institutions and Feminist Leadership," in Sweetman, ed., 74.

7. Inter-Parliamentary Union, *Women in Politics*, 6.

8. Madonna Owusuah Larbi, "New Gender Perspectives for the Millennium: Challenges and Successful Models of North-South Collaboration," *West Africa Review* 2, no. 1 (Aug. 2000). May 12, 2006, http://www.westafricareview.com/vol2.1/larbi.html.

9. Caroline Sweetman, ed., "Editorial," *Women and Leadership*, Oxfam Focus on Gender Series, Dorset, UK: Oxfam, 2000, 6.

10. Ernest Harsch, "Combating Inequality in Africa: Lessen Inequities to Reduce Poverty and Reach MDGs, says UN," *Africa Renewal* 20, no. 2 (July 2006):18.

11. Harsch, 18.

12. Paul Vallely, "From Dawn to Dusk, the Daily Struggle of Africa's Women," *The Independent*, Red ed., Sept. 21, 2006. Sept. 21, 2006, http://news.independent.co.uk/world/africa/article1655627.ece.

13. Chinua Achebe, *Anthills of the Savannah*, New York: Anchor, 1987.

14. Porter, "A New 'New' Jerusalem? West African Writers and the Dawn of the New Millennium, *JOUVERT: A Journal of Post-Colonial Studies* 4, no. 2 (Winter 2000). May 12, 2006, http://social.chass.ncsu.edu/jouvert/v4i2/porter.h*tm*.

15. Ahmadou Kourouma, *Monnè, outrages et défi*, Paris: Seuil, 1990.

16. Porter.

17. Porter.

18. Abantu for Development, "African Women and Governance: Towards Action for Women's Participation in Decision-Making," London: Abantu Publications, 1995, 4.

19. Meredeth Turshen, "Women's War Stories," in Meredeth Turshen and Clotilde Twagiramariya, eds., *What Women Do in Wartime: Gender and Conflict in Africa*, London; New York: Zed Books, 1998, 6.

20. Turshen, in Turshen, 20.

21. Michael Fleshman, "African Women Struggle for a Seat at the Peace Table," *Africa Recovery*, 16, no 4 (February 2003):1. Sept. 3, 2006, http://www.un.org/ecosocdev/geninfo/afrec/vol16no4/164wm1.htm.

22. Bisi Adeleye-Fayemi and Algresia Akwi-Ogojo, eds., *Moving from Accommodation to Transformation: New Horizons for African Women into the 21st Century*, African Women's Leadership Institute (AWLI) report, London: Akina Mama Wa Afrika, July 1998, 7.

23. BAdeleye-Fayemi and Akwi-Ogojo, eds., 7.

24. Akwe Amosu and Ofeibea Quist-Arcton, "Women in Politics," *BBC Focus on Africa* 17, no. 1 (2006): 18–22; Julie Ballington, "Conclusion: Women's Political Participation and Quotas in Africa," in Julie Ballington, ed. *The Implementation of Quotas: African Experiences, Quota Report Series No. 3*, Stockholm, Sweden: International Institute for Democracy and Electoral Assistance (IDEA), Nov. 2004. 124–128. See also at: Sept. 23, 2006, http://www.quotaproject.org/publications/Quotas_Africa.pdf.

25. Karen Fogg, "Preface," in Ballington, ed., 3.

26. Julie Ballington, "Conclusion: Women's Political Participation and Quotas in Africa," in Ballington, ed., 124.

27. Gumisai Mutume, "African Women Are Ready to Lead: But Social Beliefs and Attitudes Hinder Their Quest," *Africa Renewal* 20, no. 2 (July 2006):7. Mar. 17, 2007, http://www.un.org/ecosocdev/geninfo/afrec/vol20no2/AR-20no2-english. pdf.

28. Inter-Parliamentary Union, *Women in Politics*, 6.

29. United Nations, Economic Commission for Africa (ECA), *Promoting Gender Equality and Women's Empowerment in Africa: Questioning the Achievements and Confronting the Challenges Ten Years After Beijing*, Addis Ababa, Ethiopia, Feb. 2005, 18. Dec. 10, 2006, www.uneca.org/acgd/Publications/Gender_Equality.pdf.

30. U.N. ECA, *Promoting Gender Equality*, 19.

31. U.N. ECA, *Promoting Gender Equality*, 19.

32. U.N. ECA, *Promoting Gender Equality*, 20.

33. Aili Tripp, "Women's Movements and Challenges to Neopatrimonial Rule: Preliminary Observations from Africa," *Development and Change* 32 (Jan. 2001): 233, 253.

Bibliography

Abantu for Development. "African Women and Governance: Towards Action for Women's Participation in Decision-Making." London: Abantu Publications, 1995.

"About Amanitare." n.d. Jan. 22, 2007, http://www.rainbo.org/amanitare/about.html.

Achebe, Chinua. *Anthills of the Savannah*. New York: Anchor, 1987.

Adeleye-Fayemi, Bisi, and Algresia Akwi-Ogojo, eds. *Moving from Accommodation to Transformation: New Horizons for African Women into the 21st Century*. African Women's Leadership Institute (AWLI) report. London: Akina Mama Wa Afrika, July 1998.

AfricaFocus. "PanAfrica; Africa: Women's Rights Petition." *Bulletin*, June 30, 2004. Aug. 18, 2006, http://www.africafocus.org/docs04/wom0406.php.

African Unification Front. "AU President Gertrude Mongella: Biographical Brief." n.d. Apr. 5, 2007, http://www.africanfront.com/2004-m.php.

_____. "Continental Parliament Elects Gertrude Mongella the Leader of Africa." Mar. 18, 2004. Nov. 8, 2006, http://www.africanfront.com/2004-l.php.

African Women and Peace Support Group. *Liberian Women Peacemakers: Fighting for the Right to Be Seen, Heard, and Counted*. Trenton, N.J.: Africa World Press, 2004.

AFROL Gender Profiles: Côte d'Ivoire, Apr. 4, 2007. Apr. 4, 2007, http://www.afrol.com/Categories/Women/profiles/civ_women.htm.

_____: Equatorial Guinea, Apr. 2, 2007. Apr. 2, 2007, http://www.afrol.com/Categories/Women/profiles/equatorialguinea_women.htm.

Agence France Presse. "Women Leaders Take Hold on Power Across the Globe." Paris, Jan. 16, 2006.

_____. "Women, Power and Africa: Liberia's Sirleaf Joins Select Few." Paris, Jan. 15, 2006.

Agenda for Africa. "Person of the Month — Dec 2005A." Oct. 1, 2006, http://www.agendaafrica.com/site/en/newsletters/potm/dec2005.html.

Agozino, Bike. "What Women's Studies Offer Men: Entremesa Discussion." *West Africa Review* 2, no. 1 (Aug. 2000). May 12, 2006, http://www.westafricareview.com/vol2.1/agozino.html.

Akina Mama wa Afrika (AmwA). n.d. May 30, 2006, http://www.akinamama.org/index.html.

Algeria. "Institutions of the Government of Algeria," 2006. Jan. 4, 2007, http://www.elmouradia.dz/francais/institution/gov/GOV.htm.

Algeria. Ministry Delegated to the Minister for Health, the Population and the Hospital Reform, Responsible for the Family and the Female Condition. *National Report on the Solemn Declaration on Equality of Men and Women C.U.A.* Sec. 5, June 2006. Dec. 31, 2006, http://www.africa-union.org/root/au/Conferences/Past/2006/October/WG/Report-Algeria.doc. Translated from French to English by Alta Vista, Babel Fish Translation, http://babelfish.altavista.com/, Jan. 3, 2007.

Algeria. *Algeria: Reply to the Questionnaire to Governments on Implementation of the Beijing Platform for Action (1995) and the Outcome of the Twenty-Third Special Session of the General Assembly (2000)*, 2004:3. Mar. 15, 2007, http://www.un.org/womenwatch/daw/Review/responses/ALGERIA-English.pdf.

allAfrica.com. "Nigeria: Honoured Offshore, Ignored At Home," Oct. 22, 2006. Oct. 31, 2006, http://allafrica.com/stories/200610230442.html.

American University in Cairo. *2004–2005 Catalog*, Appendix: Personnel and Enrollment, Faculty Register, Dec. 1, 2006, http://www.aucegypt.edu/catalog04/appendix/facreg/facreg.htm.

Amosu, Akwe, and Ofeibea Quist-Arcton. "Women in Politics." *BBC Focus on Africa* 17, no. 1 (2006): 18–22.

Anbarasan, Ethirajan. "Wangari Muta Maathai: Kenya's Green Militant." *UNESCO Courier*, Dec. 1999. May 13, 2006, http://www.unesco.org/courier/1999_12/uk/dires/intro.htm.

Angola. Permanent Mission to U.N. "Government Officials in Angola," July 8, 2006. http://un.cti.depaul.edu/Countries/Angola/1142406404/GOVERNMENT%20OFFICIALSRev.pdf.

Angola. Republic of Angola. *National Report Beijing+10*, Oct. 18, 2004. Mar. 15, 2007, http://www.un.org/womenwatch/daw/Review/responses/ANGOLA-English.pdf.

Answers.com. "Maria do Carmo Silveira." n.d. Oct.

23, 2006, http://www.answers.com/topic/maria-do-carmo-silveira.

Antrobus, Peggy. "Transformational Leadership: Advancing the Agenda for Gender Justice." in Caroline Sweetman, ed. *Women and Leadership.* Oxford, UK: Oxfam GB, 2000. 50–56.

Arieff, Irwin. "UN Assembly's First Muslim Leader Vows Reform." *Reuters*, Sept. 12, 2006. Sept. 12, 2006, Reuters.com.

"Assistance for Africa: 'Don't Turn Your Back on My Country.'" *The Independent*, Jan. 3, 2007. Jan. 6, 2007, http://news.independent.co.uk/world/africa/article2121705.ece.

Association for the Progress and the Defense of Women's Rights (APDF). "Principal Activities/Achievements." Mali. Translated by Google, n.d. Feb. 21, 2007, http://translate.google. com/translate?hl=en&sl=fr&u=http://www.justicemali.org/apdf.htm&sa=X&oi=translate&resnum=1&ct=result&prev=/search%3Fq%3DAPDF%2BMali%26hl%3Den.

Ballington, Julie. "Conclusion: Women's Political Participation and Quotas in Africa." In Julie Ballington, ed. *The Implementation of Quotas: African Experiences, Quota Report Series No. 3.* Stockholm, Sweden: International Institute for Democracy and Electoral Assistance (IDEA), Nov. 2004, 124–128. See also at: Sept. 23, 2006, http://www.quotaproject.org/publications/Quotas_Africa.pdf.

Bauer, Gretchen, and Hannah E. Britton. "Women in African Parliaments: A Continental Shift?" in Gretchen Bauer and Hannah E. Britton, eds. *Women in African Parliaments.* Boulder, Colo.: Lynne Rienner Publishers, 2006. 1–30.

Biakolo, Emevwo, Maitseo Bolaane and Michelle Commeyras. "Women in Conversation with an African Man on Gender Issues." *JOUVERT: A Journal of Post-Colonial Studies* 5, no. 2 (Winter 2001). May 12, 2006, http://social.chass.ncsu.edu/jouvert/v5i2/comey.htm.

Biografias Africanas OL. "Silveira, Maria do Carmo," n.d. Oct. 25, 2006, www.ikuska.com/Africa/Historia/biografias/biografias_ol.htm.

Blau Peter M., and Marshall W. Meyers. *Bureaucracy in Modern Society.* New York: Random House, 1971. In Rosemarie Skaine. *A Study of Perceptions of Inequity Among Merit System Employees at the University of Northern Iowa.* Thesis. Cedar Falls, Ia.: University of Northern Iowa, Aug. 1977.

Boddy-Evans, Alistair. "Biography: Ellen Johnson-Sirleaf, Liberia's 'Iron Lady.'" About: African History, 2006. Oct. 7, 2006, http://africanhistory.about.com/od/liberia/p/Sirleaf.htm.

Botswana. Ministry of Labour and Home Affairs. Women's Affairs Department. *Botswana's Response to the Questionnaire to Governments on Implementation of the Beijing Platform for Action (1995) and the Outcome of the Twenty-Third Special Session of*

The General Assembly (2000): 2. Mar. 14, 2007, http://www.un.org/womenwatch/daw/Review/responses/BOTSWANA-English.pdf.

Boustany, Nora. "Rebuilding a Life and Then a Country." *Washington Post*, May 10, 2006: A21. Oct. 31, 2006, http://www.washingtonpost.com/wpdyn/content/article/2006/05/09/AR2006050901831.html.

"Bretton Woods System." *Wikipedia Encyclopedia*, Aug. 12, 2006. Aug. 12, 2006.

Brill, Alida. "Introduction." In Alida Brill, ed. *A Rising Public Voice: Women in Politics Worldwide.* New York: The Feminist Press at the City University of New York, 1995. 1–9.

British Broadcasting Corporation. "African First for Liberian Leader." Africa, Jan. 16, 2006. Oct. 1, 2006, http://news.bbc.co.uk/2/hi/africa/4615764.stm.

_____. "Country Profile: Mali." Africa, Jan. 2, 2007. Feb. 20, 2007, http://news.bbc.co.uk/2/hi/africa/country_profiles/1021454.stm.

_____. "The Green Belt Movement: Profile: Wangari Maathai," Oct. 10, 2004. Oct. 20, 2006, http://greenbeltmovement.org/a.php?id=18.

_____. "Profile: Nigeria's Respected Finance Minister," Apr. 24 2006. Oct. 31, 2006, http://odili.net/news/source/2006/apr/24/85.html.

_____. "Regions and Territories: Somaliland," Africa, Aug. 22, 2006. Jan. 26, 2007, http://news.bbc.co.uk/1/hi/world/africa/country_profiles/3794847.stm.

Brown, Mark Malloch. "Luisa Diogo Advocate for Africa." *Time 100*, Apr. 26, 2004. Oct. 27, 2006, http://www.time.com/time/magazine/article/0,9171,993968,00.html.

BuaNews. "South Africa; Mbeki Commits to Sustaining Women's Emancipation." *Africa News*, Aug. 9, 2006.

Burch, Allan. Biography for Farkhonda Hassan in Farkhonda Hassan. "Essays on Science and Society: Islamic Women in Science." *Science* 290, no. 5489 (Oct. 6, 2000): 55. Nov. 30, 2006, http://www.sciencemag.org/cgi/content/full/290/5489/55.

Burundi. Embassy of the Republic of Burundi. Addis Abeba. *Republique du Burundi Declaration Solennelle sur l'Egalité entre les Hommes et les Femmes en Afrique: Rapport Initial, Bujumbura*, Sept. 2006. Translated from French to English by Alta Vista, Babel Fish Translation, http://babelfish.altavista.com/, Dec. 31, 2006. Dec. 31, 2006, http://www.africa-union.org/root/ua/Conferences/novembre/GE/2-3%20oct/Report-Burundi.doc.

Bush, Laura. "Ellen Johnson-Sirleaf Africa's First Female President." Time.com, Apr. 30, 2006. Oct. 4, 2006, http://www.time.com/time/magazine/article/0,9171,1187159,00.html.

Cameroon. Ministry of Women's Affairs. *Replies to*

Questionnaire on the Implementation Of the Dakar and Beijing Platforms, n.d. Apr. 1, 2007, http://www.un.org/womenwatch/daw/Review/responses/CAMEROON-English.pdf.

Central African Republic. Ministry of the Family. Central African Republic Social Affairs and National Solidarity. Cabinet. *Implementation of The Beijing Platform for Action (1995) and The Outcome of the 23rd Special Session of the General Assembly (2000) in the Central African Republic*, n.d. Apr. 2, 2007, http://www.un.org/womenwatch/daw/Review/responses/CENTRAL-AFRICAN-REPUBLIC-English.pdf.

Chad. Republic of Chad. Ministry of Social Action and the Family. N'Djamena. *Reply to Questionnaires on Gender and Information and Communication Technologies in Chad*, May 14, 2004. Apr. 1, 2007, http://www.un.org/womenwatch/daw/Review/responses/CHAD-English.pdf.

Chazan, Naomi. "The New Politics of Participation in Tropical Africa." *Comparative Politics* 14, no. 2 (Jan. 1982): 169–189.

Chem@AUC. "Retirement...." *American University in Cairo: Chemistry Department Newsletter*, no. 4 (June 2004): 2. Nov. 30, 2006, http://www.aucegypt.edu/academic/chemistry/newsletters/2004.pdf.

Childs, Sarah. "The Complicated Relationship between Sex, Gender and the Substantive Representation of Women." *European Journal of Women's Studies* 13, no. 1 (2006): 7–21.

Columbia University. "World Leaders Forum: Ngozi Okonjo-Iweala," 2006. Oct. 31, 2006, http://www.worldleaders.columbia.edu/bio_okonjo-iweala.html.

Comoros. Union of Comoros. Ministere Des Affaires Sociales et Des Reformes Administratives. Direction Nationale De La Promotion De La Femme et de Groupe Vulnerable. Direction de la Promotion de la Femme. *Rapport D'Evaluation National De La Plate-Forme D'Action De Beijing (Beijing +10)*, April 2004. Mar. 29, 2007, http://www.un.org/womenwatch/daw/Review/responses/COMOROS-French.pdf. Translated from French to English by Alta Vista, Babel Fish Translation, http://babelfish.altavista.com/, Mar. 29, 2007.

Congo. Republic of the Congo. Ministry of Agriculture, Livestock, Fisheries and the Advancement of Women. Secretary of State. Cabinet. *Reply to the Questionnaire Concerning the Report of the Congo on Implementation of the Dakar Plan of Action And Beijing+10*, n.d. Apr. 1, 2007, http://www.un.org/womenwatch/daw/Review/response/CONGO-English.pdf.

Conway, Lawrence V. (President, Medical Mission Hall of Fame Foundation, Medical College of Ohio). Letter to Edna Adan Ismail, Oct. 1, 2006.

"Country Overview." *Quota Database, International IDEA and Stockholm University Global Database of Quotas for Women*, 2006. Sept. 24, 2006, http://www.quotaproject.org/ country.cfm?SortOrder=LastLowerPercentage%20DESC.

Crilly, Rob. "Liberian Leader Wants Closer Relationship with U.S." *USA Today*, Jan. 23, 2006: 6A.

Dahlerup, Drude. "Quotas — a Key to Equality?" *Quota Database, International IDEA and Stockholm University Global Database of Quotas for Women*, 2006. Sept. 24, 2006, http://www.quotaproject.org/about_research.cfm.

Daily Observer. "Gambia; Assembly Speaker Urges Children Solid Foundation." *Africa News*, May 9, 2006.

Datta, Kavita and Cathy McIlwaine. "'Empowered Leaders'? Perspectives on Women Heading Households in Latin America and Southern Africa." In Caroline Sweetman, ed. *Women and Leadership.* Oxfam Focus on Gender Series. Dorset, UK: Oxfam, 2000, 40–49.

Democracy Now! "Ellen Johnson-Sirleaf Sworn in as Liberia's New President, First Elected Female Leader of Africa," Jan. 17, 2006. June 18, 2006, http://www.democracynow.org/article.pl?sid=06/01/17/1449215.

Democratic Republic of Congo. Ministry of the Condition of Women and the Family. *National Report of the Democratic Republic of Congo on the Review and Evaluation of the Beijing+10 Plan of Action*, Feb. 2004. Mar. 29, 2007, http://www.un.org/womenwatch/daw/Review/responses/DEMREPOFTHECONGO-English.pdf.

Discover France. "Burkina Faso (Upper Volta)," n.d. Aug. 5, 2006, http://www.discoverfrance.net/Colonies/Burkina_Faso.shtml.

Djibouti. Republic of Djibouti. Office of the Prime Minister. Ministry for the Promotion of Women, Family Well-Being, and Social Affairs. *National Ten-year Evaluation Report on Implementation of the Beijing Platform for Action*, June 2004. Mar. 30, 2007, http://www.un.org/womenwatch/daw/Review/responses/DJIBOUTI-English.pdf.

Edwards, Audrey. "The Leaders of the Movement — Women's Role in Ending Apartheid in South Africa — South Africa Reborn." *Essence*, Oct. 1997. Nov. 6, 2006, http://www.findarticles.com/p/articles/mi_m1264/is_n6_v28/ai_19801496.

"Egypt: Getting Tougher on Women's Rights." *Al-Ahram Weekly.* no. 527 (Mar. 29–Apr. 4, 2001). Nov. 30, 2006, http://weekly.ahram.org.eg/2001/527/eg13.htm.

Egypt. "Mrs. Mubarak Proposes a New International Forum for Women." Mrs. Suzanne Mubarak Address, June 7, 2000. April 2, 2007, http://www.presidency.gov.eg/html/s_7-June2000_speech.htm.

Egypt. National Council for Women, 2007. Mar. 24, 2007, http://www.ncwegypt.com/english/index.jsp.

Egypt. National Council for Women. Egypt. *Beijing*

+10 report, n.d. Mar. 14, 2007, http://www.un. org/womenwatch/daw/Review/responses/EGYPT -English.pdf.

Egypt. National Council for Women. "The Secretary General Farkhonda Hassan Member of Parliament Biography," 2005. Dec. 8, 2006, http:// www.ncwegypt.com/english/coun_sec.jsp.

"Egypt: Rulers, Kings and Pharaohs of Ancient Egypt: Cleopatra VII and Ptolemy XIII Cleopatra VII: Ptolemaic Dynasty." InterCity Oz, Inc., 1996. May 11, 2006, http://touregypt.net/cleo patr.htm.

"Ellen Johnson-Sirleaf: Positions; Selected Works." *Africa Centre.* London: *Contemporary Africa Database: People: Positions; Selected Works,* Sept. 26, 2006. Oct. 11, 2006, http://people.africadatabase. org/en/person/2655.html.

Equality Now. "Protocol on the Rights of Women in Africa," n.d. Aug. 19, 2006, http://www. equalitynow.org/english/campaigns/african-protocol/ african-protocol_en.html.

_____. SOAWR Secretariat. Email from Faiza Jama Mohamed. Africa Regional Director, Aug. 21, 2006.

"Equatorial Guinea," 2006. Mar. 30, 2007, http:// www.freedomhouse.org/uploads/WoW/2006/ EquatorialGuinea2006.pdf.

Equatorial Guinea. "Government," Apr. 2, 2007. Apr. 2, 2007, http://guinea-equatorial.com/gov. asp.

Eritrea. *Implementation of the Beijing Platform for Action and The Outcome of the Twenty-Third Special Session of the General Assembly,* Mar. 2004. Mar. 30, 2007, http://www.un.org/ womenwatch/ daw/Review/responses/ERITREA-ENGLISH. pdf.

Ethiopia. *Report of the Federal Democratic Republic of Ethiopia on the Implementation of the Au Solemn Declaration on Gender Equality in Africa,* Aug. 2006. Dec. 26, 2006, http:// www.africa-union. org/root/au/Conferences/Past/2006/October/W G/Report-Ethiopia.doc.

European Union Parliamentary Support Programme. "A Poetic Politician." *PSP Newsletter,* ed. 7, Jan.–March, 2000: 3. Nov. 7, 2006, http://www. parliament.gov.za/eupsp/newsletters/07-00.html.

_____. "Style Praised." *PSP,* Newsletter, ed. 8, April-May, 2000. Nov. 7, 2006, http://www.par liament.gov.za/eupsp/newsletters/08-00.html# focus.

Fauvet, Paul. "Mozambique's Diogo Sworn in as New PM." *IOL,* Feb. 22 2004. Oct. 27, 2006, http://www.iol.co.za/index.php?click_id=84&art _id=qw1077443643261S530&set_id=1.

February, Judith. "Parliament. Parts of it were EXCELLENT." Financial Mail (South Africa), Dec. 3, 2004.

Femmes Africa Solidarité. *African Women Pioneers.* N.Y.: U.N. Liaison Office, a work in progress.

Aug. 29, 2006 http://www.fasngo.org/en/what new/african%20women%20pioneers.pdf.

_____. "Beijing Conference Chairperson: Ms. Gertrude Mongella, Teacher and Politician, Tanzania," 2006. Nov. 8, 2006, http://www.fasngo. org/en/presentation/leadbank/index.htm.

_____. *Celebrating with Her Excellency Madam Ellen Sirleaf-Johnson President of Liberia.* New York: U.N. Liaison Office, n.d. Oct. 1, 2006, http:// www.fasngo.org/en/network/index.htm.

_____. "Gertrude Mongella." Leadership Bank. Leadership Profile, 2006. Nov. 8, 2006, http:// www.fasngo.org/en/presentation/leadbank/peo ple/gertrudemong.htm.

_____. "NGO Partners," n.d. Aug. 31, 2006, http: //www.fasngo.org/en/network/index.htm.

FEMNET. "About FEMNET: Vision and Mission," Aug. 16, 2006. http://www.femnet.or.ke/subsec tion.asp?ID=2.

Fleshman, Michael. "African Women Struggle for a Seat at the Peace Table." *Africa Recovery,* 16, no. 4 (February 2003): 1. Sept. 3, 2006, http://www. un.org/ecosocdev/geninfo/afrec/vol16no4/164wm 1.htm.

Fogg, Karen. "Preface." In Julie Ballington, ed. *The Implementation of Quotas: African Experiences, Quota Report Series No. 3.* Stockholm, Sweden: International Institute for Democracy and Electoral Assistance (IDEA), Nov. 2004, 3. See also at: Sept. 23, 2006, http://www.quotaproject.org/ publications/Quotas_Africa.pdf.

Fredericks, Ilse, Bienne Huisman and Sivuyile Mbambato. "Movers and Shakers Strut Their Stuff." *Sunday Times* (South Africa), Feb. 13, 2005, Sec: Human Interest, 3.

Frontline. "The Triumph of Evil: Interviews: Philip Gourevitch." PBS. WGBH, 1995–2006. Nov. 17, 2006, http://www.pbs.org/wgbh/pages/frontline/ shows/evil/interviews/ gourevitch.html.

_____. "The Triumph of Evil: Interviews: Philip Gourevitch (continued)." PBS. WGBH, 1995– 2006. Nov. 19, 2006, http://www.pbs.org/wgbh/ pages/frontline/shows/evil/interviews/gourevitch 2.html.

Gabon. Republique Gabonaise. Ministere de LaFamille, de la Protection de L'enfance et de la Promotion de la Femme. *Rapport sur l'Evaluation Decennale de la Mise en Oeuvres des Plates-Formes d'Actions de Dakar et de Beijing,* Feb. 2004. Apr, 2, 2007, http://www.un.org/womenwatch/daw/ Review/responses/GABON-French. pdf. Translated from French to English by Alta Vista, Babel Fish Translation, http://babelfish. altavista.com/, Apr, 2, 2007.

Gambia (The). "Citation, Hon. (Mrs.) Fatoumata Jahumpa-Ceesay, Parliamentarian Par Excellence." Email attachment to the author by the Gambian Embassy in the United States, Feb. 7, 2007.

Gambia (The). Masanneh-Ceesay, Tijan (servant of the people). Embassy of the Gambia in the United States. Emails to author, Feb. 4 and 8, 2007.

Gambia (The). Njie-Saidy, Mrs. Isatou (Vice President and Secretary of State (Minister) for Women's Affairs of the Republic of the Gambia). "Statement." 49th Session. Commission on the Status of Women on the Review of the Implementation of the Beijing Platform of Action. New York, Mar. 1, 2005. Feb. 15, 2007, http://un.cti.depaul.edu/Countries/Gambia/1109710484/20050301-49thCSW.pdf.

Gambia (The). Tambajang, Mrs. Fatoumata C. M. (Minister of Health, Social Welfare and Women's Affairs of the Republic of the Gambia). "Statement." International Conference on Population and Development. Cairo, Sept. 5–3, 1994. Mar. 11, 2007, http://www.un.org/popin/icpd/conference/gov/940913142831.html.

"Gambian Parliament Gets New Speaker." Panafrican News Agency (PANA). *Daily Newswire*, Apr. 19, 2006.

"Gambian Parliament Picks First Female Speaker." *Xinhua General News Service* (Dakar), Apr. 22, 2006, World News; Political.

"Gender Insensitive Policies Keep African Women Marginalized." Panafrican News Agency (PANA). *Daily Newswire*, Oct. 9, 2004.

Ghana. Ministry of Women and Children's Affairs. *Ghana's second Progress Report on the Implementation of the African and Beijing Platform of Action and Review Report for Beijing+10*, Sept. 2004. Apr. 4, 2007, http://www.un.org/womenwatch/daw/Review/ responses/GHANA-English.pdf.

Global Alliance. "Prominent Women: Farkhonda M. Hassan, Ph.D," 2006. Nov. 30, 2006, http://www.globalalliancesmet.org/prom_hassan.html.

Goth, Bashir. "Somaliland Women: Oppressed Breadwinners and Silent Peacemakers." *Al-Jazeerah*, March 16, 2005, editorials. Jan. 27, 2007, http://www.aljazeerah.info/Opinion%20editorials/2005%20Opinion%20Editorials/March/16%20o/Somaliland%20Women%20Oppressed%20breadwinners%20and%20silent%20peacemakers%20BY%20Bashir%20Goth.htm.

Gourevitch, Philip. *We Wish to Inform You That Tomorrow We Will Be Killed with Our Families: Stories from Rwanda.* New York: Farrar, Straus, and Giroux, 1998.

Green Belt Movement. "About Wangari Maathai: Summary Biography of Professor Wangari Maathai," n.d. Oct. 20, 2006, http://greenbeltmovement.org/w.php?id=3.

_____. "Curriculum Vitae," 2006. Oct. 22, 2006, http://greenbeltmovement.org/w.php?id=47

_____. "Nobel Citation," 2004. Oct. 22, 2006, http://greenbeltmovement.org/w.php?id=45.

Guinea. Republic of Guinea. Ministry of Social Affairs and the Advancement of Women and Children. National Office for the Advancement of Women. *Reply to the United Nations Questionnaire on the Major Achievements and the Challenges Encountered in the Implementation of the Beijing Platform for Action (September 1995) and the Outcome Documents of The Twentieth Special Session of The General Assembly (June 2000)*, April 2004. Apr. 4, 2007, http://www.un.org/womenwatch/daw/Review/responses/GUINEA-English.pdf.

"Guinea-Bissau Country Report." Human Rights Violations, including Violence Against Women. WomenWarPeace.org, January 25, 2007. Mar. 28, 2007, http://www.womenwarpeace.org/guineabissau/guinea_bissau.htm#impact.

"Habyarimana, Juvénal." *Wikipedia*, Nov. 25, 2006. Nov. 26, 2006, http://en.wikipedia.org/wiki/Juv%C3%A9nal_Habyarimana.

Harris, David. "Ellen Johnson-Sirleaf: Profiles President of Liberia." *Africa Centre. Contemporary Africa Database.* London. People. Ellen Johnson-Sirleaf, main page, Sept. 26, 2006. Oct. 9, 2006, http://people.africadatabase.org/en/profile/2655.html.

Harsch, Ernest. "Combating Inequality in Africa: Lessen Inequities to Reduce Poverty and Reach MDGs, says UN." *Africa Renewal* 20, no. 2 (July 2006): 16–20.

_____. "Liberian Woman Breaks the 'Glass Ceiling': Ambitious Agenda for President Ellen Johnson-Sirleaf." *Africa Renewal* 19, no. 4 (Jan. 2005): 4. Oct. 8, 2006, http:// www.un.org/ecosocdev/geninfo/afrec/vol19no4/194sirleaf.htm.

Harter, Pascale. "Sahara Women Relish Their Rights." BBC News, Oct. 30, 2003. Mar. 24, 2007, http://news.bbc.co.uk/2/hi/africa/3227997.stm.

Hassan, Farkhonda. "Bióloga and Egyptian Química," n.d. Nov. 30, 2006, translated version of http://www.ikuska.com/Africa/Historia/biografias/biografias_g1.htm.

Hassim, Shireen. "South Africa: a Strategic Ascent." *UNESCO Courier*, June 2000. May 12, 2006, http://www.unesco.org/courier/2000_06/uk/doss12.htm.

_____. "The Virtuous Circle of Representation: Women in African Parliaments." In Gretchen Bauer and Hannah E. Britton, eds. *Women in African Parliaments.* Boulder, Colo.: Lynne Rienner Publishers, 2006, 171–185.

Independent. "Gambia; Deputy Speaker Faults Anti-Aids Workshops." *Africa News*, Dec. 9, 2005.

International IDEA. "President Johnson-Sirleaf Opens International IDEA Seminar on 'Women in Parliament.'" West Africa Office, Sept. 28, 2006. Oct. 12, 2006, http://www.idea.int/gender/wip_seminar.cfm.

International IDEA and Stockholm University. *Electoral System Design: the New IDEA Handbook*, 2005-2006. Sept. 25, 2006, http://www.idea.int/publications/esd/index.cfm.

_____. *Women in Parliament: Beyond Numbers: A Revised Edit*, 2005, 13. Sept. 25, 2006, http://www.idea.int/publications/wip2/index.cfm.

Inter-Parliamentary Union (IPU). "Gambia (The): General Information," 2002. May 16, 2006, http://www.ipu.org/english/parline/reports/2117.htm.

_____. "Gambia (The): General Information About the Parliamentary Chamber or Unicameral Parliament," Jan. 25, 2007. Feb. 13, 2007, http://www.ipu.org/parline-e/reports/2117_A.htm.

_____. "Gambia (The): Last Elections," 2002. May 16, 2006, http://www.ipu.org/english/parline/reports/2117%5Fe.htm.

_____. Guide2womenleaders.com. "Women in Government: Expert Cites Progress." *USA Today*, Jan. 23, 2006, 6A.

_____. "Women in National Parliaments: World Averages," Jul. 31, 2006. Aug. 13, 2006, http://www.ipu.org/wmn-e/world.htm.

_____. "Women in National Parliaments: World Classification," Jul. 31, 2006. Aug. 6, 2006, http://www.ipu.org/wmn-e/classif.htm.

_____. *Women in Politics: 60 Years in Retrospect* (data valid as at 1 February 2006). May 20, 2006, http://www.ipu.org/PDF/publications/wmninfokit06_en.pdf.

_____. "Women Speakers of National Parliaments: History and the Present," Feb. 28, 2007. Mar. 15, 2007, http://www.ipu.org/wmn-e/speakers.htm.

_____. "Women's Suffrage: A World Chronology of the Recognition of Women's Rights to Vote and to Stand for Election," n.d. Sept. 16, 2006, http://www.ipu.org/wmn-e/suffrage.htm.

Ismail, Edna Adan. Curriculum Vita, Aug. 1, 2006.

_____. Email interview from Hargeisa, Somaliland, Jan. 12, 2007, and follow-up email, Feb. 1, 2007.

John, Abdoulie. "My Appointment Is Women's Emancipation ... Speaker Bidwell," May 4, 2006. Nov. 11, 2006, http://observer.gm/enews/index.php?option=com_content&task=view&id=4281&pt_show=1&PHPSESSID=64eae30bbd4908155db8fb5c85e99479.

Johnson-Sirleaf, President Ellen. "Inaugural Speech." Monrovia, Liberia, Jan. 16, 2006. Oct. 5, 2006, http://www.embassyofliberia.org/news/Inaugural%20Speech.htm.

_____. "Speech to the U.S. Congress." U.S Joint Session of Congress. Washington D.C., March 15, 2006. Oct. 5, 2006, http://www.embassyofliberia.org/news/item_congressspeech.html.

_____. "Statement." 61st Regular Session of the United Nations General Assembly, New York, Sept. 19, 2006. Oct. 5, 2006, http://www.un.org/webcast/ga/61/pdfs/liberia-e.pdf.

Joof, Sulayman. "Fatou Jahumpa-Ceesay: an Amazone Queen." *Gambia News Site*, Feb. 6, 2007. Feb. 15, 2007, http://statehousenews.info/index.php?option=com_content&task=view&id=139&Itemid=9.

Karenga, Maulana. "A New President and Promise for Liberia: Searching for Signs and Wonders." *Los Angeles Sentinel*, Jan. 26, 2006: A-7. June 22, 2006, http://www.us-organization.org/position/documents/ANewPresidentandPromiseforLiberia.pdf.

Khayar, Mohamed. "Electoral Changes in Mauritania Yield Victory for Women," Feb. 14, 2007. Mar. 12, 2007, http://www.magharebia.com/cocoon/awi/print/en_GB/features/awi/features/2007/02/14/feature-02.

Kittilson, Miki Caul. *Challenging Parties, Changing Parliaments: Women and Elected Office in Contemporary Western Europe*. Columbus: Ohio State University Press, 2006.

Know Your Black History.com. "Queen Nzingha of Angola (1583–1663)." Profiles & Facts, 2005. Dec. 21, 2006, http://www.knowyourblackhistory.com/queen-nzingha.html.

Kourouma, Ahmadou. *Monnè, outrages et défis*, Paris: Seuil, 1990.

Kpayili, Michael. "Liberia: President Sirleaf Commends Women in Gov't." LiberianTimes.com, Oct. 2, 2006. Jan. 31, 2007, http://www.theliberiantimes.com/article_2006_10_2_5852.shtml.

Lacey, Marc. "Women Gain Ground in Patriarchal Rwanda." *International Herald Tribune*, Feb 28, 2005. Nov. 16, 2006, http://www.romingerlegal.com/newsviewer.php?ppa=8oplo_ZlpqspttUTmjt%3EEvbfek%5C!.

_____. "Women's Voices Rise as Rwanda Reinvents Itself." *New York Times*, Feb. 26, 2005. Nov. 16, 2006, http://www.genocidewatch.org/rwandawomensvoicesriseasrwandareinventsitself26feb05.htm.

Larbi, Madonna Owusuah. "New Gender Perspectives for the Millennium: Challenges and Successful Models of North-South Collaboration." *West Africa Review* 2, no. 1 (Aug. 2000). May 12, 2006, http://www.westafricareview.com/vol2.1/larbi.html.

Le Roux, Anita. "Addressing the Problem of the Drug Qat." Institute for Human Rights and Criminal Justice Studies. ICC, Durban, Dec. 3–7, 2001. Mar. 19, 2007, http://www.crimeinstitute.ac.za/2ndconf/papers/le_roux.pdf.

Lesotho. *Lesotho, African Union Solemn Declaration on Gender Equality in Africa*, June 2006. Dec. 26, 2006, http://www.africa-union.org/root/au/Conferences/Past/2006/October/WG/Report-Lesotho.doc.

Lesotho. Government Official Website. "The Lesotho Monarchy: Her Majesty Queen 'Masenate Mohato Seeiso," June 27, 2006. June 28, 2006, http://www.lesotho.gov.ls/articles/2004/King_Birth_2004/queen.html.

Liberia. Embassy of Liberia. Washington D.C. "President Ellen Johnson-Sirleaf and First Lady Laura Bush Receive IRI-2006 Freedom Award,"

Sept. 22, 2006. Oct. 5, 2006, http://www.em bassyofliberia.org/news/item_iriaward.html.

Liberia. Embassy of Liberia. Washington D.C. "Profile of Her Excellency Ellen Johnson-Sirleaf President of the Republic of Liberia," 2004. Oct. 5, 2006, http://www.embassyofliberia.org/biogra phy.htm.

"Liberia." *Microsoft(r) Encarta(r) Online Encyclopedia,* 2007. Feb. 28, 2007, http://ca.encarta.msn. com/text_761565772___24/Liberia.html.

"Libya: Women." *Africa Centre. Contemporary Africa Database.* London, Sept. 26, 2006. Mar. 23, 2007, http://people.africadatabase.org/en/n/cty/fem/28/.

Libya. *Reply to Questionnaire on the Implementation of the Beijing Platform for Action* (Arabic), 2000. Mar. 23, 2007, http://www.un.org/womenwatch/ daw/followup/responses/Libya.pdf.

Longwe, Sara Hlupekile. "Towards Realistic Strategies for Women's Political Empowerment in Africa." In Caroline Sweetman, ed. *Women and Leadership.* Oxfam Focus on Gender Series. Dorset, UK: Oxfam, 2000. 24–30.

Loum, Anna. "Gambia: Hon. Halifa Sallah Counters Hon. Bala Gaye On Budget." Gambianow. com's *Gambia News,* Dec. 23,2006. Feb. 15, 2007, http://www.gambianow.com/news/News/Gam bia_news_Hon_Halifa_Sallah_Counters_Hon_ Bala_Gaye_On_Budget.html.

"Luisa Diogo Biography." *Encyclopedia of World Biography.* Notable Biographies, 2006: Ca-Ge. Oct. 27, 2006, http://www.notablebiographies. com/news/Ca-Ge/Diogo-Luisa.html.

Maathai, Wangari. "Women, Information, and the Future: The Women of Kenya and the Green Belt Movement." In Alida Brill, ed. *A Rising Public Voice: Women in Politics Worldwide.* New York: The Feminist Press at the City University of New York, 1995. 241–248.

MacDonald, Elizabeth, and Chana R. Schoenberge. "Special Report: The 100 Most Powerful Women: #62 Ngozi Okonjo-Iweala, Nigeria." Forbes.com, Aug. 31, 2006. Oct. 31, 2006, http://www.forbes. com/lists/2006/11/06women_Ngozi-Okonjo-Iweala_H2RN.html.

_____. "Special Report: The 100 Most Powerful Women: #68 Wangari Maathai Nobel Laureate, Deputy Minister of Environment: Kenya." Forbes. com, Jul. 28, 2005. Sept. 1, 2006, http://www. forbes.com/lists/2005/11/BDLL.html.

_____. "Special Report: The 100 Most Powerful Women: #96 Luisa Diogo, Mozambique." Forbes. com, Aug. 31, 2006. Oct. 27, 2006, http://www. forbes.com/lists/2006/11/06women_Luisa-Diogo _ZTLN.html.

Madagascar. Republic of Madagascar. Ministere de la Population de la Protection Sociale et des Loisirs. *Rapport National sur l'Evaluation Decennale de Mise en Application du Plan d'Action de Beijing — Madagascar,* June 2004. Mar. 30, 2007,

http://www.un.org/womenwatch/daw/Review/re sponses/MADAGASCAR-French.pdf. Translated from French to English by Alta Vista, Babel Fish Translation, http://babelfish.altavista.com/, Mar. 30, 2007.

Madziwa, Miriam. "Zimbabwe — Women's 'Tough-Love' Protest Demands Change." Fahamu (Oxford). Pace e Bene. Nonviolent Service, Nov. 9, 2006. Feb. 23, 2007, http://paceebene. org/pace/ nvns/nonviolence-news-service-archive/zimbab we-womens-tough-love.

Malawi. Ministry of Gender and Community Services. *Progress on the Beijing+10 Report,* Feb. 2004. Mar. 10, 2007, http://www.un.org/womenwatch/ daw/Review/responses/MALAWI-English.pdf.

Mali. Gadiaga, Kalifa (Information Specialist at the United States Embassy in Bamako, Mali). Email to author, Feb. 22, 2007.

Mali. *Report of Mali to the Sixth Forum on Governance in Africa.* Kigali, Rwanda (Nov. 2005). Feb. 21, 2007, http://www.undp.org/agf/papers/Mali%20 Report%20on%20APRM%20for%20AGF%20 VI%20(English).pdf.

Mathaba News Service. "Africa's First Lady." Comment, posted Jan. 2006. Nov. 8, 2006, http:// www.mathaba.net/0_index.shtml?x=504287.

Mauritania. Islamic Republic of Mauritania. Secretary of State for the Condition of Women. *Evaluation of the institution of the Recommendations of the Plan of Action of Beijing: Beijing+10,* April 2004. Mar. 11, 2007, http://www.un.org/women watch/daw/Review/ responses/MAURITANIA-English.pdf.

Mauritius. *Mauritius Country Report on the Au Solemn Declaration on Gender Equality in Africa.* 2006. Dec. 26, 2006, http://www.africa-union. org/root/ua/Conferences/novembre/GE/2-3%20 oct/Report-Mauritius.doc.

Manuh, Takyiwaa. "Women in Africa's Development: Overcoming Obstacles, Pushing for Progress." *Africa Recovery* Briefing Paper. No. 11, April 1998. Aug. 25, 2006, http://www.un.org/ecosoc dev/geninfo/afrec/bpaper/maineng.htm.

"Maria do Carmo Silveira, Former Prime Minister of São Tomé and Príncipe." *Africa Centre. Contemporary Africa Database.* London. People. Positions. Selected Works, Sept. 26, 2006. Oct. 23, 2006, http://people.africadatabase.org/en/person/ 18507.html.

Mbete, Baleka. "Address by the Speaker of the National Assembly of the Parliament of the RSA." National Assembly of Parliament of the Republic of the Côte d'Ivoire, Aug. 14, 2006. Nov. 4, 2006, http://www.parliament.gov.za/pls/portal/web_ app.utl_output_doc?p_table=press_releases&p_ doc_col=press_release&p_mime_col=mime_type &p_id=638993.

McFerran, Ann. "I Keep My Ego in My Handbag." *Guardian,* Aug. 1, 2005. Oct. 31, 2006, http://

www.guardian.co.uk/g2/story/0,3604,1540043, 00.html.

"Memory of a Murdered President Disarms Egypt's Virgin Policemen; Conference Notebook: Robert Fisk Finds the Authorities Adopting a Creative Attitude to the Security Question." *The Independent* (London), Sept. 5, 1994, Sec.: International News Page, 7.

Miller, Judith. "Egypt Acts to Shield Nature from Modern Life's Ravages." *New York Times*, Jul. 29, 1983, Late City Final Ed.: A3.

Morocco. *National Report Beijing+10*, n.d., 3. Mar. 23, 2007, http://www.un.org/womenwatch/ daw/ Review/responses/MOROCCO-English.pdf.

"Mozambican Liberation Front." *Wikipedia*, Dec. 4, 2006. Dec. 5, 2006, http://en.wikipedia.org/ wiki/ FRELIMO.

Mozambique. *Mozambique Beijing+10 Report*. Summarized Version, Oct. 19, 2004. Mar. 10, 2007, http://www.un.org/womenwatch/daw/Review/res ponses/MOZAMBIQUE-English.pdf.

"Mtintso, Thenjiwe." African National Congress. Biographies of ANC Leaders, Sept. 11, 2006. Sept. 13, 2006, http://www.anc.org.za/people/mtintso_ t.html.

_____. "From Prison Cell to Parliament." In Alida Brill, ed. *A Rising Public Voice: Women in Politics Worldwide*. New York: The Feminist Press at the City University of New York, 1995. 103–117.

Mushonga, Netsai. "Democracy in the Eyes of Women in Zimbabwe." Fellowship, November/December 2006. Feb. 23, 2007, http://www. forusa.org/fellowship/nov-dec06/NetsaiMushon ga.html.

Musoke-Nteyafas, Jane. "Meet Ellen Johnson-Sirleaf First African Woman President." AfroToronto .com, Nov. 28, 2005. Oct. 7, 2006, http://www. afrotoronto.com/Articles/Nov05/JohnsonSirleaf. html.

Musoni, Edwin. "Rwanda to Participate in Global Population Forum." *The New Times* (Kigali), Nov. 20, 2006. Nov. 27, 2006, http://allafrica.com/sto ries/200611200295.html.

Mutume, Gumisai. "African Women Are Ready to Lead: But Social Beliefs and Attitudes Hinder Their Quest." *Africa Renewal* 20, no. 2 (July 2006): 6–9. Mar. 17, 2007, http://www.un.org/ ecosocdev/geninfo/afrec/vol20no2/AR-20no2-english.pdf.

_____. "Women Break into African Politics Quota Systems Allow More Women to Gain Elected Office." *Africa Recovery* 18, no. 1 (April 2004): 4. May 15, 2006, http://www.un.org/ecosocdev/gen info/afrec/vol18no1/181women.htm.

"NA Speaker Elected into Commonwealth Parliament." Yegoo: Gambia Telecommunications Co. LTD. News. Gambia, Aug. 16, 2006. Nov. 12, 2006, http://www.yegoo.gm/?part=9&spart=2& id_text=3986.

Namibia. Ministry of Gender Equality and Child Welfare. *Namibia's Country Report on the African Union Solemn Declaration on Gender Equality in Africa*, 2006. Dec. 26, 2006, http://www.africa-union.org/root/au/Conferences/Past/2006/Octob er/WG/Report-Namibia.doc.

Ndiaye, Tacko (Economic Affairs Officer, United Nations Economic Commission for Africa, Addis Ababa, Ethiopia). Email to author, Dec. 27, 2006.

Nelson, Barbara and Najma Chowdhury, eds. *Women and Politics Worldwide*. New Haven: Yale University, 1994.

"New Speaker of The National Assembly Speaks to Point." *The Point Newspaper*, Apr. 21, 2006. Nov. 11, 2006, http://www.thepoint.gm/headlines744.htm.

New Times. "Rwanda; Rusesabagina Dodges Radio Talk Show." *Africa News*, Feb. 6, 2006.

_____. "Rwanda; Senator Castigates Rusesabagina." *Africa News*, May 15, 2006.

Niger. *Initial and second report of the Niger on the Convention on the Elimination of All Forms of Discrimination against Women*. Final Document, June 2001. Mar. 9, 2007, http://daccessdds.un.org/doc/ UNDOC/GEN/N05/619/38/PDF/N0561938. pdf?OpenElement.

Nigeria. Federal Ministry of Women Affairs. *National Report on Progress Made in Implementation of the Beijing Platform for Action (Beijing+10)*, August 2004. Mar. 7, 2007, http://www.un.org/ womenwatch/daw/Review/responses/NIGERIA-English.pdf.

Nigeria. Permanent Mission of Nigeria to the United Nations. *Reply from the Government of the Federal Republic of Nigeria to the Questionnaire on the Implementation of the Beijing Platform for Action*, n.d. Mar. 7, 2007, http://www.un.org/women watch/daw/followup/responses/Nigeria.pdf.

NNDB. "Luisa Diogo," 2006. Oct. 27, 2006, http:// www.nndb.com/people/093/000044958/.

"Nyiramilimo, Odette." *Wikipedia*, Oct. 25, 2006. Nov. 17, 2006, http://en.wikipedia.org/wiki/ Odette_Nyiramilimo.

Nzegwu, Nkiru. "African Women and the Fire Dance." *West Africa Review* 2, no. 1 (Aug. 2000). May 12, 2006, http://www.westafricareview.com/ vol2.1/nzegwu2.html.

Okome, Mojúbàolú Olúfúnké. "Ellen Sirleaf-Johnson: A Tribute." *JENDA: A Journal of Culture and African Women Studies* Issue 7 (2005). Oct. 14, 2006, http://www.jendajournal.com/ issue7/okome.html.

"Okonjo-Iweala, Dr. Ngozi." *Africa Centre. Contemporary Africa Database*. London. Positions, Sept. 26, 2006. Oct. 31, 2006, http://people. africadatabase.org/en/person/16262.html.

Okoye, Michael. "The Blessing." KWENU! Our culture, Our future." Abuja, Nigeria, May 25, 2006. Nov. 1, 2006, http://www.kwenu.com/pub lications/okoye/the_blessing.htm.

Ouedraogo, Josephine. "Consolidate Progress Achieved by Women to Better Meet Development Challenges." Beijing+10 in Africa. News and Information. U.N. Economic Commission for Africa (ECA), Apr. 7, 2004. Dec. 10, 2006, http://www.uneca.org/fr/Beijing/interview%20JO.htm.

_____. "Presentation on the African Gender and Development Index (AGDI)." Beijing+10 in Africa. News and Information. U.N. Economic Commission for Africa (ECA), Oct. 6–14, 2004. Dec. 10, 2006, http://www.uneca.org/fr/Beijing/Speech_JO_AGDI.htm.

Pambazuka News. "Victory for Women's Rights in Africa!" 2006. Aug. 18, 2006, http://www.pambazuka.org/en/petition/index.php.

Pan-African Parliament. Profile of the Bureau. Profiles of the Members of the Pan-African Parliament Bureau. "The President Hon. Dr. Gertrude Ibengwe Mongella," 2005. Nov. 8, 2006, http://www.pan-african-parliament.org/profbureau.htm.

Patterson, Amy S. "A Reappraisal of Democracy in Civil Society: Evidence from Rural Senegal." *Journal of Modern Africa Studies* 36 (1998): 423–441.

"Paul Kagame." *Wikipedia*, Dec. 6, 2006. Dec. 6, 2006, http://en.wikipedia.org/wiki/Paul_Kagame.

Porter, Abioseh Michael. "A New 'New' Jerusalem? West African Writers and the Dawn of the New Millennium." *JOUVERT: A Journal of Post-Colonial Studies* 4, no. 2 (Winter 2000). May 12, 2006, http://social.chass.ncsu.edu/jouvert/v4i2/porter.htm.

Preece, Julia. "Education for Transformative Leadership in Southern Africa." *Journal of Transformative Education* 1, no. 3 (2003): 245–263.

Progressiveafricans. "Fatoumata Jahumpa-Ceesay Is New Speaker of National Assembly." *Gambia News Site*, Feb. 5, 2007. Feb. 5, 2007, http://statehousenews.info/index.php?option=com_content&task=view&id=137&Itemid=9.

Rao, Aruna, and David Kelleher. "Leadership for Social Transformation: Some Ideas and Questions on Institutions and Feminist Leadership." In Caroline Sweetman, ed. *Women and Leadership*. Oxfam Focus on Gender Series. Dorset, UK: Oxfam, 2000. 74–79.

"Reigning Queens 1945–2005," Mar. 16, 2006. July 1, 2006, http://www.terra.es/personal2/monolith/00women1.htm.

Republic of Rwanda. Ministere du Genre et De La Promotion De La Familie and Secretariat Executif Permanent De Suivi De Beijing. *Rapport D'Evaluation Decennale De La Mise en Oeuvre Du Programme D'Action De Beijing*, 1995–2004, 18. Mar. 6, 2007, http://www.un.org/womenwatch/daw/Review/responses/RWANDA-French.pdf. Translated from French to English by Alta Vista, Babel Fish Translation, http://babelfish.altavista.com/, Mar. 6, 2007.

Republic of Rwanda. Government, 2007. Mar. 31, 2007, http://www.gov.rw/government/governmentf.html.

Republic of Rwanda. Senate, Members, "Dr. Nyiramirimo, Odette," 2006. Nov. 16, 2006, http://www.rwandaparliament.gov.rw/SE/uk/compo/index.htm.

São Tomé and Príncipe. *Reply to Questionnaire on the Implementation of the Beijing Platform for Action*, Aug. 18, 2000, Feb. 28, 2007, http://www.un.org/womenwatch/daw/followup/countrylist.htm. Translated from French to English by Alta Vista. Babel Fish Translation. http://babelfish.altavista.com/, Feb. 28, 2007.

Save The Gambia Democracy Project. "First Female Speaker." *Foroyaa Newspaper Burning Issue* no. 30/2006, Apr. 20–23, 2006. Nov. 12, 2006, http://www.sunugambia.com/ modules.php?name=News&file=article&sid=102.

Senegal. Republic of Senegal. *Solemn Declaration on the Equality Between the Men and the Women in Africa*, 2006. Dec. 30, 2006, http://www.africa-union.org/root/au/ Conferences/Past/2006/October/WG/Report-Senegal.doc. Translated from French to English by Alta Vista. Babel Fish Translation. http://babelfish.altavista.com/, Jan. 5, 2007.

Seychelles. *Country Report [Beijing+10]*, n.d. Mar. 6, 2007, http://www.un.org/womenwatch/daw/Review/responses/SEYCHELLES-English.pdf.

Seychelles. Ministry of Social Affairs and Manpower Development. *Country Report: Implementation of the Beijing Platform for Action*, June 1999. Mar. 6, 2007, http://www.un.org/womenwatch/daw/followup/responses/Seychelles.pdf.

Sheppard, Gilda Louis. "Leadership Roles and Perspectives Among Ghanaian Women." The Union Institute: Dissertation, Jan. 1999.

Shvedova, Nadezhda. "Obstacles to Women's Participation in Parliament." International IDEA and Stockholm University. *Women in Parliament: Beyond Numbers: A Revised Edit*, 2005, 33–50. Sept. 25, 2006, http://www.idea.int/publications/wip2/index.cfm.

Sierra Leone. Shirley Y. Gbujama Minister of Social Welfare, Gender and Children's Affairs. Permanent Mission of the Republic of Sierra Leone to the United Nations. "Statement," 23rd Special Session. United Nations General Assembly. Women 2000: Gender Equality, Development and Peace for the 21st Century, June 9, 2000. Mar. 28, 2007, http://www.un.org/womenwatch/daw/followup/beijing+5stat/statments/sleone9.htm.

Skaine, Rosemarie. *Female Genital Mutilation: Legal, Cultural and Medical Issues*. Jefferson, N.C.: McFarland, 2005.

Somaliland. Constitution. Somaliland Forum, May 31, 2001. Mar. 31, 2007, http://www.somaliland

forum.com/somaliland/constitution/revised_con
stitution.htm.

Somaliland Republic. *Country Profile*, n.d. Jan. 26, 2007, http://www.somalilandgov.com/.

Somaliland Republic. *Country Profile*. Somaliland Net, Mar. 30, 2007. Mar. 30, 2007, http://www.somalilandnet.com/slandhome.shtml.

Somaliland Republic. Ministry of Foreign Affairs. Edna Adan Ismail. Minister. "Paper, Somaliland's Case," term June 2003 to August 2006.

Somaliland. *Wikipedia*, Mar. 27, 2007. Mar. 31, 2007, http://en.wikipedia.org/wiki/Somaliland.

South Africa. Parliament. Office of the Speaker. "Baleka Mbete, Ms.," n.d. Nov. 4, 2006, http://parliament.gov.za/pls/portal/web_app.utl_output_doc?p_table=people&p_doc_col=bio&p_mime_col=mime_type&p_id=2166.

South Africa. Presidency. Office of the Status of Women. *Global Report to Inform the Following Reports: Beijing Platform for Action, Dakar Platform for Action, Commonwealth 7WAMM, CEDAW, National Report on Ten Years of Freedom*," Oct. 19, 2004. Mar. 6, 2007, http://www.un.org/womenwatch/daw/Review/responses/SOUTH AFRICA-English.pdf.

South Africa. The Presidency. Office on the Status of Women. *South Africa's Report to the AU Secretariat on the Implementation of the AU Heads of States' Solemn Declaration on Gender Equality in Africa*, June 2006. Dec. 26, 2006, http://www.africa-union.org/root/au/Conferences/Past/2006/October/WG/Report-South% 20Africa.doc.

Southern Africa. Electoral Institute of Southern Africa (EISA). *Election Observer Mission Report, Tanzania Presidential, National Assembly and Local Government Elections*, No. 20, Dec. 14, 2005. Mar. 5, 2007, http://www.eisa.org.za/PDF/tzomr 2005.pdf.

"Stade Aline Sitoe Diatta." *Wikipedia*, Dec. 25, 2006. Jan. 17, 2007, http://en.wikipedia.org/wiki/Stade_Aline_Sitoe_Diatta.

"Status of Human Rights Organizations in Sub-Saharan Africa Mali." University of Minnesota: Human Rights Library, n.d. Feb. 21, 2007, http://www1.umn.edu/humanrts/africa/mali.htm.

Stephens, Jane Thompson. *The Rhetoric of Women's Leadership*. Dissertation. Greensboro, N.C.: University of North Carolina at Greensboro, 2000.

Sudan. Ministry of Welfare and Social Development. General Directorate for Women and the Family. *Quarter-Century Strategy for the Advancement of Women 2003–2027*, Sept. 2002. Mar. 23, 2007, http://www.un.org/womenwatch/daw/Review/responses/SUDAN-English.pdf.

Swaziland. Government. "The Kings Office: Kings of the Kingdom," n.d. June 28, 2006, http://www.gov.sz/home.asp?pid=900.

Swaziland. Government. Prime Minister's Office. "Responses to Questionnaire from Swazi TV." PM interview with Swazi TV, n.d. Mar. 4, 2007, http://www.gov.sz/home.asp?pid=4040.

Swaziland. Ministry of Home Affairs Gender Coordination Unit. *Swaziland Country Report: Sub-Regional Review on Implementation of the Beijing Platform for Action (1995) and the Outcome of the 23rd Special Session of the General Assembly (2000)*. Zambia, April 26–29, 2004. Mar. 4, 2007, http://www.un.org/womenwatch/daw/Review/responses/SWAZILAND-English.pdf.

Swaziland. *Questionnaire [Beijing+5]*, n.d., 8. Mar. 4, 2007, http://www.un.org/womenwatch/daw/followup/responses/Swaziland.pdf.

Sweetman, Caroline, ed. *Women and Leadership*. Oxfam Focus on Gender Series. Dorset, UK: Oxfam, 2000.

Tamale, Slvia. "'Point of Order, Mr. Speaker': African Women Claiming Their Space in Parliament." In Sweetman, ed., 7–15.

Tanzania. National Website. "Gender," n.d. Mar. 4, 2007, http://www.tanzania.go.tz/gender.html#Women%20Political%20Empowerment%20and%20Decision%20Making.

Tanzania. *Response to UN Questionnaire to Governments on Implementation of the Beijing Platform for Action*, n.d. Mar. 4, 2007, http://www.un.org/womenwatch/daw/followup/responses/Tanzania.pdf.

Testolin, Giorgia. *Handbook on National Machinery to Promote Gender Equality and Action Plans: Guidelines for Establishing and Implementing National Machinery to Promote Equality, with Examples of Good Practice*. Strasbourg, France: Council of Europe, May 2001 EG (2001) no. 7. Mar. 5, 2007, http://www.humanrights.coe.int/equality/Eng/WordDocs/eg(2001)7%20Handbook%20on%20National%20Machinery.doc.

Togo. Ministry for Social Affairs. Togolese Republic. The Advancement of Women and the Protection of Children. *Evaluation of the Implementation of The Beijing Platform for Action Beijing+10*, National Report, April 2004. Mar. 28, 2007, http://www.un.org/womenwatch/daw/Review/responses/TOGO-English.pdf.

Tripp, Aili Mari. "Women in Movement: Transformations in African Political Landscapes." *International Feminist Journal of Politics* 5, no. 2, (July 2003): 233–255.

Tran, Phuong. "Republic of Congo's Ruling Coalition Wins Election Amidst Accusations of Fraud." Voice of America, Dakar, Aug. 10, 2007.

Tunisia. Republic of Tunisia. Ministry for the Women's, Family, and Children's Affairs and the People. Initial Report of Tunisia. *Solemn Declaration on the Equality Between Men and Women in Africa*, June 2006. Dec. 30, 2006, http://www.africa-union.org/root/au/Conferences/Past/2006/October/WG/Report-Tunisia.doc. Translated from French to English by Alta Vista. Babel Fish

Translation. http://babelfish.altavista.com/, Jan. 7, 2007.

Tunisia. Tunisian Republic Ministry of Women's, Family and Children's Affairs Board of General Communications and Information. *Reply of Tunisia to the Questionnaire to Governments on Implementation of the Beijing Platform for Action (1995) and the Outcome of the Twenty-third Special Session of the General Assembly (2000).* Tunis, May 2005. Mar. 2, 2007, http://www.un.org/womenwatch/daw/Review/responses/ TUNISIA-English.pdf.

Turshen, Meredeth. "Women's War Stories." In Meredeth Turshen and Clotilde Twagiramariya, eds. *What Women Do in Wartime: Gender and Conflict in Africa.* London; New York: Zed Books, 1998.

Uganda. *Uganda, Report on Government of Uganda's Implementation of the Beijing Platform for Action (1995) and the Outcome of the Twenty-third Special Session of the General Assembly (2000).* Feb. 25, 2007, http://www.un.org/womenwatch/daw/Review/responses/UGANDA-English.pdf.

United Nations. *Beijing Declaration and Platform for Action. Fourth World Conference on Women.* University of Minn., Human Rights Library, Sept. 15 1995, A/CONF.177/20 (1995) and A/CONF.177/20/Add.1 (1995). Dec. 12, 2006, http://www1.umn.edu/humanrts/instree/e5dplw.htm.

United Nations. Bolton, John R. "Statement on the Situation in Liberia." USUN Press Release # 57 (06), Mar. 17, 2006. July 13, 2006, http://www.un.int/usa/06_057.htm.

United Nations Committee on the Elimination of Discrimination against Women (CEDAW). *Concluding Comments: Benin.* CEDAW/C/BEN/CO/1–3, July 22, 2005. Apr. 2, 2007, http://www.un.org/womenwatch/daw/cedaw/cedaw33/conclude/benin/0545054E.pdf.

_____. *Concluding Comments: Cape Verde.* CEDAW/C/CPV/CO/6, August 25, 2006. Apr. 2, 2007, http://www.un.org/womenwatch/daw/cedaw/cedaw36/cc/Cape%20Verde%2025 Aug.pdf.

_____. *Concluding Comments: Gabon.* CEDAW/C/GAB/CC/2–5, February 15, 2005. Apr. 2, 2007, http://www.un.org/womenwatch/daw/cedaw/cedaw32/conclude-comments/Gabon/CEDAW-CC-GAB-0523904e.pdf.

_____. *Initial Report of States Parties: Zimbabwe,* July 20, 1996. Feb. 24, 2007, http:// daccessddsun.org/doc/UNDOC/GEN/N96/311/56/IMG/N9631156.pdf?OpenElement.

_____. International Federation of Human Rights (FIDH). "Note on the Situation of Women in Gambia." 33rd session. New York, July 5–22, 2005, 4,5. Feb. 14, 2007, http://www.fidh.org/IMG/pdf/gm_cedaw2005a.pdf.

_____. *Responses to the List of Issues and Questions for Consideration of the Combined Fourth and Fifth Periodic Report Burkina Faso.* CEDAW/PSWG/2005/II/CRP.2/Add.2, April 15, 2005. Apr. 3, 2007, http://www.un.org/womenwatch/daw/cedaw/cedaw33/ responses/bfa/BFA-E.pdf.

_____. *Responses to the List of Issues and Questions for Consideration of the Combined Second, Third, Fourth and Fifth Periodic Reports, Equatorial Guinea.* CEDAW/PSWG/ 2004/II/CRP.2/Add.2, Apr. 1, 2004. Apr. 1, 2007, http://www.un.org/womenwatch/daw/ cedaw/cedaw31/EqGuinea-crp2add2-e.pdf.

_____. "Women's Anti-discrimination Committee Chides Delegation of Cape Verde over Lateness in Submitting First Report Experts Praise Female Gains in Education, Judicial, Diplomatic Fields." General Assembly. WOM/1584, August 18, 2006. Apr. 3, 2007, http://www.un.org/News/Press/docs/2006/wom1584.doc.htm.

_____. "Women's Anti-discrimination Committee Urges Gambia to Revise Discriminatory Laws Based on Religious, Cultural Practices." 697th and 698th meetings. Press release. WOM/1517, July 15, 2005. Feb. 14, 2007, http://www.un.org/News/Press/docs/2005/wom1517.doc.htm.

United Nations Development Fund for Women. "Liberia." WomenWarPeace.org, n.d., Feb. 20, 2007, http://www.womenwarpeace.org/liberia/liberia.htm.

United Nations Development Programs. *Cadre d'Orientation pour l'Integration du Genre dans les Programmes Post-Crise du Système des Nations Unies en Côte d'Ivoire 2006–2007,* Jan. 2006. Apr. 4, 2007, http://www.ci.undp.org/uploadoc/Rapport.pdf. Translated from French to English by Alta Vista, Babel Fish Translation, http://babelfish.altavista.com/, Apr. 4, 2007.

_____. Program on Governance in the Arab Region. *The Gender and Citizenship Initiative: Country Profiles: Somalia,* n.d. Mar. 30, 2007, http://gender.pogar.org/countries/gender.asp?cid=17.

United Nations Division for the Advancement of Women. Department of Economic and Social Affairs. Convention on the Elimination of All Forms of Discrimination (CEDAW). "Country Reports," Aug. 31, 2006. Mar. 23, 2007, http://www.un.org/womenwatch/daw/cedaw/reports.htm#s.

_____. Department of Economic and Social Affairs. "Member States Responses to the Questionnaire," Apr. 30, 2004. Mar. 16, 2007, http://www.un.org/womenwatch/daw/Review/english/responses.htm.

_____. Department of Economic and Social Affairs. *Platform for Action Fourth World Conference on Women.* Beijing, China, Sept. 1995. Jan, 3, 2007, http://www.un.org/womenwatch/daw/beijing/platform/index.html.

_____. Department of Economic and Social Affairs. "Replies to Questionnaire on the Implementation of the Beijing Platform for Action," Revised on

24 May 2002. Mar. 16, 2007, http://www.un.org/womenwatch/daw/followup/countrylist.htm.

_____. "Fact Sheet on Women in Government," Jan. 1996. Mar. 9, 2007, http://www.un.org/womenwatch/daw/public/percent.htm.

United Nations Economic Commission for Africa (ECA). *The African Gender and Development Index.* Addis Ababa, Ethiopia, Sept. 2004. Dec. 27, 2006, http://www.uneca.org/eca_programmes/acgd/publications/AGDI_book_final.pdf.

_____. *African Governance Report 2005.* Addis Ababa, Ethiopia, Nov. 2005. Dec. 12, 2006, http://www.uneca.org/agr2005/.

_____. *African Women's Report 1998. Post-Conflict Reconstruction in Africa: A Gender Perspective.* Addis Ababa, Ethiopia, 1999, 43, 45. Dec. 21, 2006, www.uneca.org/acgd/Publications/en_awr98.pdf.

_____. *5 Years After Beijing: What Efforts in Favor of African Women? Assessing Political Empowerment of Women.* Addis Ababa, Ethiopia, Sept. 2001. Dec. 10, 2006, http:// www.uneca.org/fr/acgd/en/1024x768/en_12areas/en_politic/en_0109_political.pdf.

_____. *Promoting Gender Equality and Women's Empowerment in Africa: Questioning the Achievements and Confronting the Challenges Ten Years After Beijing.* Addis Ababa, Ethiopia, Feb. 2005. Dec. 10, 2006, www.uneca.org/acgd/Publications/Gender_Equality.pdf.

_____. Sub-regional Offices, 2000. Mar. 16, 2007, http://www.uneca.org/eca_programmes/srdc/index.htm.

United Nations Economic and Social Commission for Western Asia (ESCWA). *Women in Decision-Making in the Arab Region.* EGM/EPWD/2005/OP.1, Dec. 12, 2005. Mar. 23, 2007, http://www.un.org/womenwatch/daw/egm/eql-men/docs/OP.1_ESCWA.pdf.

United Nations Food and Agriculture Organization (FAO). Corporate Document Repository. Sustainable Development Department. "Sharing of Power and Decision-making." *Fact sheet: Benin — Women, Agriculture and Rural Development,* n.d. Apr. 3, 2007, http://www.fao.org/docrep/V7948e/v7948e02.htm.

United Nations Foundation. "Ban Chooses Tanzanian Woman as UN No. 2." *UN Wire.* E-mail News Covering the UN and the World, Jan. 8, 2007.

United Nations. "General Assembly Reaffirms Commitment to 1995 Beijing Conference Goals, as 'Women 2000' Special Session Concludes at Headquarters." Press Release GA/9725, June 10, 2000. Feb. 28, 2007, http://www.un.org/News/Press/docs/2000/20000610.ga9725.doc.html.

United Nations High Commissioner for Refugees (UNHCR). "Rwanda: The Heart of Darkness Revisited." *Refugees Magazine* (June 2004). Nov.

16, 2006, http://www.unhcr.org/publ/PUBL/4100cd774.html.

United Nations Information Service. "Challenges of Development Require Not Only Leadership, Resources, but A Legal Response, Secretary-General Says." SG/SM/8597, Feb. 5, 2003. Aug. 25, 2006. http://www.unis.unvienna.org/unis/pressrels/2003/sgsm8597.html.

United Nations Integrated Regional Information Networks. "Egypt; Activists Call Appointments of Women, Minorities 'Fig-Leaf.'" *Africa News,* Dec. 14, 2005.

_____. "Rwanda; Government Puts Genocide Victims At 1.07 Million." *Africa News,* Dec. 19, 2001.

United Nations International Women's Day: Women in Decision Making: Meeting Challenges, Creating Change. "Baleka Mbete," Mar. 8, 2006. Nov. 5, 2006, http://www.un.org/events/women/iwd/2006/mbete.htm.

United Nations. "Networking: Directory of African NGOs," n.d. Mar. 18, 2007, http://www.un.org/africa/osaa/ngodirectory/index.htm.

United Nations. *Network: Women's Newsletter.* vol. 5. no. 1, March 2001. March 23, 2007, http://www.un.org/womenwatch/osagi/network/mar2001.htm.

United Nations Office for the Coordination of Humanitarian Affairs. "Minister's Departure Spawns Fears That Anti-graft Fight Waning." IRINnews.org, Aug. 11, 2006. Oct. 31, 2006, http://www.irinnews.org/report.asp?ReportID=55081&SelectRegion=West_Africa &SelectCountry=NIGERIA.

_____. "Niger: Humanitarian Country Profile." *IRIN,* Feb. 2007. Mar. 9, 2007, http://www.irinnews.org/country.aspx?CountryCode=NE&RegionCode=WA.

_____. "Republic of Sierra Leone Humanitarian Country Profile," Feb. 2007. Mar. 28, 2007, http://www.irinnews.org/country.aspx?CountryCode=SL&RegionCode=WA.

_____. "Somalia: Women Peace Delegates Lobby for Their Rights," Mar. 28, 2003. Mar. 30, 2007, http://www.irinnews.org/report.aspx?reportid=42312.

_____. "The Somali Democratic Republic Humanitarian Country Profile," Mar. 2007. Mar. 30, 2007, http://www.irinnews.org/country.aspx?CountryCode=SO&RegionCode=HOA.

United Nations Peace Women, Women's International League for Peace and Freedom (WILPF). "The Select Club of Women in Power," n.d. Oct. 25, 2006, http://www.peacewomen. org/news/International/Nov05/Select_Club.htm.

United Nations Security Council. *Report of the Secretary-General on Developments in Guinea-Bissau and on the Activities of the United Nations Peace-Building Support Office in that Country.* S/2004/456, June 4, 2004. Mar. 28, 2007, http://

www.womenwarpeace.org/guineabissau/docs/sgre
ptosc4jun04.pdf.

_____. *Report of the Secretary-General on the Situa-tion in Somalia*. S/2004/804, Oct. 8, 2004, no. 10, 2. Mar. 30, 2007, http://www.womenwarpeace.org/somalia/docs/sgreptosc8oct04.pdf.

_____. *Report of the Secretary-General on the Work of the Organization*. General Assembly. 60th Session, Sup. no. 1 (A/60/1), 2005, 22, no. 106. Aug. 17, 2006, http://daccessdds.un. org/doc/UNDOC/GEN/N05/453/25/PDF/N0545325.pdf?Open Element.

_____. *Twenty-second Report of the Secretary-General on the United Nations Mission in Sierra Leone*. S/2004/536, July 6, 2004. Mar. 28, 2007, http://www.womenwarpeace.org/sierra_leone/docs/sgre ptosc6jul04.pdf.

United States Agency for International Development (USAID). *Gender Assessment for USAID/Tanzania*, Sept. 2003. Mar. 4, 2007, http://www.usaid.gov/our_work/cross-cutting_programs/wid/pubs/ga_tanzania.pdf.

United States Central Intelligence Agency (CIA). "The World Fact Book," Feb. 8, 2007. Feb. 15 and Oct. 4, 2007, https://www.cia.gov/cia/publica tions/factbook/index.html.

United States Department of State. Bureau of African Affairs. "Background Note: Liberia," Sept. 2006. Jan. 29, 2007, http://www.state.gov/r/pa/ei/bgn/6618.htm.

United States Department of State. Bureau of Democracy, Human Rights, and Labor. "Comoros. Country Reports on Human Rights Practices," Feb. 25, 2004. Mar. 29, 2007, http://www.state.gov/g/drl/rls/hrrpt/2003/27720.htm.

_____. "Côte d'Ivoire. Country Reports on Human Rights Practices," Mar. 8, 2006. Apr. 4, 2007, http://www.state.gov/g/drl/rls/hrrpt/2005/61565.htm.

_____. "Niger. Country Reports on Human Rights Practices," Mar. 4, 2002. Mar. 9, 2007, http://www.state.gov/g/drl/rls/hrrpt/2001/af/8396.htm.

Usher, Rod. "A World Where Muslim Women Wear the Pants." Peace Women. Women's International League for Peace and Freedom, n.d. Mar. 24, 2007, http://www.peacewomen.org/news/West ernSahara/newsarchive/pants.html.

Vallely, Paul. "From Dawn to Dusk, the Daily Struggle of Africa's Women." *The Independent*, Red ed., Sept. 21, 2006. Sept. 21, 2006, http://news.inde pendent.co.uk/world/africa/article1655627.ece.

Vital Voices. "2006 Global Leadership Awards and Benefit: Women Changing Our World," Apr. 27, 2006. Nov. 1, 2006, http://www.vitalvoices.org/desktopdefault.aspx?page_id=372.

_____. "Women's Global Progress Watch: Strides and Setbacks for Women's Global Leadership: Strides in Political Life," Summer 2004. Feb. 20, 2007, http://www.vitalvoices.org/desktopdefault. aspx?page_id=66.

Wamala, E., A.R. Byaruhanga, A.T. Dalfovo, J.K. Kigongo, S.A. Mwanahewa and G. Tusabe, eds. "Cultural Elements in Social Reconstruction in Africa." In E. Wamala et al. ed. *Social Reconstruc-tion in Africa Ugandan Philosophical Studies, Cul-tural Heritage and Contemporary Change, Africa*: 4, II (Mar. 27, 2003): ch. 5. June 3, 2006, http://www.crvp.org/book/Series02/II-4/chapter_v.htm.

Wanyeki, L. Muthoni. Executive Director, African Women's Development and Communication Network (FEMNET). Email interview, Aug. 23, 2006.

_____. "Femme Globale: Gender Perspectives in the 21st Century: Women Contesting the Informa-tion Society: from Beijing to Geneva, Tunis and Beyond." Staff paper. FEMNET, n.d. Aug. 16, 2006, http://www.femnet.or.ke/publications.asp?documenttypeid=3.

Waring, Marilyn. "Women in Parliamentary Life 1970 to 1990." In Alida Brill. "Introduction." In Alida Brill, ed. *A Rising Public Voice: Women in Politics Worldwide*. New York: The Feminist Press at the City University of New York, 1995. 195–211.

Warsame, Amina Mohamed. "Assessment of Po-tential Women Leaders in Somaliland." Paper presented to the 2nd Post-War Reconstruction Strategies Conference. Institute for Practical Research and Training. Somaliland Women's Research and Action Group. Hargeisa, July 20–25, last Update, Aug. 12, 2006. Jan. 27, 2007, http://www.iprt.org/Amina%20Mohamed%20Warsame.htm.

"Western Sahara." People. Women in Western Sahara. *Africa Centre*. Contemporary Africa Data-base. London, Sept. 26, 2006. Mar. 24, 2007, http://people.africadatabase.org/en/n/cty/fem/51/.

Wikipedia.org. "Keorapetse Kgositsile." *Wikipedia*, 2006. Nov. 4, 2006, http://www.search.com/reference/Keorapetse_Kgositsile.

_____. "Ntombi of Swaziland." *Wikipedia*, Aug. 2006. Mar. 4, 2007, http://en.wikipedia.org/wiki/Ntombi_of_Swaziland.

"Woman to Oversee Sierra Leone Elections." The Mercury, May 18, 2005. Mar. 28, 2007. March 28, 2007, http://www.themercury.co.za/index.php?fSectionId=284&fArticleId=2524367.

"Women Who Lead Their Governments." *Toronto Star*, News, A12, Mar. 5, 2006.

Women World Leaders. Jan. 15, 2006. July 2, 2006, http://www.geocities.com/capitolHill/Lobby/4642/.

Women's eNews. *Africa's Rising Leaders*, Sept. 26, 2005. May 11, 2006, http://www.womensenews.org/article.cfm/dyn/aid/2461/.

Women's Learning Partnership. "Mauritania: Women's Status at a Glance," 2007. Mar. 12, 2007, http://www.learningpartnership.org/part ners/mauritania.

World Bank. *São Tomé and Príncipe Country Gender Assessment.* Draft for Review Only. Human Development II. Country Department 15. Africa Region, June 7, 2004. Feb. 28, 2007, http://site resources.worldbank.org/EXTAFRREGTOP GENDER/Resources/São ToméCGA.pdf.

Worldwide Guide to Women in Leadership. May 8, 2006. May 9, 2006, http://www.guide2women leaders.com/index.html.

Zambia. Republic of Zambia. Gender in Development Division. Cabinet Office. *Zambia's Progress Report on the Implementation of the Beijing Platform for Action 2000–2004.* Draft, Mar. 2004. Mar. 25, 2007, http://www.un.org/womenwatch/daw/Review/responses/ZAMBIA-English.pdf.

Zimbabwe. *Progress Report on The Implementation of The Platform for Action,* 1995–2003. Feb. 25, 2007, http://www.un.org/womenwatch/daw/Review/responses/ZIMBABWE-English.pdf.

Zimbabwe Women's Resource Centre and Network (ZWRCN). "About ZWRCN," 2002. Feb. 23, 2007, http://www.zwrcn.org.zw/about.htm.

Zimbabwe. *Zimbabwe Government Progress Report on the Implementation of the Platform for Action,* Nov. 1999. Feb. 24, 2007, http://www.un.org/women watch/daw/followup/responses/Zimbabwe.pdf.

"Zimbabwe's Women Call for Leadership Positions." *People's Daily Online,* Apr. 15, 2005. Feb. 23, 2007, http://english.people.com.cn/200504/15/eng20050415_181143.html.

Index

AAWORD *see* Association of African Women for Research and Development
abandonment 17
Abantu for Development 25
abolition 40
absence 25
access 14
accomplishment 36
accountability 31, 155, 156
Accra, Ghana 20
Achebe, Chinua 51, 154
acting head 9
action 1, 29
activist 25
Adams, Patricia vii
advancement 1, 29
Advocacy for Women in Africa (AWA) 38
affirmative action 21, 61, 62, 155
Africa 9
Africa Renewal 15
Africa World Press 51
African Center for Gender and Development (ACGD) 61
African Charter on Human and Peoples' Rights on the Rights of Women in Africa 26
African Gender and Development Index 64
African Gender Institute, University of Cape Town 21
African Governance Report 63
African National Congress (ANC) 16, 42–44
African Platform for Action (Dakar Platform for Action) 61
African Recovery 32
African Renaissance 20
African Union (AU) 26, 27, 48
African Women and Governance Seminar and Training Workshop, Entebbe, Uganda 21
African Women Pioneers 15
African Women's Development and Communication Network (FEM-NET) vii, 12, 15, 25, 28, 31
African Women's Report 64
age 17
agency 30, 32, 64
agenda 31, 155
Agenda Africa KCA Think Tank 34
Agozino, Bike 20
AIDS 1

Akina Mama wa Afrika (AmwA) 155
Akinyi, Rose vii
Al Khalifa, Haya Rashed 5, 37
Albania 6
Algeria 62, 65–67
Amara, Satta Kumba 11
ambassador 11, 15
American University in Cairo 49
Amosu, Akwe 21, 155
AmwA *see* Akina Mama wa Afrika
analysis 31
ANC *see* African National Congress
Angola 6, 8, 132–133
Annan, Kofi 31, 56
Anthills of the Savannah 154
Antigua 6
antiquity 14
Antrobus, Peggy 30
apartheid 62
Arab countries 61, 62
Arab state 9
Argentina 5
Asantewa, Yaa 6
Asia 9
Asmau, Hajiya 11
Assistant Secretary of State, Liberia 12
Associated Press vii
Association of African Women for Research and Development (AAWORD) 26
associational autonomy 14
attitude 13, 16
Austria 6, 9
authenticity 19
authority 18, 30
Aziz, Amina Abdel vii

Bahamas 6
Bahemuka, Judith Mbula 11
Bahrain 5
Bakassi Peninsula 51
Bandaranaike, Sirimavo 5
Bang, Nina 5
Bangladesh 5, 41
Bangura, Zainab Hawa 11
Ballington, Julie vii, 24
Barbuda 6
barrier 13, 19, 62
Bauer, Gretchen 9, 10, 25
Beijing Conference 21, 32
Beijing Declaration 1995 62
Beijing Platform for Action 1, 31, 49, 62, 63, 156
Beijing +5 62, 154

Beijing +10 62, 63, 154, 156
Belgium 6, 12
Belize 6
benefits 17
Benin 9, 19, 63, 64, 109–110
Biafran war 51
bias 16
bicameral 9
Bidwell, Belinda 44
Boddy-Evans, Alistair 34
Bolivia 41
Botswana 17, 30, 42, 63, 133–135
boundary 32
Boye, Madior 9
breakthrough 13
Brill, Alida 16
Britton, Hannah E. 9, 10, 25
Brook-Randolph, Angie 12
brutality 56
Bubanza, Burundi displaced persons' camps 39
Burkina Faso 20, 21, 23, 24, 63, 64, 110–111
Burundi 6, 8, 9, 38, 56, 87–88
Bush, Laura 34
Butegwa, Wa Christine vii

cabinet 5, 16, 17, 62
cabinet member 9
cabinet minister 5, 53
Camara, Mahawa Bangoura 11
Cameroon 11, 20, 51, 64, 77–78
campaign 14, 19, 20, 28, 37, 154
Canada 48
cancellation 51
candidate 7, 11, 12, 21, 62
Cape Town 16
Cape Verde 11, 111–113
career 14
caring 16
Casamance 1
case study 17, 18, 25
CEDAW *see* Convention on the Elimination of All Forms of Discrimination Against Women
Ceesay, Sulayman Masanneh 46
Central Africa 10, 77–86
Central African Empire 9
Central African Republic 78–79
Central America 17
Chad 79–80
Chadema Party (Tanzania) 11
challenge 1, 13, 14, 15, 17, 20, 24, 25, 26, 27, 35, 153, 154, 156

Chamber of Deputies 10
change 1, 12, 13, 14, 19, 21, 29, 30, 32, 153, 154, 155, 156
Charter of the United Nations 27
chieftainess 6
child care 16
children 16, 17, 20
Chili 5
China 11
Chissano, Joaquim 41
Christensen, Martin K.I. viii
circumcision 18
civil service, Somalia 54
civil society 15
civil war 155
civilian rule 21
claim 14
Clark, Helen 41
Cleopatra 6
cohabitation 17
collective 25
collective action 14
Colombia 6
colonialism 1
colonization 19
Commission on Gender Equality, South Africa 16
Commission on the Status of Women, U.N. 25, 27
commissioner 15
Committee on Social Affairs and Human Rights, Rwanda 55
Commonwealth 26
communication 25, 26, 31
community 29
Comoros 28, 61, 62, 89
compromises 19
conciliator 21
conflict 1, 17, 25, 46, 154, 155
conflict resolution 21
Conneh, Sekou 7
conservation 49
constitution 14, 17, 43, 65, 67, 69, 71, 72, 73, 75, 77, 78, 79, 80, 82, 83, 84, 87, 89, 90, 92, 93, 95, 96, 97, 99, 100, 101, 103, 105, 107, 109, 111, 112, 113, 115, 116, 118, 119, 120, 122, 124, 125, 127, 129, 130, 132, 134, 136, 137, 139, 140, 141, 143, 145, 147, 148
constitutional equal rights 61
constitutional quota system 22–24
constraint 30, 31, 32, 61
continent 153
Continental Initiative 1995 20
contribution 13
control 30
convention 26
Convention on the Elimination of All Forms of Discrimination Against Women (CEDAW) 27, 29, 32
Convention on the Rights of the Child 27
coordination 13
corruption 37
Côte d'Ivoire 113–114
country 5, 6, 9, 10, 11, 13, 14, 15, 20, 21, 22–24, 25, 28, 41, 42, 55, 57, 61, 62, 63, 64, 154, 155, 156
country report 1, 9, 154, 156

Cour Constitutionelle Conceptia, Benin 9
court 14
credit 30
Credo for Freedom of Expression and Associated Rights 28
cultural tradition 20
culture 19
Cyangugu, Rwanda 55

Dahlerup, Drude 24
Dakar Platform for Action (African Platform for Action) 61, 62
Dar es Salaam, Tanzania 42
Datta, Kavita 17
Debt Trap in Nigeria 51
decision-making 1, 6, 12, 14, 15, 17, 19, 21, 24, 25, 27, 29, 33, 53, 61, 62, 63, 64, 156
Declaration on the Elimination of Violence Against Women 27
Declaration on the Right to Development 27
decolonization 63
defeat 9
delegation 16
democracy 25, 27, 31, 44, 61, 62, 156
democratic election 156
democratic principle 23
Democratic Republic of Congo 89
Denis, Ouinsou née 9
Denmark 12
Department of Information and Publicity (Radio Freedom), ANC 42
deputy head of state 8, 9
deputy minister 16
deputy minister of environment, natural resources and wildlife, Kenya 33, 48
deputy president 12, 24
devalue 155
developed nations 13
development 21, 29, 32
development agencies 32
Diogo, Luisa 9, 40–41
Diola 1
director 15
discrimination 13, 31, 153
division of labor 16
Djibouti 53, 54, 61, 62, 91–92
Doe, Sergeant Samuel 35, 37
Dom Pedro VIII Mansala 8
Domatob, Jerry vii
dominance 20
Dominica 6
Domitien, Elisabeth 9
Dongo, Margaret 15
donor 14, 21
Dukuly-Tolbert, Neh Rita Sangai 11
Durban, South Africa 42

East Africa 10, 87–108
ECA see Economic Commission for Africa
Economic Commission for Africa (ECA) 61, 62, 63, 64, 156
economics 19, 21
Edna Adan Maternity Hospital, Hargeisa, Somaliland 54

Edna Maternity Hospital, Mogadisho, Somalia 54
education 1, 14, 16, 25, 26, 29, 30
egalitarian 17
Egypt 6, 48–50, 61, 62, 63, 64, 67–68
elected office 15, 21
election 20, 33, 42, 44, 48, 62, 66, 69, 77, 78, 79, 80, 82, 83, 84, 87, 89, 90, 92, 93, 95, 96, 98, 99, 100, 106, 107, 109, 111, 112, 113–114, 115, 116, 118, 119, 120, 122, 124, 125, 127, 129, 130, 132, 134, 136, 137, 139, 140, 141–142, 144, 145, 147, 148
election law quota system 22–24
election results 66, 77, 78, 79, 80, 82, 83, 84, 87, 89, 90, 92, 93, 95, 96, 98, 99, 100, 106, 107, 109, 111, 112, 114, 115, 116, 118, 119, 120, 122, 124, 125, 127, 129, 130, 132, 134, 136, 137, 139, 140, 142, 144, 145, 147, 148
electoral quota 29, 155
electoral system 13
electorate 23
elite 16
emancipation 20
embassy vii
employment 27
empowerment 24, 25, 29, 30, 32, 37, 50, 63, 155
enforcement 62
enfranchisement 15
entitlement 14
environment 46, 47
equal opportunity 20
equal rights 27, 32
equality 11, 17, 20, 21, 25, 29, 57, 154
Equality Now — African Region vii, 28
Equatorial Guinea 82–83
Eritrea 21, 93–94
ESCWA see United Nations Economic and Social Commission for Western Asia
Estonia 6
Ethiopia 6, 9, 21, 63, 64, 94–96
Europe 9, 11
European Union 12, 43
European Union Parliamentary Support Programme 43
executive 6
exile 7

Fahamu Networks for Social Justice 28
family 13, 16, 19
famine 1
father tongue 19
FAWE see Forum for African Women Educationalists
Federation of African Women's Peace Networks (FERFAP) 26
feminism 21, 30
feminization 13
Femmes Africa Solidarité 1, 15
FEMNET see African Women's Development and Communication Network

FERFAP *see* Federation of African Women's Peace Networks
Ferreira, Domingos vii
finance 21
Finance Minister, Nigeria 50, 51
Finland 5, 12
First Lady 19
First Past the Post (FPTP) system 24
First World Conference on Women, 1975, Mexico 61
Fleshman, Michael 155
Fogg, Karen 14, 24
food 17
Forbes 46, 51
Foreign Affairs Minister 15
Foreign Minister 5, 11
Forum for African Women Educationalists (FAWE) 26
Fourth World Conference on Women, Beijing 27, 29, 62
France 11
FREMILO *see* Mozambique Liberation Front
freedom 44
freedom fighter 15
freedom of expression 33
freedom of information 33

Gabarone, Botswana 42
Gabon 56, 63, 83–84
Gadiaga, Kalifa vii
gain 1, 21
The Gambia 8, 9, 44–46, 63, 114–116
Gambia News 44
Garba, Alhagi Ibrahima Muhammadu 44
Gasasira, Jean-Baptiste 56
gatekeeper 15
Gawanas, Bience 19
gender 13, 14, 17, 18, 20, 21, 25, 26, 62, 64, 153
Gender Affairs Ministry 11
gender balance 11
gender constraint 16
gender equality 14, 29, 31, 37, 40, 63, 154, 155
gender imbalance 30
gender inequality 27
gender quota 14, 15, 155
gender relations 155
gender role 1
gender stereotype 16
General Assembly 27
General Secretarial, Political Office, National Democratic Party, Egypt 48
Geneva, Switzerland viii
genocide 1, 10, 21, 56–57
Georgia 6
Germany 5, 12, 41
Ghana 6, 19, 20, 21, 63, 64, 116–117
Ginwala, Frene 16
Githumu, Kenya 18
glass ceiling 25
Global Finance Minister of the Year 2005 51
Global Platform for Action 27
globalism 27
goal 1, 25, 26, 27, 41, 155

godfather 19
Gould, Margot vii
Gourevitch, Philip 55
governance 19, 26, 31, 32, 153, 156
government 5, 6, 8, 13, 15, 19, 20, 21, 24, 28, 30, 32, 44, 51, 53, 55, 61, 64, 154, 155
government type 65, 67, 69, 71, 73, 75, 77, 78, 79, 80, 82, 83, 84, 87, 89, 90, 91, 93, 94, 96, 97, 98, 100, 101, 103, 105, 107, 109, 110, 111, 113, 114, 116, 117, 119, 120, 122, 123, 125, 127, 128, 130, 132, 133, 135, 137, 139, 140, 141, 143, 145, 148
grandparents 35
grassroots 17, 25, 29, 47
Great She-Elephant 6
Greece 6
Green, Rosario 15
Green Belt Movement 47
Grenada 6
group 14
guarantees 14
Guebuza, Armando 41
Guinea 11, 12, 117–119
Guinea-Bissau 8, 11, 119–120

Habib, Hajia Maira Baturiya 11
Habyarimana, Juvénal 56
Harare, Zimbabwe 42
Hargeisa, Somaliland 54
Harris, David 37
Harris, Parleh D. 11
Hassan, Farkhonda vii, 48–50
Hassim, Shireen 31
Hatshepsut 6
head 18
head of household 13
head of state 6, 8, 153, 154
health collective 18
hierarchy 25, 30
HIV-AIDS 26, 27, 62
homemaker 21
honesty 19
hostility 153
house arrest 35, 54
household 17, 32
Human Development Report 2005 154
human rights 12, 23, 27, 32
Hungary 6
Hutu 56, 57

Iceland 6, 12
IDEA *see* International Institute for Democracy and Electoral Assistance
identification 14
ideology 18
imperialism 20
implementation 28
inauguration 11, 34
incidence 5
income 154
independence 14, 19, 21, 31, 55, 65, 67, 69, 70, 71, 72, 73, 75, 77, 78, 79, 80, 82, 84, 87, 89, 90, 91–92, 93, 94–95, 96, 97, 98–99, 100, 101, 103, 105, 107, 109, 110, 111,

113, 114, 116, 118, 119, 120, 122, 123–124, 125, 127, 128–129, 130, 132, 133–134, 135–136, 137, 139, 140, 141, 143, 145, 147, 148, 154, 156
independence movement 14, 20
Indlovukaz 6, 8
inequality 13, 27, 29, 154
influence 18
information 29
inheritance 14, 57
Institute of Women and Children, Guinea Bissau 11
institution 1, 9, 13, 19, 25, 30, 154
Inter-African Committee for Traditional Practices Affecting the Health of Women and Children 54
Inter-Parliamentary Union (IPU) viii, 10, 26, 29, 45, 48, 154, 155
international community 29, 155
international conferences 25, 26
international discourses 27, 29, 32
International Institute for Democracy and Electoral Assistance (IDEA) vii, 12, 14, 24
international instruments 32
international law 27, 32
International Monetary Fund (IMF) 32
International Parliamentary Union 6
international women's movement 14
internet 14
intimidation 19
invasion 37
IPU *see* Inter-Parliamentary Union
Ireland 5
Ismail, Edna Adan vii, 52–55
issue 1, 17, 21, 26
Italy 48
Ivory Coast *see* Côte d'Ivoire

Jagne, Dodou Bammy vii
Jahumpa-Ceesay, Fatoumata vii, 44–46
jail 34
Jaló, Luzéria Dos Santos 11
Jamaica 6
Japan 6
Jaramillo, Jorge A. vii
Jiabao, Wen 43
Jidawi, Naila 11
Jidawi, Naila Majid 11
Johnson Sirleaf, Ellen 6, 7, 11, 12, 13, 14, 15, 20, 21, 33–37, 153
Jones, Hanna Abedou Bowen 11
journalist 46
judge 12

Kagame, Paul 57
Kahin, Dahir Rayale 53
Kaurouma, Ahmadou 154
Kawira, Esther vii
Kekeh, Biyémi 11
Kelleher, David 30, 153
Kenya 11, 18, 33, 46–48, 56, 63, 96–97
Kgositsile, Keorapetse 42
Kigali, Rwanda 56
Ki-moon, Ban 5

king 6, 8
King Dom Antonio III 8
King Mswati 6
King Sobhuza II 8
kingdom 6
Kiota, Rukia Omar 11
Kittilson, Miki Caul 15, 16
Komu, Anna Valerian 11
Konie, Gwendoline C. 12
Koran 49, 50
Kramer, Robert vii
Kuehner, Carolyn E. Guenther viii
Kuehner, Nancy L. Craft viii
Kuehner, Richard L. viii
Kuehner, William V. viii

labor 24
Labour Party (Tanzania) 11
land 14, 27, 30
land claim 14
land rights 154
language 18, 19, 29
Larbi, Madonna Owusuah 20
Latvia 5, 6
law 14, 20, 26, 28, 31, 154
law enforcement 12
leader 1, 5, 6, 12, 13, 15, 19, 20, 25,
    28, 33, 48, 57, 154, 155, 156
leadership 1, 5, 9, 11, 13, 17, 18, 19,
    20, 25, 26, 27, 29, 30, 31, 32, 37,
    40, 48, 49, 62, 153
legacy 6, 14, 153
legislature 14, 65, 67, 69, 71, 72,
    73, 75, 77, 78, 79, 80, 82, 83,
    84, 87, 89, 90, 92, 93, 95, 96,
    97, 99, 100, 101, 103, 105, 107,
    109, 111, 112, 113, 115, 116, 118, 119,
    120, 122, 124, 125, 127, 129, 130,
    132, 134, 136, 137, 139, 140, 141,
    143, 145, 147, 148
legitimacy 19
Lempinen, Edward W. vii
Lesotho 6, 8, 9, 11, 63, 135–137
level 1, 6, 13, 19
level playing field 13
Libandla 8
Liberal Party or PL (Parti Liberal),
    Rwanda 55
liberation 155
liberation movement 6, 25
Liberia 5, 8, 9, 11, 12, 13, 14, 19, 20,
    33–37, 120–122, 153
Libya 62, 68–69
limitation 13, 17, 24, 153
lobby 25, 29
location 65, 67, 68, 69, 71, 72, 73,
    75, 77, 78, 79, 80, 82, 83, 84,
    87, 89, 91, 93, 94, 96, 97, 98,
    100, 101, 102, 105, 107, 109, 110,
    111, 113, 114, 116, 117, 119, 120,
    122, 123, 125, 127, 128, 129, 132,
    133, 135, 137, 139, 140, 141, 143,
    145, 146, 148
Longwe, Sara Hlupekile 29
Lusaka, Zambia 42
Luxembourg 11

Maathai, Wangari Muta 33, 46–48
Madagascar 64, 97–98
Maendeleo Ya Wana Wake 18

Magaia, Lina 1
Mahfouz, Azza vii
mainstream 25, 26
Mairie, Simone 11
Malawi 20, 63, 137–139
male domination 13, 17, 31, 55
male privilege 17, 19
Mali 20, 21, 63, 122–123
Mama, Amina 21
MaMohato Tabitha' Masentle
    Lerotholi 6
management 44
Mandela, Winnie 6
Maputo, Mozambique 27
marginalization 61, 63
marriage 17
Martin-Cisse, Jeanne 12
Marxist coup 54
Masai 18
Masanneh-Ceesay, Tijan vii
Mauritania 62, 69–71
Mauritius 63, 139–140
Mbabane, Swaziland 42
Mbeki, Thabo 43
Mbete, Baleka 41–44
Mbikusita-Lewanika, Inonge 15
McIlwaine, Cathy 17
measures 29
mechanism 1, 29, 156
media 1, 13, 30
media representation 154
Mediterranean 48
member states 28
mentor 25
Merkel, Angela 41
Mexico 15
middle-class 21
military 14, 19, 155
military coup 35
military regime 20, 35
military rule 14
Millennium Declaration 27
Millennium Development Goals
    (MDGs) 29
minister 5, 16, 39, 40–41, 62
Minister of Communication,
    Liberia 11
Minister of Education 5
Minister of Family Welfare and
    Social Development, Somaliland
    vii, 52
Minister of Finance, Nigeria 21
Minister of Foreign Affairs, Cape
    Verde 11
Minister of Foreign Affairs, Somali-
    land 52
Minister of Health and Social Secu-
    rity, Liberia 12
Minister of Health, Kenya 15
Minister of Post, Liberia 11
Minister of Social Affairs 12
ministry 17, 39, 156
Ministry of Finance 11
mobilization 14, 21, 29, 31
Mogadishu, Somalia 54, 55
Mohammed, Asmau Aliyu vii, 11
Monaco 5
monarchy 8
money 17
Mongella, Gertrude Ibengwe 5, 38–40

Monrovia, Liberia 7, 34
Morocco 71–72
motherhood 14
movement 14
Movement for the Liberation, São
    Tomé and Príncipe Social Demo-
    cratic Party (MLSTP-PSD) 41–42
Mozambican Liberation Front
    (FREMILO 41
Mozambique 1, 5, 8, 9, 22, 24,
    40–41, 63, 64, 140–141
Mtengeti-Migiro, Asha-Rose 5
Mtintso, Thenjiwe 16
Mubarak, Hosni 48, 49
Mubarak, Mrs. Suzanne 61
Muhtar, Mansur 51
Mujuru, Joyce 24
multi-partyism 14
murder 56
Muslim 5
Musyimi-Ogana, Litha vii
Mutume, Gumisai 15, 21, 24, 25

Nairobi, Kenya vii, 12
Namibia 9, 19, 63, 141–143, 154
nation 5, 12
National Assembly 9, 12, 42–46
National Council for Women,
    Egypt vii, 50
National Democratic Party (NDP),
    Egypt 49
National Women's Council 49
Ndiaye, Tacko viii, viii
negotiations 13, 20, 26, 51
NEPAD see New Partnership for
    Africa's Development
net worth 19
Netherlands 6
networking 25, 26, 61
Neves, Maria das 9
New Partnership for Africa's Devel-
    opment (NEPAD), vii, 45, 156
New Zealand 5, 6, 41
Ngilu, Charity 15
Niger 123–125
Nigeria 11, 19, 20, 21, 50–52, 63,
    125–127
Njathi, Esther 18
Nobel Peace Prize Laureate 46
nominee 14
non-governmental organization
    (NGO) 13, 15, 25
Nordic states 10
North Africa 10, 65–76
Norway 12, 46
Nshingmateka, Inama 9
Ntolia aNtino ne Kongo 8
Ntombi 6
Ntombi Thwala 6, 8
number 5, 9, 12, 19, 20, 57, 62, 63,
    156
nuns, Maryknoll, Tanzania 39
Nyeri, Kenya 47
Nyiramirimo, Odette 55–57
Nzegwu, Nkiru 19, 20
Nzingha 6

Obasanjo, Olusegun 51
objectives 1
obligation 13

office 14
Office of the Ombudsman, Namibia 19
Okome, Mojúbàolú Olúfúnké 37
Okonjo-Iweala, Ngozi 21, 50–52
opponent 37
opportunity 15, 19, 21, 25, 64, 155
opposition 13, 24, 47
oppression 20
organization 1, 13, 14, 15, 20, 24, 25, 26, 28, 29, 64, 153
Organization of African Unity (OAU) 39
Ouedraogo, Joseshine 64
outcome 27
Oxfam GB — Pan African Policy 28

Pacific 9
Paley, Cass viii
Pan African Parliament 5, 38–40
paramount chieftainess 6
parity 1
parliament 6, 9, 12, 15, 16, 17, 25, 29, 42–44, 47, 48, 57, 61, 62, 64, 156
parliamentarian 15
participation 12, 14, 15, 19, 20, 21, 25, 26, 27, 29, 64
partner 20
party 9, 13, 14, 16, 19, 20
party support 13
party system 16
patriarchy 17, 19, 24, 30, 31, 63, 153, 155
pay 1, 13
peace 1, 13, 20, 25, 26, 156
peacemaking 46, 155
people 55, 57
people's assembly, Egypt 49
per capita income 65, 67, 68, 69, 71, 72, 73, 75, 77, 78, 79, 80, 82, 83, 84, 87, 89, 91, 93, 94, 96, 97, 98, 100, 101, 103, 105, 107, 109, 110, 111, 113, 114, 116, 117, 119, 120, 122, 125, 127, 128, 129, 132, 133, 135, 137, 139, 140, 141, 143, 145, 146, 148
percent 9, 11, 14, 22–23, 25, 62, 63, 64
percentage 10, 11, 13, 22–23, 57
Periera, Carman 9
permanent mission vii
Permanent Mission of São Tomé and Príncipe, U.N. vii
Perón, Isabel 5
persuasion 18
petition 28
pharaoh 6
Philippines 5
philosophy 12
platform for action 61
policy 32
political party 14, 15, 22–24, 29, 66, 67, 69, 70, 71, 73, 74, 75, 77, 78, 79, 80–81, 82, 83–84, 85, 88, 89, 90, 92, 93, 95, 97, 98, 99, 100, 101, 103, 106, 107, 109–110, 111, 112, 114, 115, 116, 118, 119, 121, 122, 124, 125–126, 127, 129, 132, 134, 136, 137, 139, 140, 142, 144, 145–146, 147, 148; quotas 22–24
political rights 61
political system 21
political will 29
politician 33
politics 12, 14, 19, 30, 62, 64, 153
population 32, 65, 67, 68, 69, 71, 72, 73, 75, 77, 78, 79, 80, 82, 83, 84, 87, 89, 91, 93, 94, 96, 97, 98, 100, 101, 103, 105, 107, 109, 110, 111, 113, 114, 116, 117, 119, 120, 122, 123, 125, 127, 128, 129, 132, 133, 135, 137, 139, 140, 141, 143, 145, 146, 148
Porter, Abioseh Michael 154
position 1, 6
post colonial 13, 20
post-conflict 13
post independence 14
poverty 13, 32
power 1, 5, 8, 12, 15, 16, 17, 18, 19, 21, 24, 25, 27, 29, 30, 32, 55, 56, 64, 154, 155
Preece, Julia 30
presidency 5, 6, 8, 9, 11, 12, 13, 14, 15, 20, 45, 48, 51
presidential candidate 7
presiding officer 6
prime minister vii, 5, 8, 9, 40–41, 63
Prime Minister, Somalia 54
private sector 12
private sphere 14
process 30, 32, 153
production 32
profile 33
progress 1, 5, 6, 13, 21, 23, 27, 29, 32, 57, 62, 64, 156
progressive change 20
Progressive Women's Movement, South Africa 44
property 27, 154
Prophet Mohamed 50
proportion 6, 16, 25, 29
Proportional Representation (PR) system 24
protocol 28
Protocol on the Rights of Women in Africa 27
province 1
provision 29
Ptolemy Auletes 6
public 16, 23, 25, 29
public office 12, 61
public sphere 14

Qat 55
queen 6, 8
queen mother 6, 8
queen regent 8
queen sister 6
Quist-Arcton, Ofeibea 21, 155
quota 13, 14, 31, 62, 155
quota policy 16
quota provisions 13
quota systems 22–24, 26, 49
quota type 22–24

rally 7
Rao, Aruna 30, 153

rape 20
ratification 28
reality 13
reason 21, 24
rebel leader 7
rebel movements 155
reconciliation 37
reconstruction 1, 13, 19, 25
recruits 20
redistribution 154
reform 29
regent 6
regent queen 8
regulation 14
rehabilitation 13
relationship 18
religious offices 12
renewal 32
report 27
representation 9, 12, 14, 25, 31, 57, 62
reproduction 24
reproductive rights 27
Republic of Congo 80–81
research 26
resistance 19, 153
resolution 29
resources 17, 21, 24, 30, 31, 51
responsibility 16
revenue 51
rhetoric 13, 18, 20
right 12, 25, 26, 28, 31, 49, 61
role 5, 13, 15, 19, 20, 23, 29, 32, 154, 155
role model 55
Rugendo, Rose 15
rule 19, 153
rule change 19
rule of law 31
ruler 6
Rwanda 9, 10, 11, 21, 24, 25, 55–57, 62, 63, 98–99
Rwandan Patriotic Front 56, 57

sacrifice 1, 5
Saidy, Aisatou N'Jie 9
Saint Kitts and Nevis 6
Salaam, Deborah 11
Sallah, Tijan 51
São Tomé and Príncipe vii, 5, 8, 9, 41–42, 84–86
Saudi Arabia 5
Scandinavian countries 11
school 14
Schulte, Christopher M. vii
seats 9, 29
Secretary General, United Nations 27
Secretary of State of Foreign Affairs 11
Security Council, United Nations 12
segregation 13
self-confidence 13
self-esteem 13
self-protectiveness 19
senate 9
senator 16, 55
Senegal 1, 9, 21, 63, 127–128
senior position 25
senior wife 8

sexism 19, 153
Seychelles 9, 63, 100–101
Shirati Health, Education, and
    Development Foundation
    (SHED) vii
Shirati, Tanzania vii
Shongwe, Dzeliwe 6, 8
Shoura Council, Egypt 48
Shvedova, Nadezhda 13
siege 7
Sierra Leone 11, 19, 20, 128–129
Sigcau, Stella 16
signatory 28
Silveira, Maria do Carmo Trovoada
    vii, 9, 41–42
Sirleaf, James 35
sister 1
Skaine, James C. vii
skill 21
slavery 34, 40
soccer legend 7
Social and Human Sciences
    National Committee, UNESCO
    11
social change 30
Social Democratic Party, Zambia 12
social justice 20
social norm 17
societal transformation 14, 153, 156
society 14, 20, 24, 25, 27, 63
sociocultural 1
Soludo, Charles C. 51
Somalia 11, 20, 101–102
Somaliland vii, 52–55, 102–105
South Africa 6, 8, 9, 11, 16, 21, 22,
    24, 42–44, 62, 63, 64, 143–145,
    156
Southern Africa 10, 15, 30, 132–151
Southern African Development
    Community (SADC) 15, 64
sovereign state 9
Spain 11
speaker 8
speaker of the house 16
speaker of the national assembly
    vii, 42–46
Sri Lanka 5
state 6, 9
statistics 154
status 15, 20, 28
status and progress of women
    66–67, 68, 69, 70–71, 72, 74,
    75, 76, 77–78, 79, 81, 82–83,
    84, 85–86, 88, 89, 90–91, 92,
    93–94, 95–96, 97, 98, 99, 100–
    101, 102, 104–105, 106–107, 108,
    110, 111, 112–113, 115–116, 116–117,
    118–119, 120, 121–122, 123, 124–
    125, 126–127, 128, 129, 130–131,
    133, 134–135, 136–137, 138–139,
    140, 141, 142–143, 144–145, 146,
    147–148, 149–151
Stephens, Jane Thompson 18, 20
strategies 1, 14, 16, 19, 30, 31, 32,
    64, 153
structure 153
struggle 1, 153
study 1, 64
sub-minister 5

success 13, 14, 15, 25
Sudan 24, 62, 72–73
support 25, 28
support structure 17
Supreme Court, Liberia 12
survey 16
Swazi National Council 8
Swaziland 6, 8, 9, 11, 20, 52–55,
    63, 145–146
Sweden 5, 11, 12
Sweetmand, Caroline 154
Switzerland 11

Tamale, Slvia 14, 15, 153
Tanzania 5, 11, 15, 18, 20, 38–40,
    42, 56, 63, 64, 105–107
Taphorn, Rita vii
tasks 17
Taylor, Charles 7, 37
theory 1
Time magazine 48
Togo 11, 19, 129–131
Tombai, Maimunatu Lata 11
tool 29
tradition 6, 13, 18, 19, 24
traditional male-driven fields 20
training 1, 17, 25, 29
transformation 30, 31, 154, 155
transformational leadership 30, 153
transformative education 30
treason 37
treaties 31
tree-planting project 47
tribe 18
Trinidad and Tobago 6
Tripp, Aili Mari 14, 156
troops 51
Tunisia 61, 62, 64, 73–75
Turshen, Meredeth, 155
Tutsi 55, 56
two party system 47

Uganda 9, 15, 21, 22, 24, 25, 41,
    63, 64, 107–108
United Nations 11, 15, 26, 27, 32,
    48, 61
United Nations Commission on
    Science and Technology for
    Development, co-chair, Gender
    Advisory Board 48
United Nations Development Pro-
    gram (UNDP) 35
United Nations Economic and
    Social Commission for Western
    Asia (ESCWA) 61
United Nations Economic Commis-
    sion for Africa (ECA) 10, 156
United Nations Educational, Sci-
    entific and Cultural Organization
    (UNESCO) 11, 43
United Nations General Assembly
    5, 12
United Nations High Commissioner
    for Refugees (UNHCR) 56
United Nations Secretary-General 5
United States 1, 9, 11, 15, 48
United States Peace Corps mission
    56
Unity Party, Liberia 7, 33

Universal Declaration of Human
    Rights 27
University of Ibadan, Nigeria 52
University of Nairobi, Kenya 46,
    47
University of Northern Iowa, Cedar
    Falls vii
Upper Volta 20
Uruguay 6
USAID vii
Uwilingiyimana, Agathe 9

Vallely, Paul 154
Veiga, María de Fátima Lima 11
vice chairperson 11
vice president 9, 11, 12, 15, 63
victim 20, 56
violence 13, 19, 20, 27, 56
voice 18, 45
voluntary party quotas 24
voting 24, 61

Waldman, Kimberly D. vii
Wandira-Kazibwe, Specioza 15
Wanyeki, L. Muthoni vii, 12, 15,
    21, 23, 24, 25, 26, 31
war 20, 21, 37, 46, 155
Ward, Amelia 11
warlord 7
We Wish to Inform You That Tomor-
    row We Will Be Killed with Our
    Families 55
Weah, George 7, 37
wealth 19
West Africa 10, 19, 109–131
West African Networking for Peace
    Gambia Charter, The Gambia
    45
Western Europe 1
Western Sahara 20, 75–76
wife/wives 19
witch burning 18
women-headed households 17
Women in Decision-Making in the
    Arab Region 61
Women in Law and Development
    in Africa (WiLDAF) 26
women in parliaments, world
    classification 157–162
Women in Power and Decision
    Making 27
Women's eNews 1
women's rights 49
work 13, 16, 17, 20, 25, 32
workshop 21
world 9, 13, 24, 33, 153
World Bank 32, 35, 51, 154
World Health Organization
    (WHO) 54; Regional Office
    for the Eastern Mediterranean
    (WHO/EMRO) 54

Zambia 11, 12, 15, 20, 24, 42, 63,
    146–148
Zanzibar 11
Zia, Begum Khaleda 41
Zimbabwe 6, 8, 9, 11, 15, 20, 21,
    24, 42, 63, 148–151
Zuma-Dlamini, Nkosazana 16